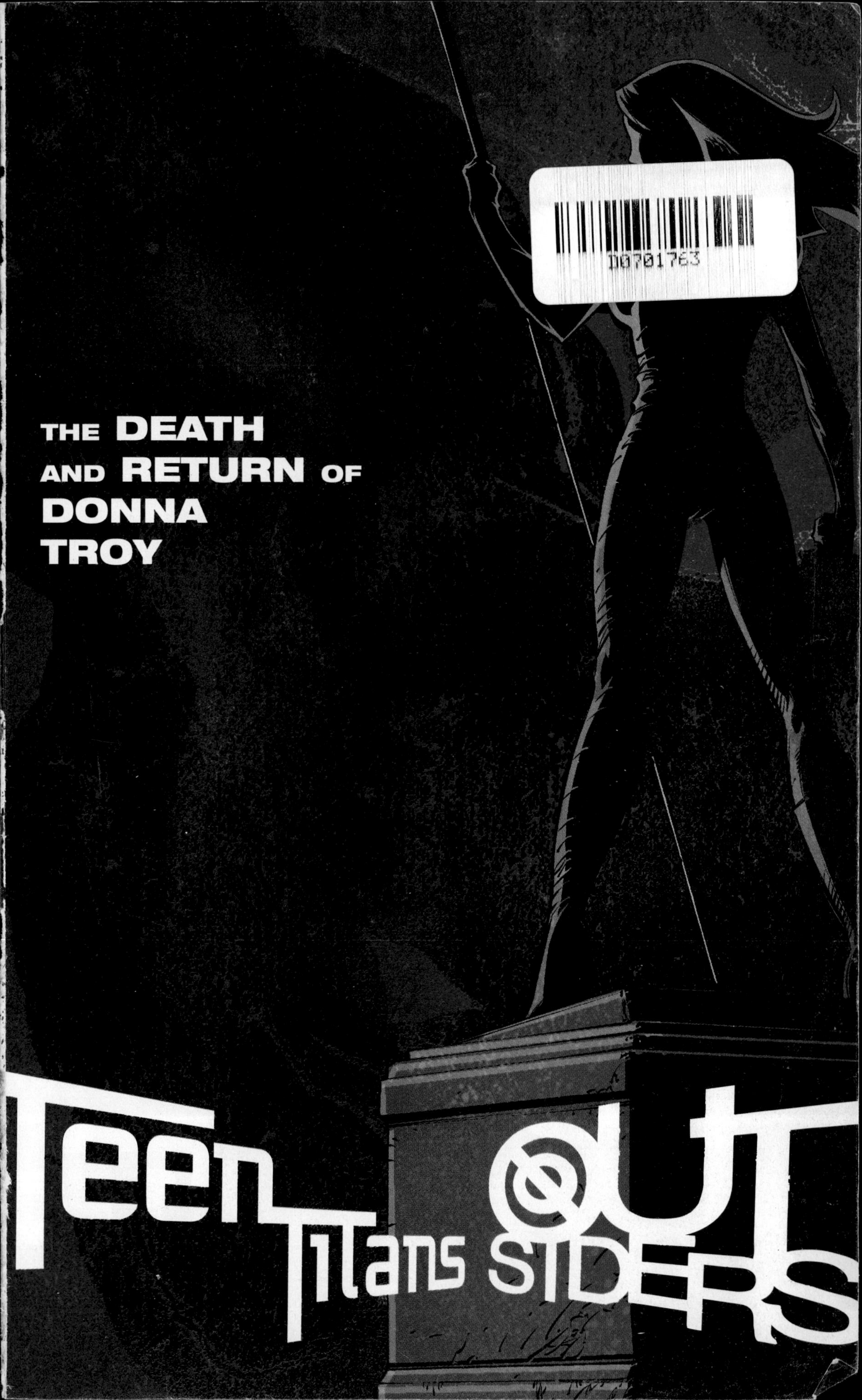
THE DEATH
AND RETURN OF
DONNA
TROY
Teen Titans
Outsiders

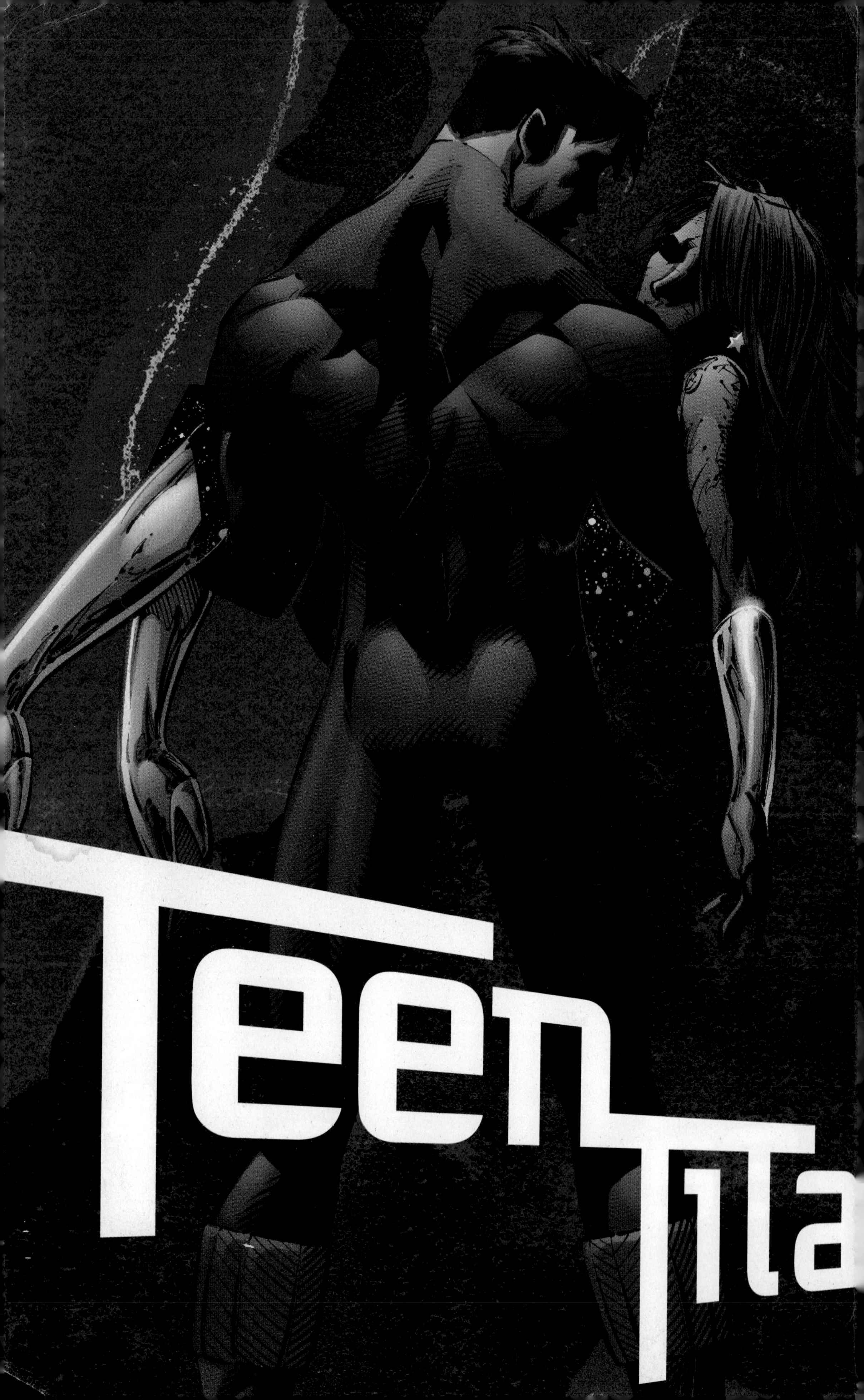
Teen Tita

THE **DEATH** AND **RETURN** OF **DONNA TROY**

OUT
15 SIDERS
WITHDRAWN

TEEN TITANS/OUTSIDERS:
THE DEATH AND RETURN
OF DONNA TROY

Published by DC Comics. Cover and
compilation copyright © 2006 DC Comics.
All Rights Reserved.

Originally published in single
magazine form in TITANS/YOUNG JUSTICE:
GRADUATION DAY #1-3, TEEN TITANS/
OUTSIDERS SECRET FILES 2003, DC SPECIAL:
THE RETURN OF DONNA TROY #1-4.
Copyright © 2003, 2005 DC Comics. All
Rights Reserved. All characters, their
distinctive likenesses and related
elements featured in this publication are
trademarks of DC Comics. The stories,
characters and incidents featured in this
publication are entirely fictional. DC Comics
does not read or accept unsolicited submis-
sions of ideas, stories or artwork.

DC Comics, 1700 Broadway,
New York, NY 10019
A Warner Bros. Entertainment Company

Printed in Canada. First Printing.
ISBN: 1-4012-0931-9
ISBN: 13 978-1-4012-0931-5

Special thanks to Erik Merk
and Spencer Beck and Drew R. Moore
Cover illustration by Phil Jimenez &
George Pérez with Lee Loughridge
Teen Titans Logo designed by Terry Marks
Outsiders Logo designed by Glenn Parsons

CAST OF CHARACTERS

ARGENT

Toni Monetti led a very pampered life until she turned 16, when she began to manifest her then-unknown alien D.N.A. — which gave her the power to create various plasma energy constructs, and turned her skin to a pale silver complexion. She has been a member of two different incarnations of the Teen Titans.

ARSENAL

Idolizing Green Arrow, orphan Roy Harper had mastered archery when he was a teenager on a Navajo reservation. Harper became billionaire Oliver Queen's ward, and his guardian named him Speedy because of the quickness he exhibited with his bow. Renaming himself Arsenal, Harper went on to work for the U.S. government, lead the Titans, and fall in love with the assassin Cheshire. Together they have a child, Lian.

BEAST BOY

Garfield Logan was poisoned with sakutia by a rare African primate. His geneticist parents used an experimental treatment to save his life, and in so doing imbued him with green skin and the ability to transform him-self into any animal life form. When his parents died in an accident, he was adopted by Rita Farr and Steve Dayton of the Doom Patrol. Gar des-perately wants to be an actor but finds himself most comfortable in the role of hero, serving with the various incarnations of the Titans. At age 19, Beast Boy finds himself acting as the mediator between the older and younger Titans, a task he readily accepts.

CYBORG

Victor Stone's parents were research scientists for S.T.A.R. Labs. During an experiment his mother accidentally unleashed a destructive force that killed her instantly and destroyed most of Vic's body. His father saved the youth's life by grafting cybernetic components to his body, leaving Vic feeling utterly alienated from his fellow man. He only came to accept his fate when he joined the Titans. Through many changes, Vic has remained committed to the team. Currently, Cyborg has taken it upon himself to re-form the Titans and usher in today's incarnation of the teenaged super-heroes at the new Titans Tower in San Francisco.

JADE

Jenny-Lynn Hayden's normal adolescence came to an abrupt end when the green birthmark on her left palm began to pulse, giving her power over a strange green energy similar to the type used by Green Lanterns. Jenny-Lynn, along with her long-lost brother Todd (a.k.a. Obsidian), learned that their biological father was the World War II-era Green Lantern, Alan Scott. After being a member of the group Infinity Inc., and the girlfriend of Green Lantern Kyle Rayner, Jenny-Lynn felt she needed to define herself on her own and joined the Outsiders.

JESSE QUICK

Jesse Chambers is the daughter of two Golden Age heroes, from whom she has inherited her powers: Johnny Quick (speed and flight) and Liberty Belle (strength). She is the successful head of QuickStart Enterprises, and has a hard time balancing her super-hero, business and personal lives.

IMPULSE/KID FLASH

Bart Allen has quite a legacy to live up to. His grandfather was Barry Allen, the second Flash. Born in the 30th century, Bart was brought to the 21st century by his grandmother to be properly schooled in the use of his natural super-speed. For a time, he operated as Impulse, under the tutelage of Max Mercury, Zen Master of speed. A dramatic turn of events led Bart to decide it was time to grow up, and toward that goal he has speed-read and memorized the contents of the San Francisco Public Library. He has the knowledge, but now needs the experience that will make him worthy of the Flash mantle. Taking the next step in that process, he has changed his name to Kid Flash.

NIGHTWING

Former partner to Batman as Robin, Dick Grayson has left Gotham City for nearby Blüdhaven, where he fights crime as Nightwing. He is a master of several martial arts disciplines, and is armed with escrima sticks, batarangs, jumplines and gas capsules. As sometimes leader of the new Outsiders (which he named as a nod to Batman's former team), Dick sees this group as hunters — they will seek out the world's villains and bring them in.

OMEN

Lilith Clay was only 13 when her mental powers began to manifest. At age 16, she left her foster parents to try to uncover her true origins. She ultimately discovered Mr. Jupiter — a millionaire philanthropist who was funding the Teen Titans — and began to aid his cause, before eventually learning that Jupiter was her true father. After untapping further abilities of teleportation and enhanced mystical skills, Lilith took the name Omen.

RAVEN

The daughter of a human mother and the demon Trigon, Raven has spent much of her life trying to escape her father's influence. She was warned to always keep her anger and frustrations in check, lest she give in to her father's demonic influence. When Trigon set his sights on Earth, Raven got there ahead of him, helping form one version of the Titans in order to stop him. Since then, she has opposed Trigon frequently, losing her mortal body in the process. Without a body to inhabit, Raven's soul-self wandered the world aimlessly until recently. Now she's trying to adapt to her new surroundings.

SHIFT

Metamorpho was a member of the original Outsiders, who could transform his body into any element on the periodic table. When the Outsiders disbanded, he joined the Justice League for a mission which left him a comatose, inert mass. Fragments of Metamorpho were scattered all over the United States, and the hero collected each one he could find. But one fragment developed into a full-bodied replica of Metamorpho, with no memories of his own. This replica joined the new Outsiders, and has since learned the truth of his origin. Now called Shift, he too has the ability to transform his body into any element he wishes.

STARFIRE

Princess Koriand'r of Tamaran was sacrificed by her father to save their world. Subjected to horrendous experiments, she gained the ability to generate energy bolts, this in addition to her natural gift of flight. Escaping her tormentors, she made her way to Earth and found a new life as Starfire. Her world is now gone, a victim of the alien warlord Imperiex. Starfire tends to be impatient, which has recently led to her leaving the Titans and working with the Outsiders.

TEMPEST

Garth was abandoned at birth by superstitious Atlanteans due to his purple eyes, and survived alone in the ocean depths for years before being discovered by Aquaman. As Aqualad, Garth became a charter member of the Teen Titans. But he was often seen as one of the least-powerful members — that is, until he realized his potential for wizardry and became the powerful mage Tempest!

WONDER GIRL

Cassie Sandsmark was thrilled to befriend Diana, the Themysciran princess known as Wonder Woman — so much so that during a crisis, she borrowed the Sandals of Hermes and the Gauntlet of Atlas in order to aid Diana. Emboldened by her success, she asked Zeus for additional powers. Amused and impressed, he granted her strength and flight, and she became the heroine known as Wonder Girl. Cassie's secret identity has since been exposed, and arrangements have been made for her to attend private school. Cassie continues to grow into her extraordinary role, discovering the extent of her powers and finding new allies and enemies lurking among the ancient myths. These include the war god Ares, who, for reasons unknown, gave her a golden lasso. She has also faced an astonishing revelation — that Zeus is her true father.

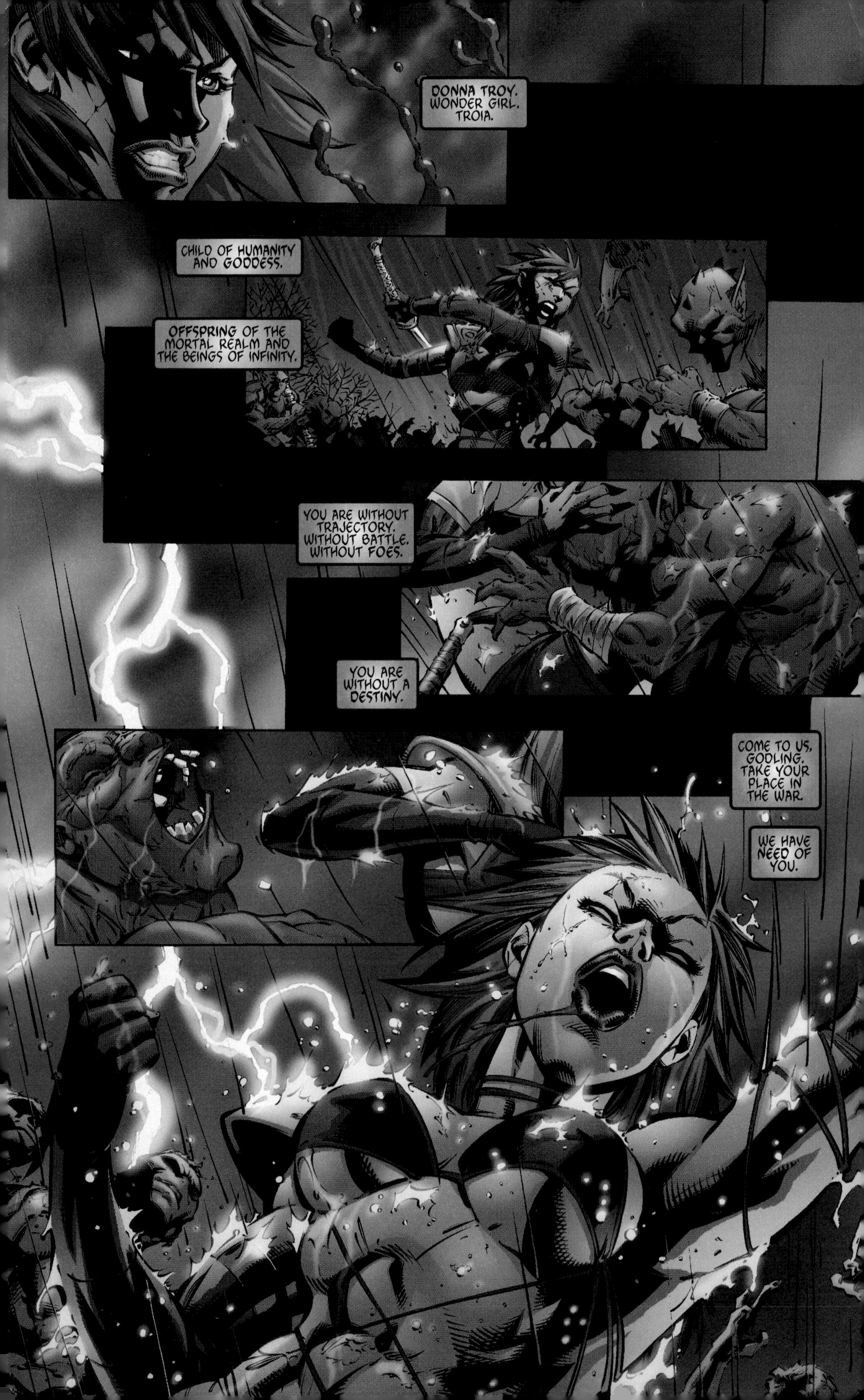
DONNA TROY. WONDER GIRL. TROIA.
CHILD OF HUMANITY AND GODDESS.
OFFSPRING OF THE MORTAL REALM AND THE BEINGS OF INFINITY.
YOU ARE WITHOUT TRAJECTORY. WITHOUT BATTLE. WITHOUT FOES.
YOU ARE WITHOUT A DESTINY.
COME TO US, GODLING. TAKE YOUR PLACE IN THE WAR.
WE HAVE NEED OF YOU.

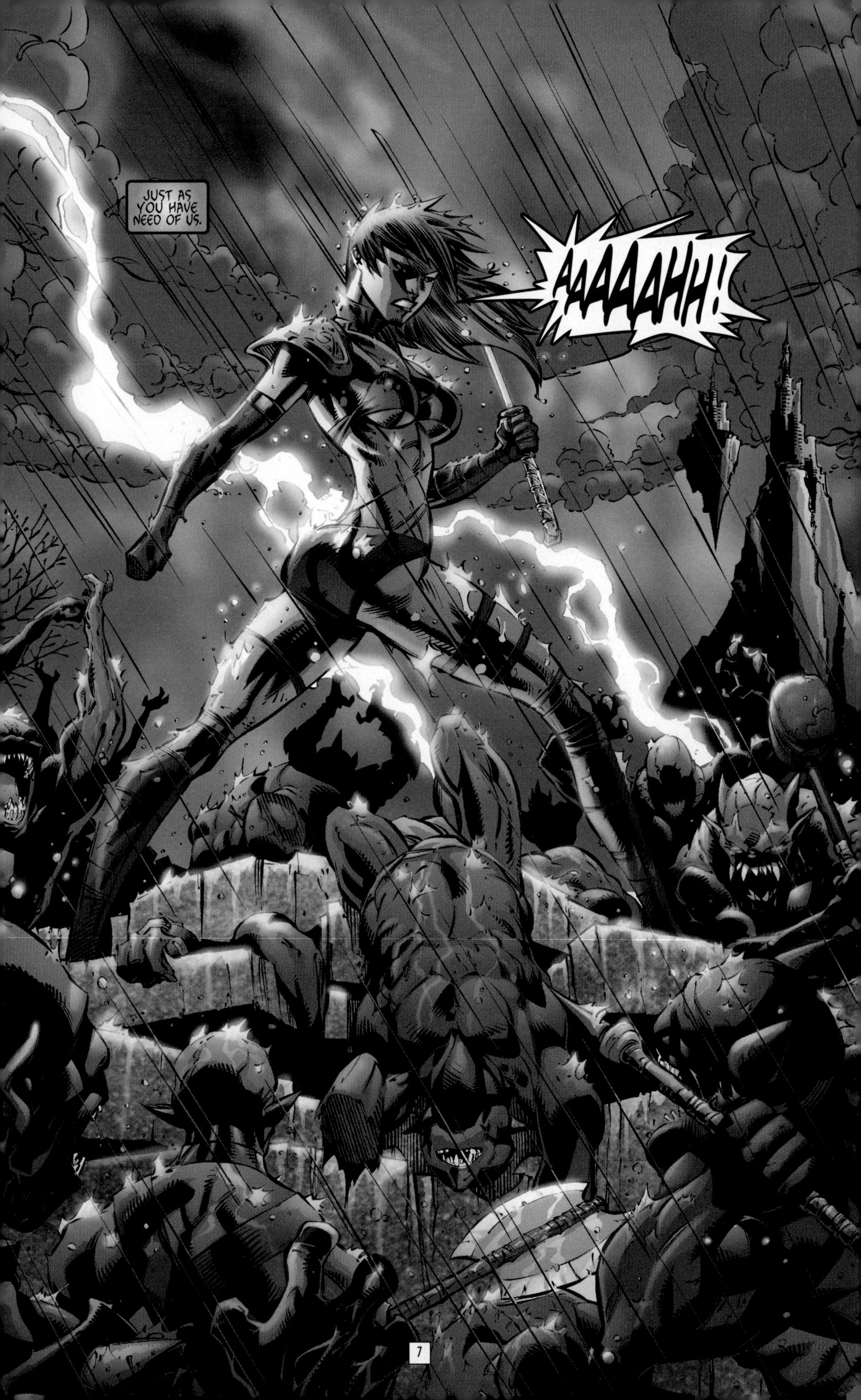
JUST AS YOU HAVE NEED OF US.
AAAAAHH!

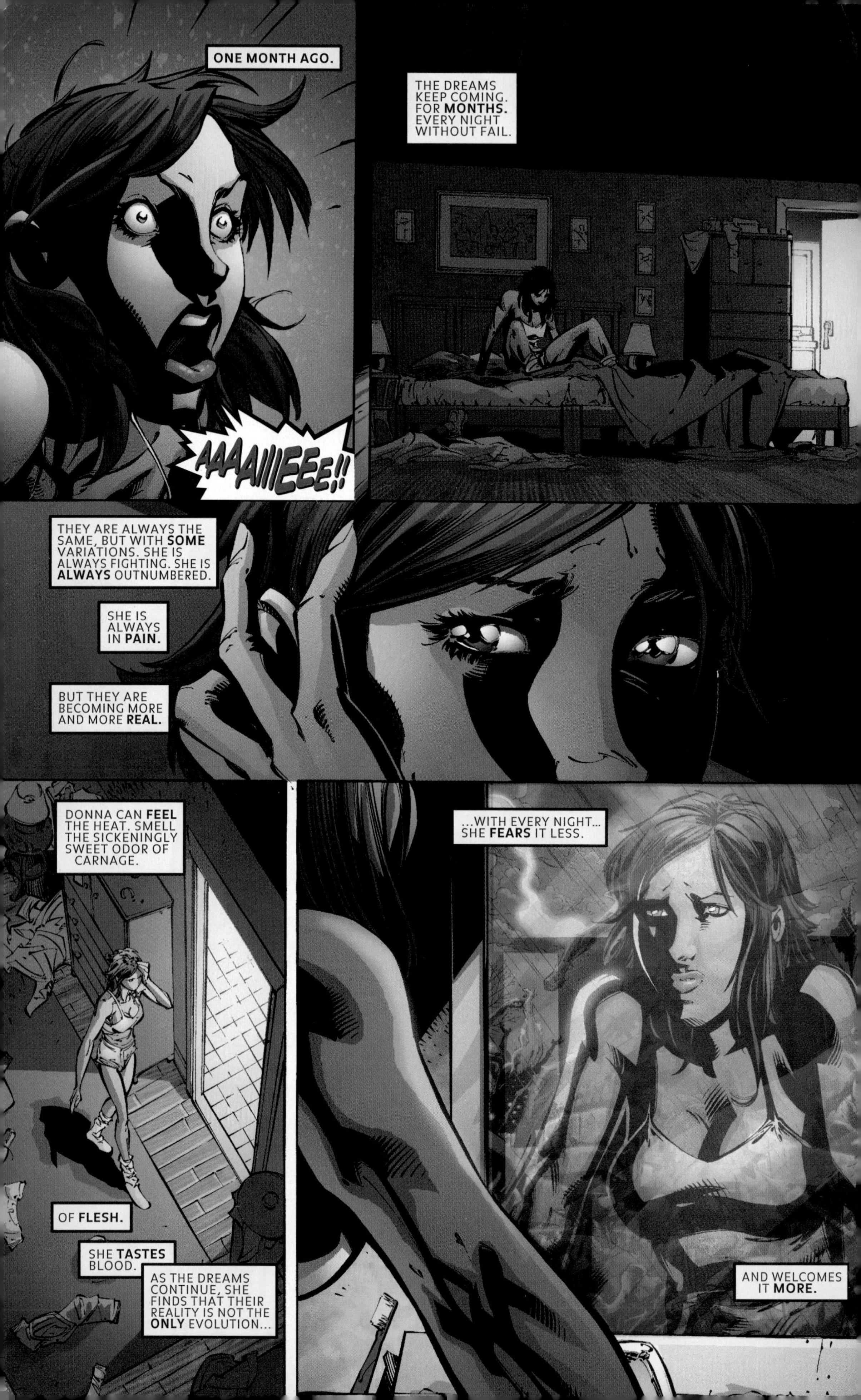
ONE MONTH AGO.
AAAAIIIEEE!!
THE DREAMS KEEP COMING. FOR MONTHS. EVERY NIGHT WITHOUT FAIL.
THEY ARE ALWAYS THE SAME, BUT WITH SOME VARIATIONS. SHE IS ALWAYS FIGHTING. SHE IS ALWAYS OUTNUMBERED.
SHE IS ALWAYS IN PAIN.
BUT THEY ARE BECOMING MORE AND MORE REAL.
DONNA CAN FEEL THE HEAT. SMELL THE SICKENINGLY SWEET ODOR OF CARNAGE.
OF FLESH.
SHE TASTES BLOOD.
AS THE DREAMS CONTINUE, SHE FINDS THAT THEIR REALITY IS NOT THE ONLY EVOLUTION...
...WITH EVERY NIGHT... SHE FEARS IT LESS.
AND WELCOMES IT MORE.

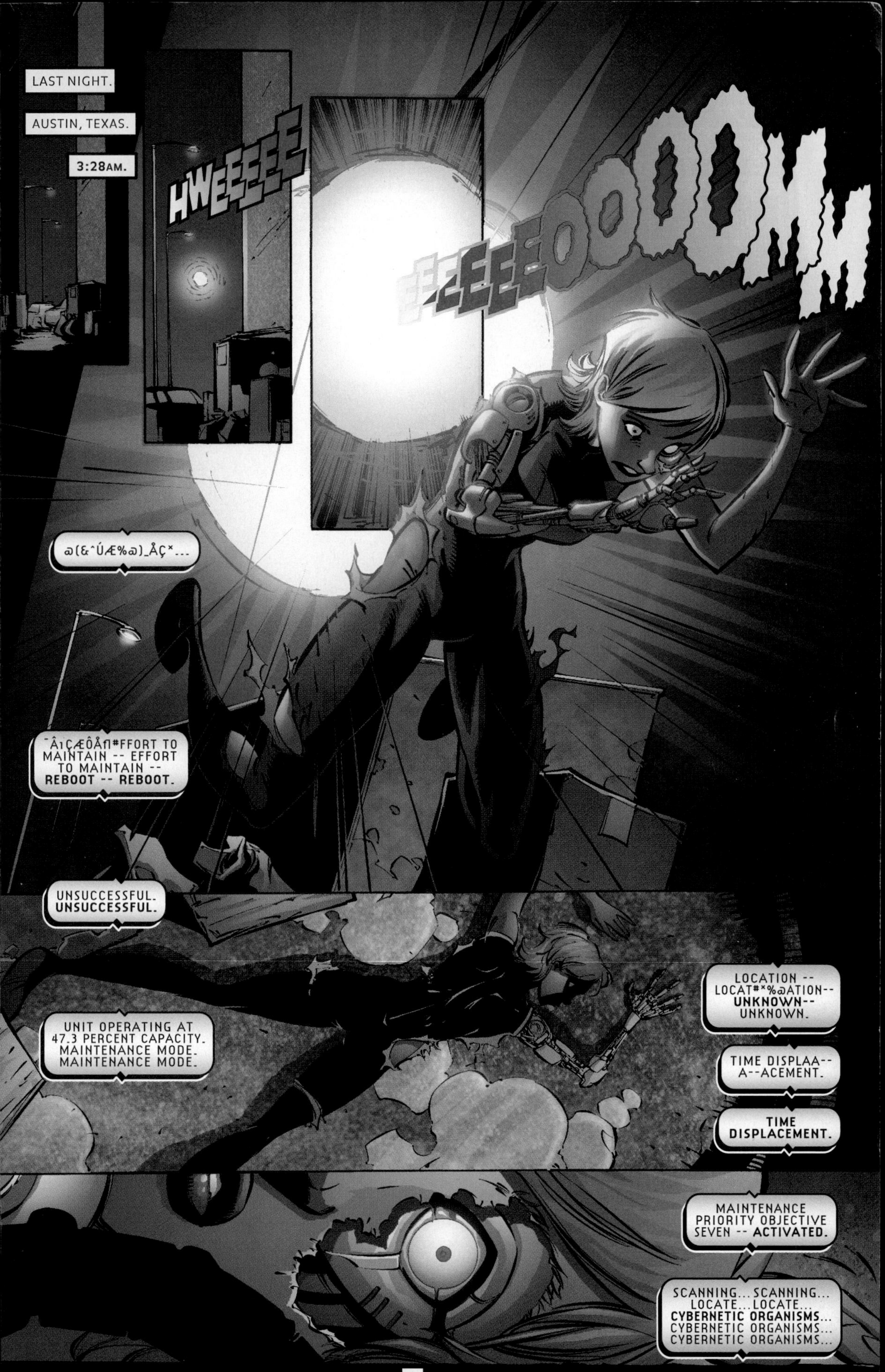
LAST NIGHT.
AUSTIN, TEXAS.
3:28AM.
HWEEEEE
EEEEEEOOOOOMM
@(&^ÚÆ%@)_ÅÇ*...
¯ÂıÇÆÔÅΠ#FFORT TO MAINTAIN -- EFFORT TO MAINTAIN -- REBOOT -- REBOOT.
UNSUCCESSFUL. UNSUCCESSFUL.
UNIT OPERATING AT 47.3 PERCENT CAPACITY. MAINTENANCE MODE. MAINTENANCE MODE.
LOCATION -- LOCAT#*%@ATION-- UNKNOWN-- UNKNOWN.
TIME DISPLAA-- A--ACEMENT.
TIME DISPLACEMENT.
MAINTENANCE PRIORITY OBJECTIVE SEVEN -- ACTIVATED.
SCANNING... SCANNING... LOCATE... LOCATE... CYBERNETIC ORGANISMS... CYBERNETIC ORGANISMS... CYBERNETIC ORGANISMS...

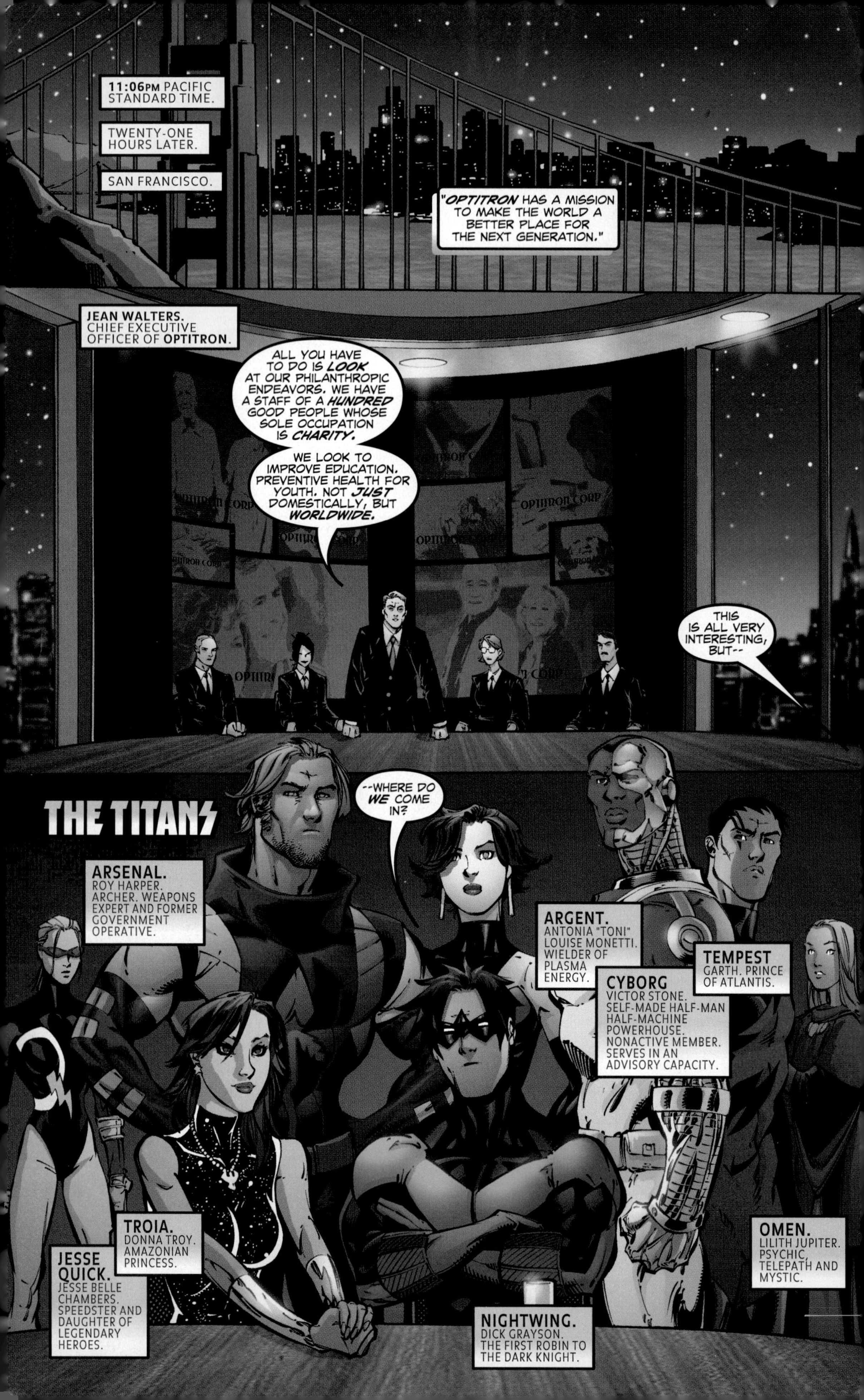
11:06PM PACIFIC STANDARD TIME.
TWENTY-ONE HOURS LATER.
SAN FRANCISCO.
"OPTITRON HAS A MISSION TO MAKE THE WORLD A BETTER PLACE FOR THE NEXT GENERATION."
JEAN WALTERS. CHIEF EXECUTIVE OFFICER OF OPTITRON.
ALL YOU HAVE TO DO IS LOOK AT OUR PHILANTHROPIC ENDEAVORS. WE HAVE A STAFF OF A HUNDRED GOOD PEOPLE WHOSE SOLE OCCUPATION IS CHARITY.
WE LOOK TO IMPROVE EDUCATION. PREVENTIVE HEALTH FOR YOUTH. NOT JUST DOMESTICALLY, BUT WORLDWIDE.
THIS IS ALL VERY INTERESTING, BUT--
THE TITANS
--WHERE DO WE COME IN?
ARSENAL. ROY HARPER. ARCHER. WEAPONS EXPERT AND FORMER GOVERNMENT OPERATIVE.
ARGENT. ANTONIA "TONI" LOUISE MONETTI. WIELDER OF PLASMA ENERGY.
TEMPEST GARTH. PRINCE OF ATLANTIS.
CYBORG VICTOR STONE. SELF-MADE HALF-MAN HALF-MACHINE POWERHOUSE. NONACTIVE MEMBER. SERVES IN AN ADVISORY CAPACITY.
TROIA. DONNA TROY. AMAZONIAN PRINCESS.
JESSE QUICK. JESSE BELLE CHAMBERS. SPEEDSTER AND DAUGHTER OF LEGENDARY HEROES.
NIGHTWING. DICK GRAYSON. THE FIRST ROBIN TO THE DARK KNIGHT.
OMEN. LILITH JUPITER. PSYCHIC, TELEPATH AND MYSTIC.

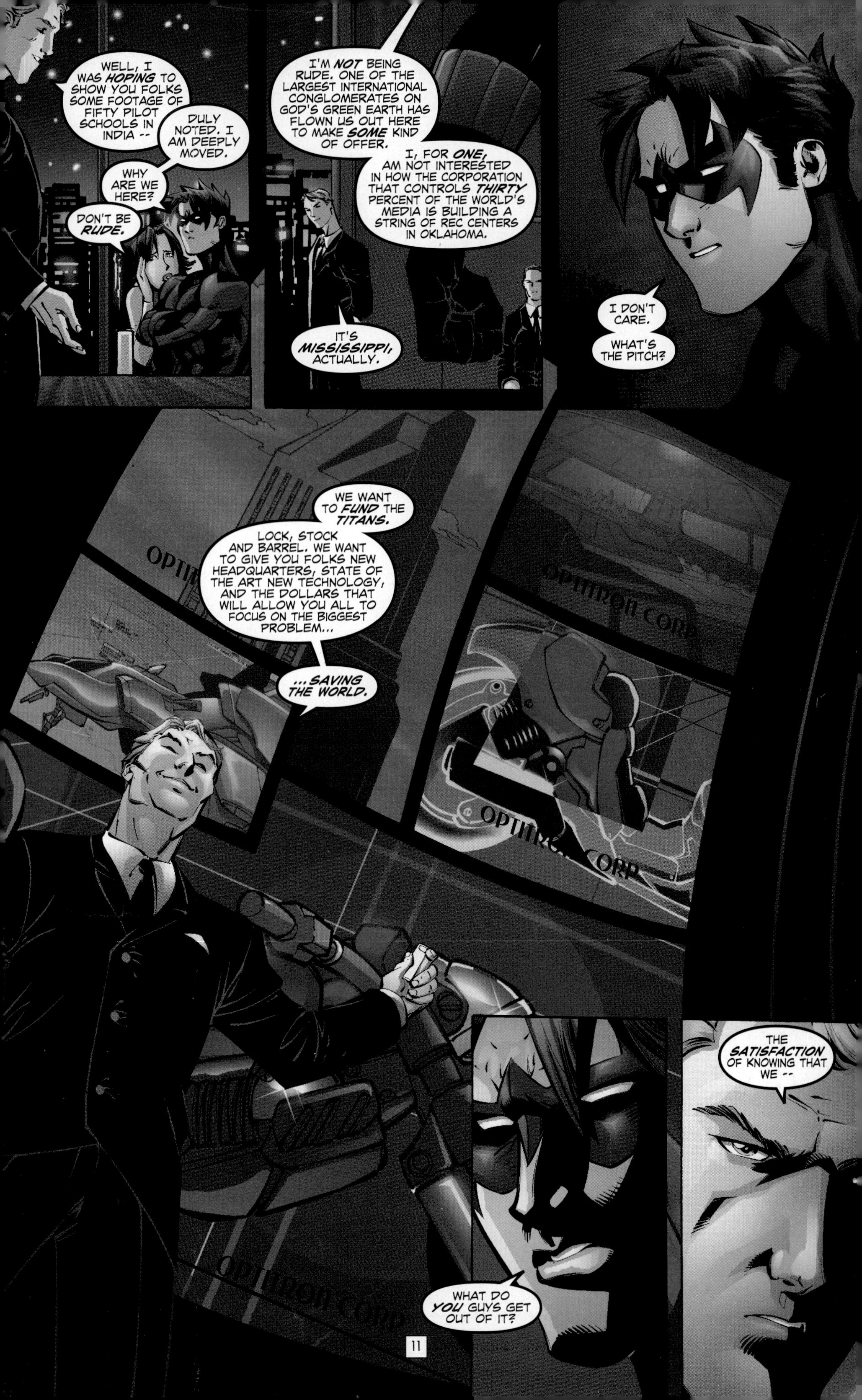
WELL, I WAS HOPING TO SHOW YOU FOLKS SOME FOOTAGE OF FIFTY PILOT SCHOOLS IN INDIA --
DULY NOTED. I AM DEEPLY MOVED.
WHY ARE WE HERE?
DON'T BE RUDE.
I'M NOT BEING RUDE. ONE OF THE LARGEST INTERNATIONAL CONGLOMERATES ON GOD'S GREEN EARTH HAS FLOWN US OUT HERE TO MAKE SOME KIND OF OFFER.
I, FOR ONE, AM NOT INTERESTED IN HOW THE CORPORATION THAT CONTROLS THIRTY PERCENT OF THE WORLD'S MEDIA IS BUILDING A STRING OF REC CENTERS IN OKLAHOMA.
IT'S MISSISSIPPI, ACTUALLY.
I DON'T CARE.
WHAT'S THE PITCH?
WE WANT TO FUND THE TITANS.
LOCK, STOCK AND BARREL. WE WANT TO GIVE YOU FOLKS NEW HEADQUARTERS, STATE OF THE ART NEW TECHNOLOGY, AND THE DOLLARS THAT WILL ALLOW YOU ALL TO FOCUS ON THE BIGGEST PROBLEM...
...SAVING THE WORLD.
OPTITRON CORP
OPTITRON CORP
OPTITRON CORP
THE SATISFACTION OF KNOWING THAT WE --
WHAT DO YOU GUYS GET OUT OF IT?

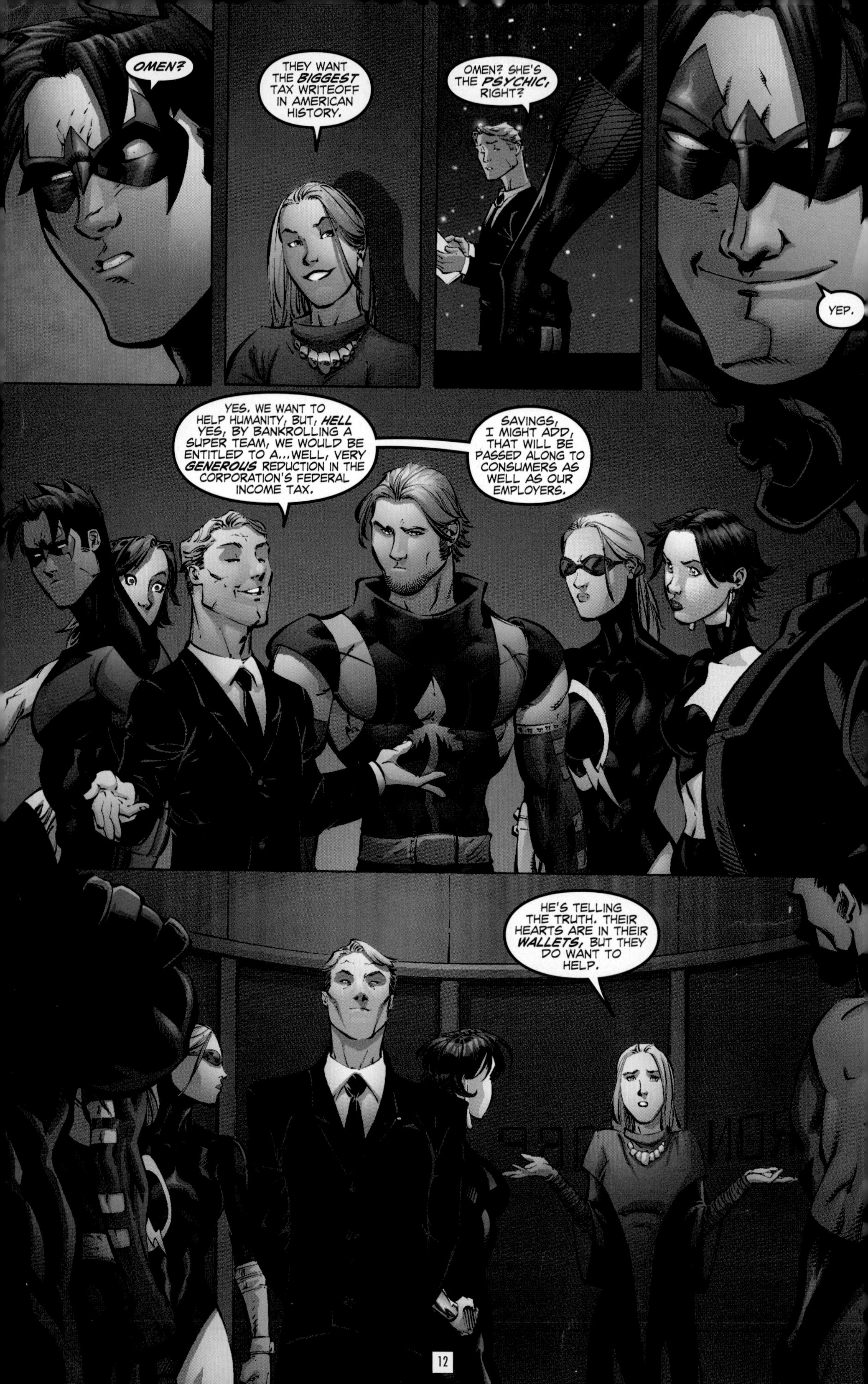
OMEN?
THEY WANT THE BIGGEST TAX WRITEOFF IN AMERICAN HISTORY.
OMEN? SHE'S THE PSYCHIC, RIGHT?
YEP.
YES. WE WANT TO HELP HUMANITY, BUT, HELL YES, BY BANKROLLING A SUPER TEAM, WE WOULD BE ENTITLED TO A...WELL, VERY GENEROUS REDUCTION IN THE CORPORATION'S FEDERAL INCOME TAX.
SAVINGS, I MIGHT ADD, THAT WILL BE PASSED ALONG TO CONSUMERS AS WELL AS OUR EMPLOYERS.
HE'S TELLING THE TRUTH. THEIR HEARTS ARE IN THEIR WALLETS, BUT THEY DO WANT TO HELP.

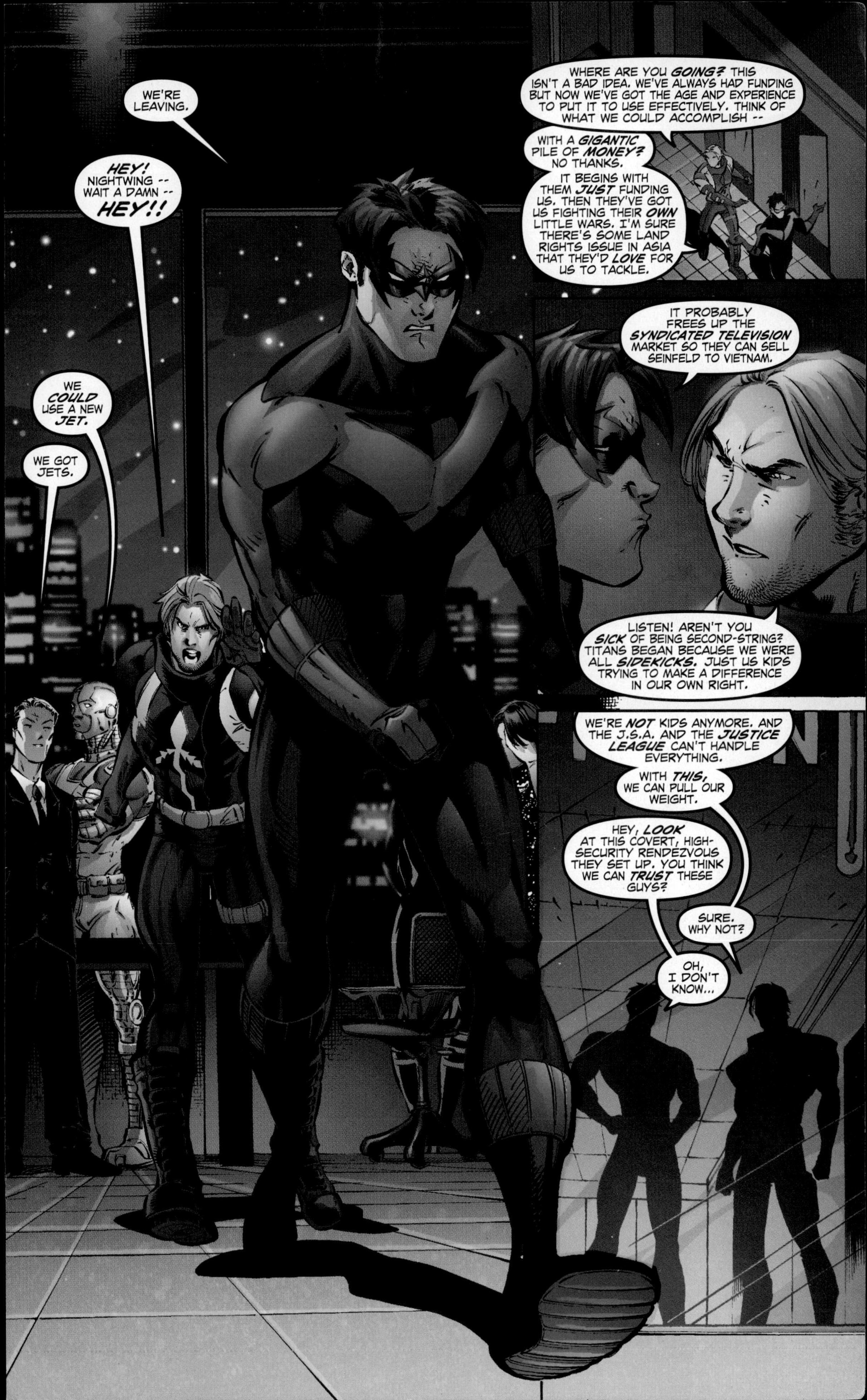
WE'RE LEAVING.
HEY! NIGHTWING -- WAIT A DAMN -- HEY!!
WE COULD USE A NEW JET.
WE GOT JETS.
WHERE ARE YOU GOING? THIS ISN'T A BAD IDEA. WE'VE ALWAYS HAD FUNDING BUT NOW WE'VE GOT THE AGE AND EXPERIENCE TO PUT IT TO USE EFFECTIVELY. THINK OF WHAT WE COULD ACCOMPLISH --
WITH A GIGANTIC PILE OF MONEY? NO THANKS.
IT BEGINS WITH THEM JUST FUNDING US. THEN THEY'VE GOT US FIGHTING THEIR OWN LITTLE WARS. I'M SURE THERE'S SOME LAND RIGHTS ISSUE IN ASIA THAT THEY'D LOVE FOR US TO TACKLE.
IT PROBABLY FREES UP THE SYNDICATED TELEVISION MARKET SO THEY CAN SELL SEINFELD TO VIETNAM.
LISTEN! AREN'T YOU SICK OF BEING SECOND-STRING? TITANS BEGAN BECAUSE WE WERE ALL SIDEKICKS. JUST US KIDS TRYING TO MAKE A DIFFERENCE IN OUR OWN RIGHT.
WE'RE NOT KIDS ANYMORE. AND THE J.S.A. AND THE JUSTICE LEAGUE CAN'T HANDLE EVERYTHING.
WITH THIS, WE CAN PULL OUR WEIGHT.
HEY, LOOK AT THIS COVERT, HIGH-SECURITY RENDEZVOUS THEY SET UP. YOU THINK WE CAN TRUST THESE GUYS?
SURE. WHY NOT?
OH, I DON'T KNOW...

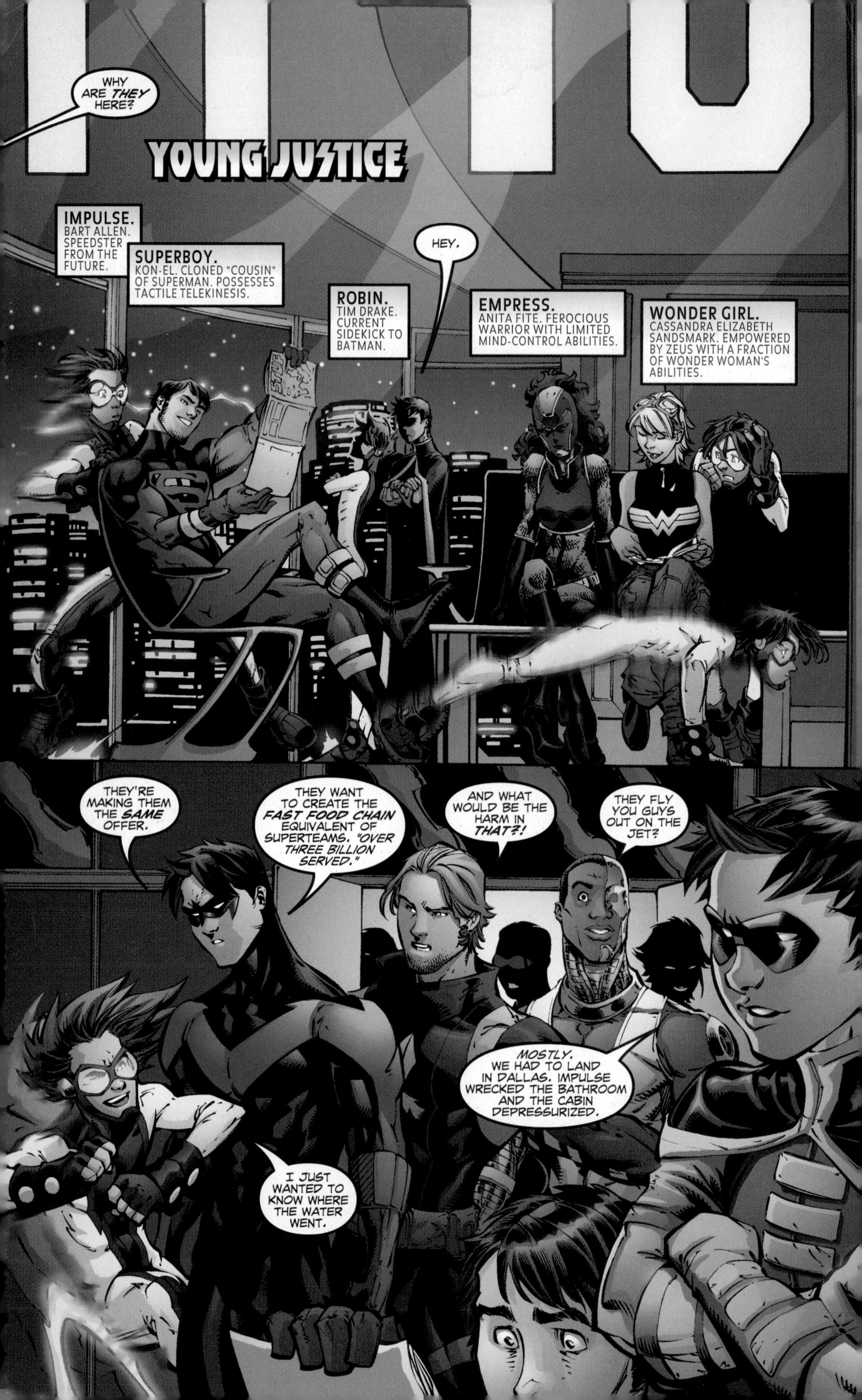
WHY ARE *THEY* HERE?
YOUNG JUSTICE
IMPULSE. BART ALLEN. SPEEDSTER FROM THE FUTURE.
SUPERBOY. KON-EL. CLONED "COUSIN" OF SUPERMAN. POSSESSES TACTILE TELEKINESIS.
HEY.
ROBIN. TIM DRAKE. CURRENT SIDEKICK TO BATMAN.
EMPRESS. ANITA FITE. FEROCIOUS WARRIOR WITH LIMITED MIND-CONTROL ABILITIES.
WONDER GIRL. CASSANDRA ELIZABETH SANDSMARK. EMPOWERED BY ZEUS WITH A FRACTION OF WONDER WOMAN'S ABILITIES.
THEY'RE MAKING THEM THE *SAME* OFFER.
THEY WANT TO CREATE THE *FAST FOOD CHAIN* EQUIVALENT OF SUPERTEAMS. "OVER THREE BILLION SERVED."
AND WHAT WOULD BE THE HARM IN *THAT?!*
THEY FLY YOU GUYS OUT ON THE JET?
MOSTLY. WE HAD TO LAND IN DALLAS. IMPULSE WRECKED THE BATHROOM AND THE CABIN DEPRESSURIZED.
I JUST WANTED TO KNOW WHERE THE WATER WENT.

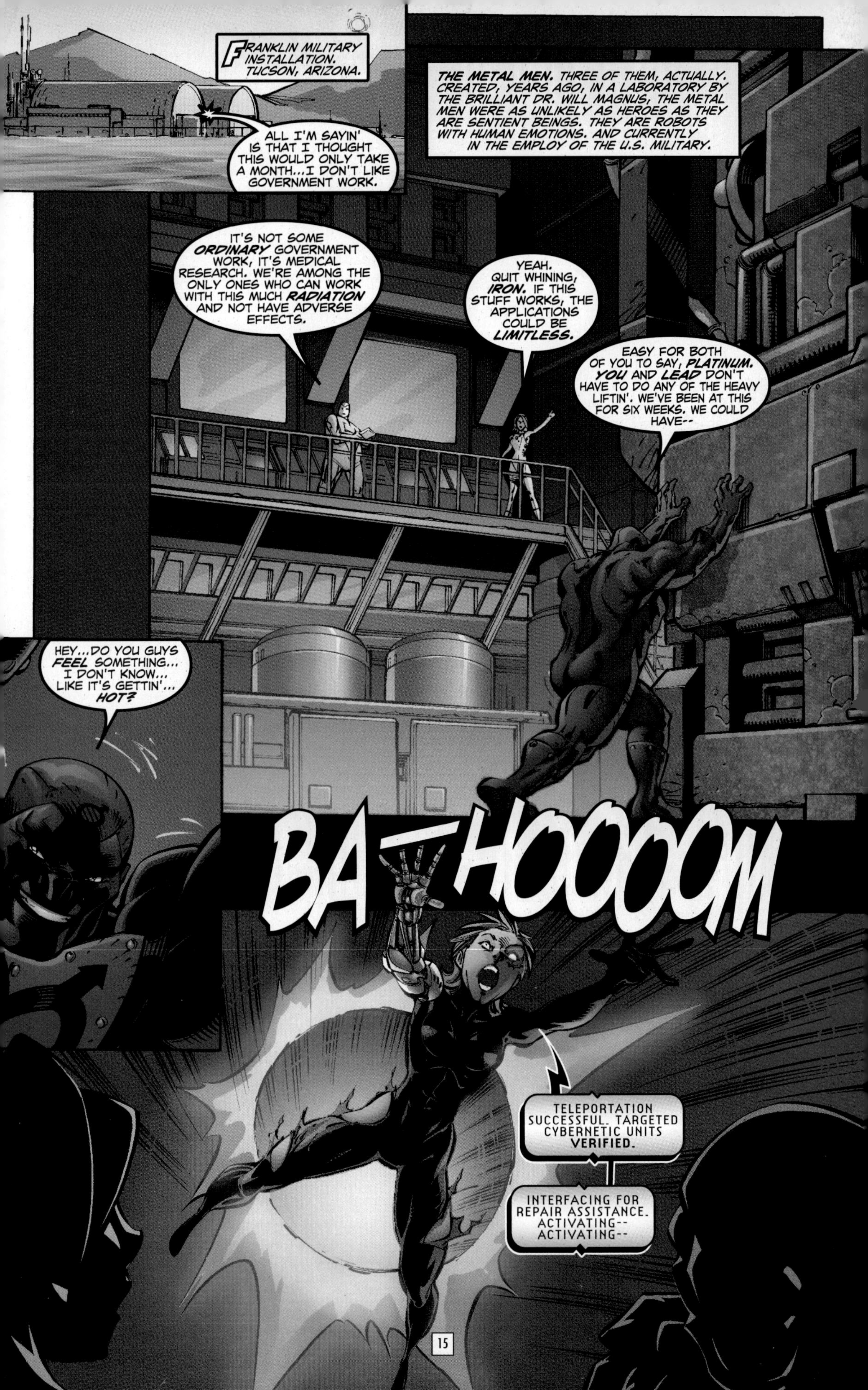
FRANKLIN MILITARY INSTALLATION. TUCSON, ARIZONA.
ALL I'M SAYIN' IS THAT I THOUGHT THIS WOULD ONLY TAKE A MONTH...I DON'T LIKE GOVERNMENT WORK.
THE METAL MEN. THREE OF THEM, ACTUALLY. CREATED, YEARS AGO, IN A LABORATORY BY THE BRILLIANT DR. WILL MAGNUS, THE METAL MEN WERE AS UNLIKELY AS HEROES AS THEY ARE SENTIENT BEINGS. THEY ARE ROBOTS WITH HUMAN EMOTIONS. AND CURRENTLY IN THE EMPLOY OF THE U.S. MILITARY.
IT'S NOT SOME ORDINARY GOVERNMENT WORK, IT'S MEDICAL RESEARCH. WE'RE AMONG THE ONLY ONES WHO CAN WORK WITH THIS MUCH RADIATION AND NOT HAVE ADVERSE EFFECTS.
YEAH. QUIT WHINING, IRON. IF THIS STUFF WORKS, THE APPLICATIONS COULD BE LIMITLESS.
EASY FOR BOTH OF YOU TO SAY, PLATINUM. YOU AND LEAD DON'T HAVE TO DO ANY OF THE HEAVY LIFTIN'. WE'VE BEEN AT THIS FOR SIX WEEKS. WE COULD HAVE--
HEY...DO YOU GUYS FEEL SOMETHING... I DON'T KNOW... LIKE IT'S GETTIN'... HOT?
BA-HOOOOM
TELEPORTATION SUCCESSFUL. TARGETED CYBERNETIC UNITS VERIFIED.
INTERFACING FOR REPAIR ASSISTANCE. ACTIVATING-- ACTIVATING--

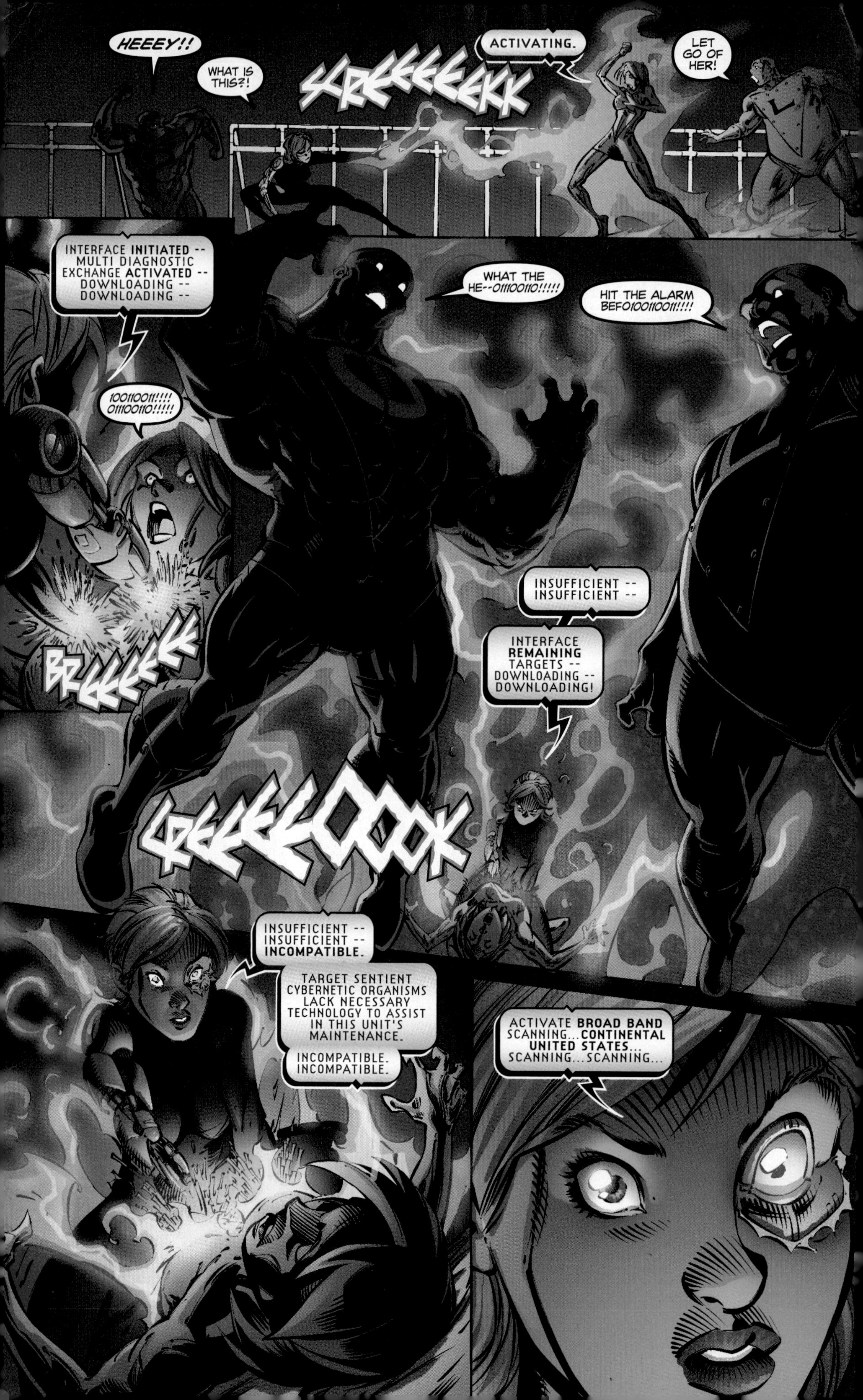
HEEEY!!
WHAT IS THIS?!
ACTIVATING.
SCREEEEEEKK
LET GO OF HER!
INTERFACE INITIATED -- MULTI DIAGNOSTIC EXCHANGE ACTIVATED -- DOWNLOADING -- DOWNLOADING --
100110011!!!! 01110011O!!!!!
WHAT THE HE--01110011O!!!!!
HIT THE ALARM BEFO100110011!!!!!
BREEEEEE
INSUFFICIENT -- INSUFFICIENT --
INTERFACE REMAINING TARGETS -- DOWNLOADING -- DOWNLOADING!
CREEEOOOK
INSUFFICIENT -- INSUFFICIENT -- INCOMPATIBLE.
TARGET SENTIENT CYBERNETIC ORGANISMS LACK NECESSARY TECHNOLOGY TO ASSIST IN THIS UNIT'S MAINTENANCE.
INCOMPATIBLE. INCOMPATIBLE.
ACTIVATE BROAD BAND SCANNING...CONTINENTAL UNITED STATES... SCANNING...SCANNING...

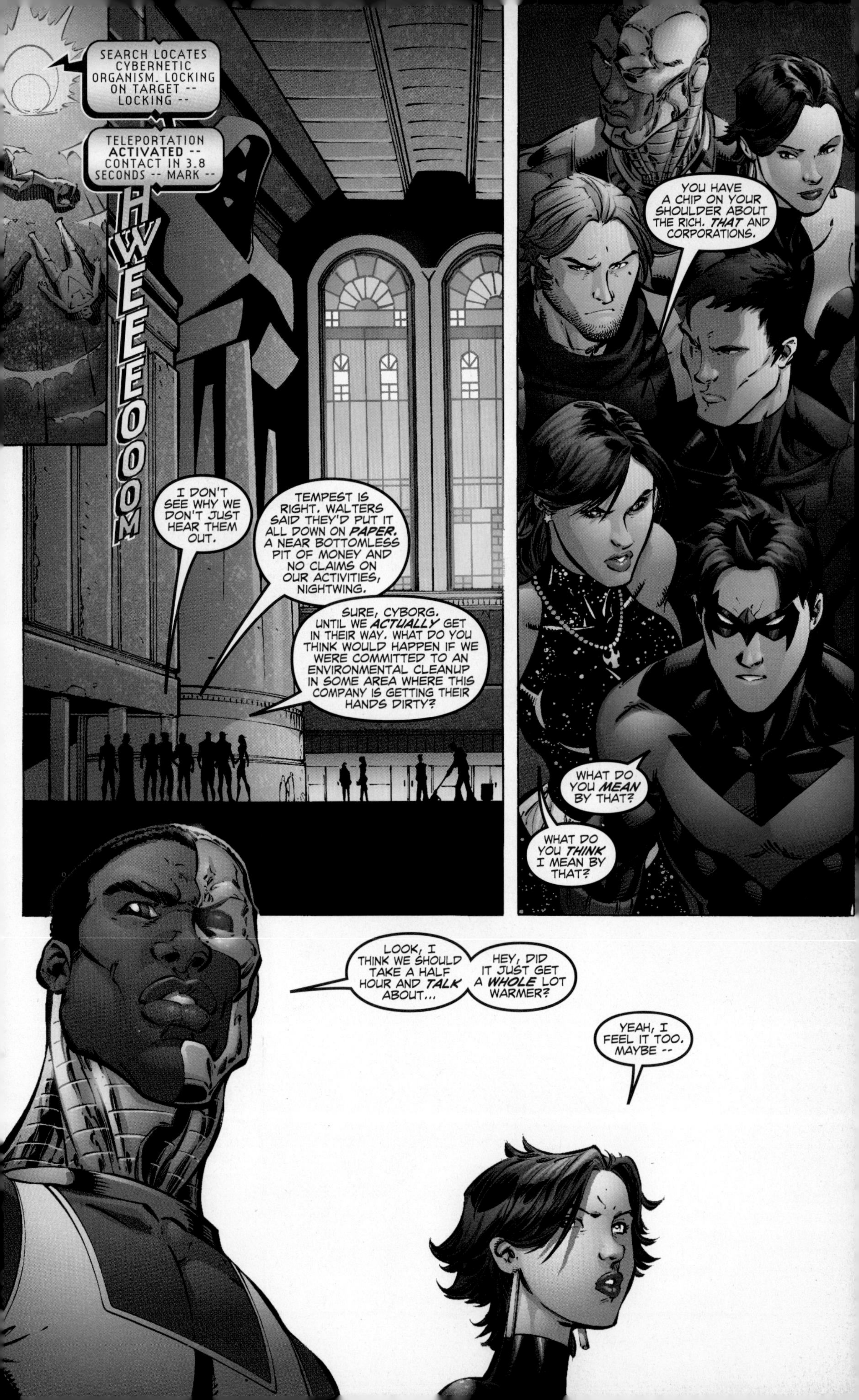
SEARCH LOCATES CYBERNETIC ORGANISM. LOCKING ON TARGET -- LOCKING --
TELEPORTATION ACTIVATED -- CONTACT IN 3.8 SECONDS -- MARK --
HWEEEEOOOOM
I DON'T SEE WHY WE DON'T JUST HEAR THEM OUT.
TEMPEST IS RIGHT. WALTERS SAID THEY'D PUT IT ALL DOWN ON PAPER. A NEAR BOTTOMLESS PIT OF MONEY AND NO CLAIMS ON OUR ACTIVITIES, NIGHTWING.
SURE, CYBORG. UNTIL WE ACTUALLY GET IN THEIR WAY. WHAT DO YOU THINK WOULD HAPPEN IF WE WERE COMMITTED TO AN ENVIRONMENTAL CLEANUP IN SOME AREA WHERE THIS COMPANY IS GETTING THEIR HANDS DIRTY?
YOU HAVE A CHIP ON YOUR SHOULDER ABOUT THE RICH. THAT AND CORPORATIONS.
WHAT DO YOU MEAN BY THAT?
WHAT DO YOU THINK I MEAN BY THAT?
LOOK, I THINK WE SHOULD TAKE A HALF HOUR AND TALK ABOUT...
HEY, DID IT JUST GET A WHOLE LOT WARMER?
YEAH, I FEEL IT TOO. MAYBE --

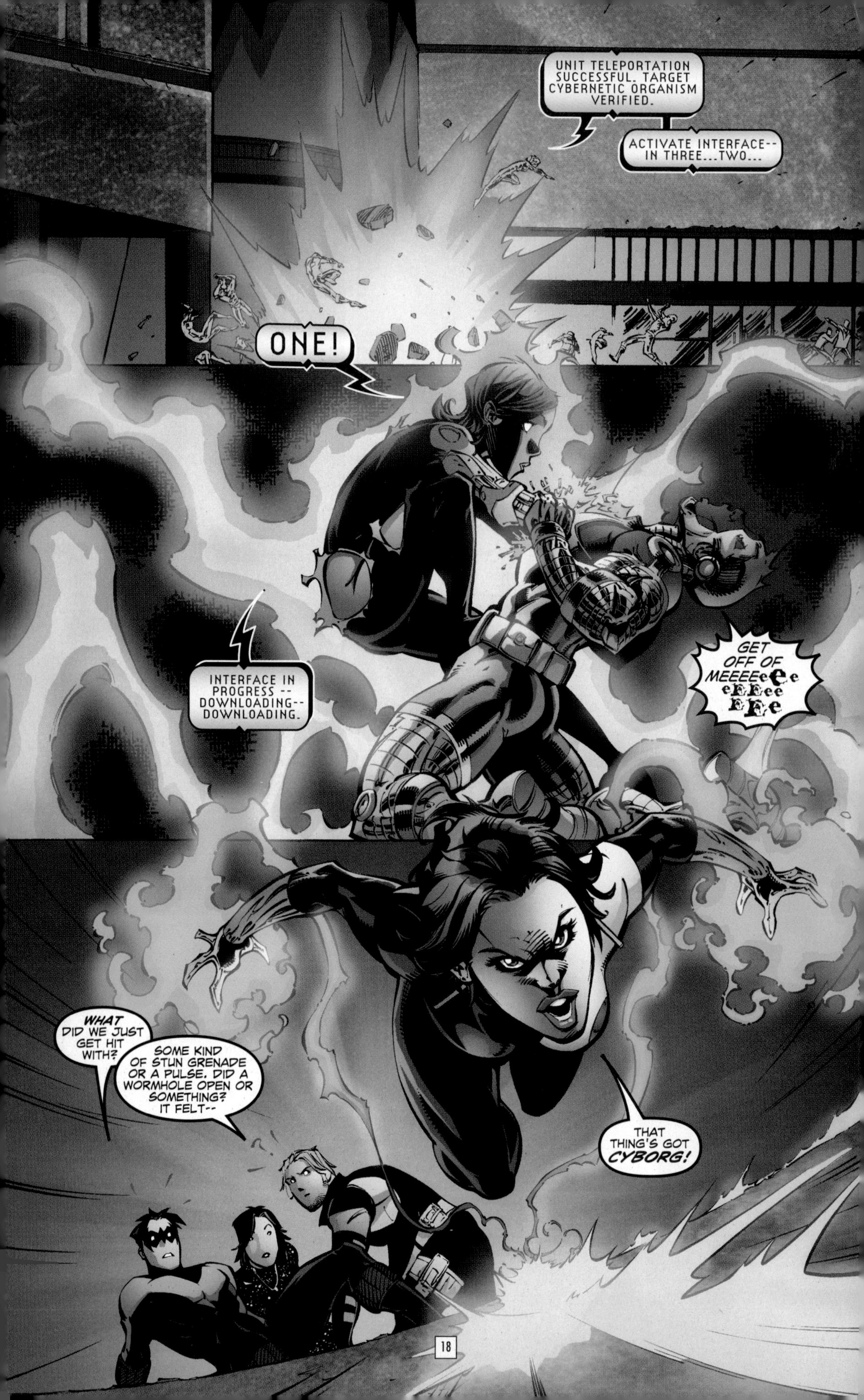
UNIT TELEPORTATION SUCCESSFUL. TARGET CYBERNETIC ORGANISM VERIFIED.
ACTIVATE INTERFACE-- IN THREE...TWO...
ONE!
INTERFACE IN PROGRESS -- DOWNLOADING-- DOWNLOADING.
GET OFF OF MEEEEeEe eEEee EEe
WHAT DID WE JUST GET HIT WITH?
SOME KIND OF STUN GRENADE OR A PULSE. DID A WORMHOLE OPEN OR SOMETHING? IT FELT--
THAT THING'S GOT CYBORG!

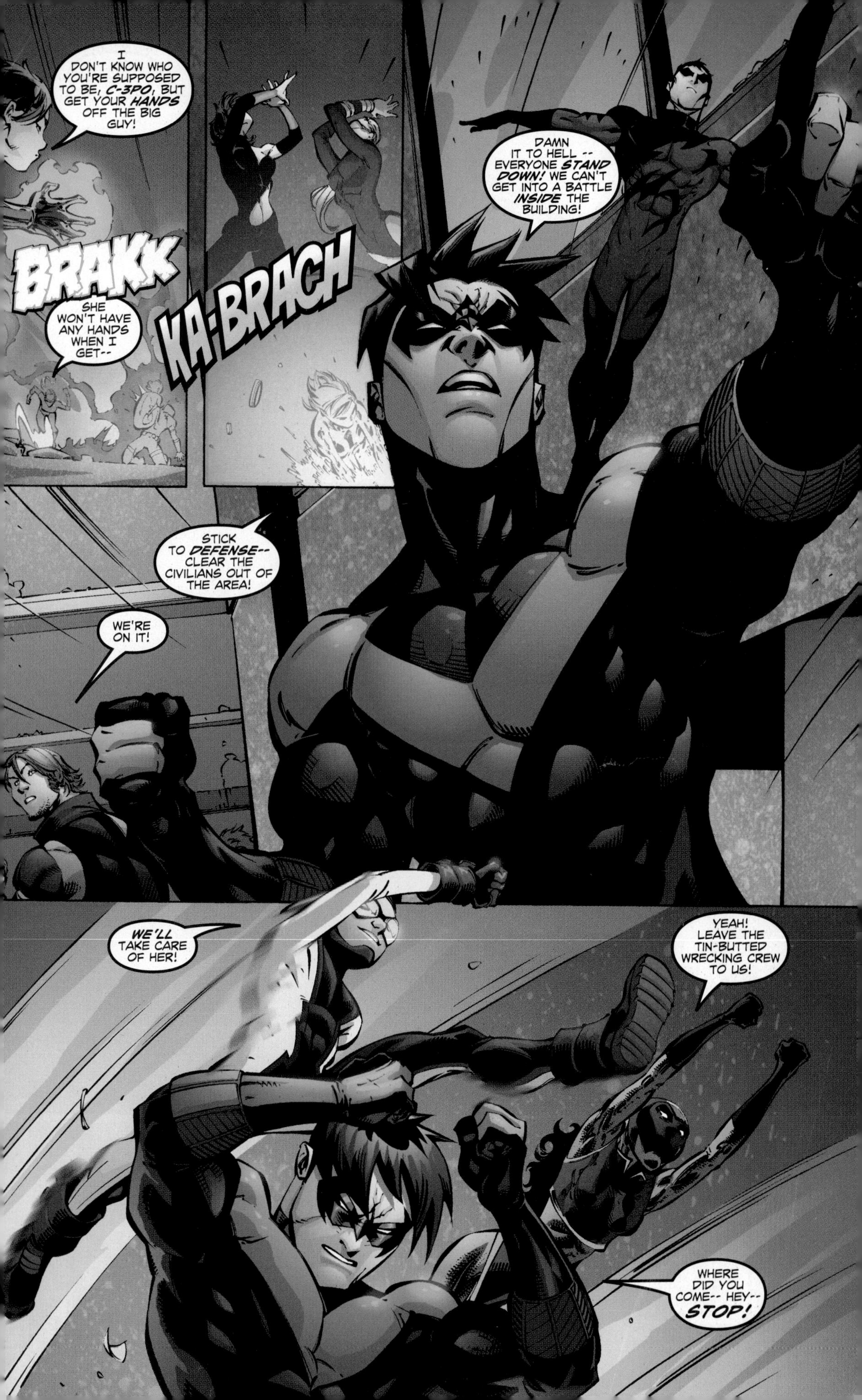
I DON'T KNOW WHO YOU'RE SUPPOSED TO BE, C-3PO, BUT GET YOUR HANDS OFF THE BIG GUY!
BRAKK
SHE WON'T HAVE ANY HANDS WHEN I GET--
KA-BRACH
DAMN IT TO HELL -- EVERYONE STAND DOWN! WE CAN'T GET INTO A BATTLE INSIDE THE BUILDING!
STICK TO DEFENSE-- CLEAR THE CIVILIANS OUT OF THE AREA!
WE'RE ON IT!
WE'LL TAKE CARE OF HER!
YEAH! LEAVE THE TIN-BUTTED WRECKING CREW TO US!
WHERE DID YOU COME-- HEY-- STOP!

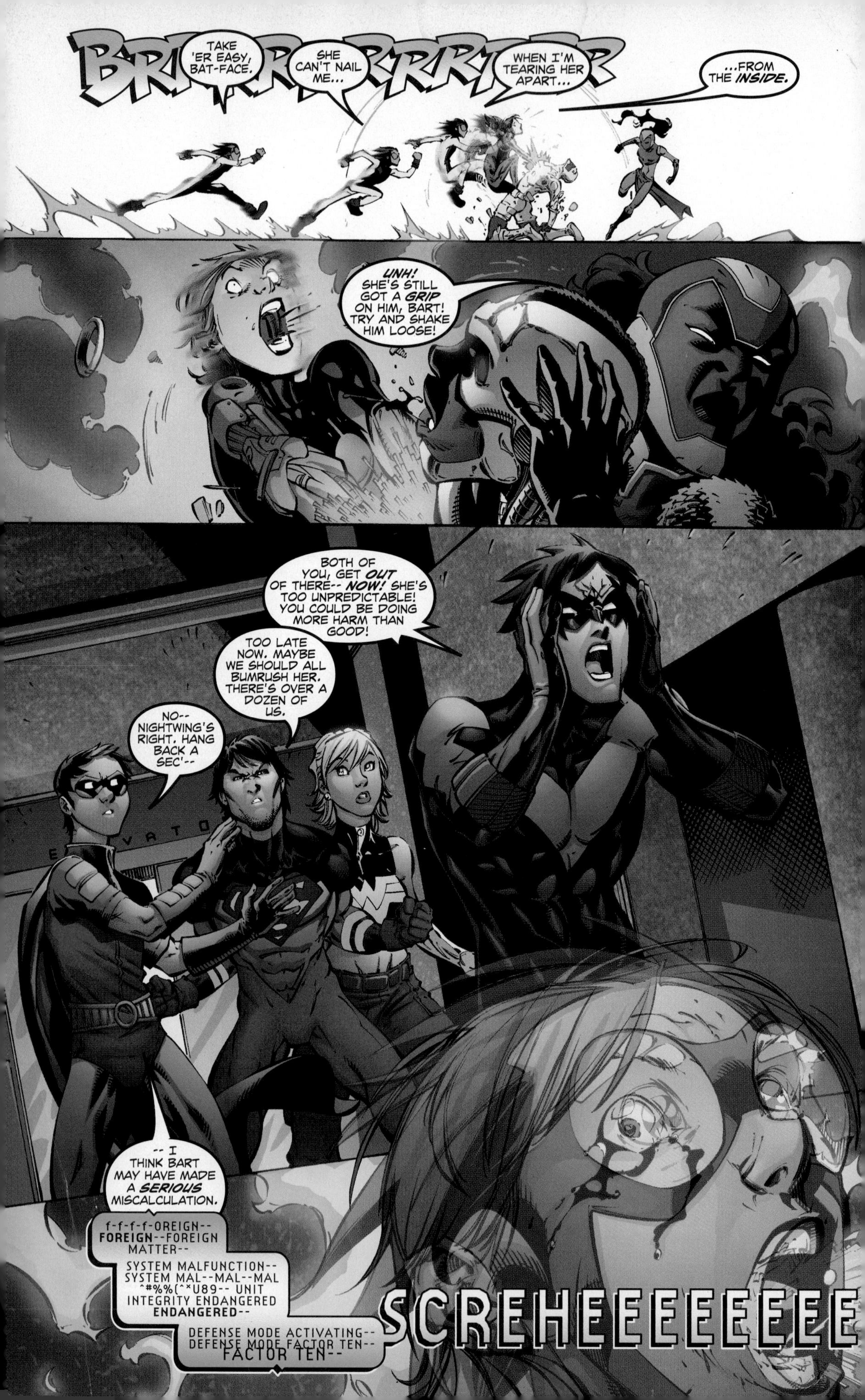
BRRRRRRRRRRRRRRRR
TAKE 'ER EASY, BAT-FACE.
SHE CAN'T NAIL ME...
WHEN I'M TEARING HER APART...
...FROM THE *INSIDE.*
UNH! SHE'S STILL GOT A *GRIP* ON HIM, BART! TRY AND SHAKE HIM LOOSE!
BOTH OF YOU, GET *OUT* OF THERE-- *NOW!* SHE'S TOO UNPREDICTABLE! YOU COULD BE DOING MORE HARM THAN GOOD!
TOO LATE NOW. MAYBE WE SHOULD ALL BUMRUSH HER. THERE'S OVER A DOZEN OF US.
NO-- NIGHTWING'S RIGHT. HANG BACK A SEC'--
-- I THINK BART MAY HAVE MADE A *SERIOUS* MISCALCULATION.
f-f-f-f-OREIGN-- **FOREIGN**--FOREIGN MATTER--
SYSTEM MALFUNCTION-- SYSTEM MAL--MAL--MAL ^#%%(^*U89-- UNIT INTEGRITY ENDANGERED **ENDANGERED**--
DEFENSE MODE ACTIVATING-- DEFENSE MODE FACTOR TEN-- FACTOR TEN--
SCREHEEEEEEEEE

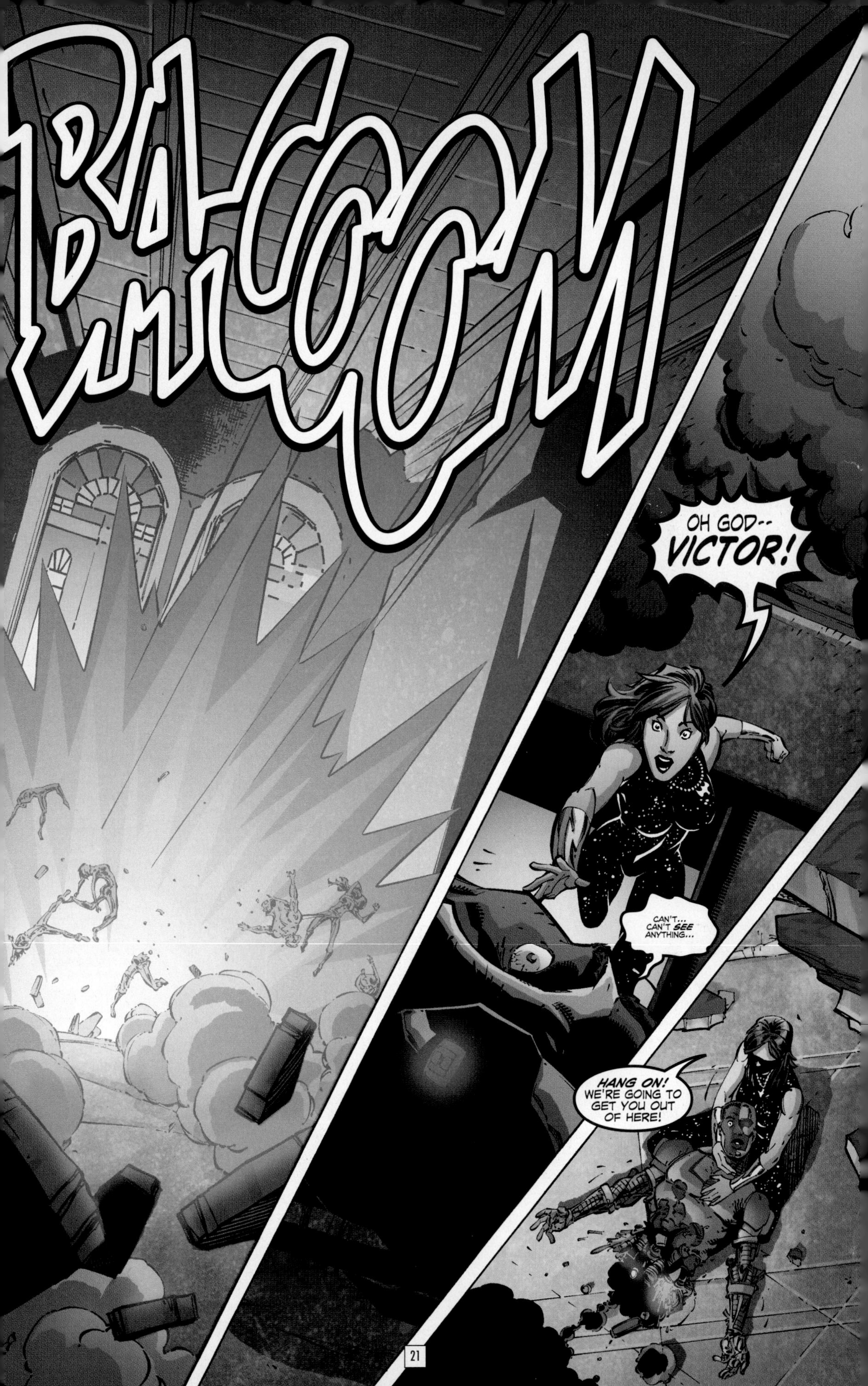
BRACOOM
OH GOD-- VICTOR!
CAN'T... CAN'T SEE ANYTHING...
HANG ON! WE'RE GOING TO GET YOU OUT OF HERE!

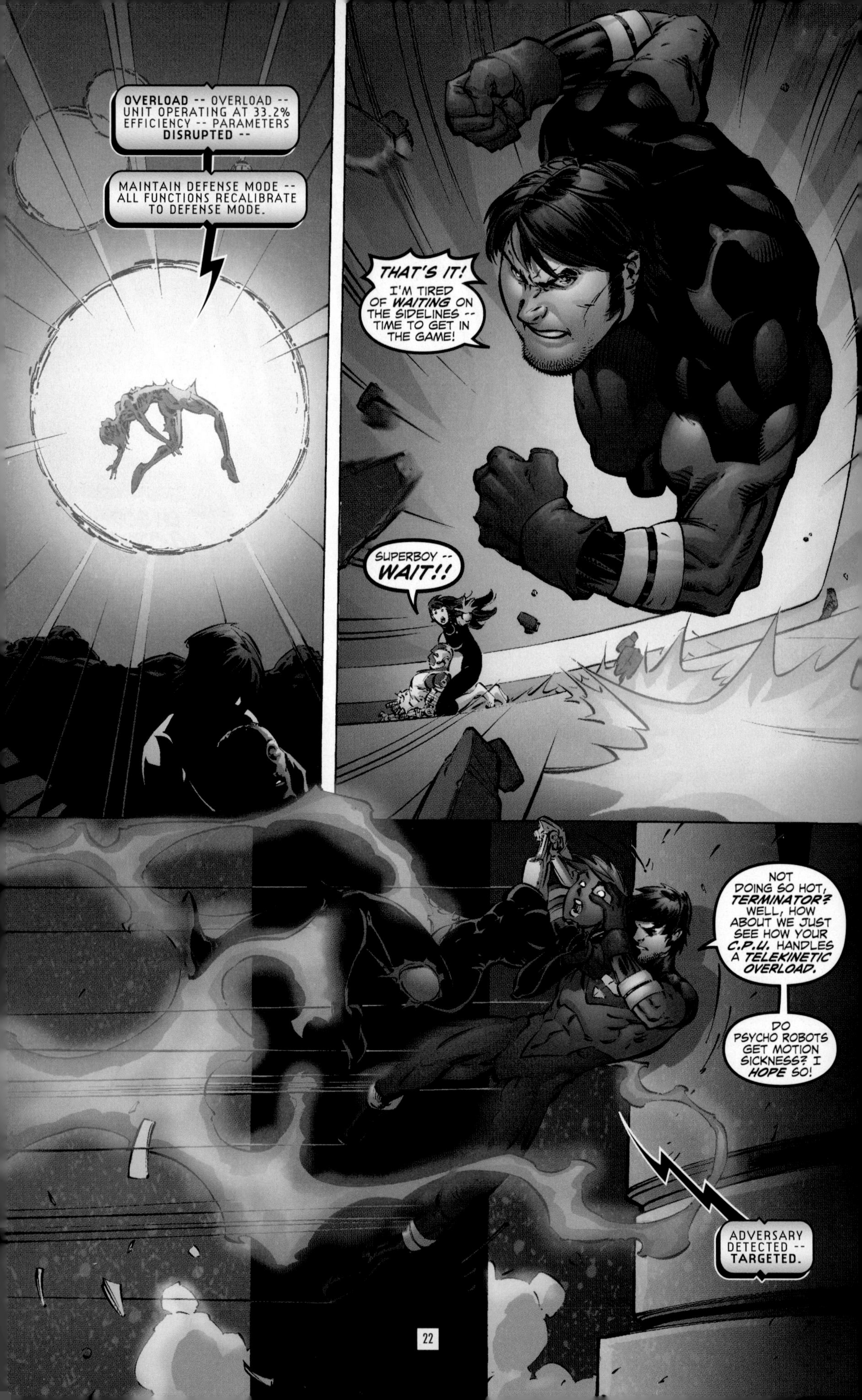

OVERLOAD -- OVERLOAD -- UNIT OPERATING AT 33.2% EFFICIENCY -- PARAMETERS DISRUPTED --
MAINTAIN DEFENSE MODE -- ALL FUNCTIONS RECALIBRATE TO DEFENSE MODE.
THAT'S IT! I'M TIRED OF WAITING ON THE SIDELINES -- TIME TO GET IN THE GAME!
SUPERBOY -- WAIT!!
NOT DOING SO HOT, TERMINATOR? WELL, HOW ABOUT WE JUST SEE HOW YOUR C.P.U. HANDLES A TELEKINETIC OVERLOAD.
DO PSYCHO ROBOTS GET MOTION SICKNESS? I HOPE SO!
ADVERSARY DETECTED -- TARGETED.

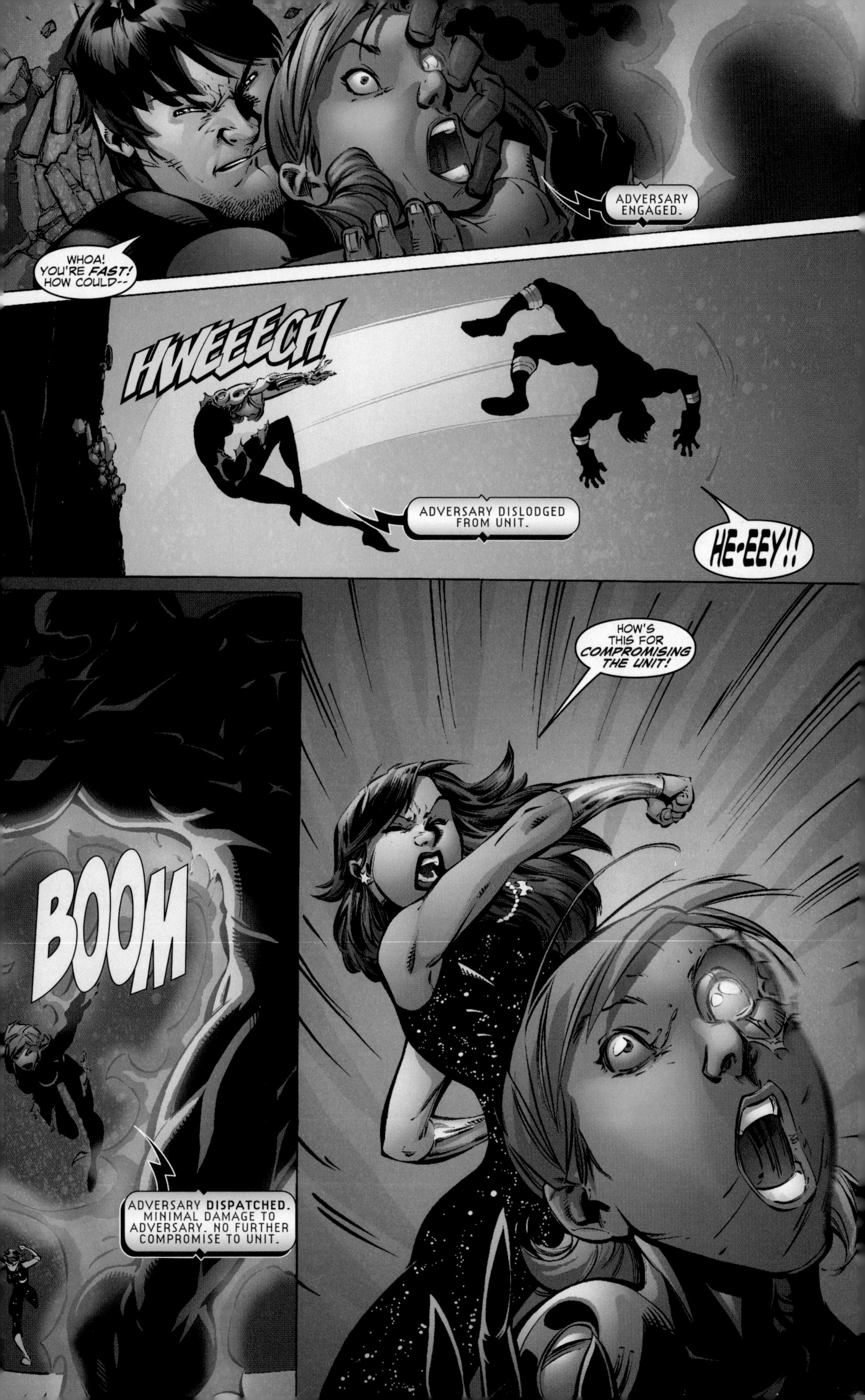
ADVERSARY ENGAGED.
WHOA! YOU'RE *FAST!* HOW COULD--
HWEEECH
ADVERSARY DISLODGED FROM UNIT.
HE-EEY!!
HOW'S THIS FOR *COMPROMISING THE UNIT!*
BOOM
ADVERSARY **DISPATCHED.** MINIMAL DAMAGE TO ADVERSARY. NO FURTHER COMPROMISE TO UNIT.

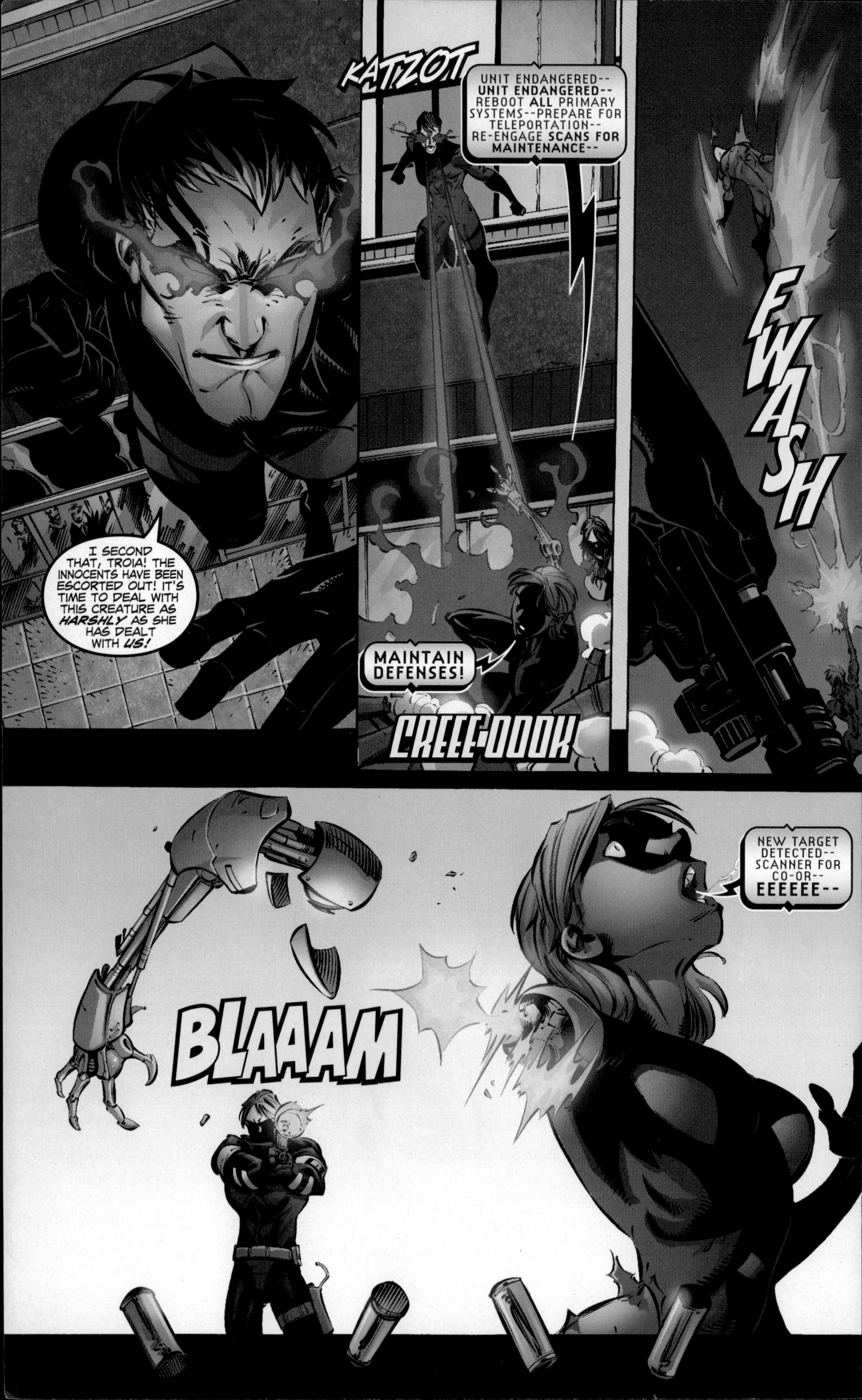
KATZOT
UNIT ENDANGERED-- UNIT ENDANGERED-- REBOOT ALL PRIMARY SYSTEMS--PREPARE FOR TELEPORTATION-- RE-ENGAGE SCANS FOR MAINTENANCE--
FWASH
I SECOND THAT, TROIA! THE INNOCENTS HAVE BEEN ESCORTED OUT! IT'S TIME TO DEAL WITH THIS CREATURE AS *HARSHLY* AS SHE HAS DEALT WITH *US!*
MAINTAIN DEFENSES!
CREEE-DOOK
NEW TARGET DETECTED-- SCANNER FOR CO-OR-- EEEEEE--
BLAAAM

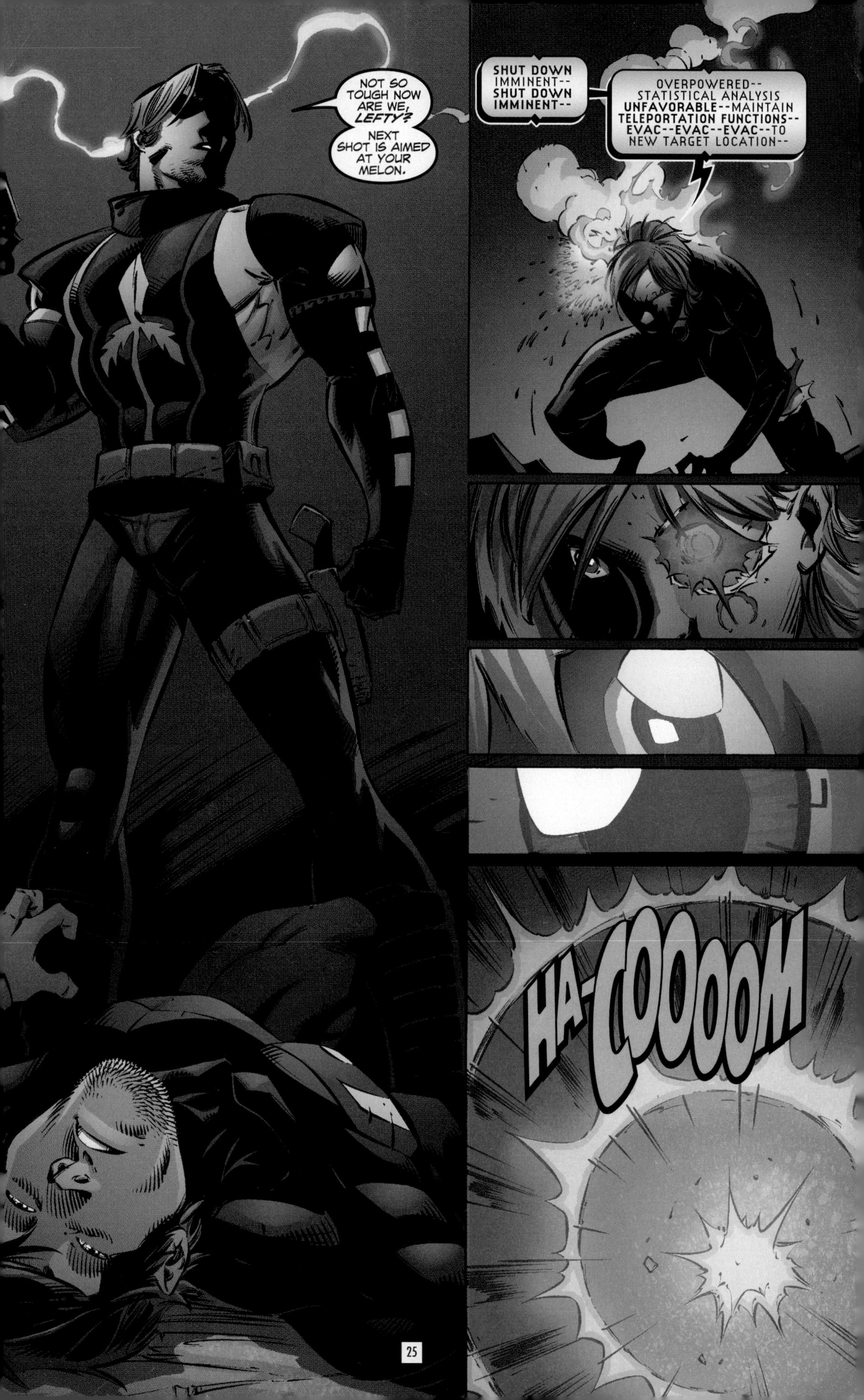
NOT SO TOUGH NOW ARE WE, LEFTY? NEXT SHOT IS AIMED AT YOUR MELON.
SHUT DOWN IMMINENT-- SHUT DOWN IMMINENT--
OVERPOWERED-- STATISTICAL ANALYSIS UNFAVORABLE--MAINTAIN TELEPORTATION FUNCTIONS-- EVAC--EVAC--EVAC--TO NEW TARGET LOCATION--
HA-COOOOM

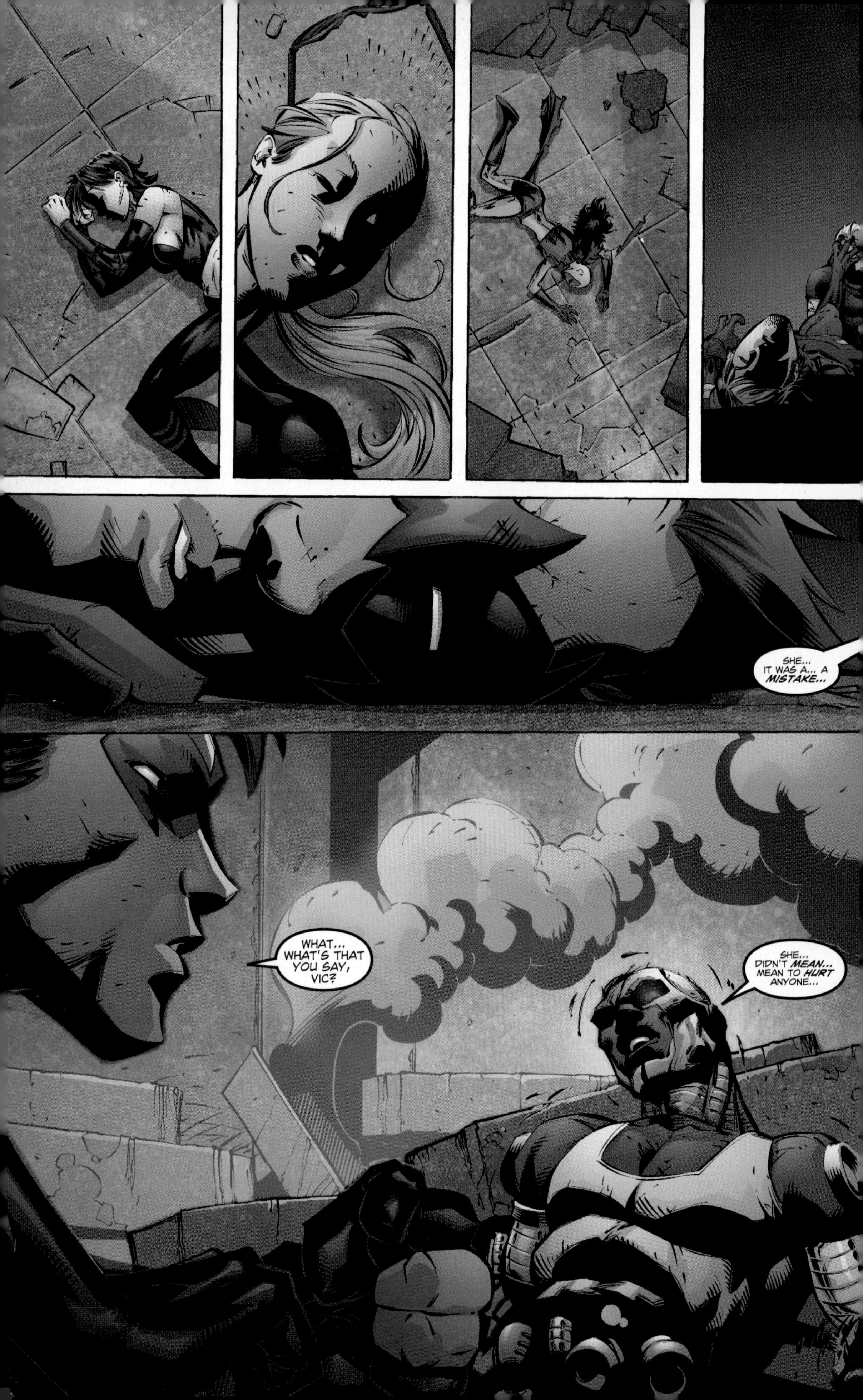
SHE... IT WAS A... A MISTAKE...
WHAT... WHAT'S THAT YOU SAY, VIC?
SHE... DIDN'T MEAN... MEAN TO HURT ANYONE...

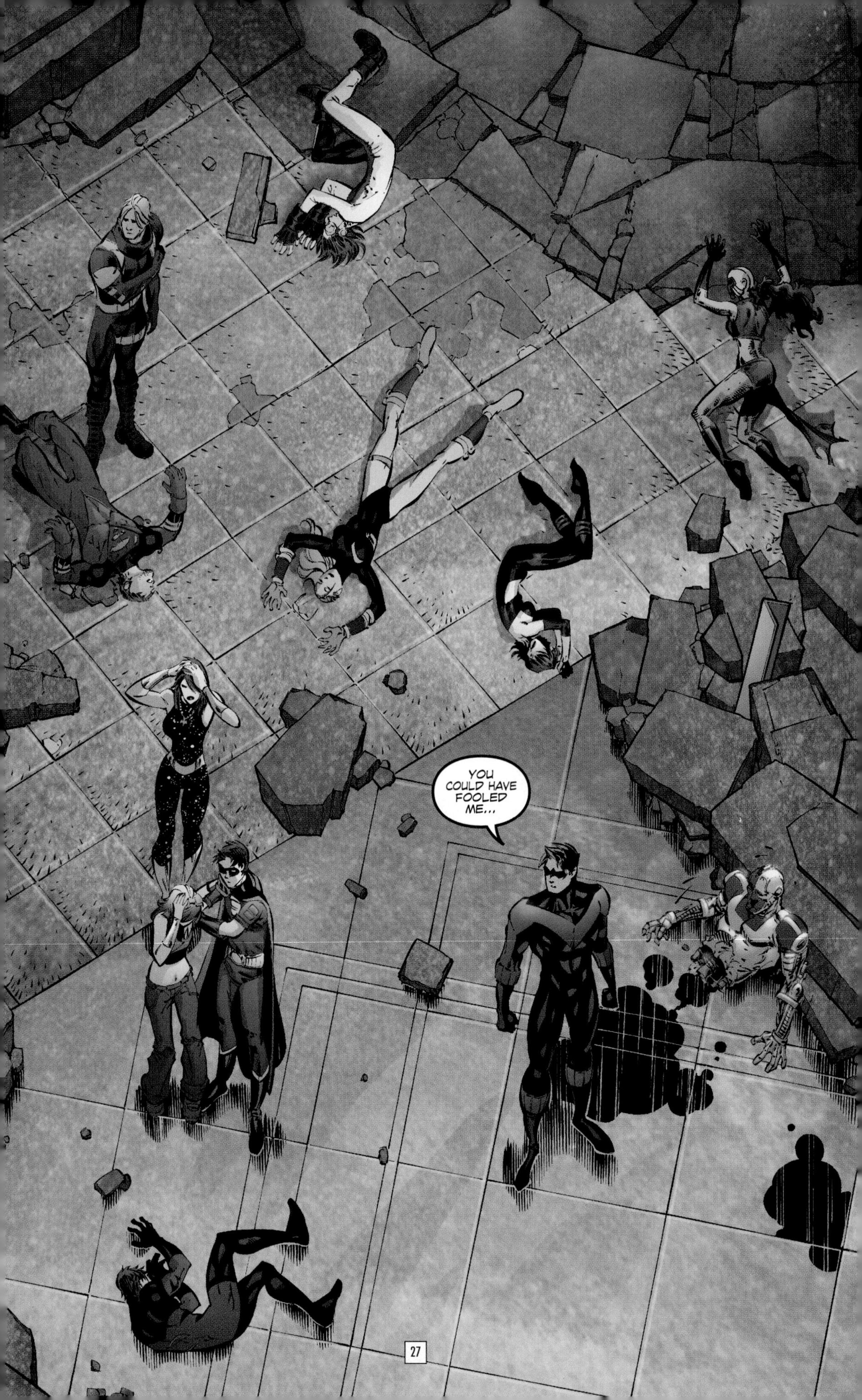
YOU COULD HAVE FOOLED ME...

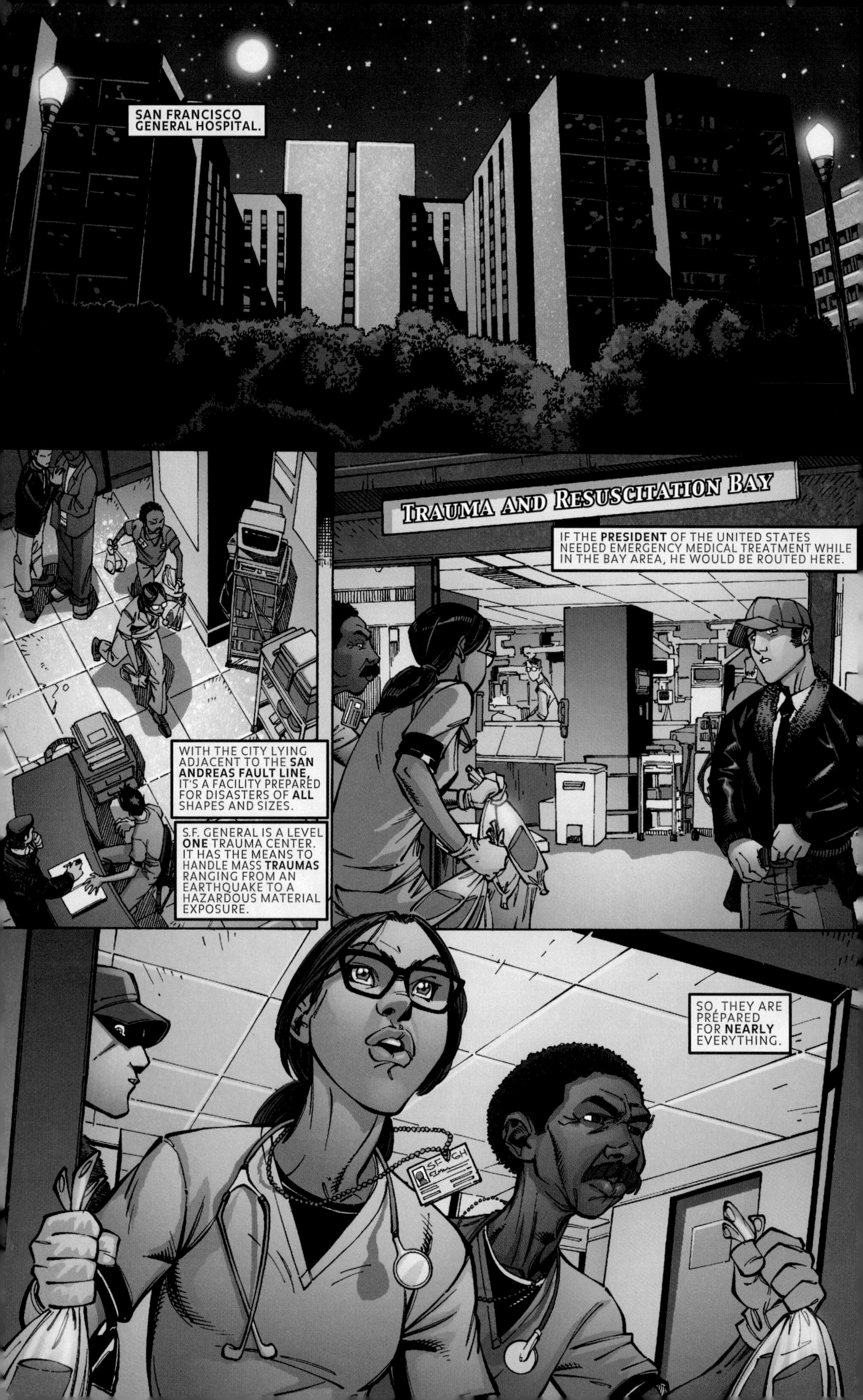
SAN FRANCISCO GENERAL HOSPITAL.
WITH THE CITY LYING ADJACENT TO THE SAN ANDREAS FAULT LINE, IT'S A FACILITY PREPARED FOR DISASTERS OF ALL SHAPES AND SIZES.
S.F. GENERAL IS A LEVEL ONE TRAUMA CENTER. IT HAS THE MEANS TO HANDLE MASS TRAUMAS RANGING FROM AN EARTHQUAKE TO A HAZARDOUS MATERIAL EXPOSURE.
TRAUMA AND RESUSCITATION BAY
IF THE PRESIDENT OF THE UNITED STATES NEEDED EMERGENCY MEDICAL TREATMENT WHILE IN THE BAY AREA, HE WOULD BE ROUTED HERE.
SO, THEY ARE PREPARED FOR NEARLY EVERYTHING.

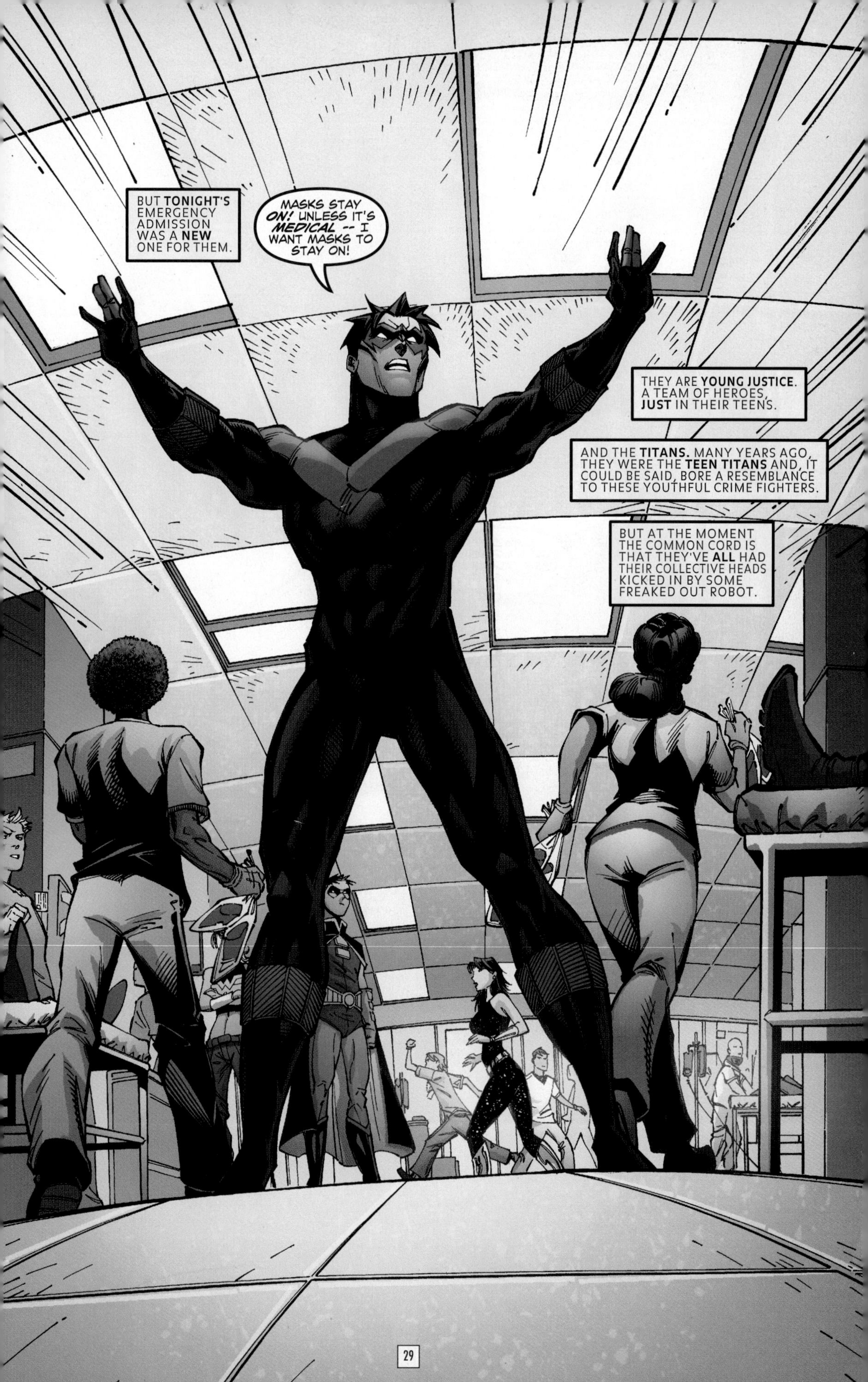
BUT TONIGHT'S EMERGENCY ADMISSION WAS A NEW ONE FOR THEM.
MASKS STAY ON! UNLESS IT'S MEDICAL -- I WANT MASKS TO STAY ON!
THEY ARE YOUNG JUSTICE. A TEAM OF HEROES, JUST IN THEIR TEENS.
AND THE TITANS. MANY YEARS AGO, THEY WERE THE TEEN TITANS AND, IT COULD BE SAID, BORE A RESEMBLANCE TO THESE YOUTHFUL CRIME FIGHTERS.
BUT AT THE MOMENT THE COMMON CORD IS THAT THEY'VE ALL HAD THEIR COLLECTIVE HEADS KICKED IN BY SOME FREAKED OUT ROBOT.

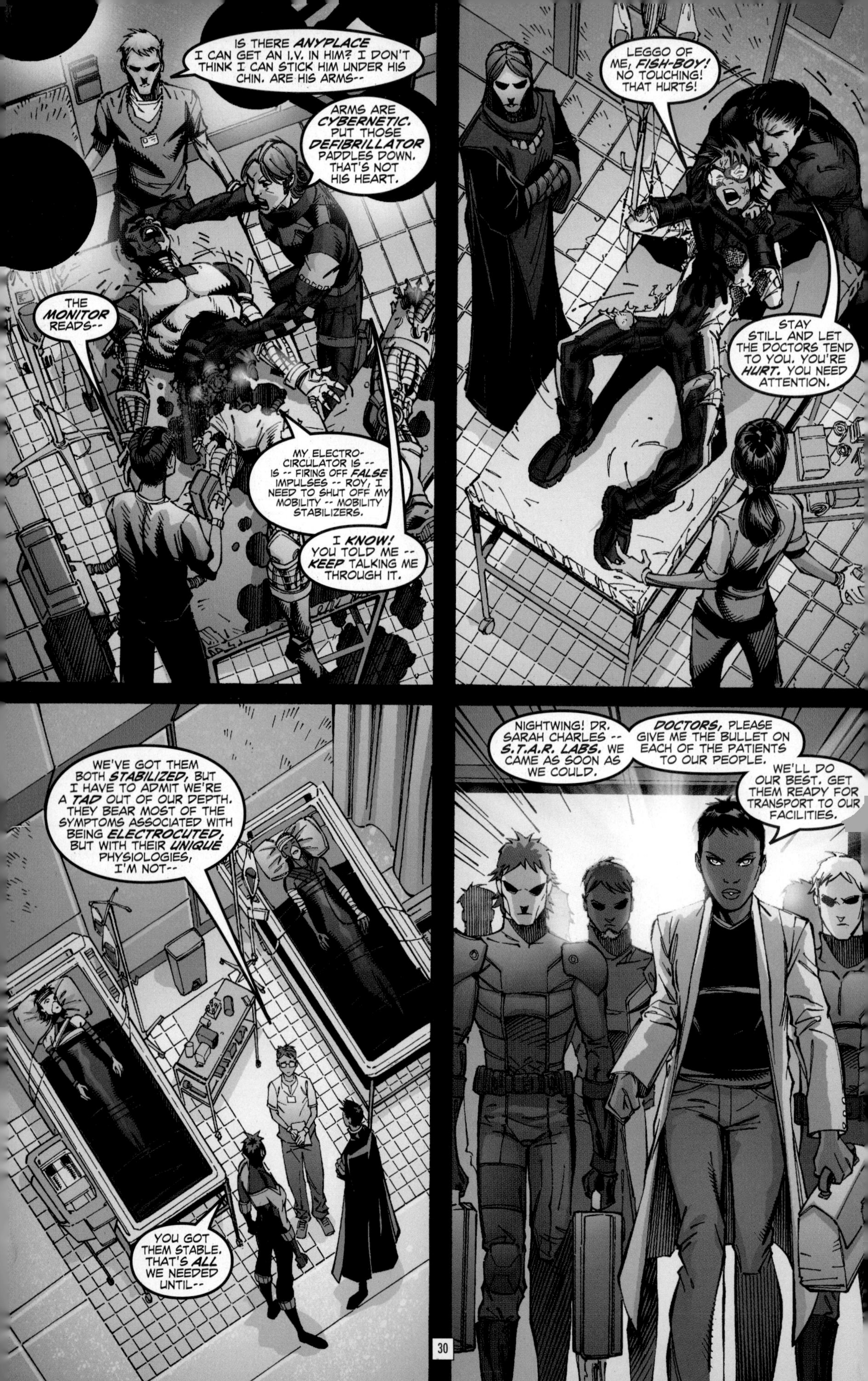
IS THERE ANYPLACE I CAN GET AN I.V. IN HIM? I DON'T THINK I CAN STICK HIM UNDER HIS CHIN. ARE HIS ARMS--
ARMS ARE CYBERNETIC. PUT THOSE DEFIBRILLATOR PADDLES DOWN. THAT'S NOT HIS HEART.
THE MONITOR READS--
MY ELECTRO-CIRCULATOR IS -- IS -- FIRING OFF FALSE IMPULSES -- ROY, I NEED TO SHUT OFF MY MOBILITY -- MOBILITY STABILIZERS.
I KNOW! YOU TOLD ME -- KEEP TALKING ME THROUGH IT.
LEGGO OF ME, FISH-BOY! NO TOUCHING! THAT HURTS!
STAY STILL AND LET THE DOCTORS TEND TO YOU. YOU'RE HURT. YOU NEED ATTENTION.
WE'VE GOT THEM BOTH STABILIZED, BUT I HAVE TO ADMIT WE'RE A TAD OUT OF OUR DEPTH. THEY BEAR MOST OF THE SYMPTOMS ASSOCIATED WITH BEING ELECTROCUTED, BUT WITH THEIR UNIQUE PHYSIOLOGIES, I'M NOT--
YOU GOT THEM STABLE. THAT'S ALL WE NEEDED UNTIL--
NIGHTWING! DR. SARAH CHARLES -- S.T.A.R. LABS. WE CAME AS SOON AS WE COULD.
DOCTORS, PLEASE GIVE ME THE BULLET ON EACH OF THE PATIENTS TO OUR PEOPLE.
WE'LL DO OUR BEST. GET THEM READY FOR TRANSPORT TO OUR FACILITIES.

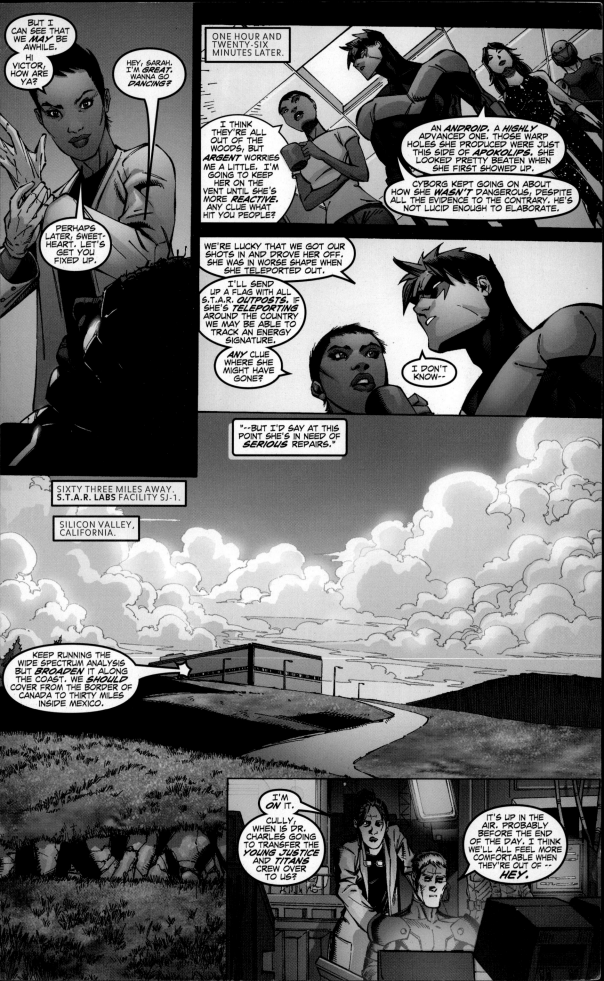

BUT I CAN SEE THAT WE *MAY* BE AWHILE.

HI VICTOR, HOW ARE YA?

HEY, SARAH. I'M *GREAT*. WANNA GO *DANCING*?

PERHAPS LATER, SWEET-HEART. LET'S GET YOU FIXED UP.

ONE HOUR AND TWENTY-SIX MINUTES LATER.

I THINK THEY'RE ALL OUT OF THE WOODS, BUT *ARGENT* WORRIES ME A LITTLE. I'M GOING TO KEEP HER ON THE VENT UNTIL SHE'S MORE *REACTIVE*. ANY CLUE WHAT HIT YOU PEOPLE?

AN *ANDROID*. A *HIGHLY* ADVANCED ONE. THOSE WARP HOLES SHE PRODUCED WERE JUST THIS SIDE OF *APOKOLIPS*. SHE LOOKED PRETTY BEATEN WHEN SHE FIRST SHOWED UP.

CYBORG KEPT GOING ON ABOUT HOW SHE *WASN'T* DANGEROUS, DESPITE ALL THE EVIDENCE TO THE CONTRARY. HE'S NOT LUCID ENOUGH TO ELABORATE.

WE'RE LUCKY THAT WE GOT OUR SHOTS IN AND DROVE HER OFF. SHE WAS IN WORSE SHAPE WHEN SHE TELEPORTED OUT.

I'LL SEND UP A FLAG WITH ALL S.T.A.R. *OUTPOSTS*. IF SHE'S *TELEPORTING* AROUND THE COUNTRY WE MAY BE ABLE TO TRACK AN ENERGY SIGNATURE.

ANY CLUE WHERE SHE MIGHT HAVE GONE?

I DON'T KNOW--

"--BUT I'D SAY AT THIS POINT SHE'S IN NEED OF *SERIOUS* REPAIRS."

SIXTY THREE MILES AWAY. **S.T.A.R. LABS** FACILITY SJ-1.

SILICON VALLEY, CALIFORNIA.

KEEP RUNNING THE WIDE SPECTRUM ANALYSIS BUT *BROADEN* IT ALONG THE COAST. WE *SHOULD* COVER FROM THE BORDER OF CANADA TO THIRTY MILES INSIDE MEXICO.

I'M *ON* IT.

CULLY, WHEN IS DR. CHARLES GOING TO TRANSFER THE *YOUNG JUSTICE* AND *TITANS* CREW OVER TO US?

IT'S UP IN THE AIR. PROBABLY BEFORE THE END OF THE DAY. I THINK WE'LL ALL FEEL MORE COMFORTABLE WHEN THEY'RE OUT OF -- *HEY.*

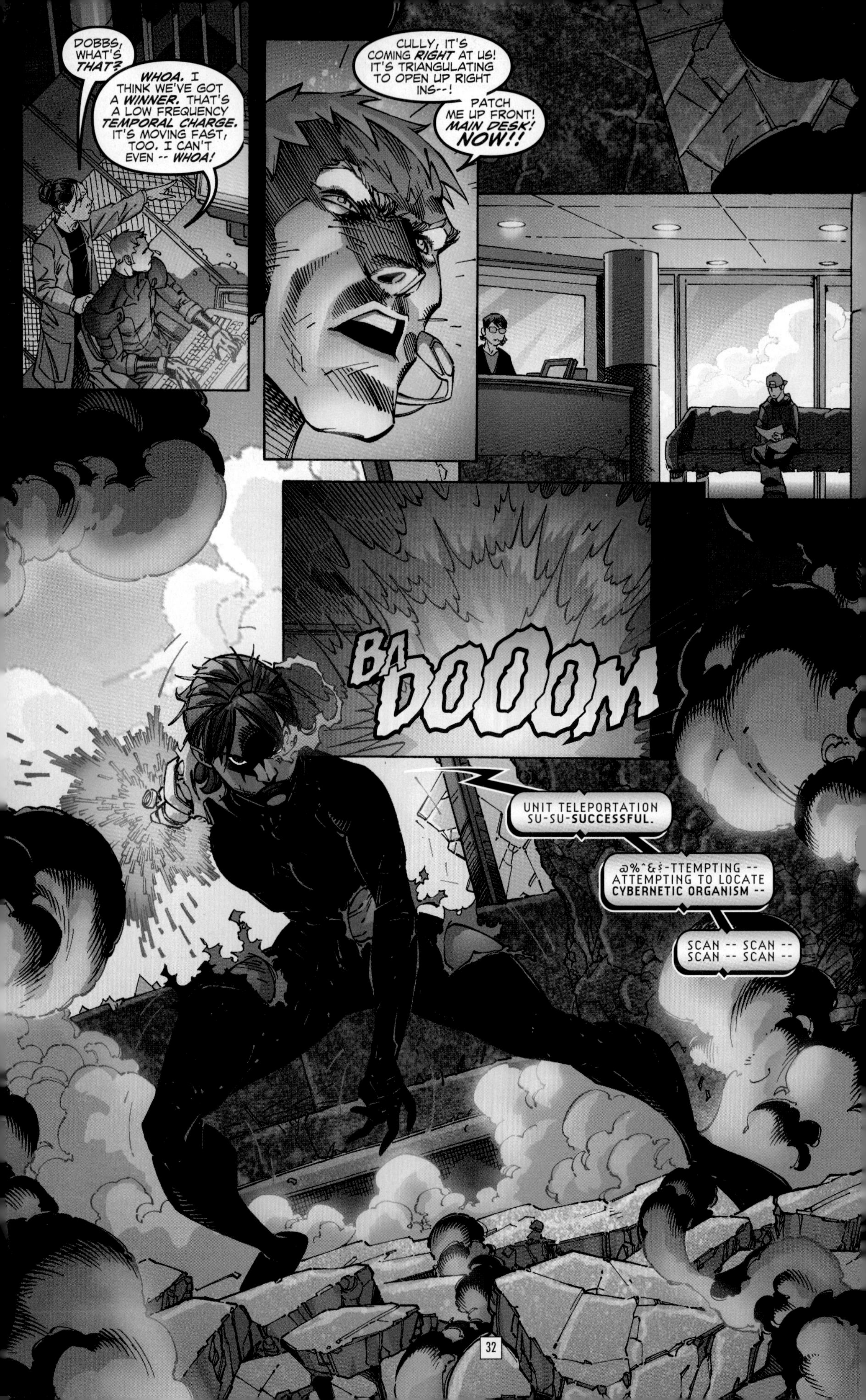
DOBBS, WHAT'S *THAT?*
WHOA. I THINK WE'VE GOT A *WINNER.* THAT'S A LOW FREQUENCY *TEMPORAL CHARGE.* IT'S MOVING FAST, TOO. I CAN'T EVEN -- *WHOA!*
CULLY, IT'S COMING *RIGHT* AT US! IT'S TRIANGULATING TO OPEN UP RIGHT INS--!
PATCH ME UP FRONT! *MAIN DESK! NOW!!*
BA DOOOM
UNIT TELEPORTATION SU-SU-**SUCCESSFUL.**
@%^&$-TTEMPTING -- ATTEMPTING TO LOCATE **CYBERNETIC ORGANISM** --
SCAN -- SCAN -- SCAN -- SCAN --

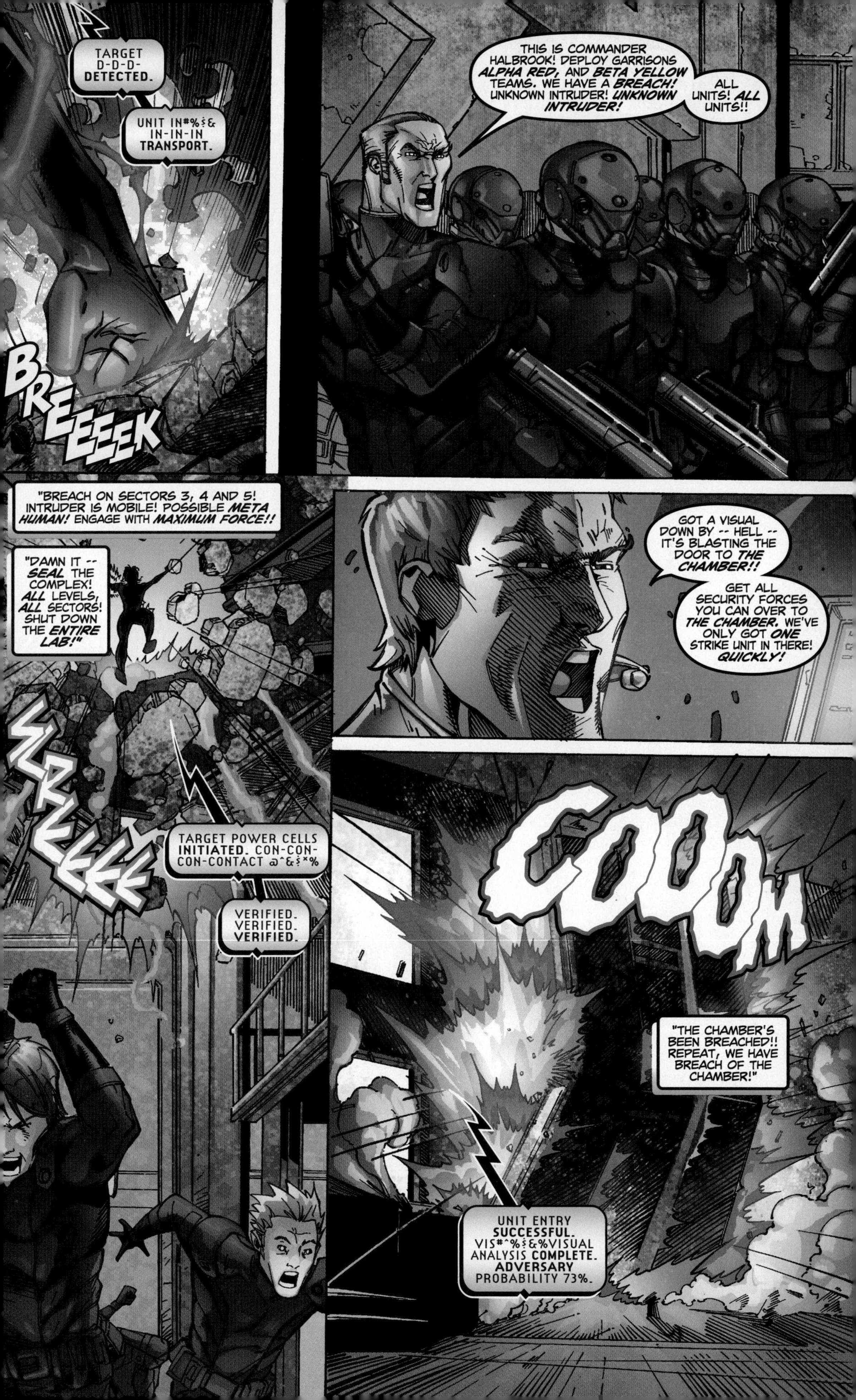
TARGET D-D-D-DETECTED.
UNIT IN#%$& IN-IN-IN TRANSPORT.
BREEEEK
THIS IS COMMANDER HALBROOK! DEPLOY GARRISONS ALPHA RED, AND BETA YELLOW TEAMS. WE HAVE A BREACH! UNKNOWN INTRUDER! UNKNOWN INTRUDER!
ALL UNITS! ALL UNITS!!
"BREACH ON SECTORS 3, 4 AND 5! INTRUDER IS MOBILE! POSSIBLE META HUMAN! ENGAGE WITH MAXIMUM FORCE!!
"DAMN IT -- SEAL THE COMPLEX! ALL LEVELS, ALL SECTORS! SHUT DOWN THE ENTIRE LAB!"
GOT A VISUAL DOWN BY -- HELL -- IT'S BLASTING THE DOOR TO THE CHAMBER!!
GET ALL SECURITY FORCES YOU CAN OVER TO THE CHAMBER. WE'VE ONLY GOT ONE STRIKE UNIT IN THERE! QUICKLY!
TARGET POWER CELLS INITIATED. CON-CON-CON-CONTACT @^&$*%
VERIFIED. VERIFIED. VERIFIED.
COOOM
"THE CHAMBER'S BEEN BREACHED!! REPEAT, WE HAVE BREACH OF THE CHAMBER!"
UNIT ENTRY SUCCESSFUL. VIS#^%$&%VISUAL ANALYSIS COMPLETE. ADVERSARY PROBABILITY 73%.

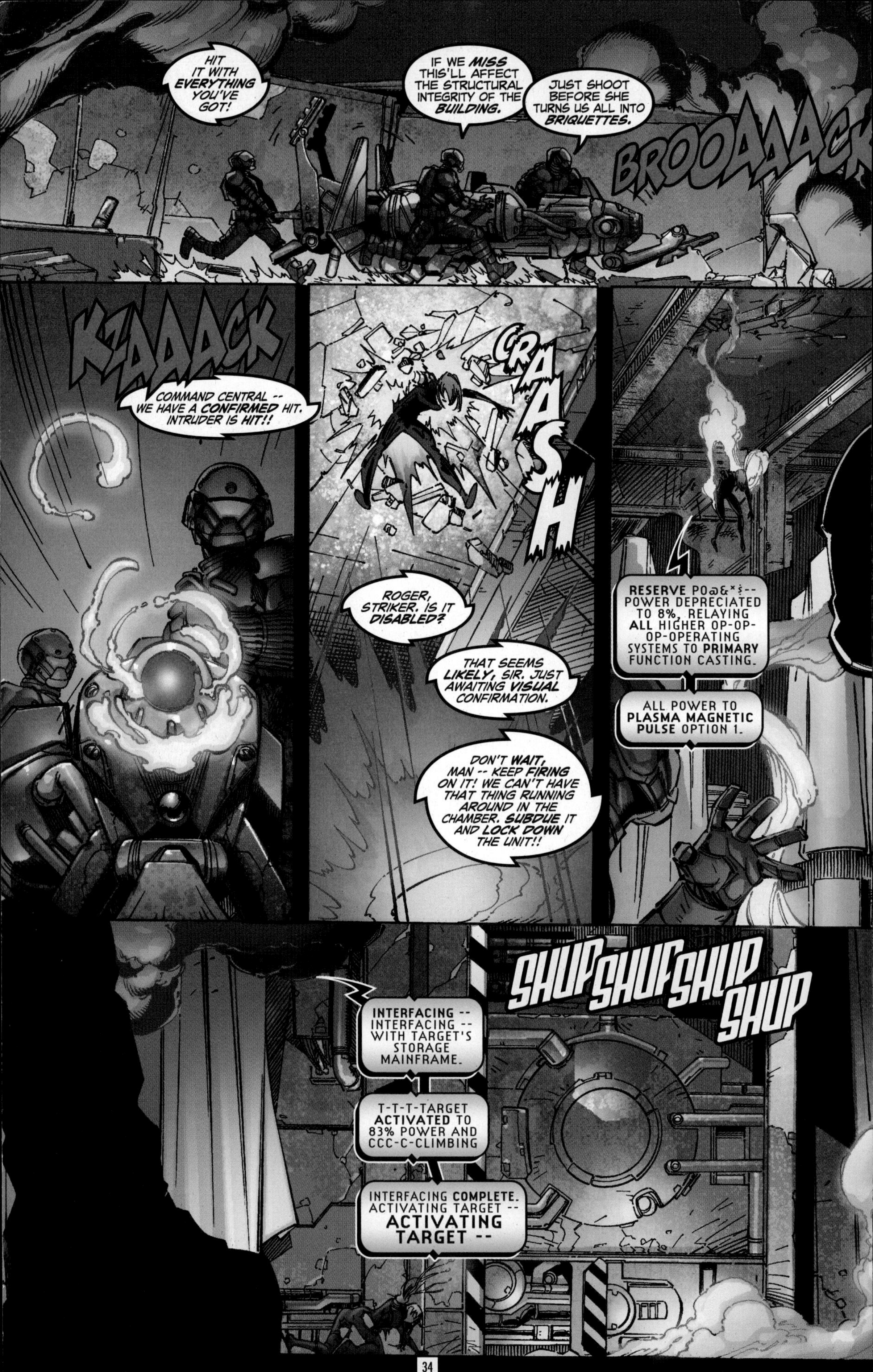
HIT IT WITH EVERYTHING YOU'VE GOT!
IF WE MISS THIS'LL AFFECT THE STRUCTURAL INTEGRITY OF THE BUILDING.
JUST SHOOT BEFORE SHE TURNS US ALL INTO BRIQUETTES.
BROOAAACK
KZAAACK
COMMAND CENTRAL -- WE HAVE A CONFIRMED HIT. INTRUDER IS HIT!!
CRAASH
ROGER, STRIKER. IS IT DISABLED?
THAT SEEMS LIKELY, SIR. JUST AWAITING VISUAL CONFIRMATION.
DON'T WAIT, MAN -- KEEP FIRING ON IT! WE CAN'T HAVE THAT THING RUNNING AROUND IN THE CHAMBER. SUBDUE IT AND LOCK DOWN THE UNIT!!
RESERVE PO@&*§-- POWER DEPRECIATED TO 8%, RELAYING ALL HIGHER OP-OP-OP-OPERATING SYSTEMS TO PRIMARY FUNCTION CASTING.
ALL POWER TO PLASMA MAGNETIC PULSE OPTION 1.
SHUP SHUP SHUP SHUP
INTERFACING -- INTERFACING -- WITH TARGET'S STORAGE MAINFRAME.
T-T-T-TARGET ACTIVATED TO 83% POWER AND CCC-C-CLIMBING
INTERFACING COMPLETE. ACTIVATING TARGET -- ACTIVATING TARGET --

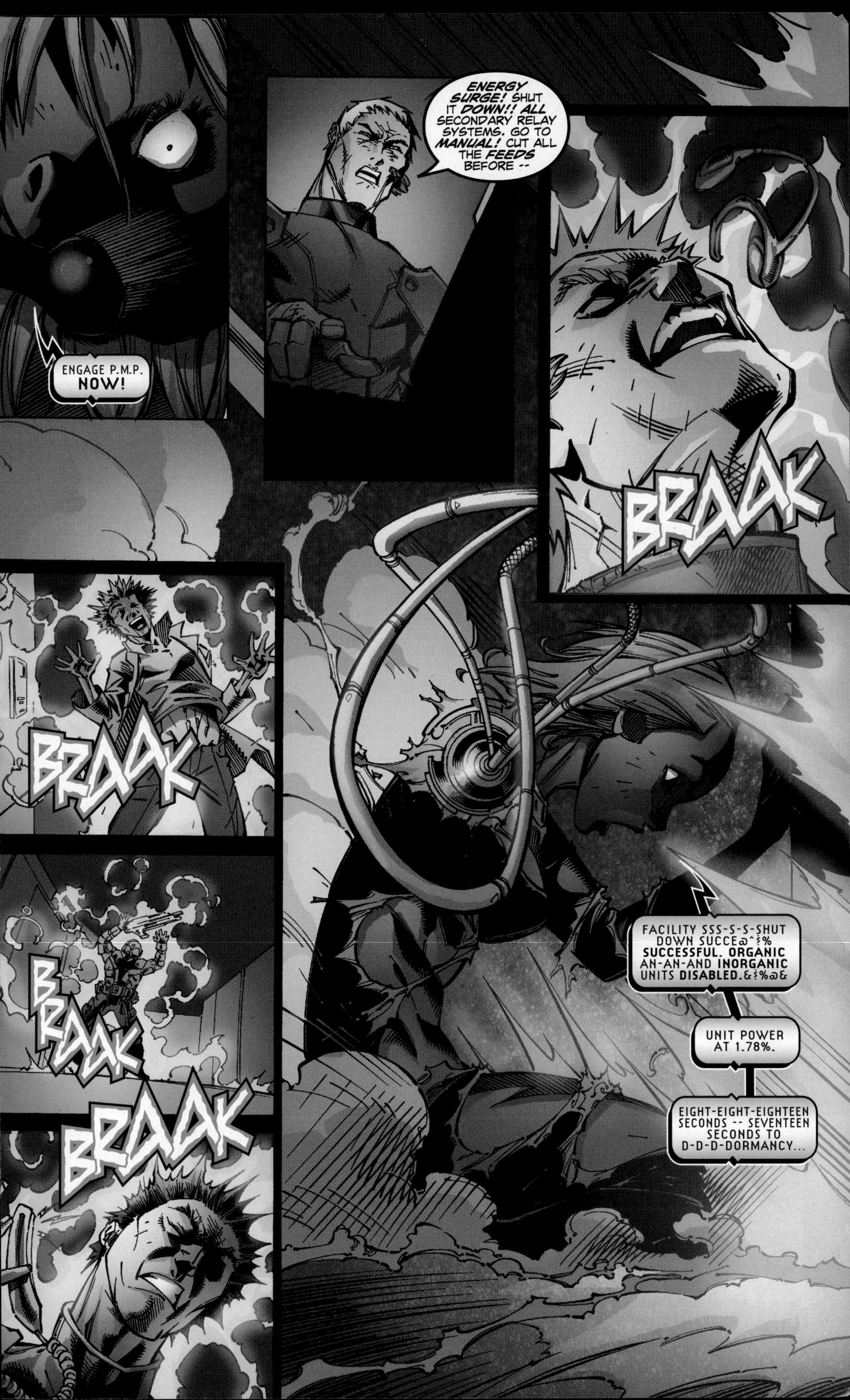
ENGAGE P.M.P. NOW!
ENERGY SURGE! SHUT IT DOWN!! ALL SECONDARY RELAY SYSTEMS. GO TO MANUAL! CUT ALL THE FEEDS BEFORE --
BRAAK
BRAAK
BRAAK
BRAAK
FACILITY SSS-S-S-SHUT DOWN SUCCE@^$% SUCCESSFUL. ORGANIC AN-AN-AND INORGANIC UNITS DISABLED.&$%@&
UNIT POWER AT 1.78%.
EIGHT-EIGHT-EIGHTEEN SECONDS -- SEVENTEEN SECONDS TO D-D-D-DORMANCY...

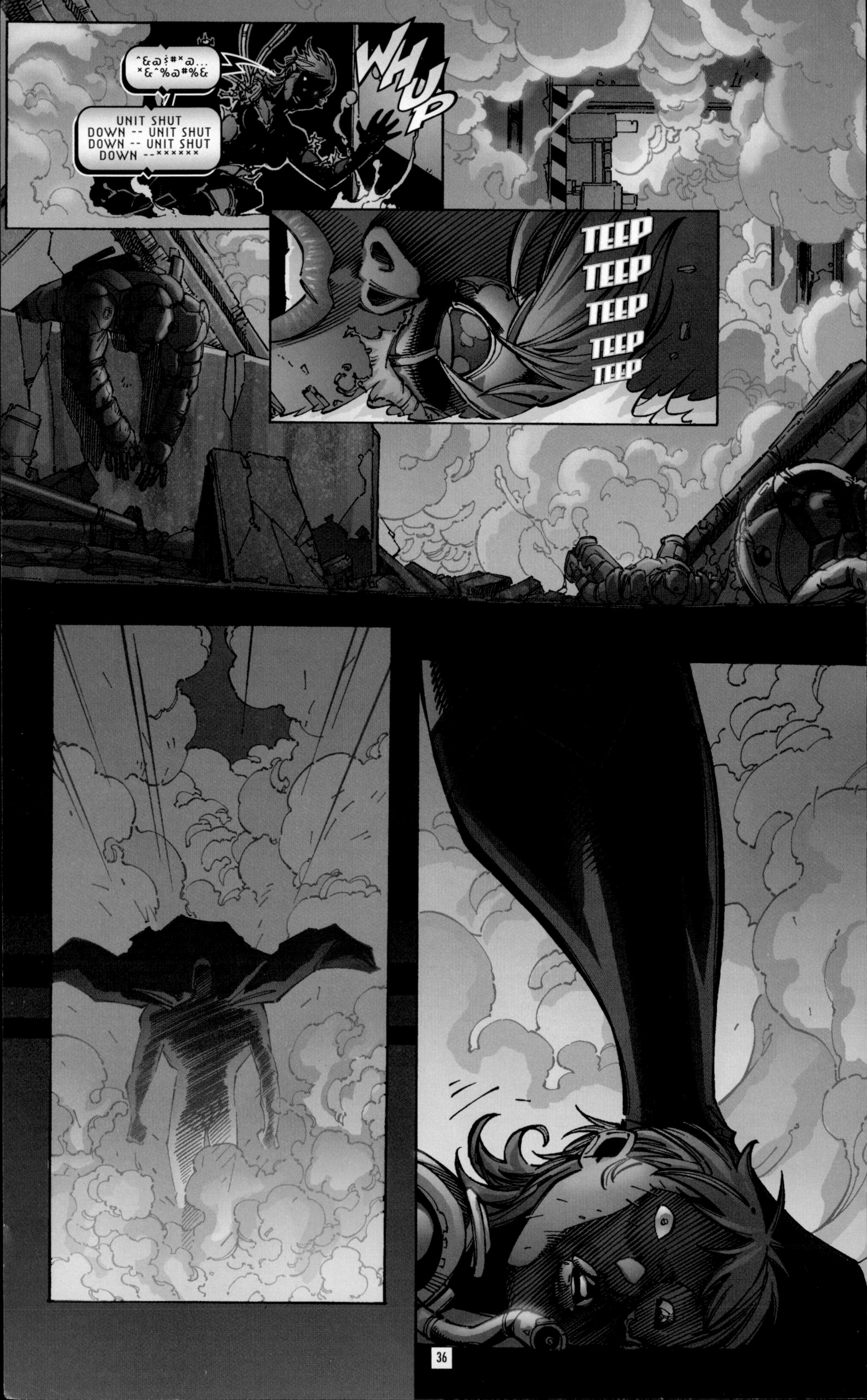
^&@$#*@...
*&^%@#%&
UNIT SHUT DOWN -- UNIT SHUT DOWN -- UNIT SHUT DOWN --******
WHUP
TEEP TEEP TEEP TEEP TEEP

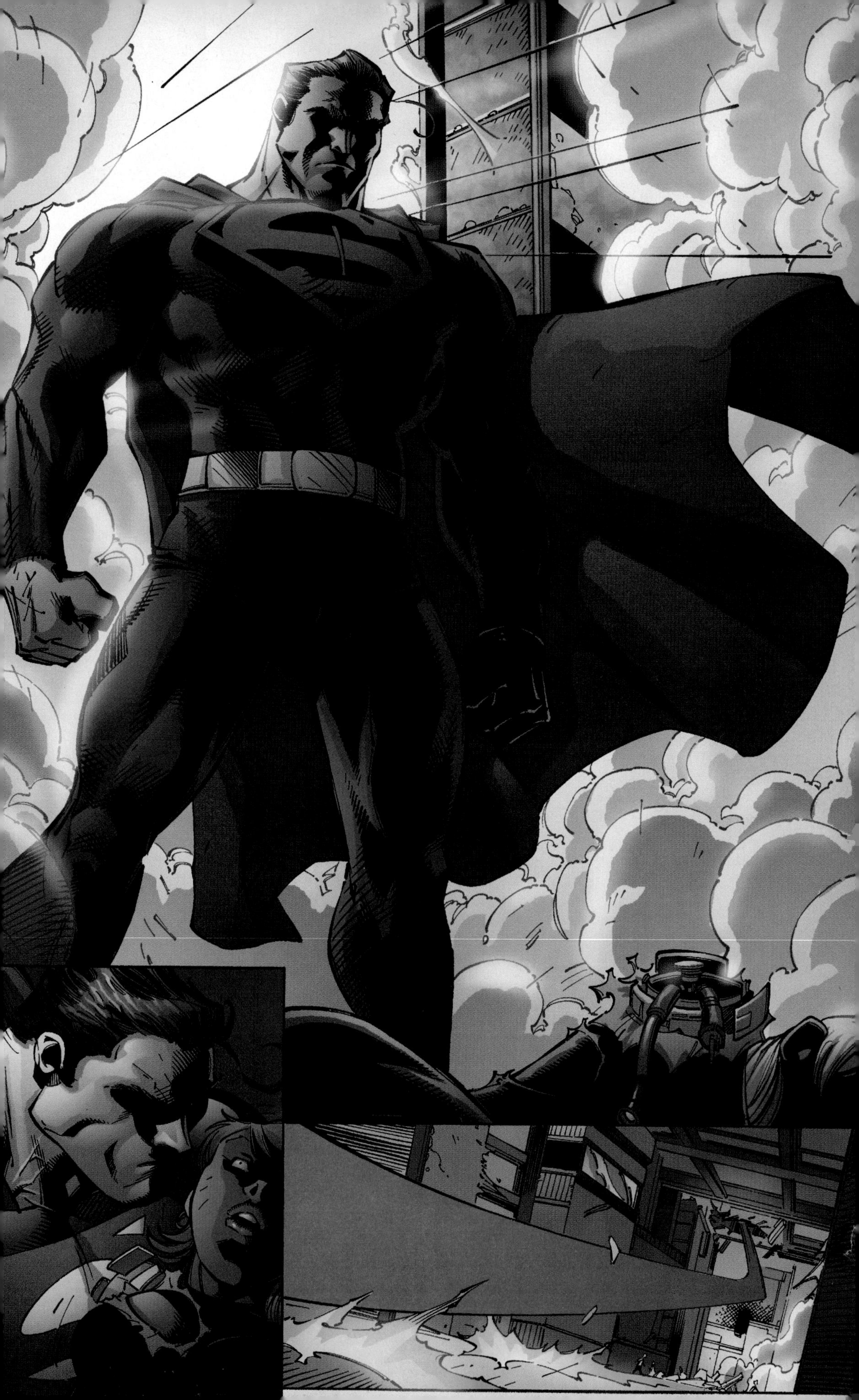

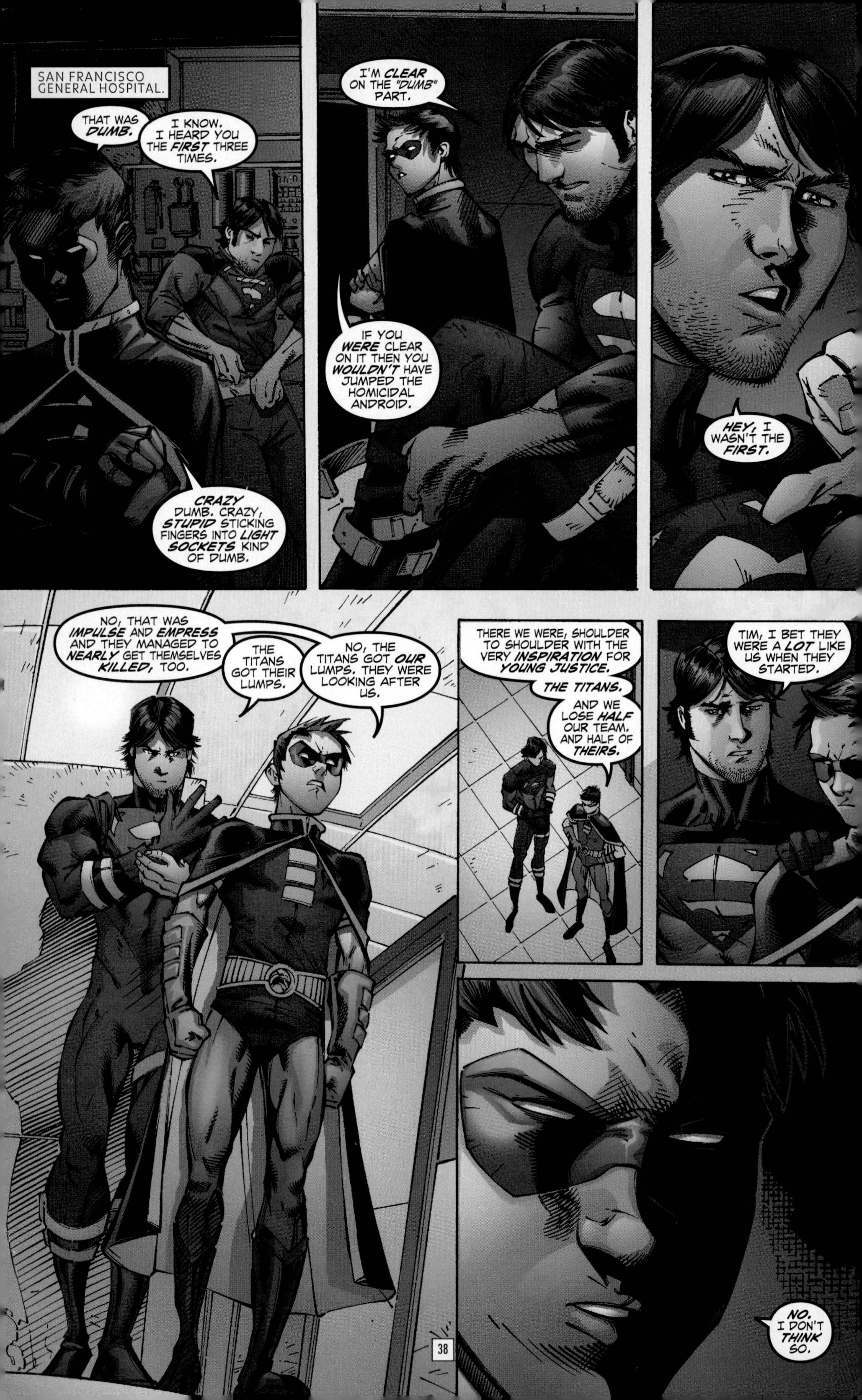
SAN FRANCISCO GENERAL HOSPITAL.
THAT WAS DUMB.
I KNOW. I HEARD YOU THE FIRST THREE TIMES.
CRAZY DUMB. CRAZY, STUPID STICKING FINGERS INTO LIGHT SOCKETS KIND OF DUMB.
I'M CLEAR ON THE "DUMB" PART.
IF YOU WERE CLEAR ON IT THEN YOU WOULDN'T HAVE JUMPED THE HOMICIDAL ANDROID.
HEY, I WASN'T THE FIRST.
NO, THAT WAS IMPULSE AND EMPRESS AND THEY MANAGED TO NEARLY GET THEMSELVES KILLED, TOO.
THE TITANS GOT THEIR LUMPS.
NO, THE TITANS GOT OUR LUMPS. THEY WERE LOOKING AFTER US.
THERE WE WERE, SHOULDER TO SHOULDER WITH THE VERY INSPIRATION FOR YOUNG JUSTICE.
THE TITANS.
AND WE LOSE HALF OUR TEAM. AND HALF OF THEIRS.
TIM, I BET THEY WERE A LOT LIKE US WHEN THEY STARTED.
NO. I DON'T THINK SO.

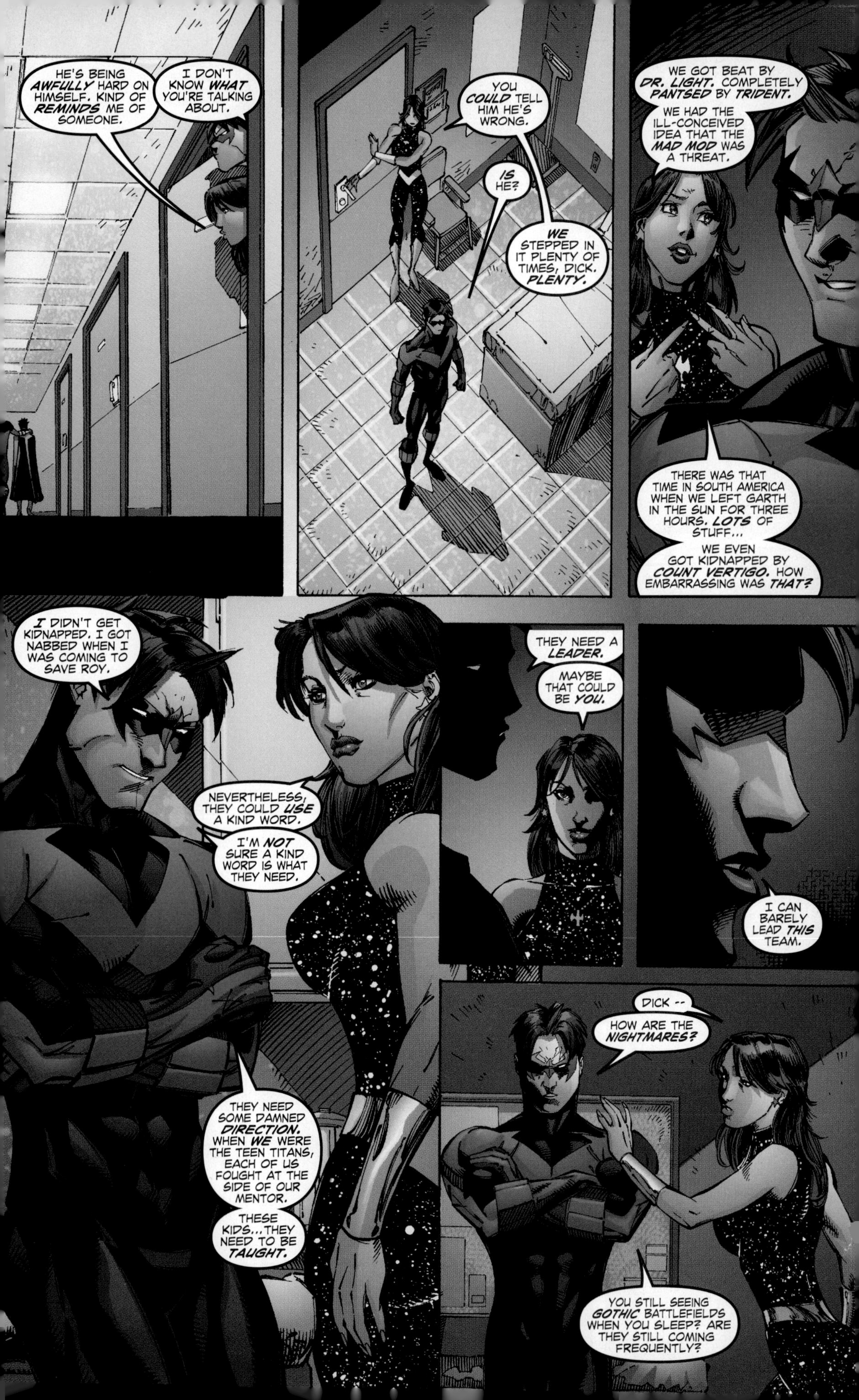
HE'S BEING AWFULLY HARD ON HIMSELF. KIND OF REMINDS ME OF SOMEONE.
I DON'T KNOW WHAT YOU'RE TALKING ABOUT.
YOU COULD TELL HIM HE'S WRONG.
IS HE?
WE STEPPED IN IT PLENTY OF TIMES, DICK. PLENTY.
WE GOT BEAT BY DR. LIGHT. COMPLETELY PANTSED BY TRIDENT.
WE HAD THE ILL-CONCEIVED IDEA THAT THE MAD MOD WAS A THREAT.
THERE WAS THAT TIME IN SOUTH AMERICA WHEN WE LEFT GARTH IN THE SUN FOR THREE HOURS. LOTS OF STUFF...
WE EVEN GOT KIDNAPPED BY COUNT VERTIGO. HOW EMBARRASSING WAS THAT?
I DIDN'T GET KIDNAPPED. I GOT NABBED WHEN I WAS COMING TO SAVE ROY.
NEVERTHELESS, THEY COULD USE A KIND WORD.
I'M NOT SURE A KIND WORD IS WHAT THEY NEED.
THEY NEED SOME DAMNED DIRECTION. WHEN WE WERE THE TEEN TITANS, EACH OF US FOUGHT AT THE SIDE OF OUR MENTOR.
THESE KIDS...THEY NEED TO BE TAUGHT.
THEY NEED A LEADER.
MAYBE THAT COULD BE YOU.
I CAN BARELY LEAD THIS TEAM.
DICK --
HOW ARE THE NIGHTMARES?
YOU STILL SEEING GOTHIC BATTLEFIELDS WHEN YOU SLEEP? ARE THEY STILL COMING FREQUENTLY?

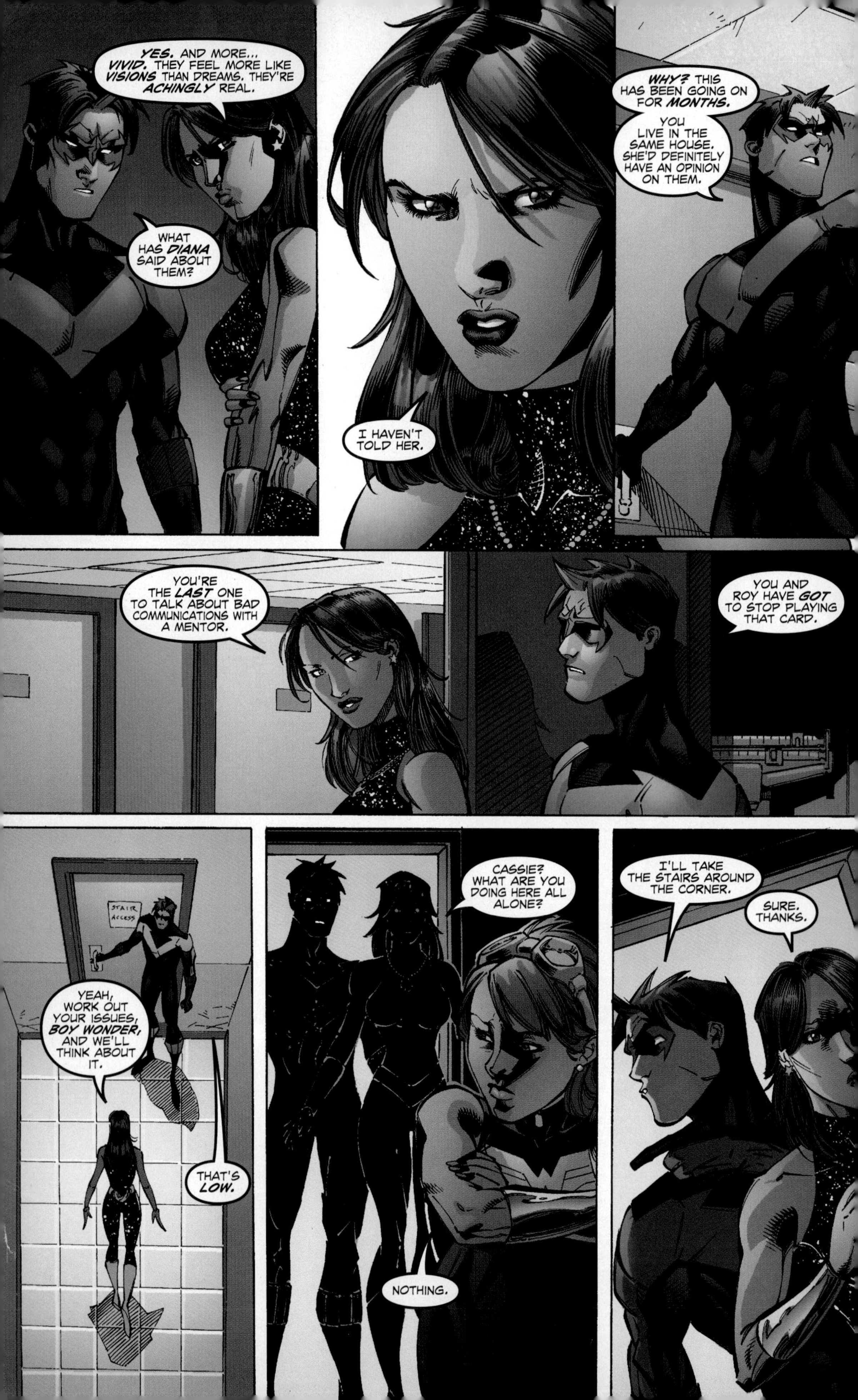
YES. AND MORE... VIVID. THEY FEEL MORE LIKE VISIONS THAN DREAMS. THEY'RE ACHINGLY REAL.
WHAT HAS DIANA SAID ABOUT THEM?
I HAVEN'T TOLD HER.
WHY? THIS HAS BEEN GOING ON FOR MONTHS.
YOU LIVE IN THE SAME HOUSE. SHE'D DEFINITELY HAVE AN OPINION ON THEM.
YOU'RE THE LAST ONE TO TALK ABOUT BAD COMMUNICATIONS WITH A MENTOR.
YOU AND ROY HAVE GOT TO STOP PLAYING THAT CARD.
STAIR ACCESS
YEAH, WORK OUT YOUR ISSUES, BOY WONDER, AND WE'LL THINK ABOUT IT.
THAT'S LOW.
CASSIE? WHAT ARE YOU DOING HERE ALL ALONE?
NOTHING.
I'LL TAKE THE STAIRS AROUND THE CORNER.
SURE. THANKS.

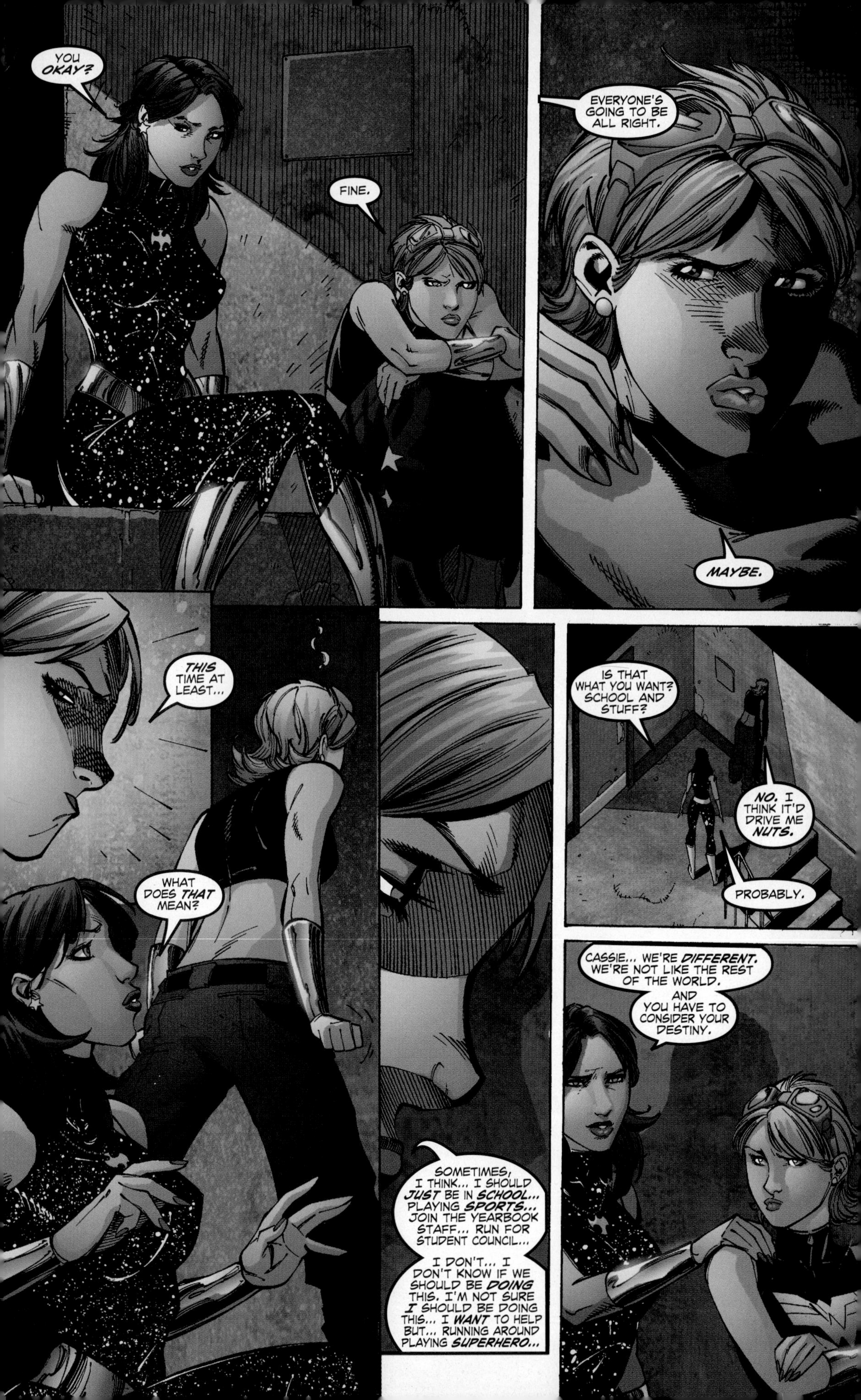
YOU OKAY?
FINE.
EVERYONE'S GOING TO BE ALL RIGHT.
MAYBE.
THIS TIME AT LEAST...
WHAT DOES THAT MEAN?
SOMETIMES, I THINK... I SHOULD JUST BE IN SCHOOL... PLAYING SPORTS... JOIN THE YEARBOOK STAFF... RUN FOR STUDENT COUNCIL...
I DON'T... I DON'T KNOW IF WE SHOULD BE DOING THIS. I'M NOT SURE I SHOULD BE DOING THIS... I WANT TO HELP BUT... RUNNING AROUND PLAYING SUPERHERO...
IS THAT WHAT YOU WANT? SCHOOL AND STUFF?
NO. I THINK IT'D DRIVE ME NUTS.
PROBABLY.
CASSIE... WE'RE DIFFERENT. WE'RE NOT LIKE THE REST OF THE WORLD.
AND YOU HAVE TO CONSIDER YOUR DESTINY.

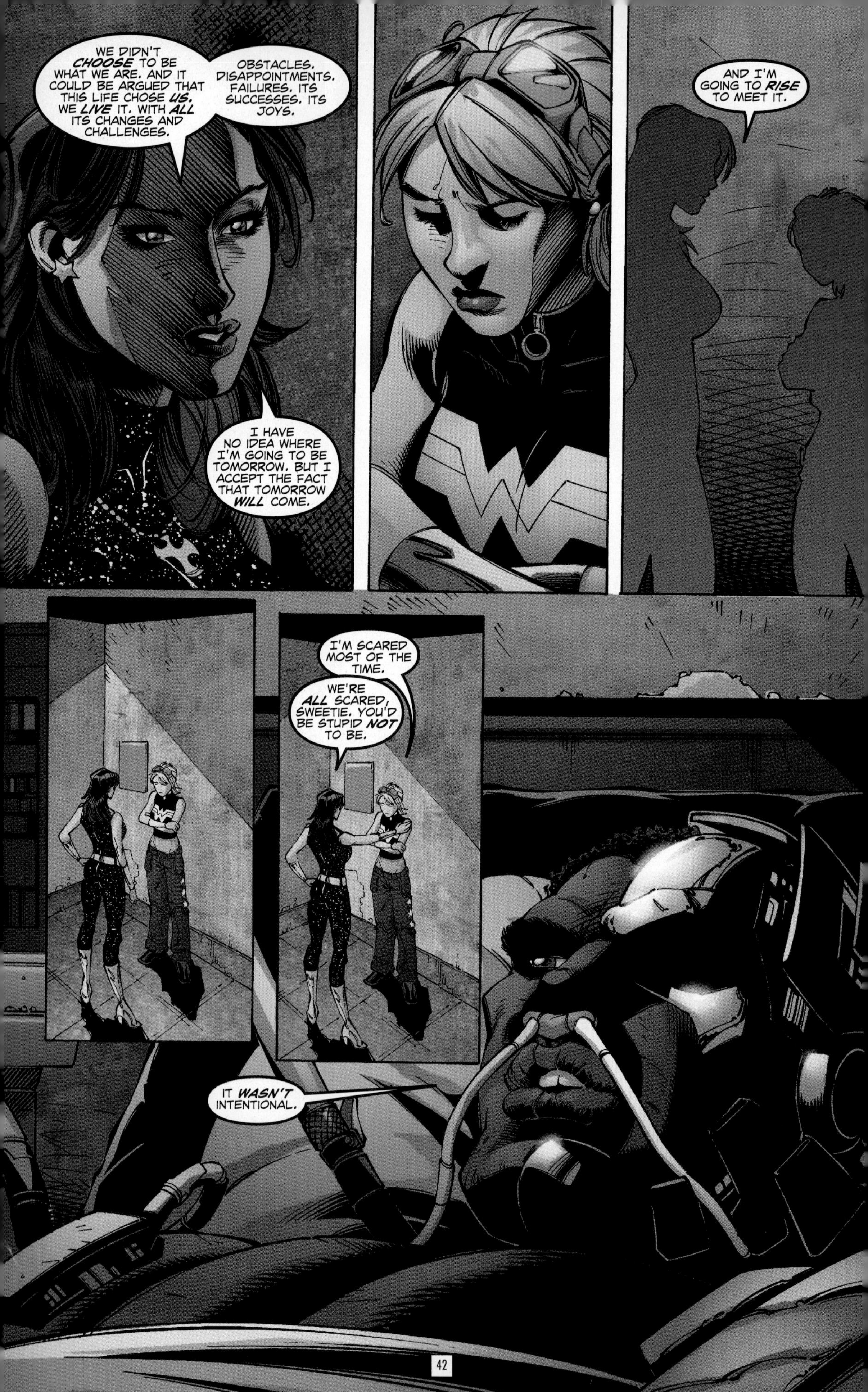
WE DIDN'T CHOOSE TO BE WHAT WE ARE. AND IT COULD BE ARGUED THAT THIS LIFE CHOSE US. WE LIVE IT. WITH ALL ITS CHANGES AND CHALLENGES.
OBSTACLES. DISAPPOINTMENTS. FAILURES. ITS SUCCESSES. ITS JOYS.
I HAVE NO IDEA WHERE I'M GOING TO BE TOMORROW. BUT I ACCEPT THE FACT THAT TOMORROW WILL COME.
AND I'M GOING TO RISE TO MEET IT.
I'M SCARED MOST OF THE TIME.
WE'RE ALL SCARED, SWEETIE. YOU'D BE STUPID NOT TO BE.
IT WASN'T INTENTIONAL.

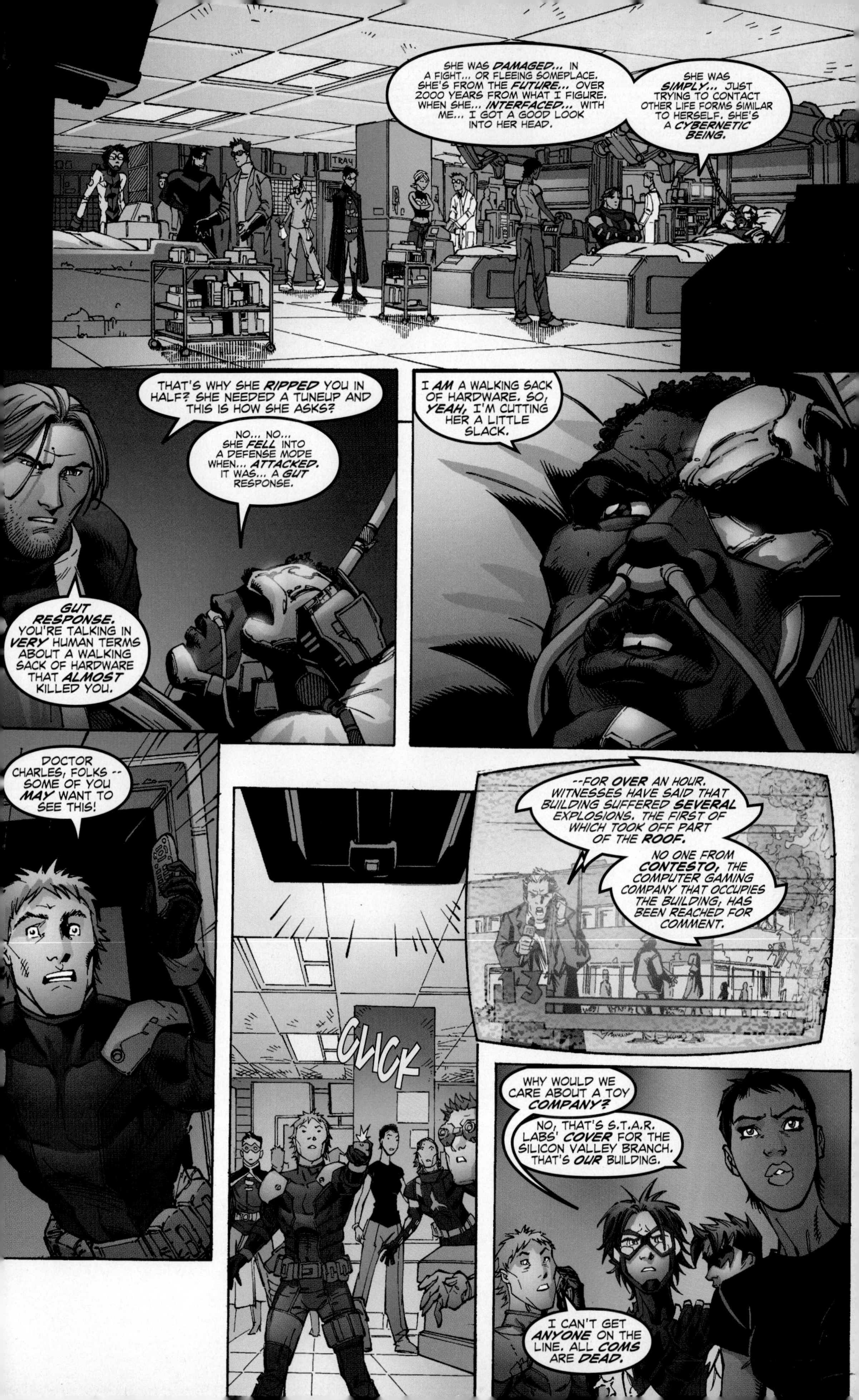

SHE WAS DAMAGED... IN A FIGHT... OR FLEEING SOMEPLACE. SHE'S FROM THE FUTURE... OVER 2000 YEARS FROM WHAT I FIGURE. WHEN SHE... INTERFACED... WITH ME... I GOT A GOOD LOOK INTO HER HEAD.
SHE WAS SIMPLY... JUST TRYING TO CONTACT OTHER LIFE FORMS SIMILAR TO HERSELF. SHE'S A CYBERNETIC BEING.
THAT'S WHY SHE RIPPED YOU IN HALF? SHE NEEDED A TUNEUP AND THIS IS HOW SHE ASKS?
NO... NO... SHE FELL INTO A DEFENSE MODE WHEN... ATTACKED. IT WAS... A GUT RESPONSE.
GUT RESPONSE. YOU'RE TALKING IN VERY HUMAN TERMS ABOUT A WALKING SACK OF HARDWARE THAT ALMOST KILLED YOU.
I AM A WALKING SACK OF HARDWARE. SO, YEAH, I'M CUTTING HER A LITTLE SLACK.
DOCTOR CHARLES, FOLKS -- SOME OF YOU MAY WANT TO SEE THIS!
CLICK
--FOR OVER AN HOUR. WITNESSES HAVE SAID THAT BUILDING SUFFERED SEVERAL EXPLOSIONS, THE FIRST OF WHICH TOOK OFF PART OF THE ROOF.
NO ONE FROM CONTESTO, THE COMPUTER GAMING COMPANY THAT OCCUPIES THE BUILDING, HAS BEEN REACHED FOR COMMENT.
WHY WOULD WE CARE ABOUT A TOY COMPANY?
NO, THAT'S S.T.A.R. LABS' COVER FOR THE SILICON VALLEY BRANCH. THAT'S OUR BUILDING.
I CAN'T GET ANYONE ON THE LINE. ALL COMS ARE DEAD.

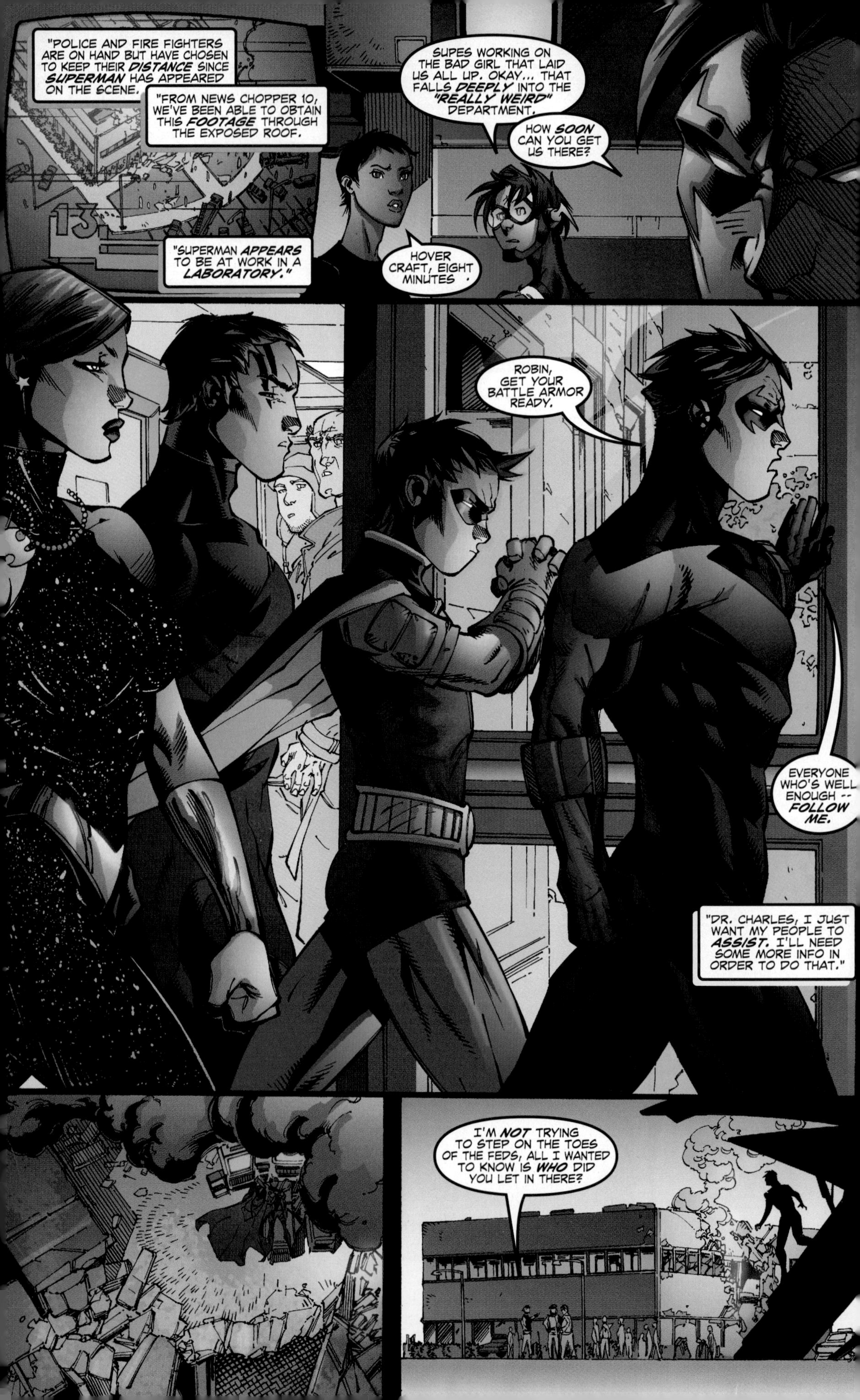
"POLICE AND FIRE FIGHTERS ARE ON HAND BUT HAVE CHOSEN TO KEEP THEIR DISTANCE SINCE SUPERMAN HAS APPEARED ON THE SCENE.
"FROM NEWS CHOPPER 10, WE'VE BEEN ABLE TO OBTAIN THIS FOOTAGE THROUGH THE EXPOSED ROOF.
"SUPERMAN APPEARS TO BE AT WORK IN A LABORATORY."
SUPES WORKING ON THE BAD GIRL THAT LAID US ALL UP. OKAY... THAT FALLS DEEPLY INTO THE "REALLY WEIRD" DEPARTMENT.
HOW SOON CAN YOU GET US THERE?
HOVER CRAFT, EIGHT MINUTES.
ROBIN, GET YOUR BATTLE ARMOR READY.
EVERYONE WHO'S WELL ENOUGH -- FOLLOW ME.
"DR. CHARLES, I JUST WANT MY PEOPLE TO ASSIST. I'LL NEED SOME MORE INFO IN ORDER TO DO THAT."
I'M NOT TRYING TO STEP ON THE TOES OF THE FEDS, ALL I WANTED TO KNOW IS WHO DID YOU LET IN THERE?

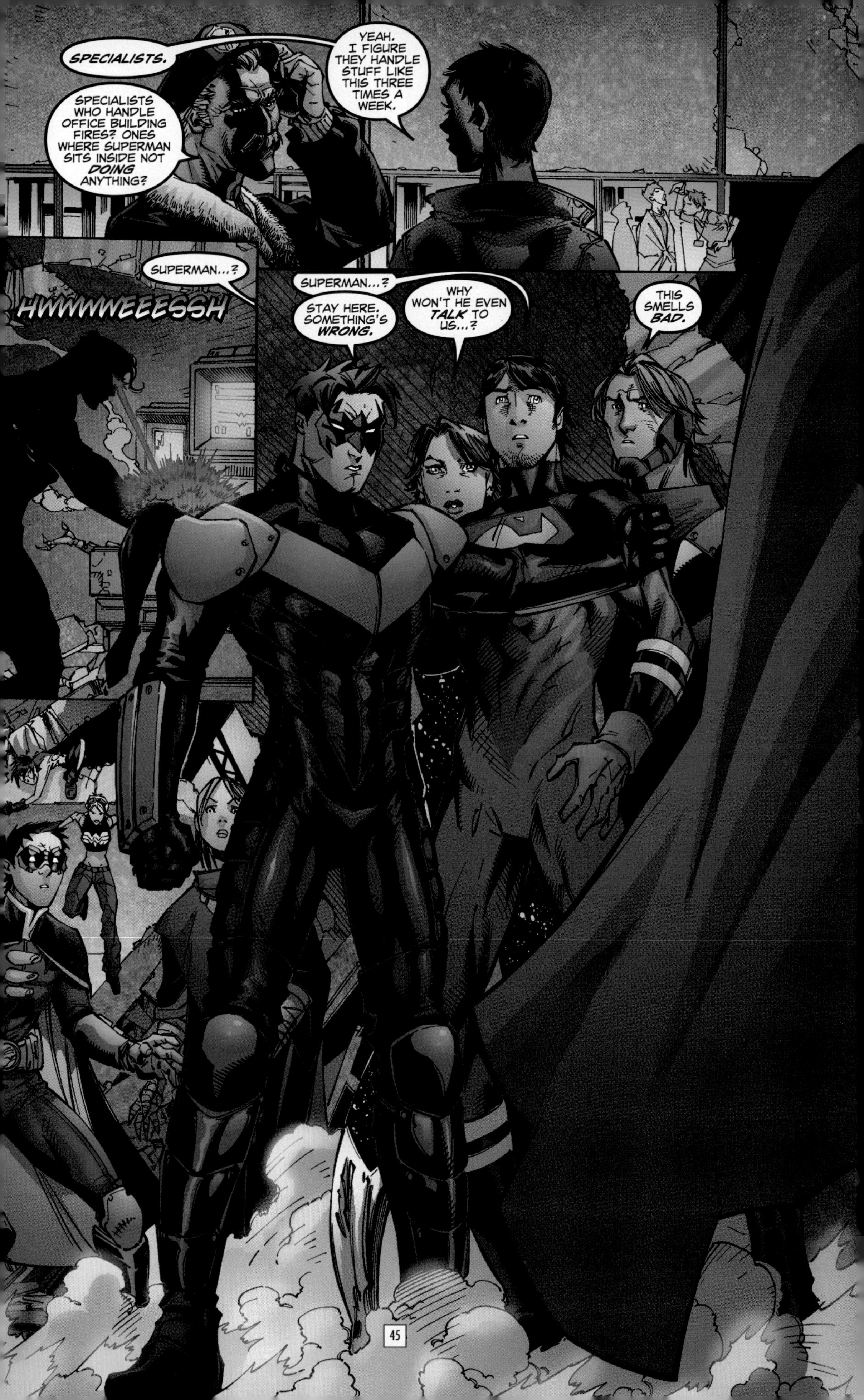
SPECIALISTS.
YEAH. I FIGURE THEY HANDLE STUFF LIKE THIS THREE TIMES A WEEK.
SPECIALISTS WHO HANDLE OFFICE BUILDING FIRES? ONES WHERE SUPERMAN SITS INSIDE NOT DOING ANYTHING?
SUPERMAN...?
HWWWWEEEESSH
SUPERMAN...?
STAY HERE. SOMETHING'S WRONG.
WHY WON'T HE EVEN TALK TO US...?
THIS SMELLS BAD.

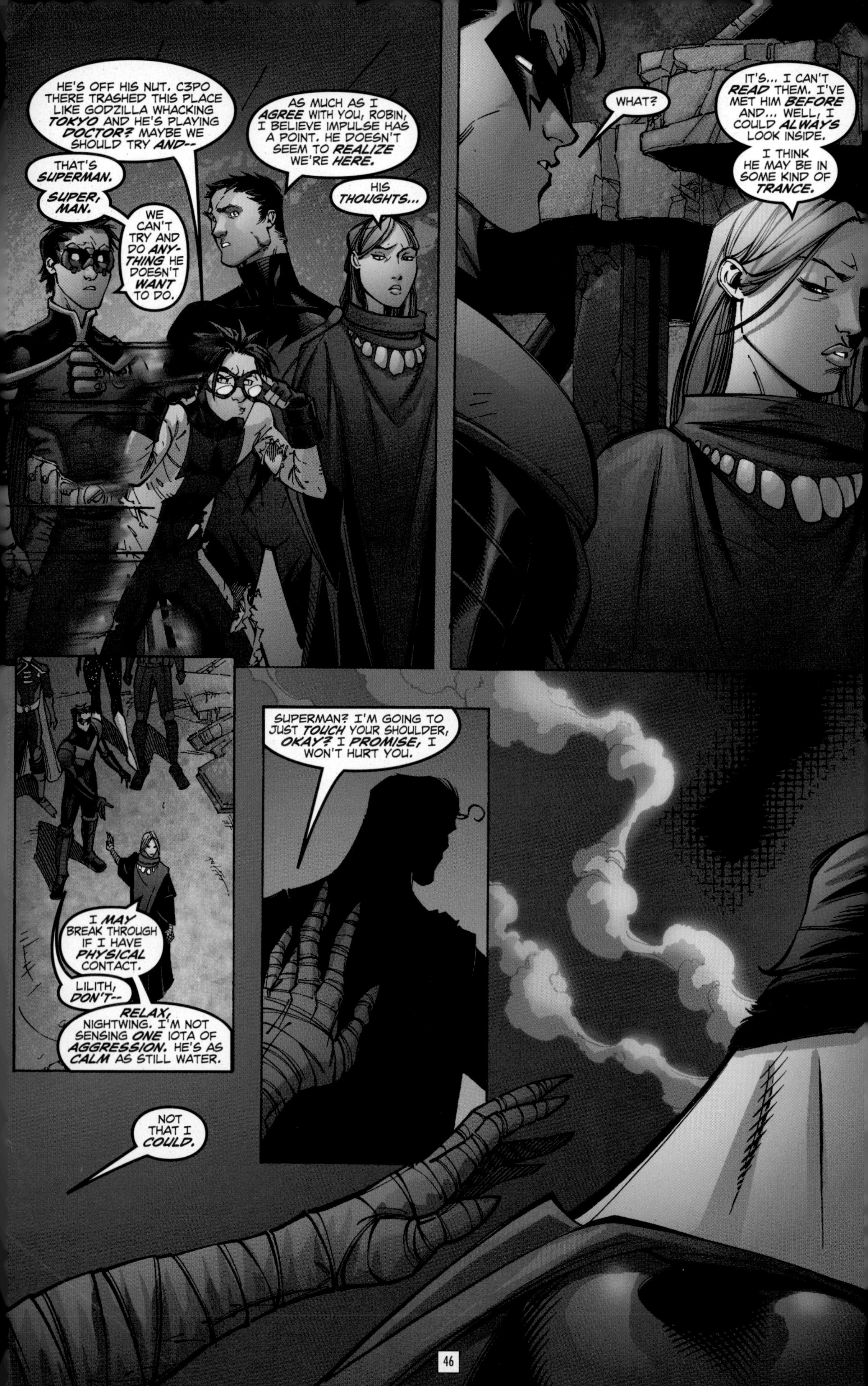
HE'S OFF HIS NUT. C3PO THERE TRASHED THIS PLACE LIKE GODZILLA WHACKING TOKYO AND HE'S PLAYING DOCTOR? MAYBE WE SHOULD TRY AND--
THAT'S SUPERMAN.
SUPER, MAN.
WE CAN'T TRY AND DO ANYTHING HE DOESN'T WANT TO DO.
AS MUCH AS I AGREE WITH YOU, ROBIN, I BELIEVE IMPULSE HAS A POINT. HE DOESN'T SEEM TO REALIZE WE'RE HERE.
HIS THOUGHTS...
WHAT?
IT'S... I CAN'T READ THEM. I'VE MET HIM BEFORE AND... WELL, I COULD ALWAYS LOOK INSIDE.
I THINK HE MAY BE IN SOME KIND OF TRANCE.
I MAY BREAK THROUGH IF I HAVE PHYSICAL CONTACT.
LILITH, DON'T--
RELAX, NIGHTWING. I'M NOT SENSING ONE IOTA OF AGGRESSION. HE'S AS CALM AS STILL WATER.
NOT THAT I COULD.
SUPERMAN? I'M GOING TO JUST TOUCH YOUR SHOULDER, OKAY? I PROMISE, I WON'T HURT YOU.

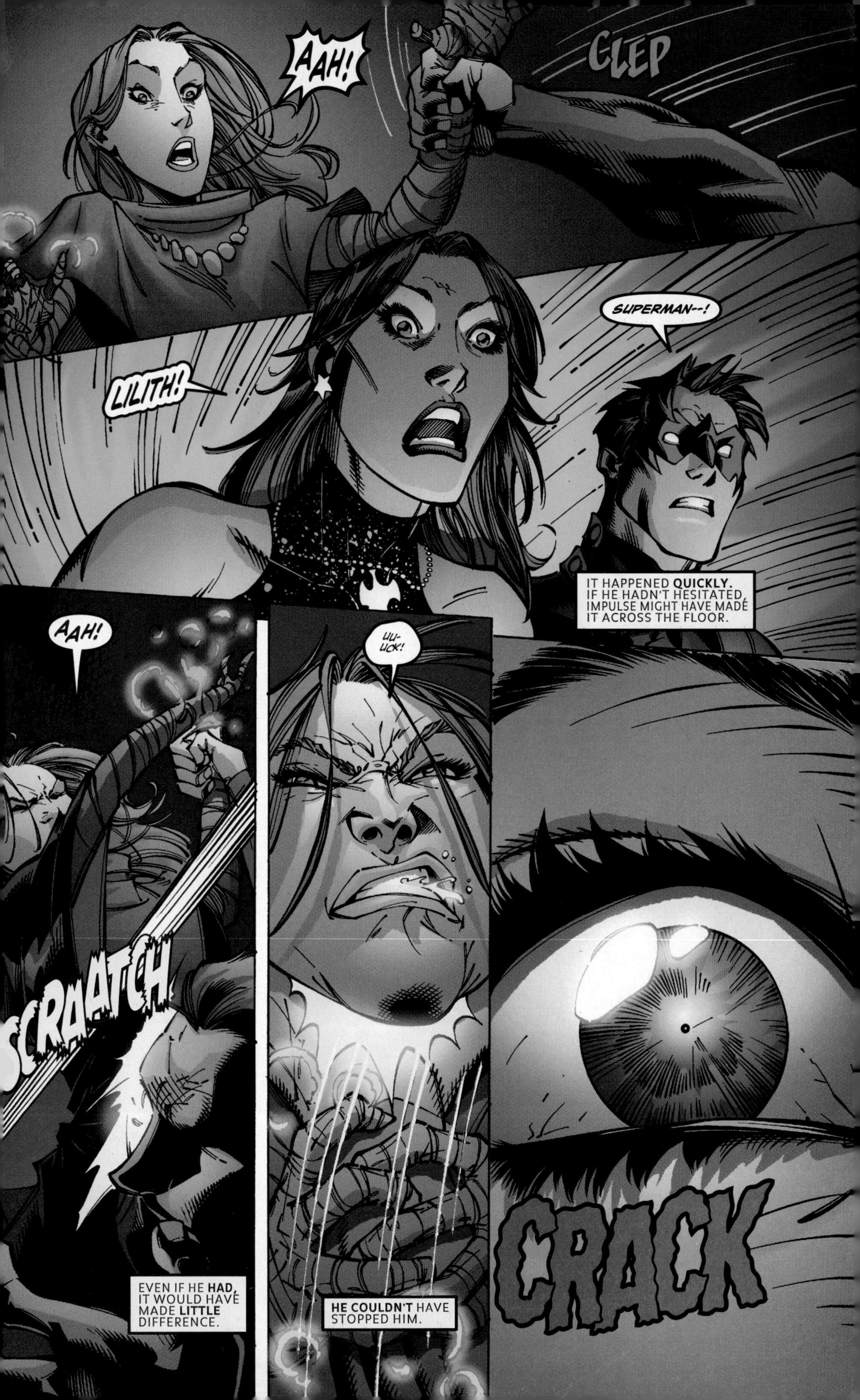

AAH!
CLEP
SUPERMAN--!
LILITH!
IT HAPPENED QUICKLY. IF HE HADN'T HESITATED, IMPULSE MIGHT HAVE MADE IT ACROSS THE FLOOR.
AAH!
SCRAATCH
EVEN IF HE HAD, IT WOULD HAVE MADE LITTLE DIFFERENCE.
UU-UCK!
HE COULDN'T HAVE STOPPED HIM.
CRACK

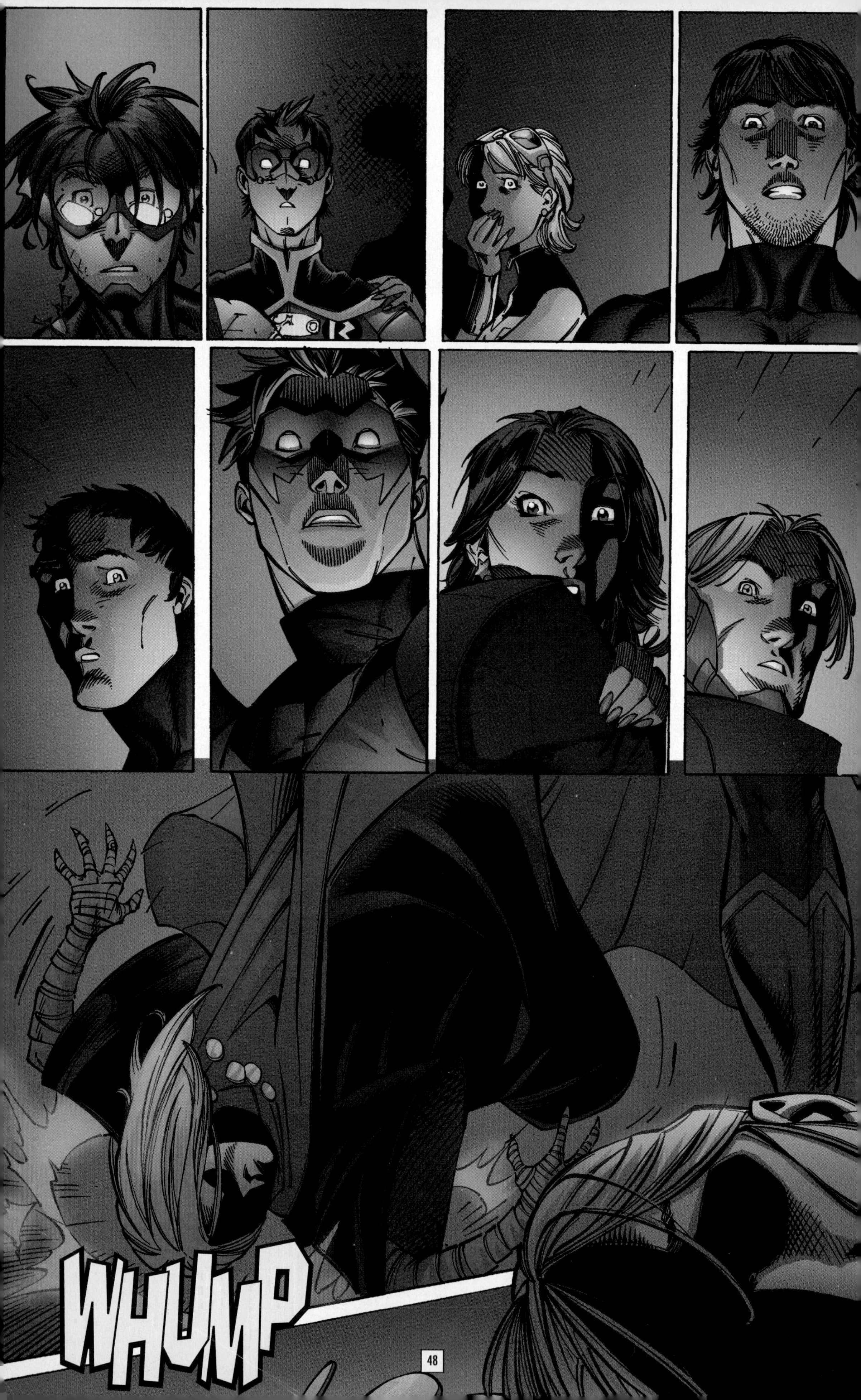
WHUMP

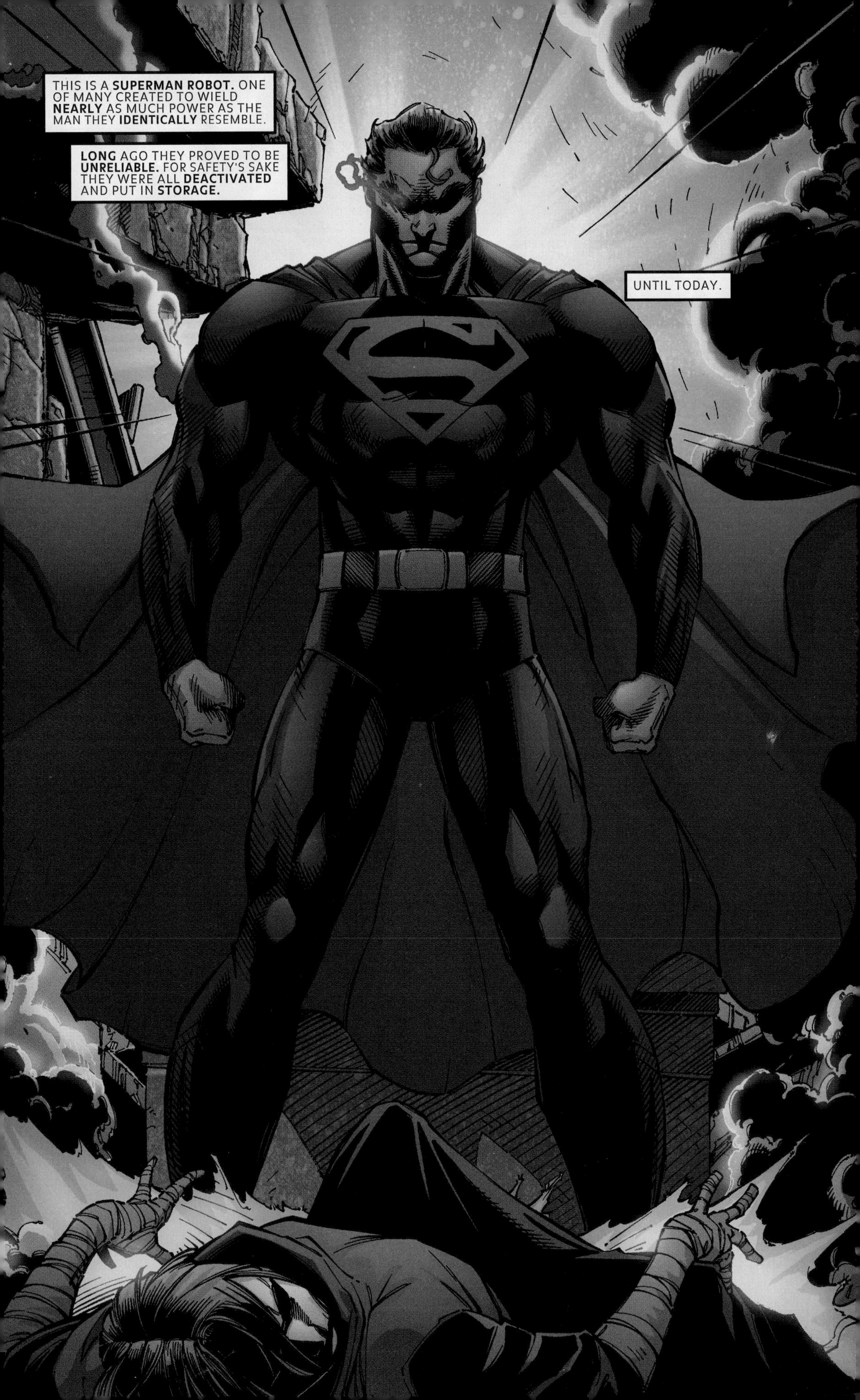

THIS IS A SUPERMAN ROBOT. ONE OF MANY CREATED TO WIELD NEARLY AS MUCH POWER AS THE MAN THEY IDENTICALLY RESEMBLE.
LONG AGO THEY PROVED TO BE UNRELIABLE. FOR SAFETY'S SAKE THEY WERE ALL DEACTIVATED AND PUT IN STORAGE.
UNTIL TODAY.

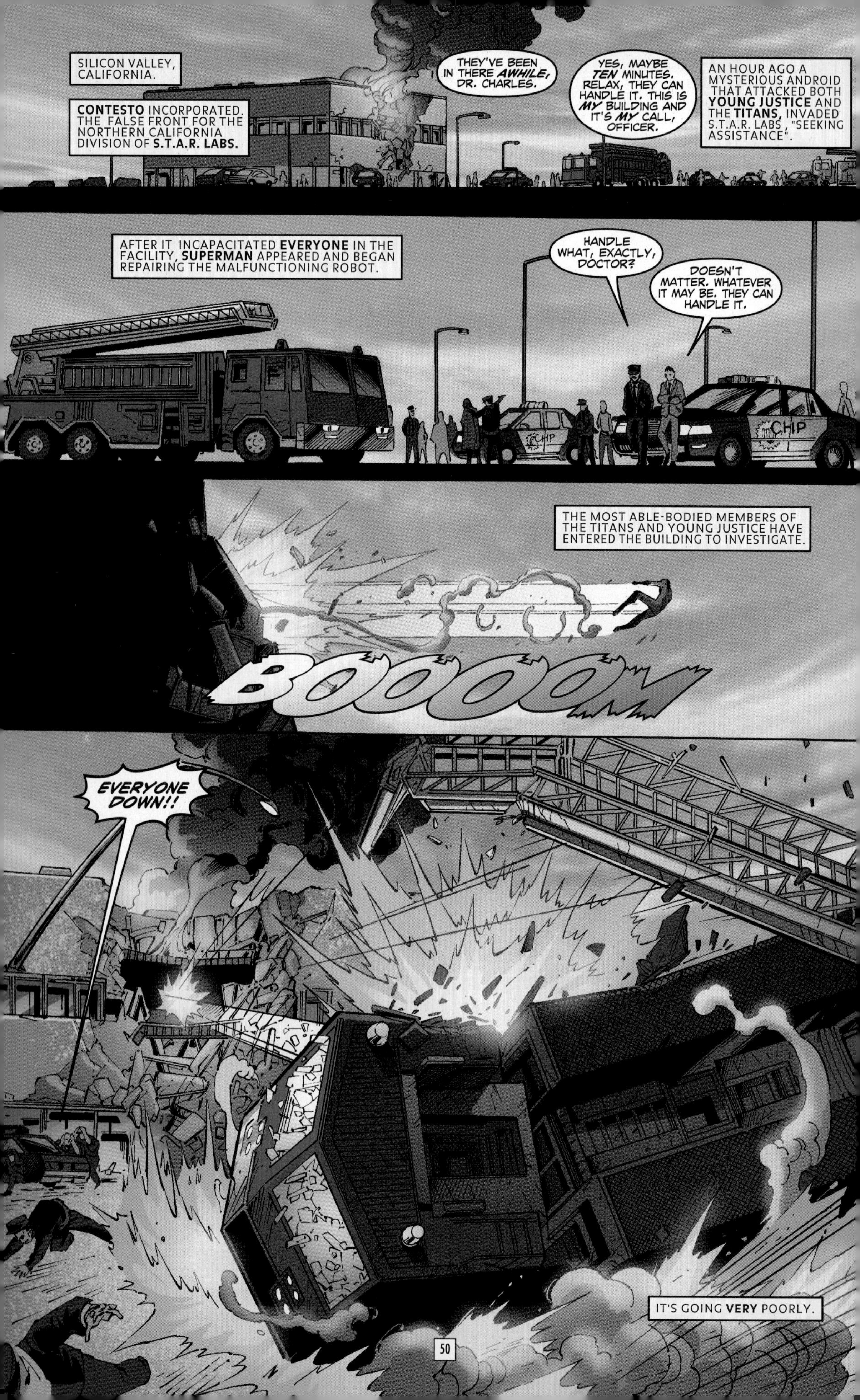
SILICON VALLEY, CALIFORNIA.
CONTESTO INCORPORATED. THE FALSE FRONT FOR THE NORTHERN CALIFORNIA DIVISION OF S.T.A.R. LABS.
THEY'VE BEEN IN THERE AWHILE, DR. CHARLES.
YES, MAYBE TEN MINUTES. RELAX, THEY CAN HANDLE IT. THIS IS MY BUILDING AND IT'S MY CALL, OFFICER.
AN HOUR AGO A MYSTERIOUS ANDROID THAT ATTACKED BOTH YOUNG JUSTICE AND THE TITANS, INVADED S.T.A.R. LABS, "SEEKING ASSISTANCE".
AFTER IT INCAPACITATED EVERYONE IN THE FACILITY, SUPERMAN APPEARED AND BEGAN REPAIRING THE MALFUNCTIONING ROBOT.
HANDLE WHAT, EXACTLY, DOCTOR?
DOESN'T MATTER. WHATEVER IT MAY BE, THEY CAN HANDLE IT.
CHP
CHP
THE MOST ABLE-BODIED MEMBERS OF THE TITANS AND YOUNG JUSTICE HAVE ENTERED THE BUILDING TO INVESTIGATE.
BOOOOM
EVERYONE DOWN!!
IT'S GOING VERY POORLY.

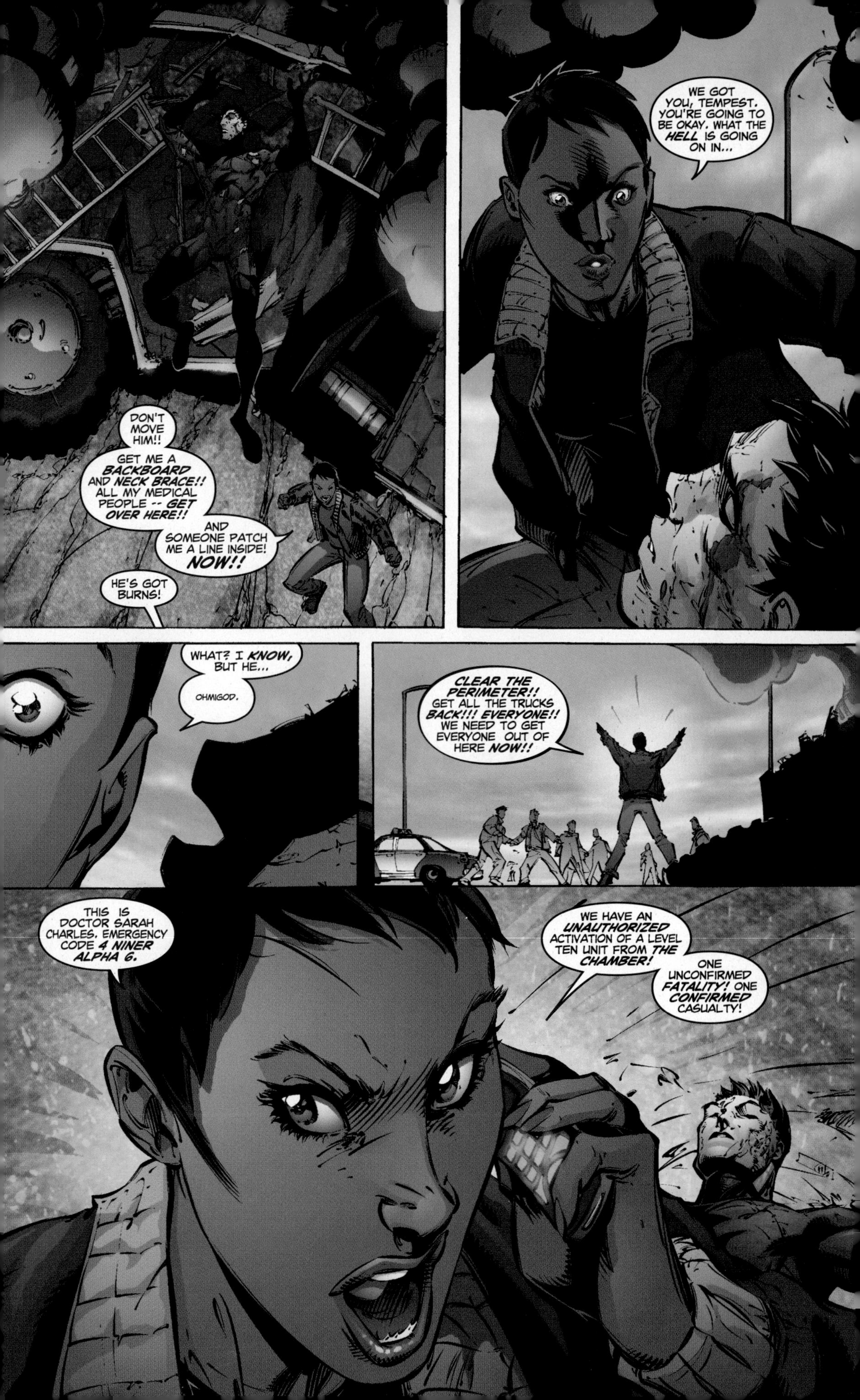
DON'T MOVE HIM!!
GET ME A BACKBOARD AND NECK BRACE!! ALL MY MEDICAL PEOPLE -- GET OVER HERE!!
AND SOMEONE PATCH ME A LINE INSIDE! NOW!!
HE'S GOT BURNS!
WE GOT YOU, TEMPEST. YOU'RE GOING TO BE OKAY. WHAT THE HELL IS GOING ON IN...
WHAT? I KNOW, BUT HE...
OHMIGOD.
CLEAR THE PERIMETER!! GET ALL THE TRUCKS BACK!!! EVERYONE!! WE NEED TO GET EVERYONE OUT OF HERE NOW!!
THIS IS DOCTOR SARAH CHARLES. EMERGENCY CODE 4 NINER ALPHA 6.
WE HAVE AN UNAUTHORIZED ACTIVATION OF A LEVEL TEN UNIT FROM THE CHAMBER!
ONE UNCONFIRMED FATALITY! ONE CONFIRMED CASUALTY!

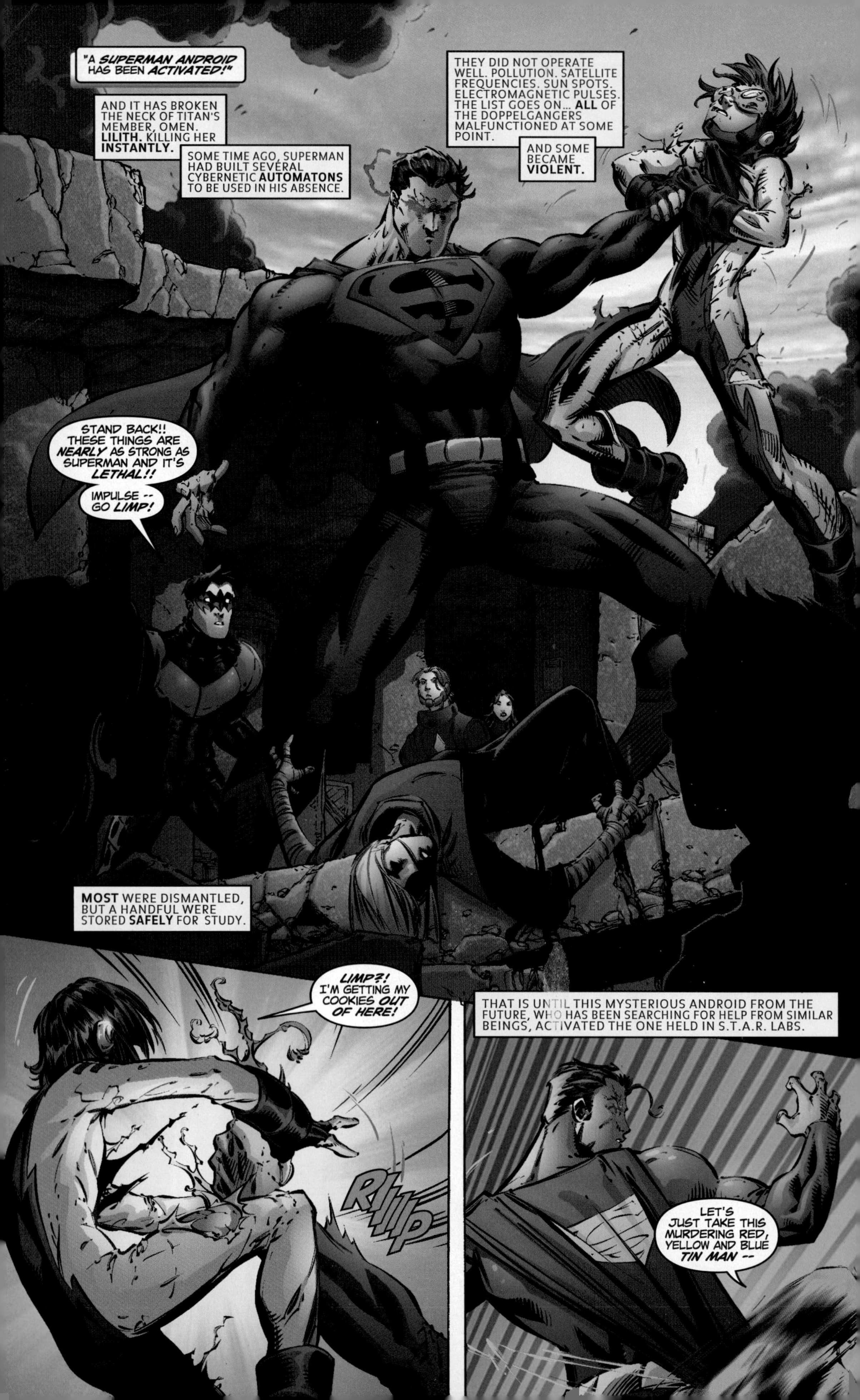

"A SUPERMAN ANDROID HAS BEEN ACTIVATED!"
AND IT HAS BROKEN THE NECK OF TITAN'S MEMBER, OMEN. LILITH. KILLING HER INSTANTLY.
SOME TIME AGO, SUPERMAN HAD BUILT SEVERAL CYBERNETIC AUTOMATONS TO BE USED IN HIS ABSENCE.
THEY DID NOT OPERATE WELL. POLLUTION. SATELLITE FREQUENCIES. SUN SPOTS. ELECTROMAGNETIC PULSES. THE LIST GOES ON... ALL OF THE DOPPELGANGERS MALFUNCTIONED AT SOME POINT.
AND SOME BECAME VIOLENT.
STAND BACK!! THESE THINGS ARE NEARLY AS STRONG AS SUPERMAN AND IT'S LETHAL!!
IMPULSE -- GO LIMP!
MOST WERE DISMANTLED, BUT A HANDFUL WERE STORED SAFELY FOR STUDY.
LIMP?! I'M GETTING MY COOKIES OUT OF HERE!
RIIIP
THAT IS UNTIL THIS MYSTERIOUS ANDROID FROM THE FUTURE, WHO HAS BEEN SEARCHING FOR HELP FROM SIMILAR BEINGS, ACTIVATED THE ONE HELD IN S.T.A.R. LABS.
LET'S JUST TAKE THIS MURDERING RED, YELLOW AND BLUE TIN MAN --

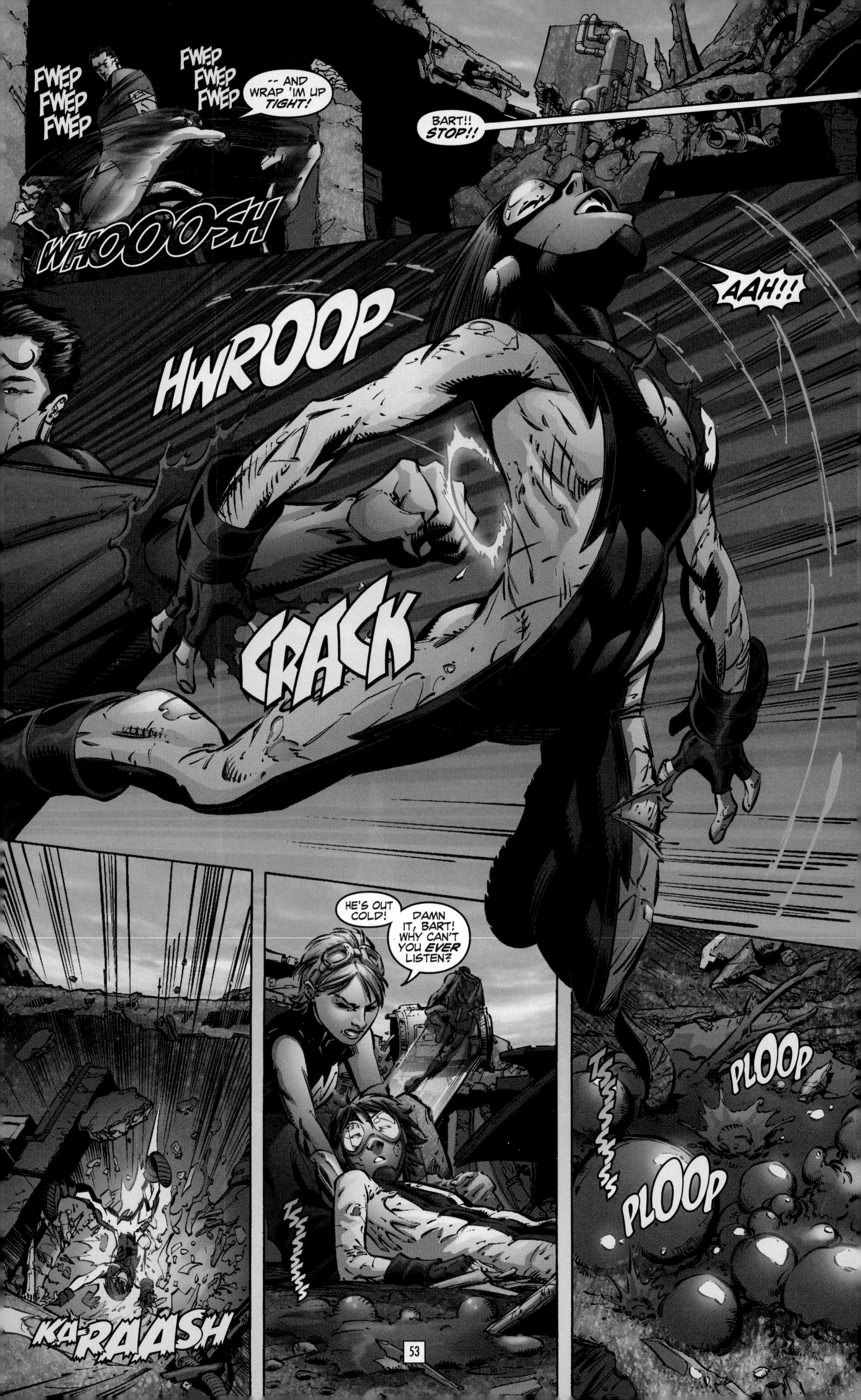
FWEP FWEP FWEP
FWEP FWEP FWEP
-- AND WRAP 'IM UP TIGHT!
BART!! STOP!!
WHOOOSH
HWROOP
AAH!!
CRACK
KA-RAASH
HE'S OUT COLD!
DAMN IT, BART! WHY CAN'T YOU EVER LISTEN?
PLOOP
PLOOP

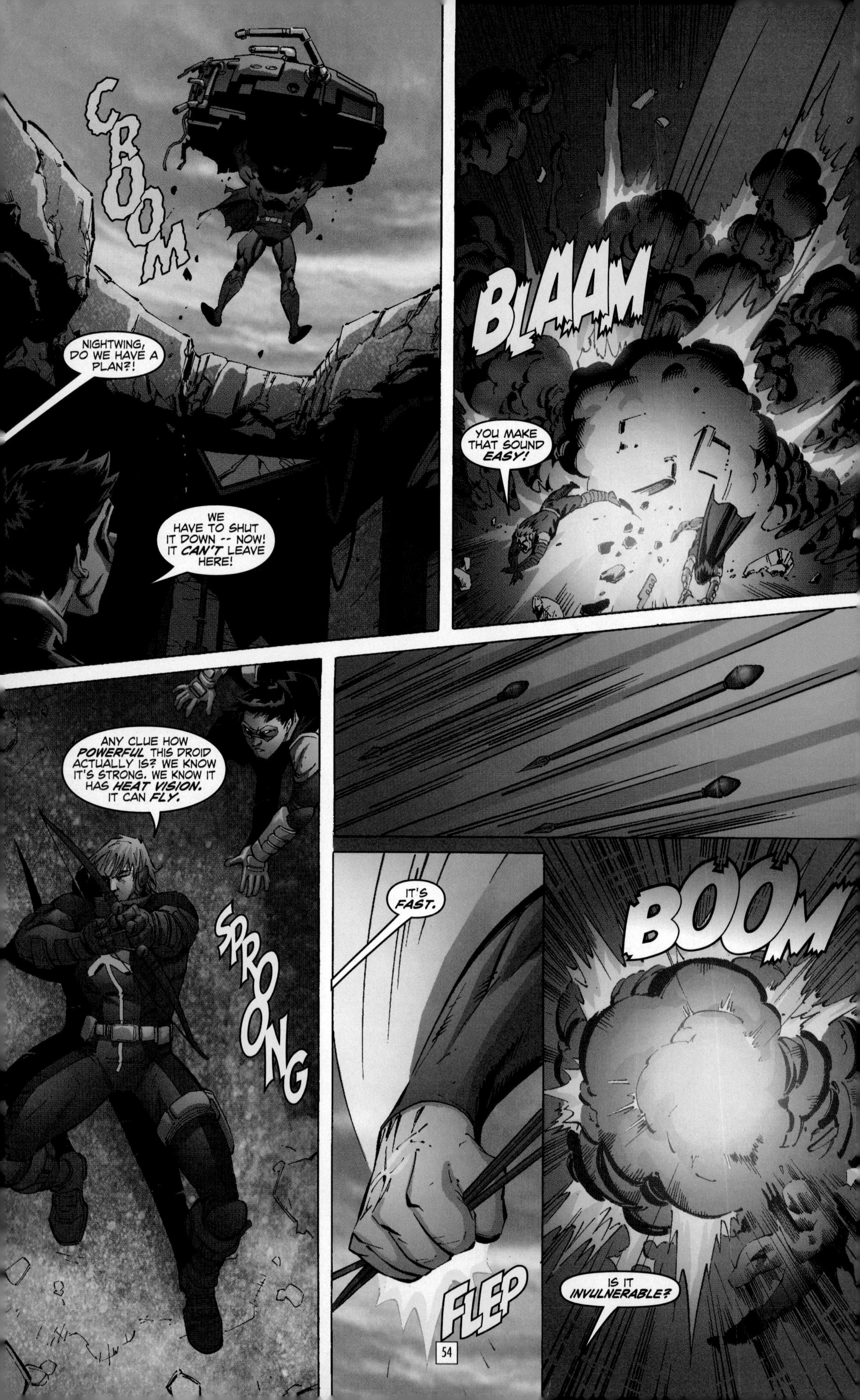
CROOM
NIGHTWING, DO WE HAVE A PLAN?!
WE HAVE TO SHUT IT DOWN -- NOW! IT CAN'T LEAVE HERE!
BLAAM
YOU MAKE THAT SOUND EASY!
ANY CLUE HOW POWERFUL THIS DROID ACTUALLY IS? WE KNOW IT'S STRONG. WE KNOW IT HAS HEAT VISION. IT CAN FLY.
SPROONG
IT'S FAST.
FLEP
BOOM
IS IT INVULNERABLE?

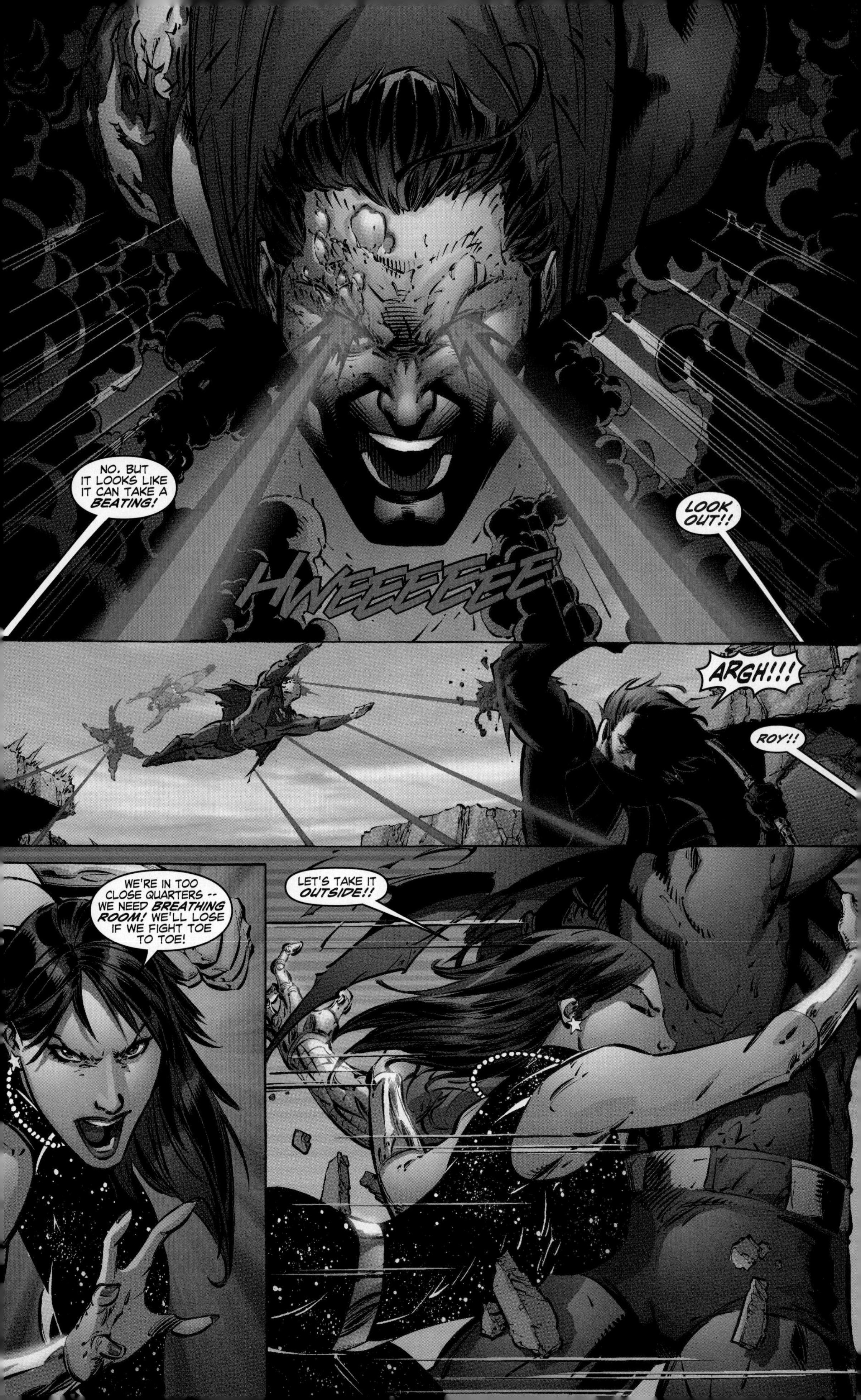
NO. BUT IT LOOKS LIKE IT CAN TAKE A BEATING!
LOOK OUT!!
HWEEEEEEE
ARGH!!!
ROY!!
WE'RE IN TOO CLOSE QUARTERS -- WE NEED BREATHING ROOM! WE'LL LOSE IF WE FIGHT TOE TO TOE!
LET'S TAKE IT OUTSIDE!!

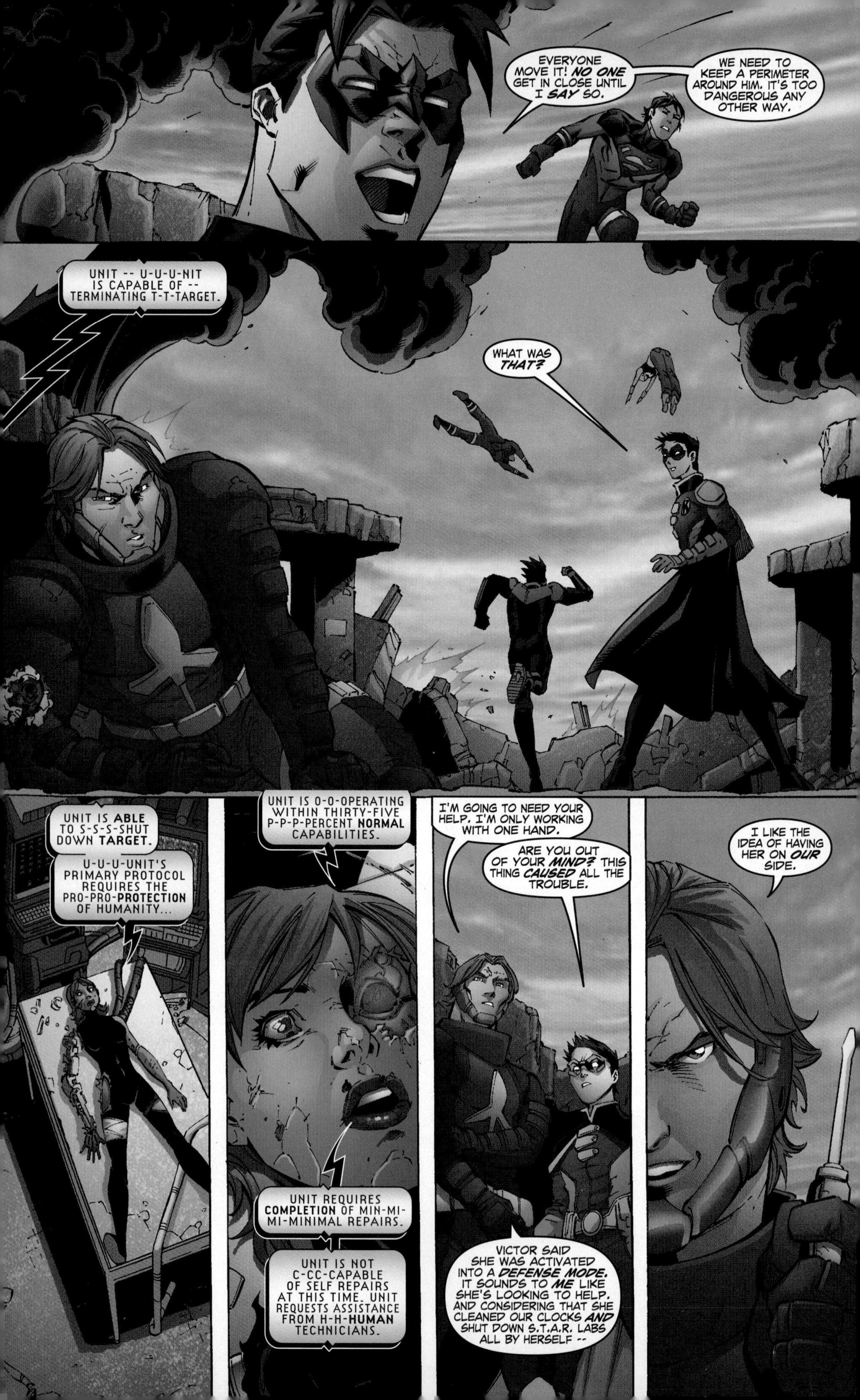
EVERYONE MOVE IT! NO ONE GET IN CLOSE UNTIL I SAY SO.
WE NEED TO KEEP A PERIMETER AROUND HIM. IT'S TOO DANGEROUS ANY OTHER WAY.
UNIT -- U-U-U-NIT IS CAPABLE OF -- TERMINATING T-T-TARGET.
WHAT WAS THAT?
UNIT IS ABLE TO S-S-S-SHUT DOWN TARGET.
U-U-U-UNIT'S PRIMARY PROTOCOL REQUIRES THE PRO-PRO-PROTECTION OF HUMANITY...
UNIT IS O-O-OPERATING WITHIN THIRTY-FIVE P-P-P-PERCENT NORMAL CAPABILITIES.
UNIT REQUIRES COMPLETION OF MIN-MI-MI-MINIMAL REPAIRS.
UNIT IS NOT C-CC-CAPABLE OF SELF REPAIRS AT THIS TIME. UNIT REQUESTS ASSISTANCE FROM H-H-HUMAN TECHNICIANS.
I'M GOING TO NEED YOUR HELP. I'M ONLY WORKING WITH ONE HAND.
ARE YOU OUT OF YOUR MIND? THIS THING CAUSED ALL THE TROUBLE.
VICTOR SAID SHE WAS ACTIVATED INTO A DEFENSE MODE. IT SOUNDS TO ME LIKE SHE'S LOOKING TO HELP. AND CONSIDERING THAT SHE CLEANED OUR CLOCKS AND SHUT DOWN S.T.A.R. LABS ALL BY HERSELF --
I LIKE THE IDEA OF HAVING HER ON OUR SIDE.

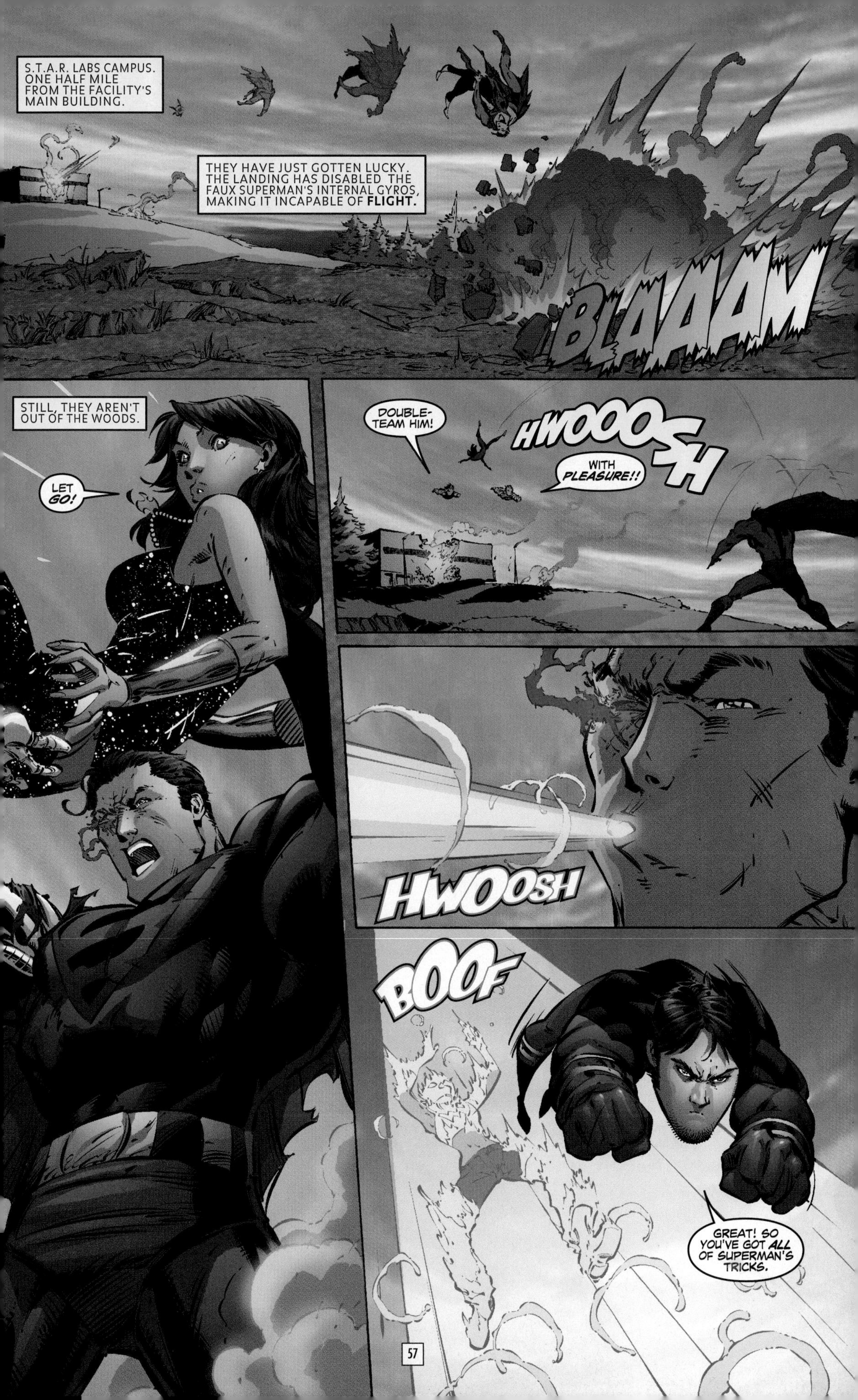

S.T.A.R. LABS CAMPUS. ONE HALF MILE FROM THE FACILITY'S MAIN BUILDING.
THEY HAVE JUST GOTTEN LUCKY. THE LANDING HAS DISABLED THE FAUX SUPERMAN'S INTERNAL GYROS, MAKING IT INCAPABLE OF **FLIGHT.**
BLAAAM
STILL, THEY AREN'T OUT OF THE WOODS.
LET *GO!*
DOUBLE-TEAM HIM!
HWOOOSH
WITH *PLEASURE!!*
HWOOSH
BOOF
GREAT! SO YOU'VE GOT *ALL* OF SUPERMAN'S TRICKS.

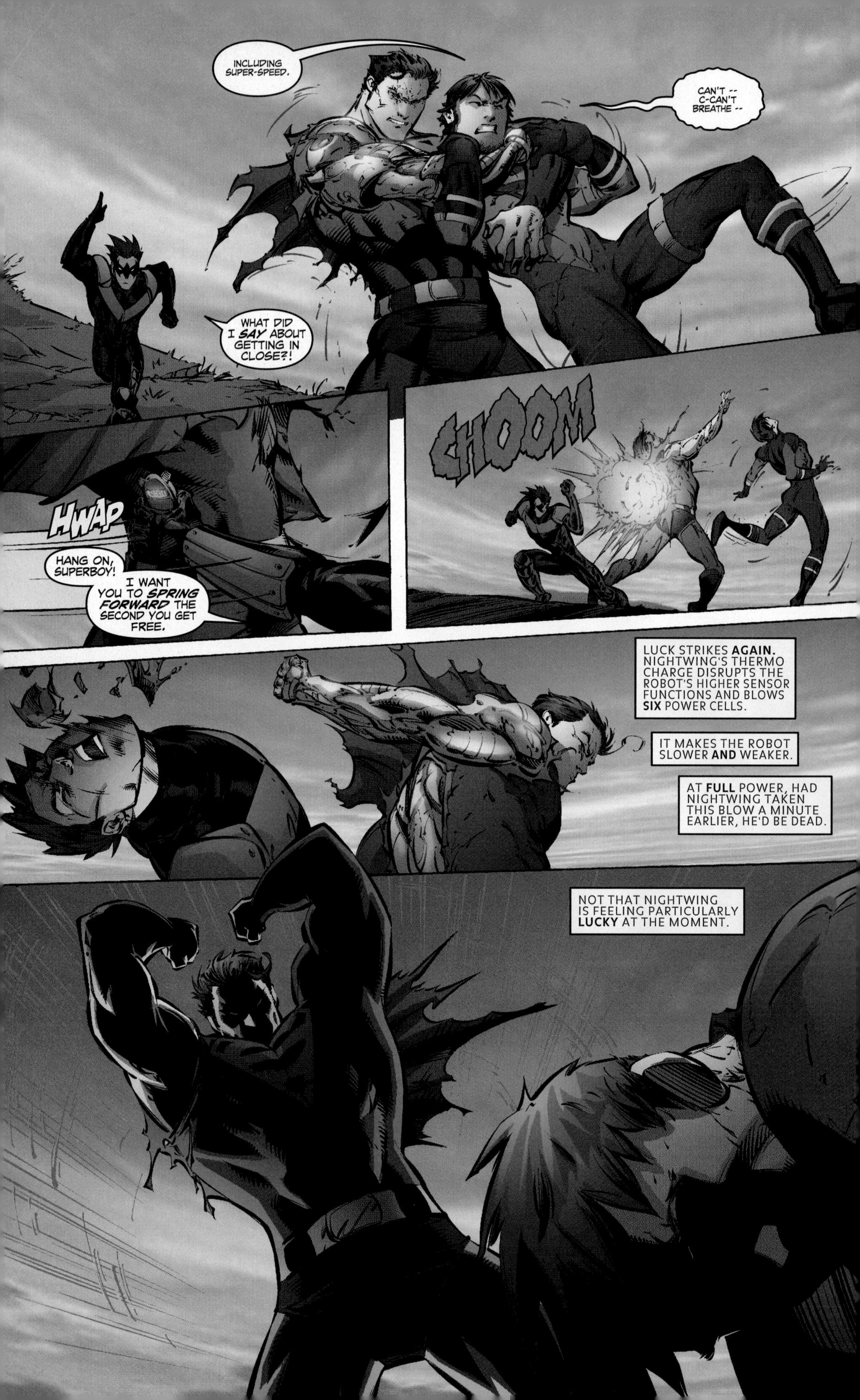
INCLUDING SUPER-SPEED.
CAN'T -- C-CAN'T BREATHE --
WHAT DID I SAY ABOUT GETTING IN CLOSE?!
HWAP
HANG ON, SUPERBOY!
I WANT YOU TO SPRING FORWARD THE SECOND YOU GET FREE.
CHOOM
LUCK STRIKES AGAIN. NIGHTWING'S THERMO CHARGE DISRUPTS THE ROBOT'S HIGHER SENSOR FUNCTIONS AND BLOWS SIX POWER CELLS.
IT MAKES THE ROBOT SLOWER AND WEAKER.
AT FULL POWER, HAD NIGHTWING TAKEN THIS BLOW A MINUTE EARLIER, HE'D BE DEAD.
NOT THAT NIGHTWING IS FEELING PARTICULARLY LUCKY AT THE MOMENT.

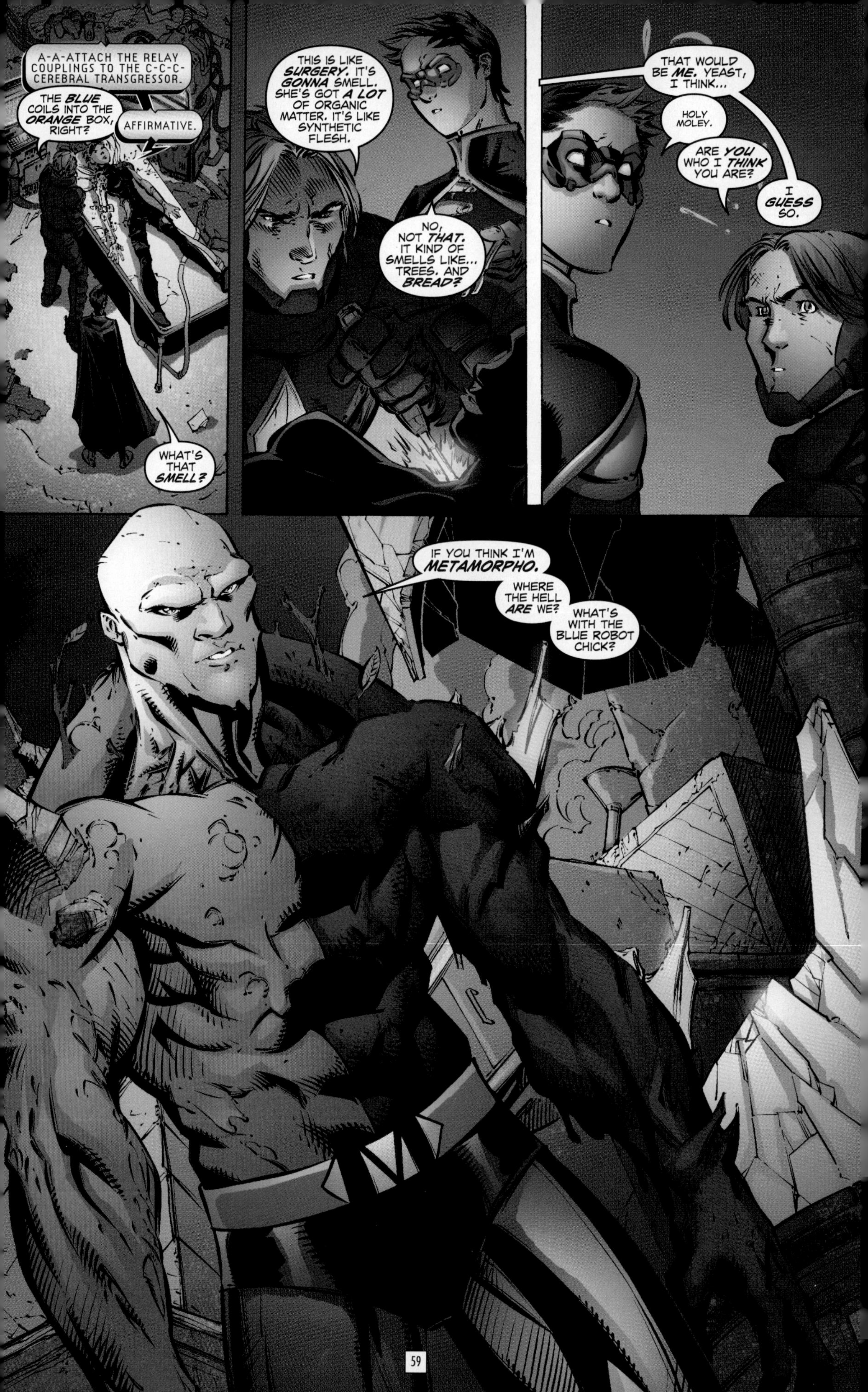
A-A-ATTACH THE RELAY COUPLINGS TO THE C-C-C-CEREBRAL TRANSGRESSOR.
THE BLUE COILS INTO THE ORANGE BOX, RIGHT?
AFFIRMATIVE.
WHAT'S THAT SMELL?
THIS IS LIKE SURGERY. IT'S GONNA SMELL. SHE'S GOT A LOT OF ORGANIC MATTER. IT'S LIKE SYNTHETIC FLESH.
NO, NOT THAT. IT KIND OF SMELLS LIKE... TREES. AND BREAD?
THAT WOULD BE ME. YEAST, I THINK...
HOLY MOLEY.
ARE YOU WHO I THINK YOU ARE?
I GUESS SO.
IF YOU THINK I'M METAMORPHO.
WHERE THE HELL ARE WE?
WHAT'S WITH THE BLUE ROBOT CHICK?

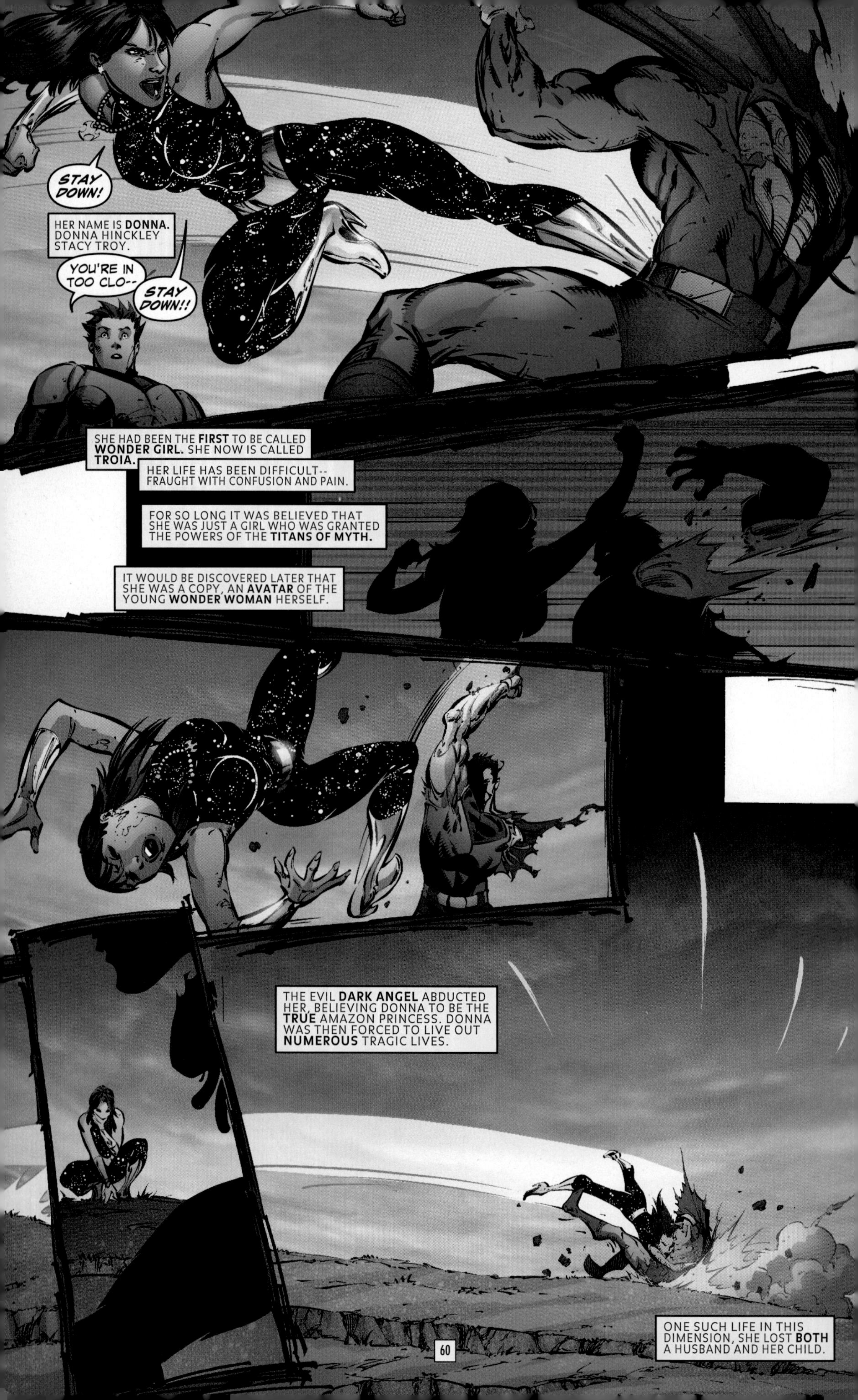
STAY DOWN!
HER NAME IS DONNA. DONNA HINCKLEY STACY TROY.
YOU'RE IN TOO CLO--
STAY DOWN!!
SHE HAD BEEN THE FIRST TO BE CALLED WONDER GIRL. SHE NOW IS CALLED TROIA.
HER LIFE HAS BEEN DIFFICULT-- FRAUGHT WITH CONFUSION AND PAIN.
FOR SO LONG IT WAS BELIEVED THAT SHE WAS JUST A GIRL WHO WAS GRANTED THE POWERS OF THE TITANS OF MYTH.
IT WOULD BE DISCOVERED LATER THAT SHE WAS A COPY, AN AVATAR OF THE YOUNG WONDER WOMAN HERSELF.
THE EVIL DARK ANGEL ABDUCTED HER, BELIEVING DONNA TO BE THE TRUE AMAZON PRINCESS. DONNA WAS THEN FORCED TO LIVE OUT NUMEROUS TRAGIC LIVES.
ONE SUCH LIFE IN THIS DIMENSION, SHE LOST BOTH A HUSBAND AND HER CHILD.

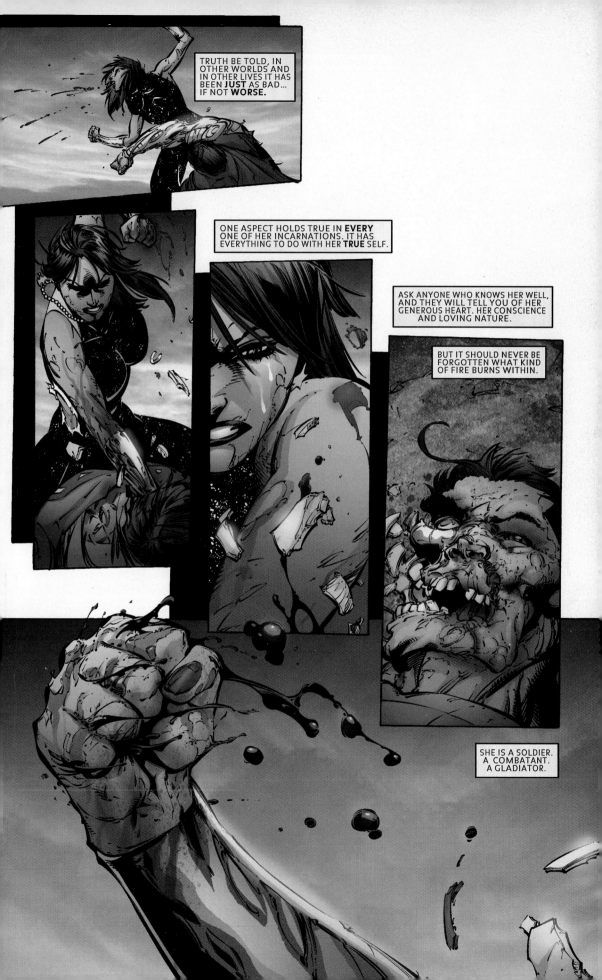

TRUTH BE TOLD, IN OTHER WORLDS AND IN OTHER LIVES IT HAS BEEN **JUST** AS BAD... IF NOT **WORSE**.

ONE ASPECT HOLDS TRUE IN **EVERY** ONE OF HER INCARNATIONS. IT HAS EVERYTHING TO DO WITH HER **TRUE** SELF.

ASK ANYONE WHO KNOWS HER WELL, AND THEY WILL TELL YOU OF HER GENEROUS HEART. HER CONSCIENCE AND LOVING NATURE.

BUT IT SHOULD NEVER BE FORGOTTEN WHAT KIND OF FIRE BURNS WITHIN.

SHE IS A SOLDIER. A COMBATANT. A GLADIATOR.

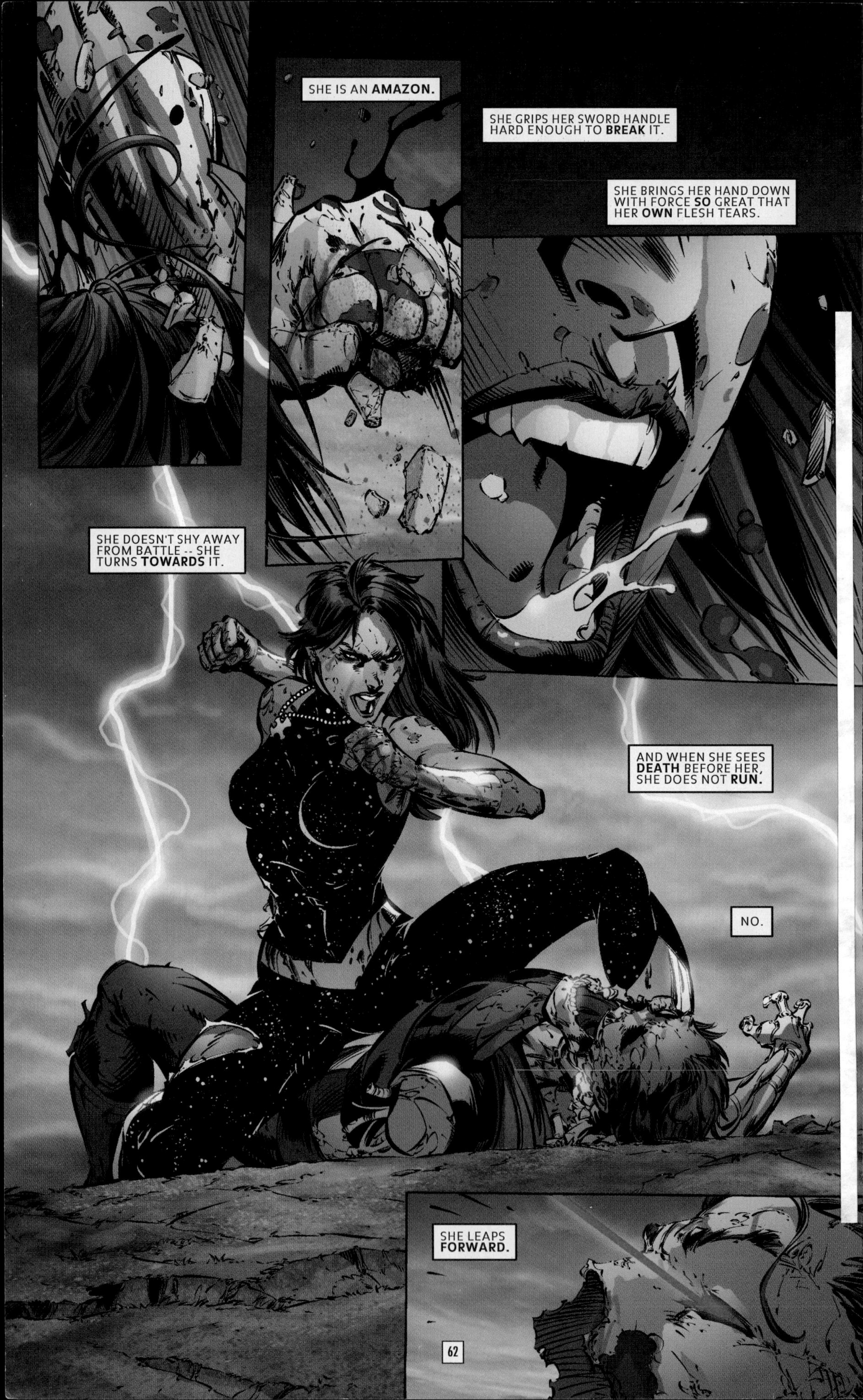
SHE IS AN **AMAZON.**
SHE GRIPS HER SWORD HANDLE HARD ENOUGH TO **BREAK** IT.
SHE BRINGS HER HAND DOWN WITH FORCE **SO** GREAT THAT HER **OWN** FLESH TEARS.
SHE DOESN'T SHY AWAY FROM BATTLE -- SHE TURNS **TOWARDS** IT.
AND WHEN SHE SEES **DEATH** BEFORE HER, SHE DOES NOT **RUN.**
NO.
SHE LEAPS **FORWARD.**

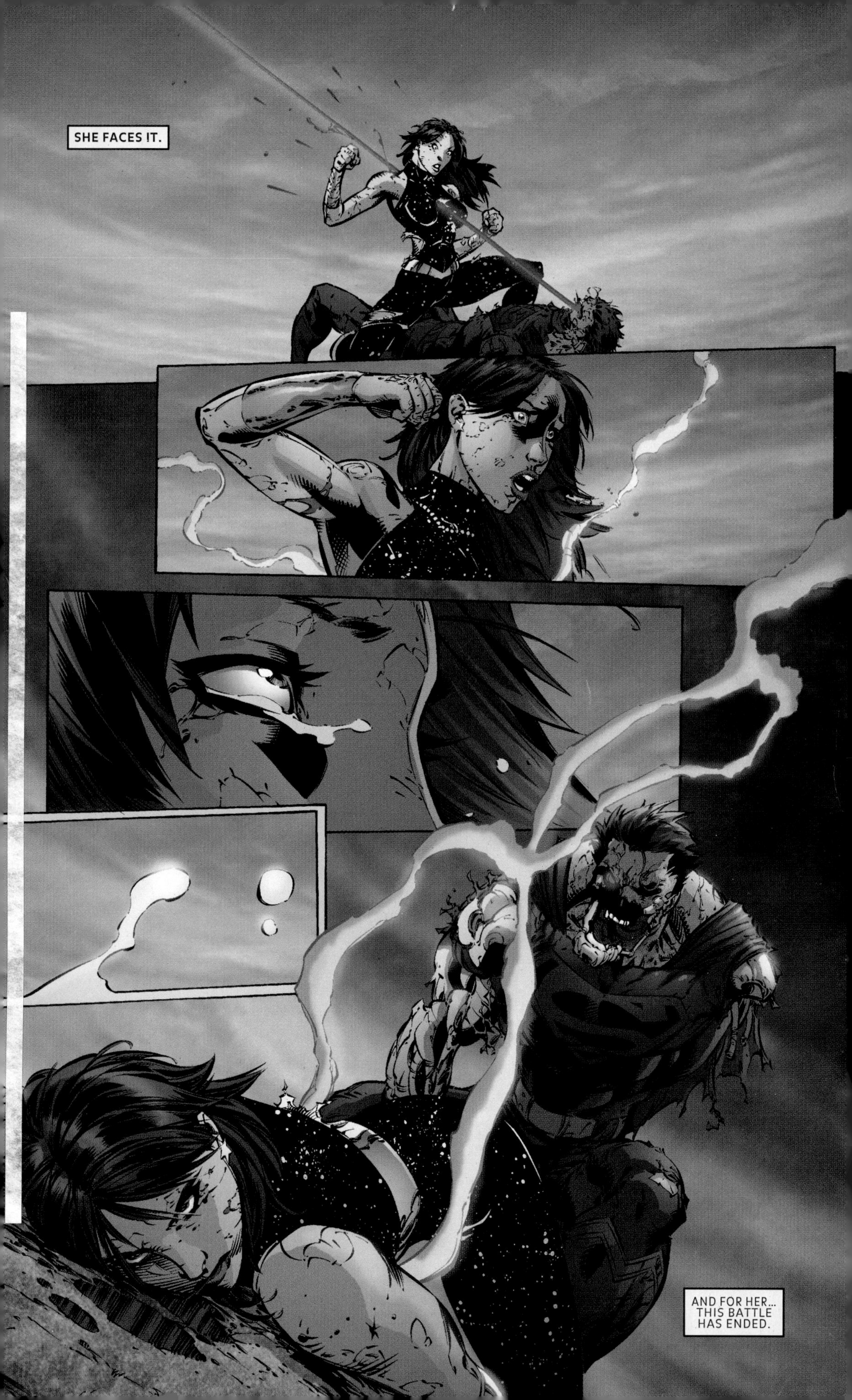
SHE FACES IT.
AND FOR HER... THIS BATTLE HAS ENDED.

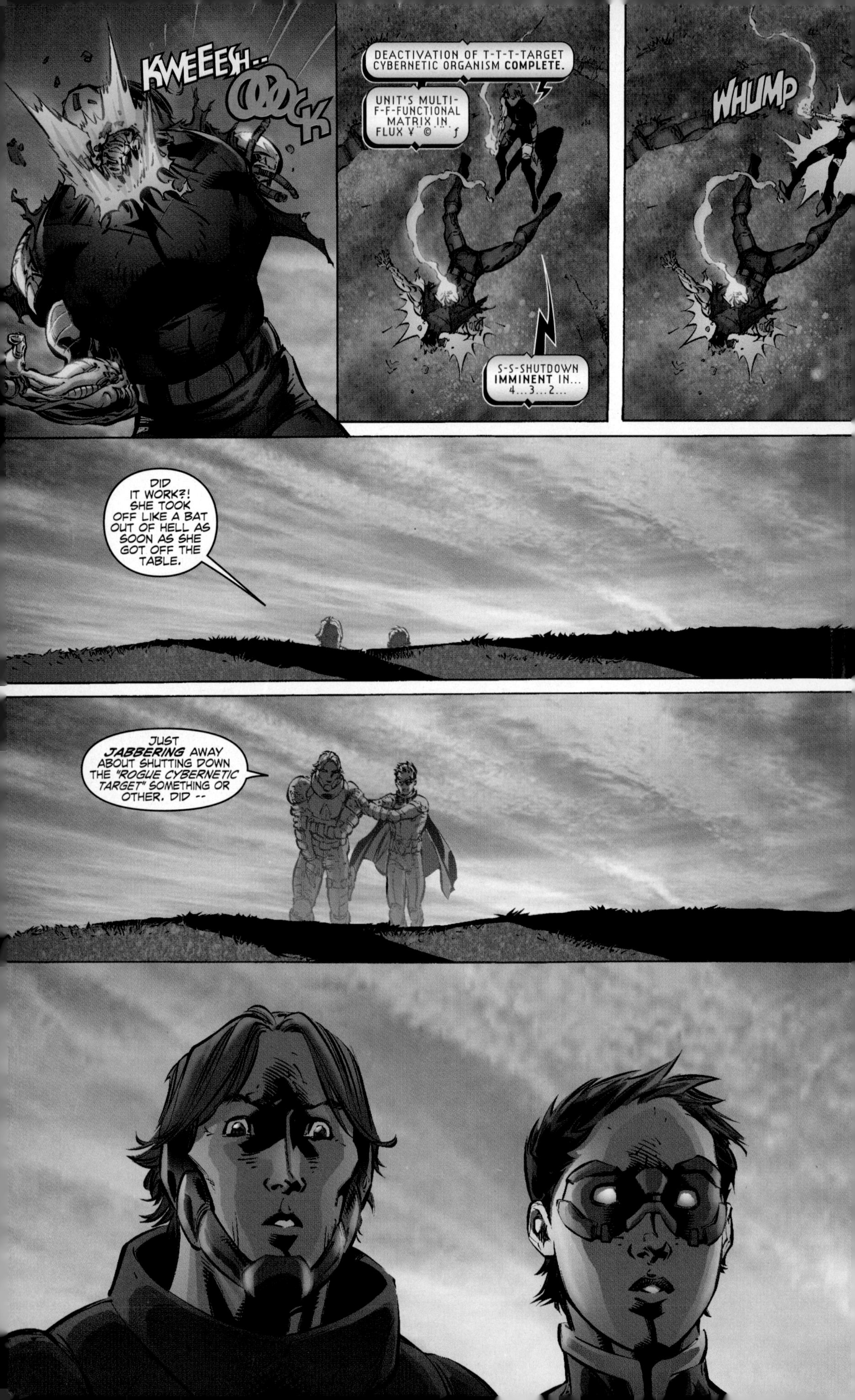
KWEEESH..
CHOOCK
DEACTIVATION OF T-T-T-TARGET CYBERNETIC ORGANISM COMPLETE.
UNIT'S MULTI-F-F-FUNCTIONAL MATRIX IN FLUX ¥¨©˙˙˙ƒ
S-S-SHUTDOWN IMMINENT IN... 4...3...2...
WHUMP
DID IT WORK?! SHE TOOK OFF LIKE A BAT OUT OF HELL AS SOON AS SHE GOT OFF THE TABLE.
JUST JABBERING AWAY ABOUT SHUTTING DOWN THE "ROGUE CYBERNETIC TARGET" SOMETHING OR OTHER. DID --

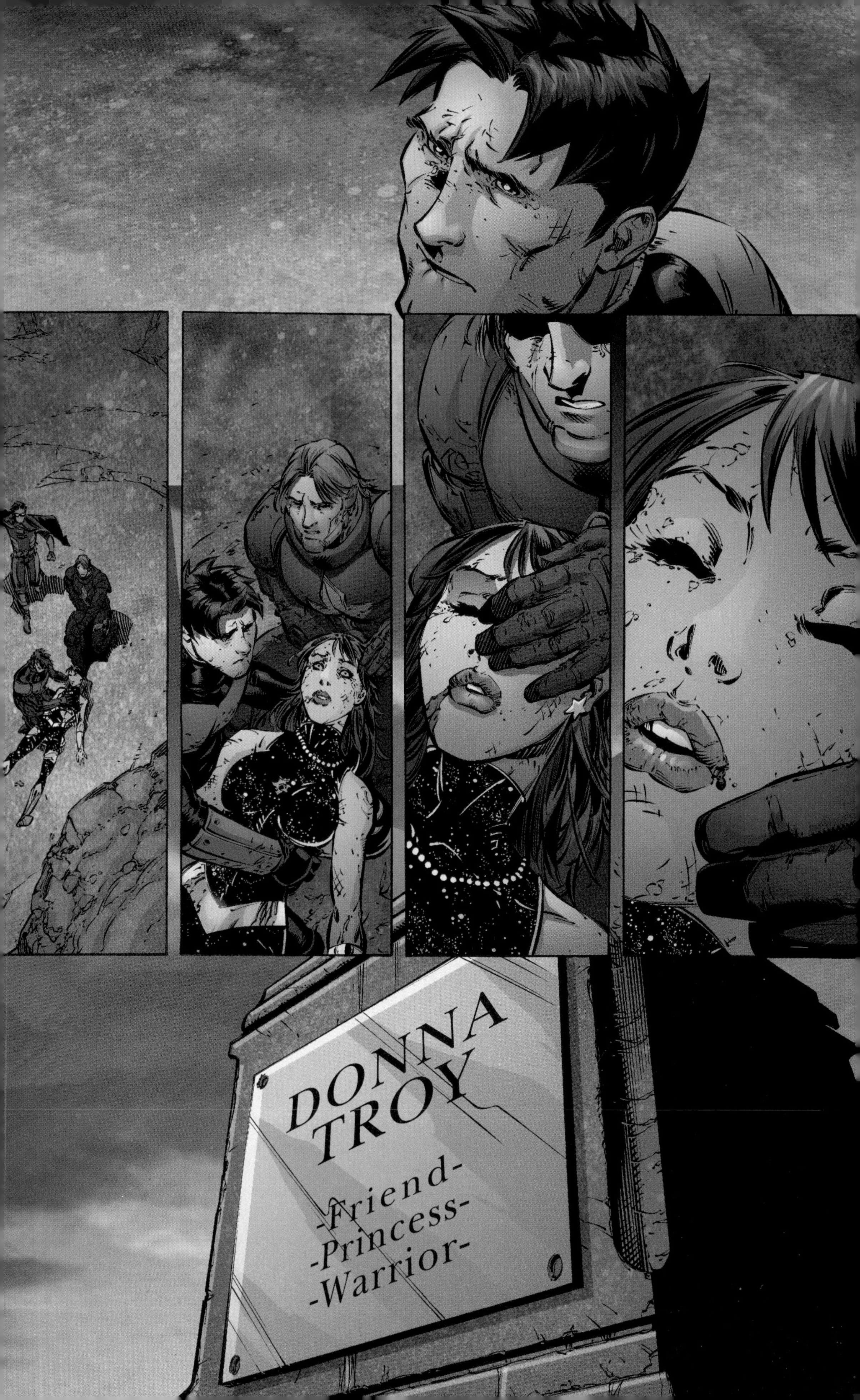
DONNA TROY
-Friend-
-Princess-
-Warrior-

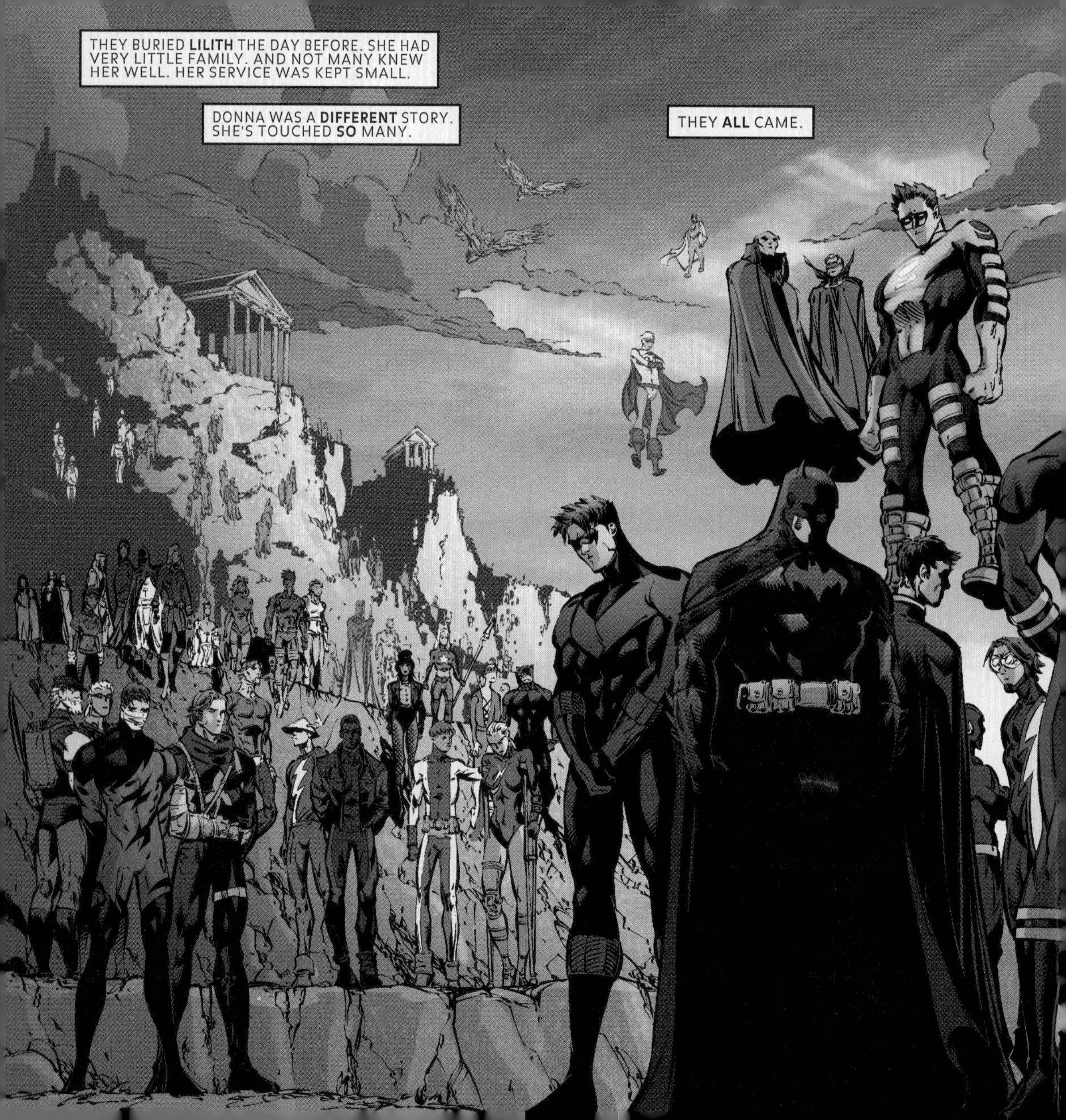
THEY BURIED **LILITH** THE DAY BEFORE. SHE HAD VERY LITTLE FAMILY. AND NOT MANY KNEW HER WELL. HER SERVICE WAS KEPT SMALL.
DONNA WAS A **DIFFERENT** STORY. SHE'S TOUCHED **SO** MANY.
THEY **ALL** CAME.

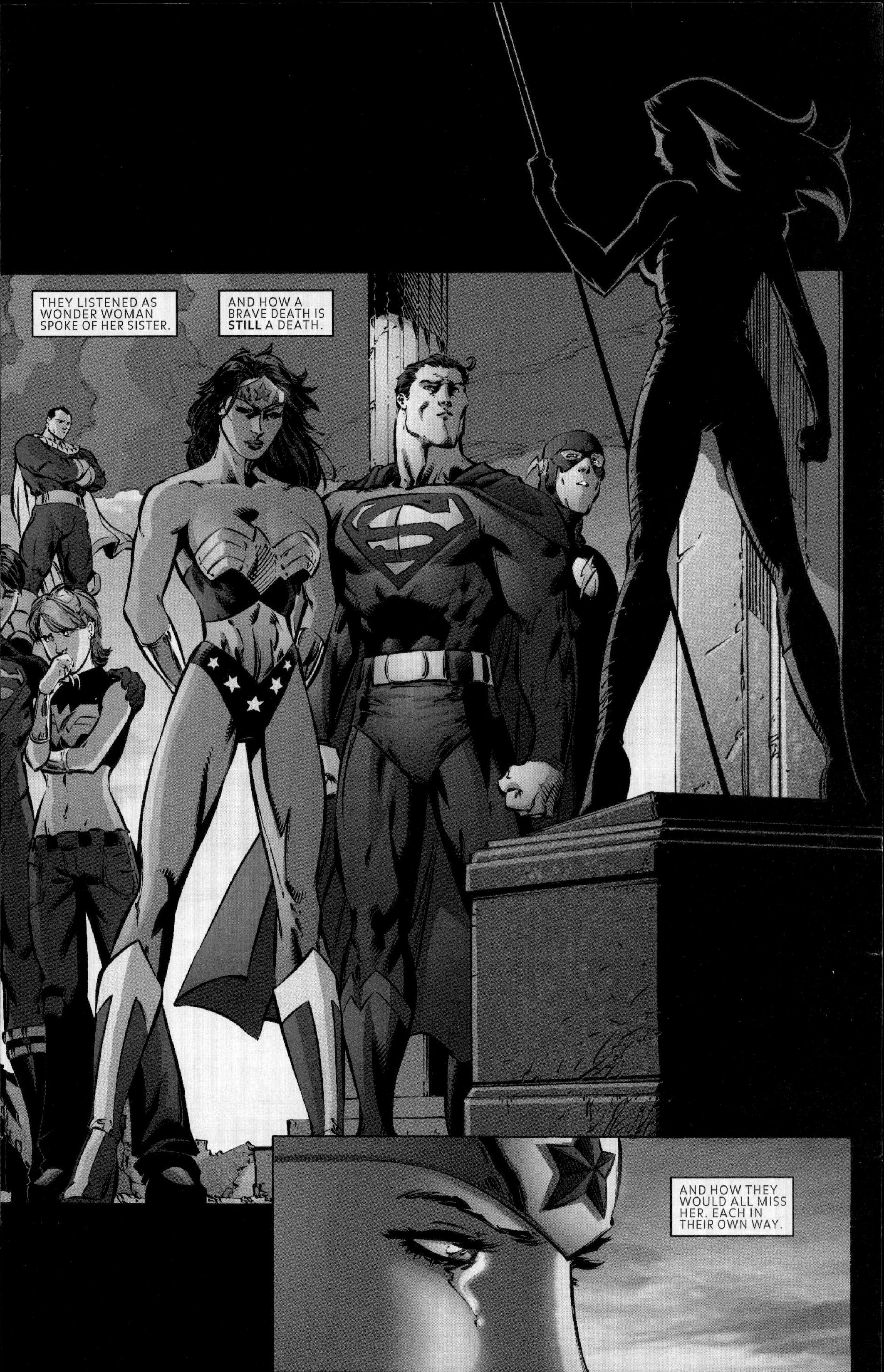
THEY LISTENED AS WONDER WOMAN SPOKE OF HER SISTER.
AND HOW A BRAVE DEATH IS **STILL** A DEATH.
AND HOW THEY WOULD ALL MISS HER. EACH IN THEIR OWN WAY.

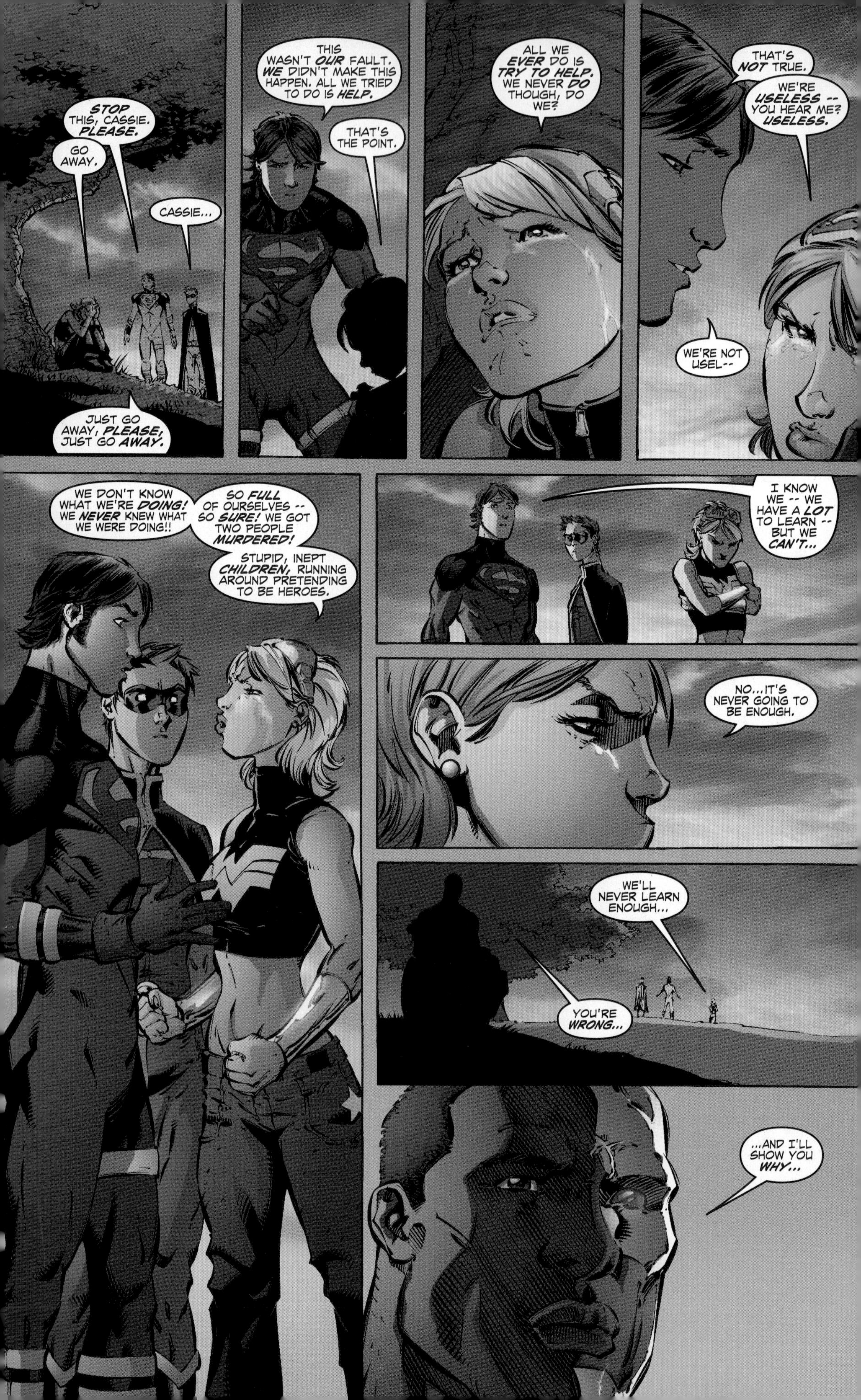

STOP THIS, CASSIE. PLEASE.
GO AWAY.
CASSIE...
JUST GO AWAY, PLEASE, JUST GO AWAY.
THIS WASN'T OUR FAULT. WE DIDN'T MAKE THIS HAPPEN. ALL WE TRIED TO DO IS HELP.
THAT'S THE POINT.
ALL WE EVER DO IS TRY TO HELP. WE NEVER DO THOUGH, DO WE?
THAT'S NOT TRUE.
WE'RE USELESS -- YOU HEAR ME? USELESS.
WE'RE NOT USEL--
WE DON'T KNOW WHAT WE'RE DOING! WE NEVER KNEW WHAT WE WERE DOING!!
SO FULL OF OURSELVES -- SO SURE! WE GOT TWO PEOPLE MURDERED!
STUPID, INEPT CHILDREN, RUNNING AROUND PRETENDING TO BE HEROES.
I KNOW WE -- WE HAVE A LOT TO LEARN -- BUT WE CAN'T...
NO...IT'S NEVER GOING TO BE ENOUGH.
WE'LL NEVER LEARN ENOUGH...
YOU'RE WRONG...
...AND I'LL SHOW YOU WHY...

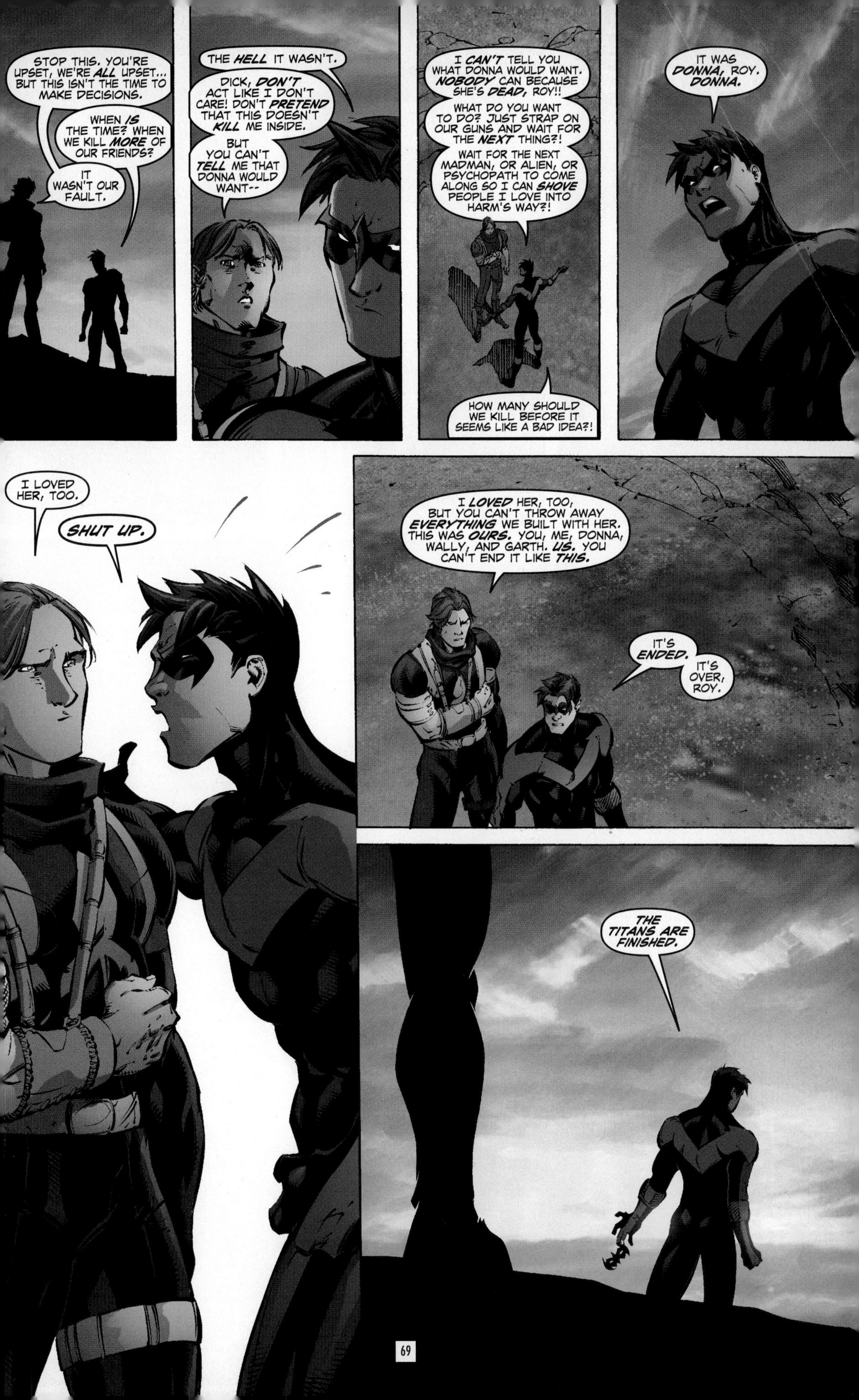
STOP THIS. YOU'RE UPSET, WE'RE ALL UPSET... BUT THIS ISN'T THE TIME TO MAKE DECISIONS.
WHEN IS THE TIME? WHEN WE KILL MORE OF OUR FRIENDS?
IT WASN'T OUR FAULT.
THE HELL IT WASN'T.
DICK, DON'T ACT LIKE I DON'T CARE! DON'T PRETEND THAT THIS DOESN'T KILL ME INSIDE.
BUT YOU CAN'T TELL ME THAT DONNA WOULD WANT--
I CAN'T TELL YOU WHAT DONNA WOULD WANT. NOBODY CAN BECAUSE SHE'S DEAD, ROY!!
WHAT DO YOU WANT TO DO? JUST STRAP ON OUR GUNS AND WAIT FOR THE NEXT THING?!
WAIT FOR THE NEXT MADMAN, OR ALIEN, OR PSYCHOPATH TO COME ALONG SO I CAN SHOVE PEOPLE I LOVE INTO HARM'S WAY?!
HOW MANY SHOULD WE KILL BEFORE IT SEEMS LIKE A BAD IDEA?!
IT WAS DONNA, ROY. DONNA.
I LOVED HER, TOO.
SHUT UP.
I LOVED HER, TOO, BUT YOU CAN'T THROW AWAY EVERYTHING WE BUILT WITH HER. THIS WAS OURS. YOU, ME, DONNA, WALLY, AND GARTH. US. YOU CAN'T END IT LIKE THIS.
IT'S ENDED.
IT'S OVER, ROY.
THE TITANS ARE FINISHED.

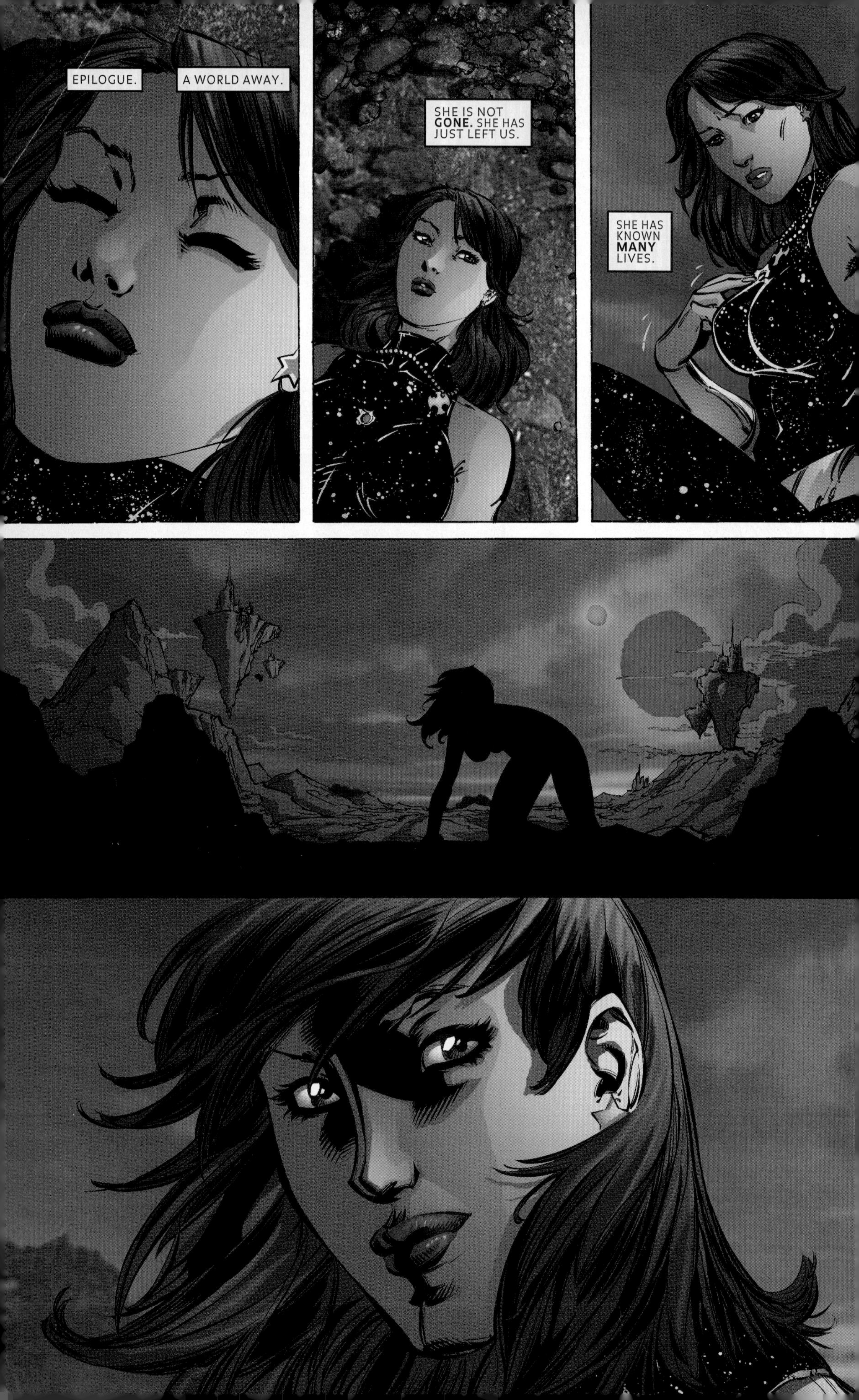
EPILOGUE.
A WORLD AWAY.
SHE IS NOT GONE. SHE HAS JUST LEFT US.
SHE HAS KNOWN MANY LIVES.

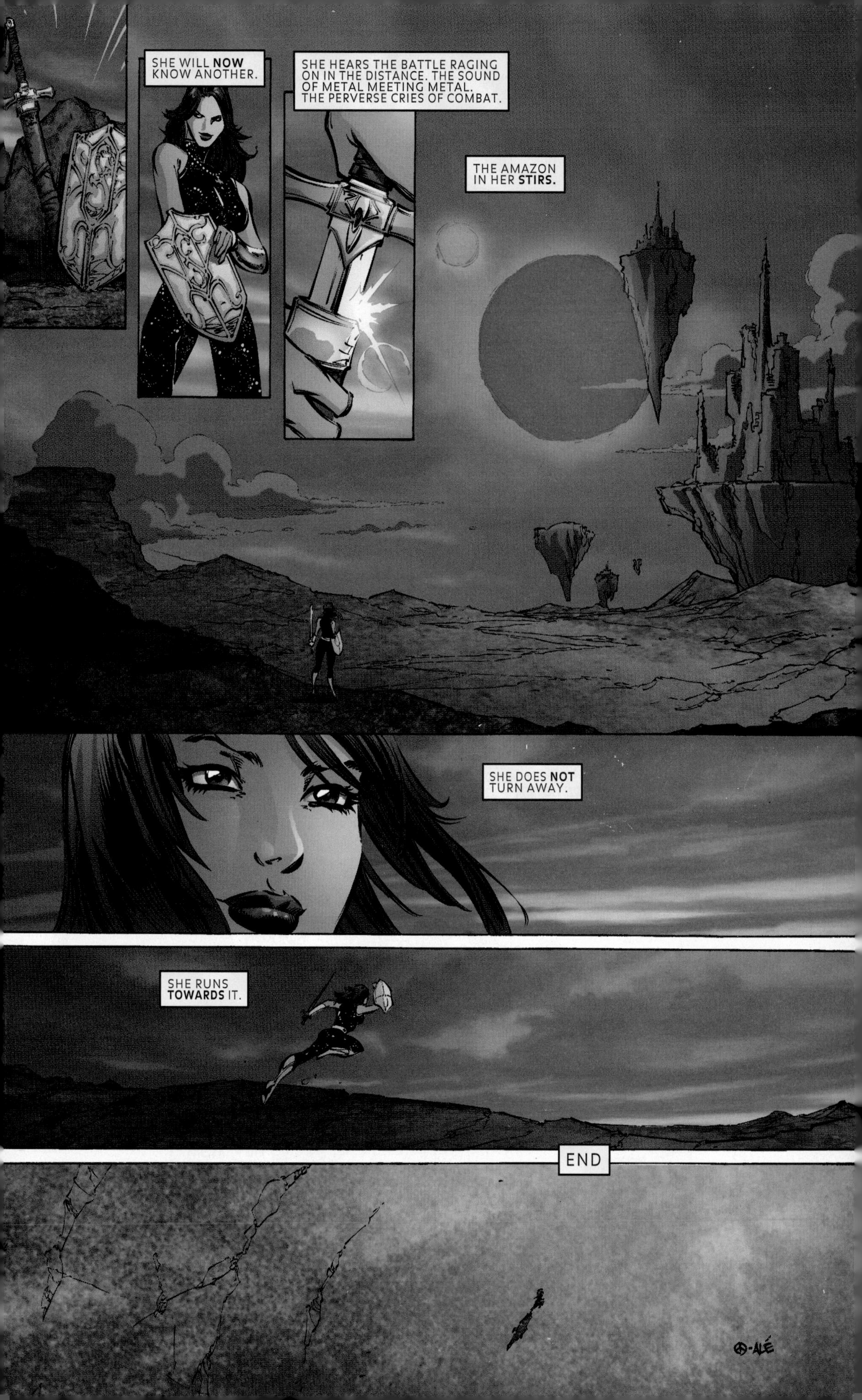
SHE WILL **NOW** KNOW ANOTHER.
SHE HEARS THE BATTLE RAGING ON IN THE DISTANCE. THE SOUND OF METAL MEETING METAL. THE PERVERSE CRIES OF COMBAT.
THE AMAZON IN HER **STIRS.**
SHE DOES **NOT** TURN AWAY.
SHE RUNS **TOWARDS** IT.
END
ALÉ

<LORD HADES, MOST INEVITABLE OF THE GODS-->

<--WE BESEECH THAT YOU HONOR OUR FALLEN QUEEN, THE NOBLE HIPPOLYTA, BY ESCORTING HER ADOPTED DAUGHTER SAFELY BEYOND THE TOWER OF CRONUS, TO THE BLESSED ISLANDS OF THE ELYSIAN FIELDS-->

<--TO AN AFTERLIFE WORTHY OF THE FAVORED OF ATHENA AND ARTEMIS, OF APHRODITE AND DEMETER-->

<--ONE FITTING AN AMAZON.>

DONNA TROY
FRIEND
PRINCE
WARRI

CASSIE, YOU GONNA BE OKAY?

NO, KON.
I'M NOT.

HEY, MOM? CAN YOU HANDLE THE CLEANUP FOR A MINUTE?

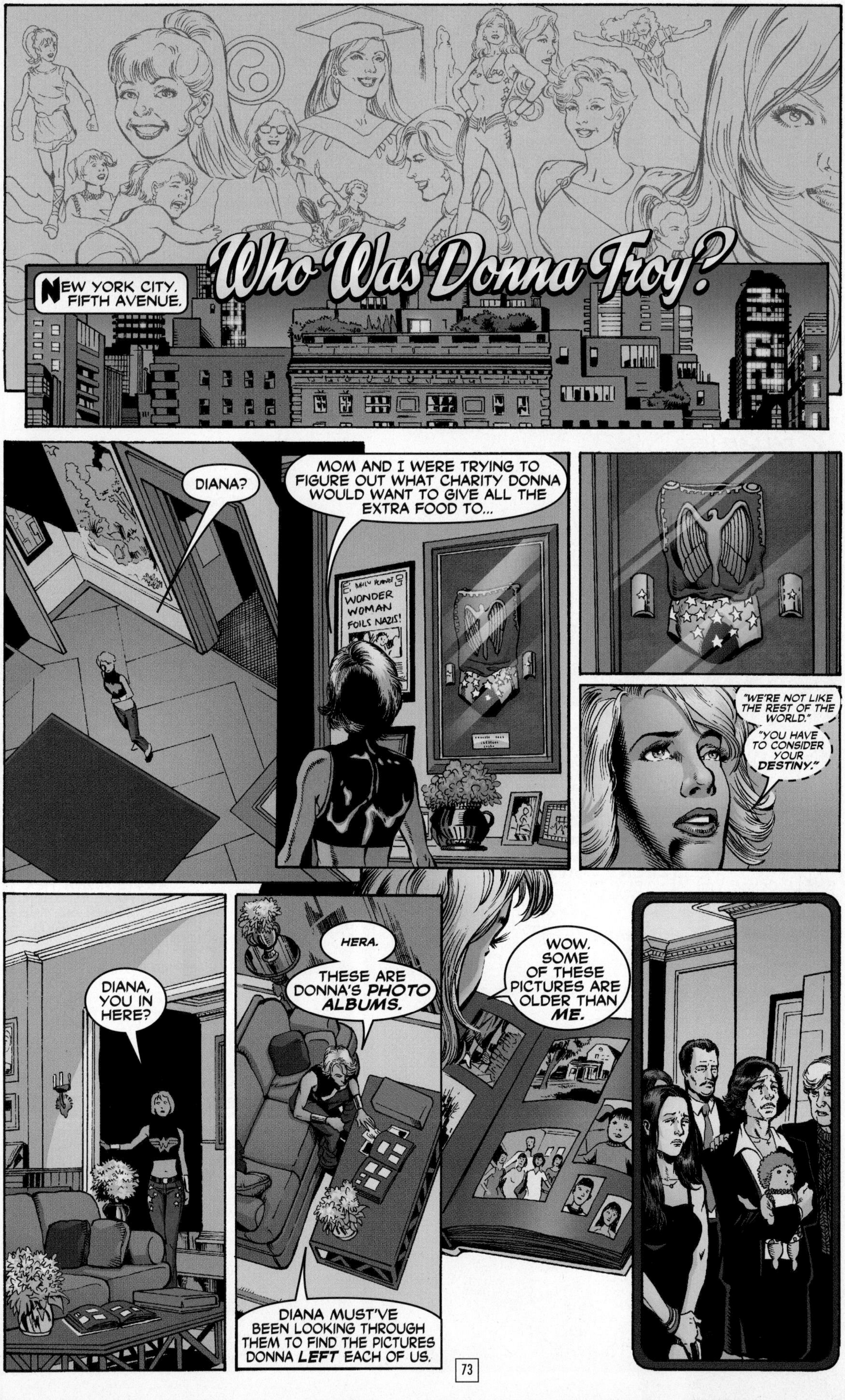

Who Was Donna Troy?
NEW YORK CITY. FIFTH AVENUE.
DIANA?
MOM AND I WERE TRYING TO FIGURE OUT WHAT CHARITY DONNA WOULD WANT TO GIVE ALL THE EXTRA FOOD TO...
DAILY PLANET
WONDER WOMAN FOILS NAZIS!
"WE'RE NOT LIKE THE REST OF THE WORLD."
"YOU HAVE TO CONSIDER YOUR DESTINY."
DIANA, YOU IN HERE?
HERA.
THESE ARE DONNA'S PHOTO ALBUMS.
WOW. SOME OF THESE PICTURES ARE OLDER THAN ME.
DIANA MUST'VE BEEN LOOKING THROUGH THEM TO FIND THE PICTURES DONNA LEFT EACH OF US.

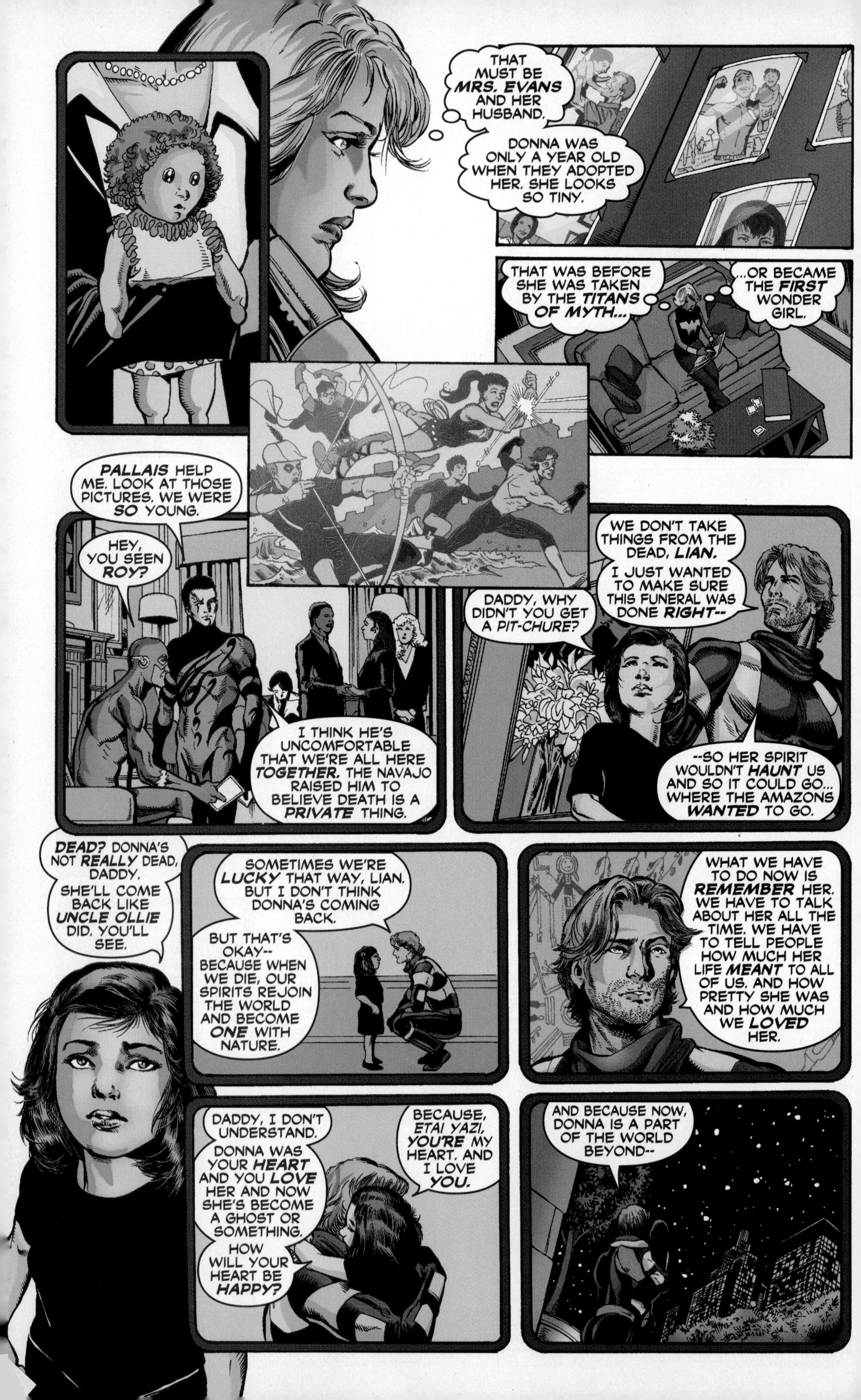
THAT MUST BE MRS. EVANS AND HER HUSBAND.
DONNA WAS ONLY A YEAR OLD WHEN THEY ADOPTED HER. SHE LOOKS SO TINY.
THAT WAS BEFORE SHE WAS TAKEN BY THE TITANS OF MYTH...
...OR BECAME THE FIRST WONDER GIRL.
PALLAIS HELP ME. LOOK AT THOSE PICTURES. WE WERE SO YOUNG.
HEY, YOU SEEN ROY?
I THINK HE'S UNCOMFORTABLE THAT WE'RE ALL HERE TOGETHER. THE NAVAJO RAISED HIM TO BELIEVE DEATH IS A PRIVATE THING.
DADDY, WHY DIDN'T YOU GET A PIT-CHURE?
WE DON'T TAKE THINGS FROM THE DEAD, LIAN.
I JUST WANTED TO MAKE SURE THIS FUNERAL WAS DONE RIGHT--
--SO HER SPIRIT WOULDN'T HAUNT US AND SO IT COULD GO... WHERE THE AMAZONS WANTED TO GO.
DEAD? DONNA'S NOT REALLY DEAD, DADDY.
SHE'LL COME BACK LIKE UNCLE OLLIE DID. YOU'LL SEE.
SOMETIMES WE'RE LUCKY THAT WAY, LIAN. BUT I DON'T THINK DONNA'S COMING BACK.
BUT THAT'S OKAY-- BECAUSE WHEN WE DIE, OUR SPIRITS REJOIN THE WORLD AND BECOME ONE WITH NATURE.
WHAT WE HAVE TO DO NOW IS REMEMBER HER. WE HAVE TO TALK ABOUT HER ALL THE TIME. WE HAVE TO TELL PEOPLE HOW MUCH HER LIFE MEANT TO ALL OF US. AND HOW PRETTY SHE WAS AND HOW MUCH WE LOVED HER.
DADDY, I DON'T UNDERSTAND.
DONNA WAS YOUR HEART AND YOU LOVE HER AND NOW SHE'S BECOME A GHOST OR SOMETHING.
HOW WILL YOUR HEART BE HAPPY?
BECAUSE, ETAI YAZI, YOU'RE MY HEART. AND I LOVE YOU.
AND BECAUSE NOW, DONNA IS A PART OF THE WORLD BEYOND--

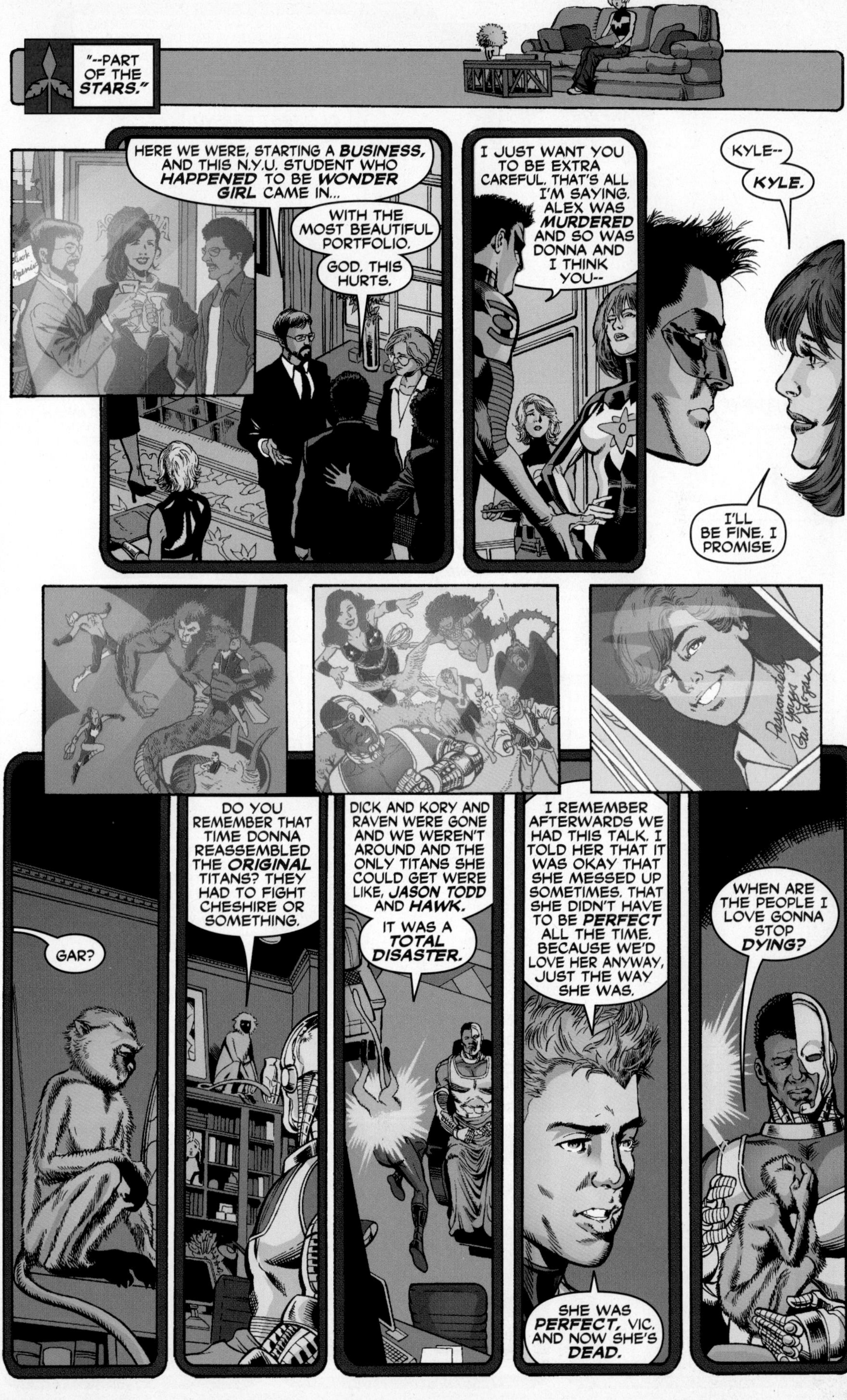

"--PART OF THE STARS."
HERE WE WERE, STARTING A BUSINESS, AND THIS N.Y.U. STUDENT WHO HAPPENED TO BE WONDER GIRL CAME IN...
WITH THE MOST BEAUTIFUL PORTFOLIO.
GOD, THIS HURTS.
I JUST WANT YOU TO BE EXTRA CAREFUL. THAT'S ALL I'M SAYING. ALEX WAS MURDERED AND SO WAS DONNA AND I THINK YOU--
KYLE--
KYLE.
I'LL BE FINE. I PROMISE.
GAR?
DO YOU REMEMBER THAT TIME DONNA REASSEMBLED THE ORIGINAL TITANS? THEY HAD TO FIGHT CHESHIRE OR SOMETHING.
DICK AND KORY AND RAVEN WERE GONE AND WE WEREN'T AROUND AND THE ONLY TITANS SHE COULD GET WERE LIKE, JASON TODD AND HAWK.
IT WAS A TOTAL DISASTER.
I REMEMBER AFTERWARDS WE HAD THIS TALK. I TOLD HER THAT IT WAS OKAY THAT SHE MESSED UP SOMETIMES. THAT SHE DIDN'T HAVE TO BE PERFECT ALL THE TIME. BECAUSE WE'D LOVE HER ANYWAY, JUST THE WAY SHE WAS.
SHE WAS PERFECT, VIC. AND NOW SHE'S DEAD.
WHEN ARE THE PEOPLE I LOVE GONNA STOP DYING?

I WAS GIVING A PERSONAL OFFERING TO THE SUPREME GODDESS X'HAL. STORIES OF DONNA'S BRAVERY WILL BE SPREAD ACROSS THE VEGAN STAR SYSTEM.

SHE WAS MY **CLOSEST FRIEND,** CASSIE.

ᐸᔕᑕᑕᗅ ᑕᔨᑕᔕᔕ, Yᔕ ᒪᔔᑌᔨᑌ, ᔕᗅᔨ ᑕᔨᒪᒍᑕ ᗅ ᑕᔐᒍᒍᗅᔐ

STARFIRE? WHAT ARE YOU DOING IN DONNA'S **BEDROOM?**

SHE WON'T BE **FORGOTTEN.**

AAAHH!

MAN--YOU'RE LIKE A NINJA BACK THERE!

HONEY! IT'S ME!

I DIDN'T MEAN TO STARTLE YOU, I WAS JUST ASKING IF YOU KNEW WHAT DIANA HAD PLANNED ON DOING WITH DONNA'S **APARTMENT--?**

SELLING IT, I GUESS. SHE DOESN'T NEED A PLACE THIS BIG, SHE'D LIVE IN A CARDBOARD **BOX** AND FIND A WAY TO BE COMFORTABLE.

WHAT ARE THESE?

CHECK IT OUT. THEY'RE ALL OF DONNA'S PICTURES.

"THIS IS HER **WEDDING.** SHE WAS, LIKE, 19 WHEN SHE GOT MARRIED, CAN YOU BELIEVE THAT?

"THAT WAS HER HUSBAND **TERRY** AND THEIR KID, **ROBERT,** AND HER STEPDAUGHTER **JENNIFER.**"

"WOW, I JUST REALIZED. THEY'RE ALL **DEAD** NOW. ALL OF 'EM."

HOW **DARE** YOU?

YOU LET YOUR LITTLE SIDEKICKS RUN AROUND IN THOSE **HORRIBLE** COSTUMES, AND CHILDREN EVERYWHERE THINK IT'S "COOL" AND "HIP."

ALL MY DAUGHTER JENNIFER EVER WANTED TO **BE** WAS DONNA TROY, **WONDER GIRL NUMBER TWO.**

AND NOW MY WHOLE FAMILY'S **GONE** BECAUSE OF THAT WOMAN.

BECAUSE OF ALL OF **YOU.**

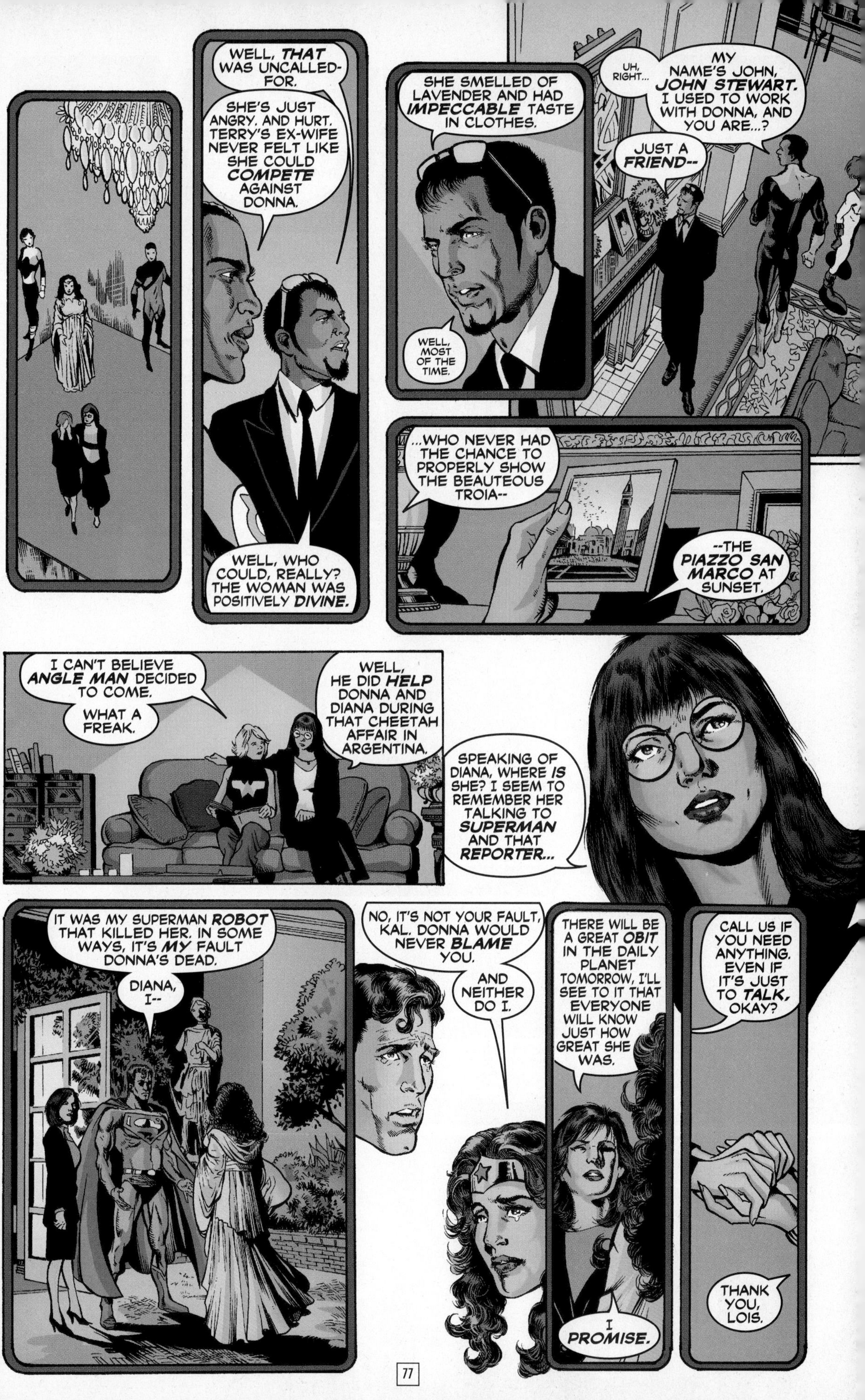

WELL, *THAT* WAS UNCALLED-FOR.
SHE'S JUST ANGRY. AND HURT. TERRY'S EX-WIFE NEVER FELT LIKE SHE COULD *COMPETE* AGAINST DONNA.
WELL, WHO COULD, REALLY? THE WOMAN WAS POSITIVELY *DIVINE.*
SHE SMELLED OF LAVENDER AND HAD *IMPECCABLE* TASTE IN CLOTHES.
WELL, MOST OF THE TIME.
UH, RIGHT...
MY NAME'S JOHN, *JOHN STEWART.* I USED TO WORK WITH DONNA, AND YOU ARE...?
JUST A *FRIEND--*
...WHO NEVER HAD THE CHANCE TO PROPERLY SHOW THE BEAUTEOUS TROIA--
--THE *PIAZZO SAN MARCO* AT SUNSET.
I CAN'T BELIEVE *ANGLE MAN* DECIDED TO COME.
WHAT A FREAK.
WELL, HE DID *HELP* DONNA AND DIANA DURING THAT CHEETAH AFFAIR IN ARGENTINA.
SPEAKING OF DIANA, WHERE *IS* SHE? I SEEM TO REMEMBER HER TALKING TO *SUPERMAN* AND THAT *REPORTER...*
IT WAS MY SUPERMAN *ROBOT* THAT KILLED HER. IN SOME WAYS, IT'S *MY* FAULT DONNA'S DEAD.
DIANA, I--
NO, IT'S NOT YOUR FAULT, KAL. DONNA WOULD NEVER *BLAME* YOU.
AND NEITHER DO I.
THERE WILL BE A GREAT *OBIT* IN THE DAILY PLANET TOMORROW, I'LL SEE TO IT THAT EVERYONE WILL KNOW JUST HOW GREAT SHE WAS.
I *PROMISE.*
CALL US IF YOU NEED ANYTHING. EVEN IF IT'S JUST TO *TALK,* OKAY?
THANK YOU, LOIS.

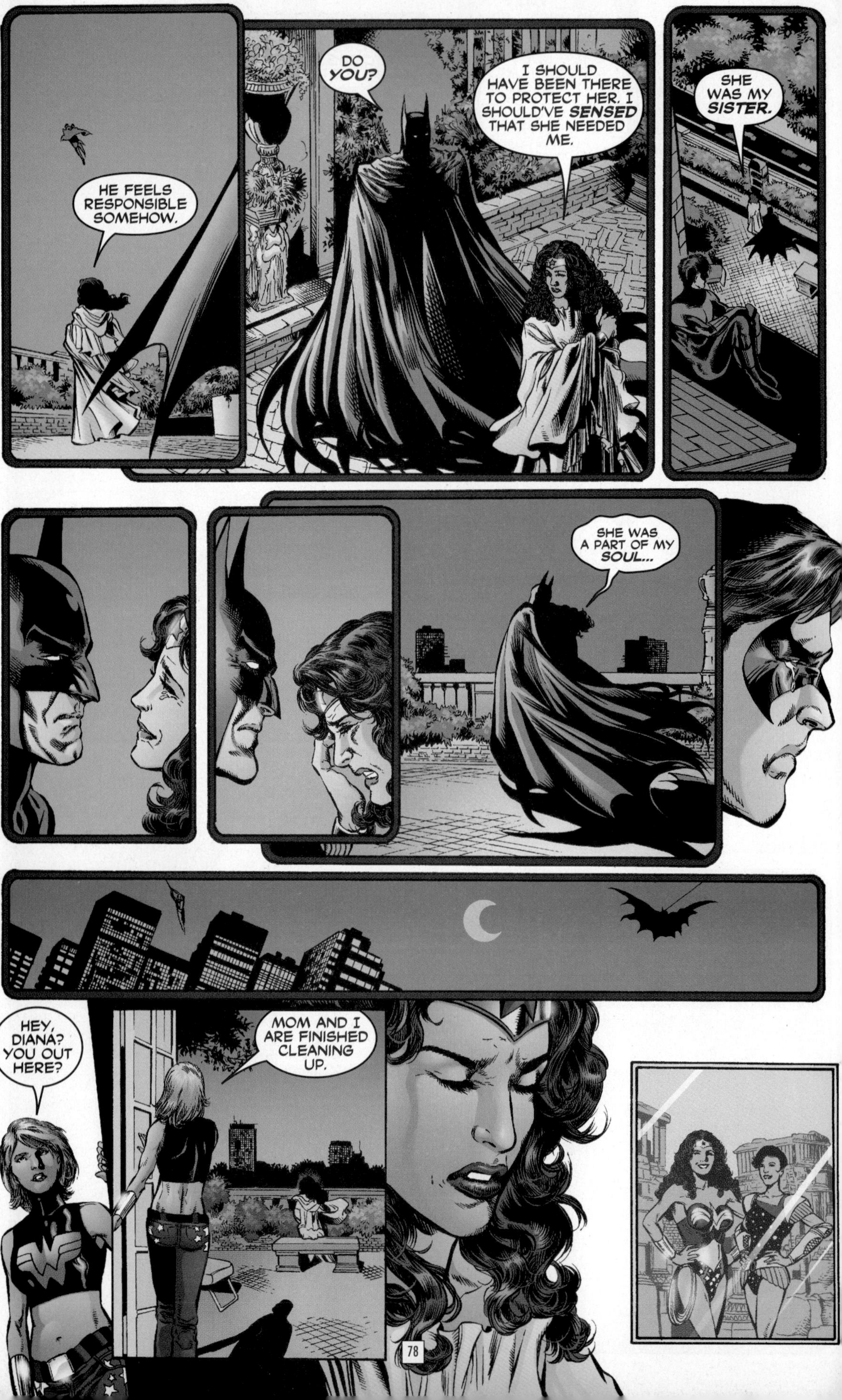
HE FEELS RESPONSIBLE SOMEHOW.
DO YOU?
I SHOULD HAVE BEEN THERE TO PROTECT HER. I SHOULD'VE SENSED THAT SHE NEEDED ME.
SHE WAS MY SISTER.
SHE WAS A PART OF MY SOUL...
HEY, DIANA? YOU OUT HERE?
MOM AND I ARE FINISHED CLEANING UP.

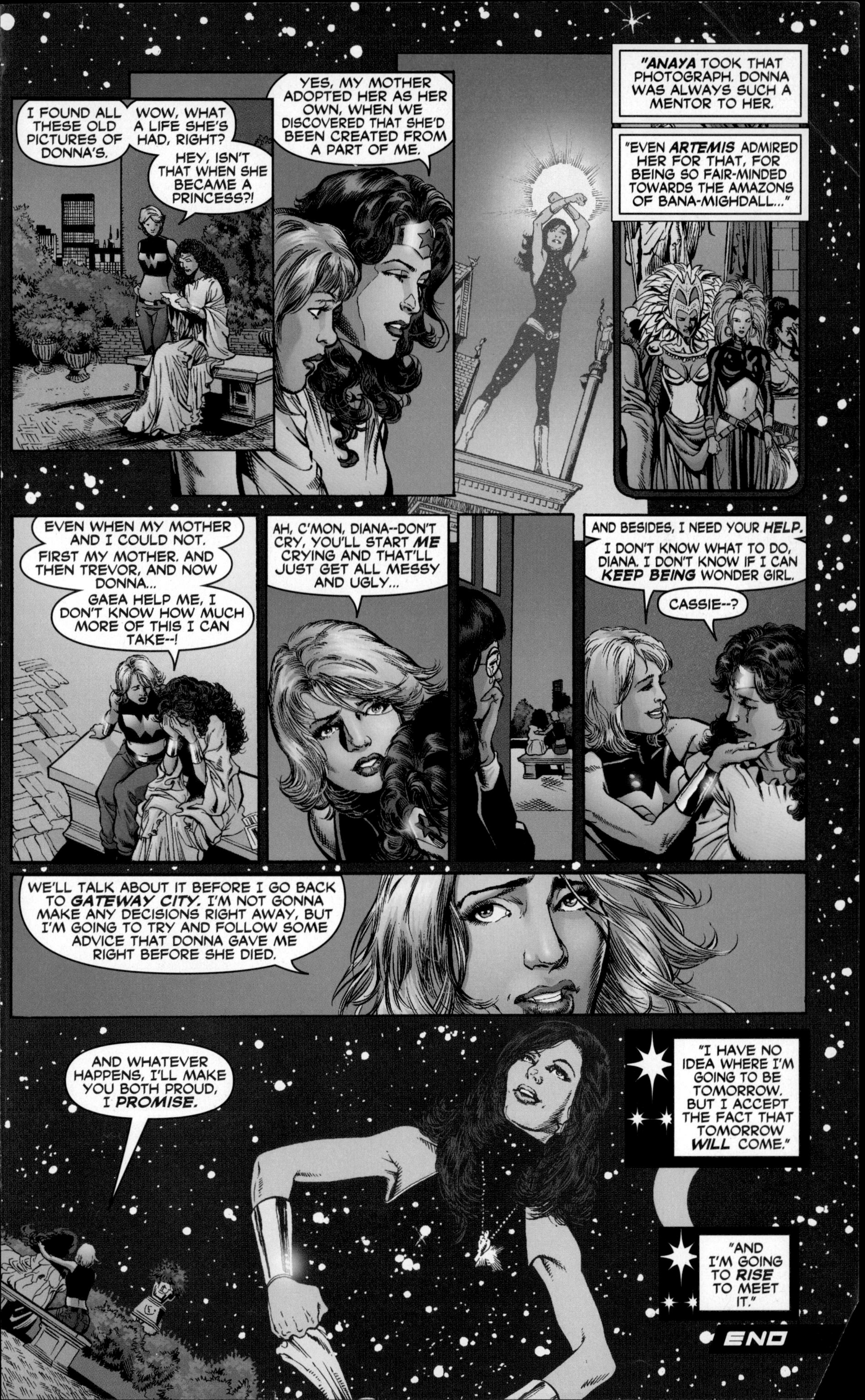

I FOUND ALL THESE OLD PICTURES OF DONNA'S.
WOW, WHAT A LIFE SHE'S HAD, RIGHT?
HEY, ISN'T THAT WHEN SHE BECAME A PRINCESS?!
YES, MY MOTHER ADOPTED HER AS HER OWN, WHEN WE DISCOVERED THAT SHE'D BEEN CREATED FROM A PART OF ME.
"ANAYA TOOK THAT PHOTOGRAPH. DONNA WAS ALWAYS SUCH A MENTOR TO HER.
"EVEN ARTEMIS ADMIRED HER FOR THAT, FOR BEING SO FAIR-MINDED TOWARDS THE AMAZONS OF BANA-MIGHDALL..."
EVEN WHEN MY MOTHER AND I COULD NOT. FIRST MY MOTHER, AND THEN TREVOR, AND NOW DONNA...
GAEA HELP ME, I DON'T KNOW HOW MUCH MORE OF THIS I CAN TAKE--!
AH, C'MON, DIANA--DON'T CRY, YOU'LL START ME CRYING AND THAT'LL JUST GET ALL MESSY AND UGLY...
AND BESIDES, I NEED YOUR HELP. I DON'T KNOW WHAT TO DO, DIANA. I DON'T KNOW IF I CAN KEEP BEING WONDER GIRL.
CASSIE--?
WE'LL TALK ABOUT IT BEFORE I GO BACK TO GATEWAY CITY. I'M NOT GONNA MAKE ANY DECISIONS RIGHT AWAY, BUT I'M GOING TO TRY AND FOLLOW SOME ADVICE THAT DONNA GAVE ME RIGHT BEFORE SHE DIED.
AND WHATEVER HAPPENS, I'LL MAKE YOU BOTH PROUD, I PROMISE.
"I HAVE NO IDEA WHERE I'M GOING TO BE TOMORROW. BUT I ACCEPT THE FACT THAT TOMORROW WILL COME."
"AND I'M GOING TO RISE TO MEET IT."
END

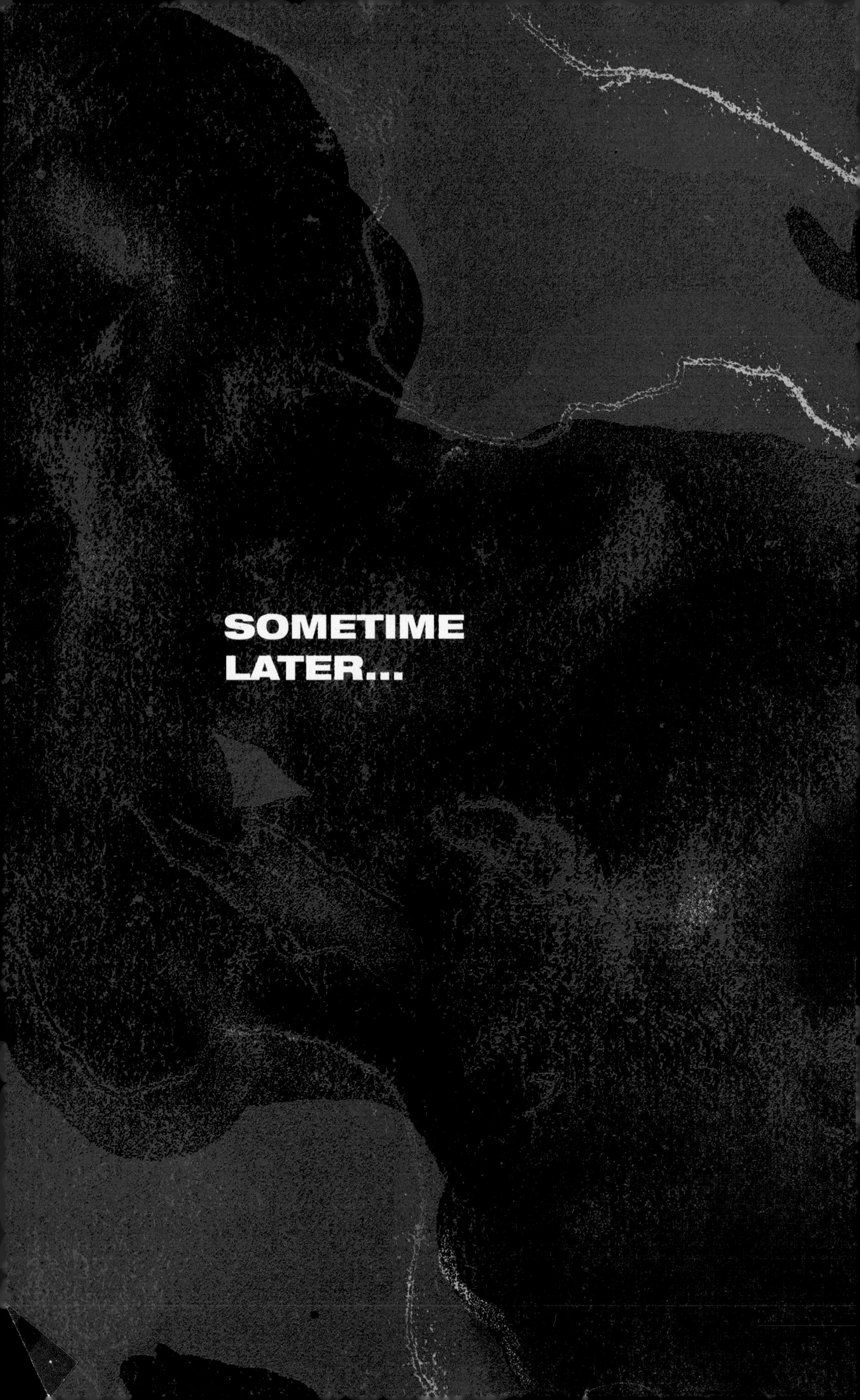
SOMETIME LATER...

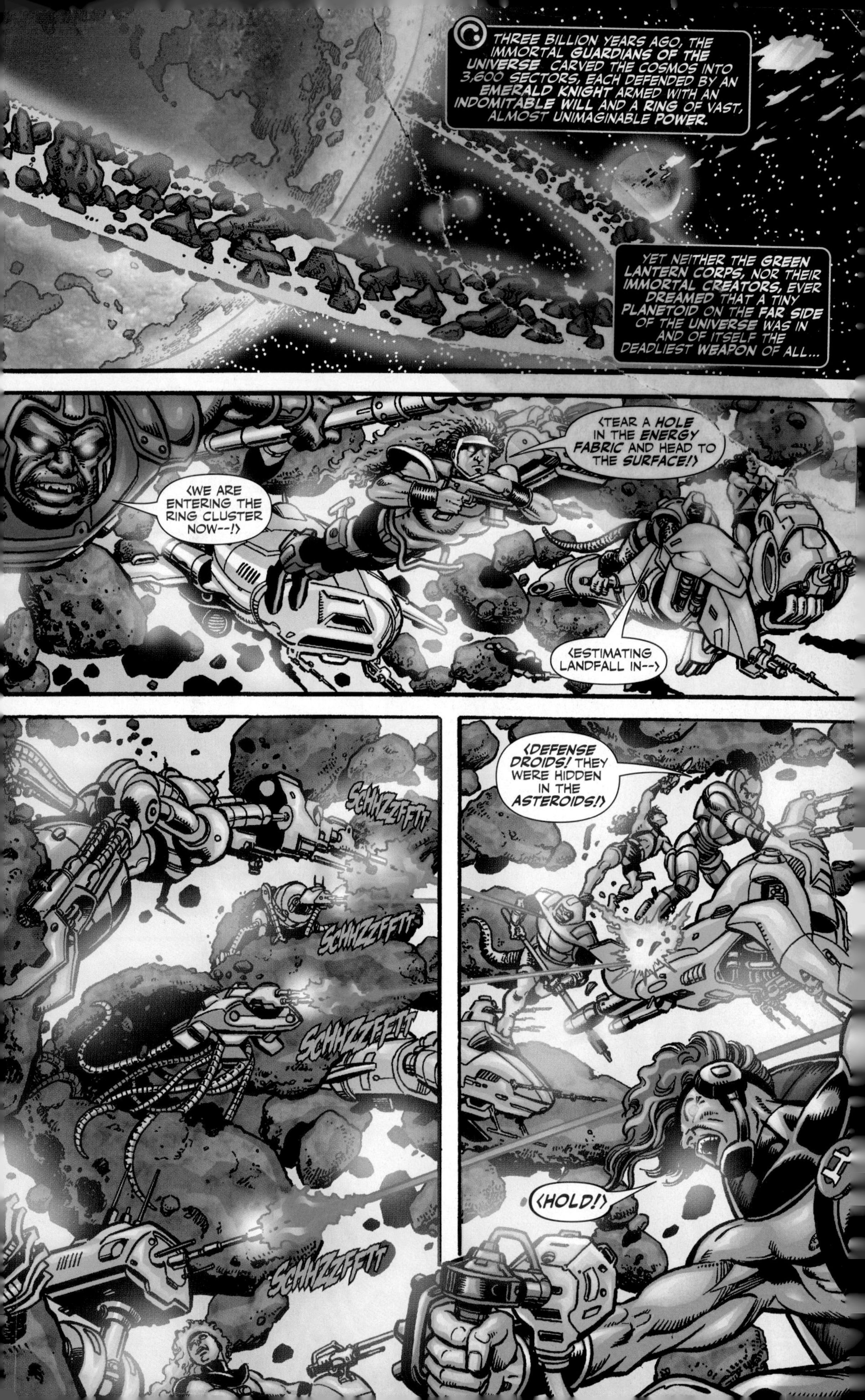
THREE BILLION YEARS AGO, THE IMMORTAL GUARDIANS OF THE UNIVERSE CARVED THE COSMOS INTO 3,600 SECTORS, EACH DEFENDED BY AN EMERALD KNIGHT ARMED WITH AN INDOMITABLE WILL AND A RING OF VAST, ALMOST UNIMAGINABLE POWER.
YET NEITHER THE GREEN LANTERN CORPS, NOR THEIR IMMORTAL CREATORS, EVER DREAMED THAT A TINY PLANETOID ON THE FAR SIDE OF THE UNIVERSE WAS IN AND OF ITSELF THE DEADLIEST WEAPON OF ALL...
<WE ARE ENTERING THE RING CLUSTER NOW--!>
<TEAR A HOLE IN THE ENERGY FABRIC AND HEAD TO THE SURFACE!>
<ESTIMATING LANDFALL IN-->
SCHZZFFTT
SCHZZZFFTT
SCHZZFFTT
SCHZZFFTT
<DEFENSE DROIDS! THEY WERE HIDDEN IN THE ASTEROIDS!>
<HOLD!>

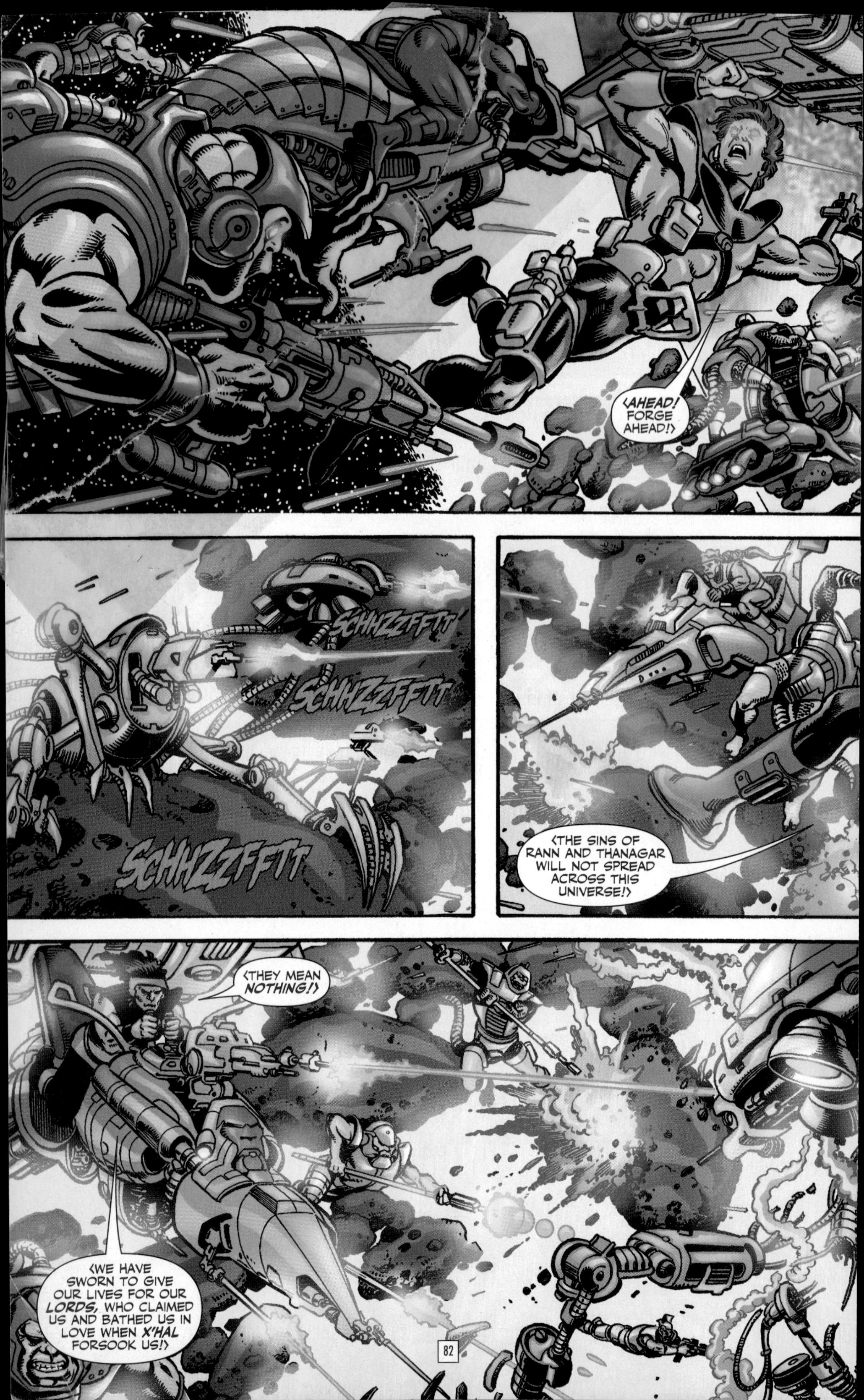
‹AHEAD! FORGE AHEAD!›
SCHHZZFFTT
SCHHZZFFTT
SCHHZZFFTT
‹THE SINS OF RANN AND THANAGAR WILL NOT SPREAD ACROSS THIS UNIVERSE!›
‹THEY MEAN NOTHING!›
‹WE HAVE SWORN TO GIVE OUR LIVES FOR OUR LORDS, WHO CLAIMED US AND BATHED US IN LOVE WHEN X'HAL FORSOOK US!›

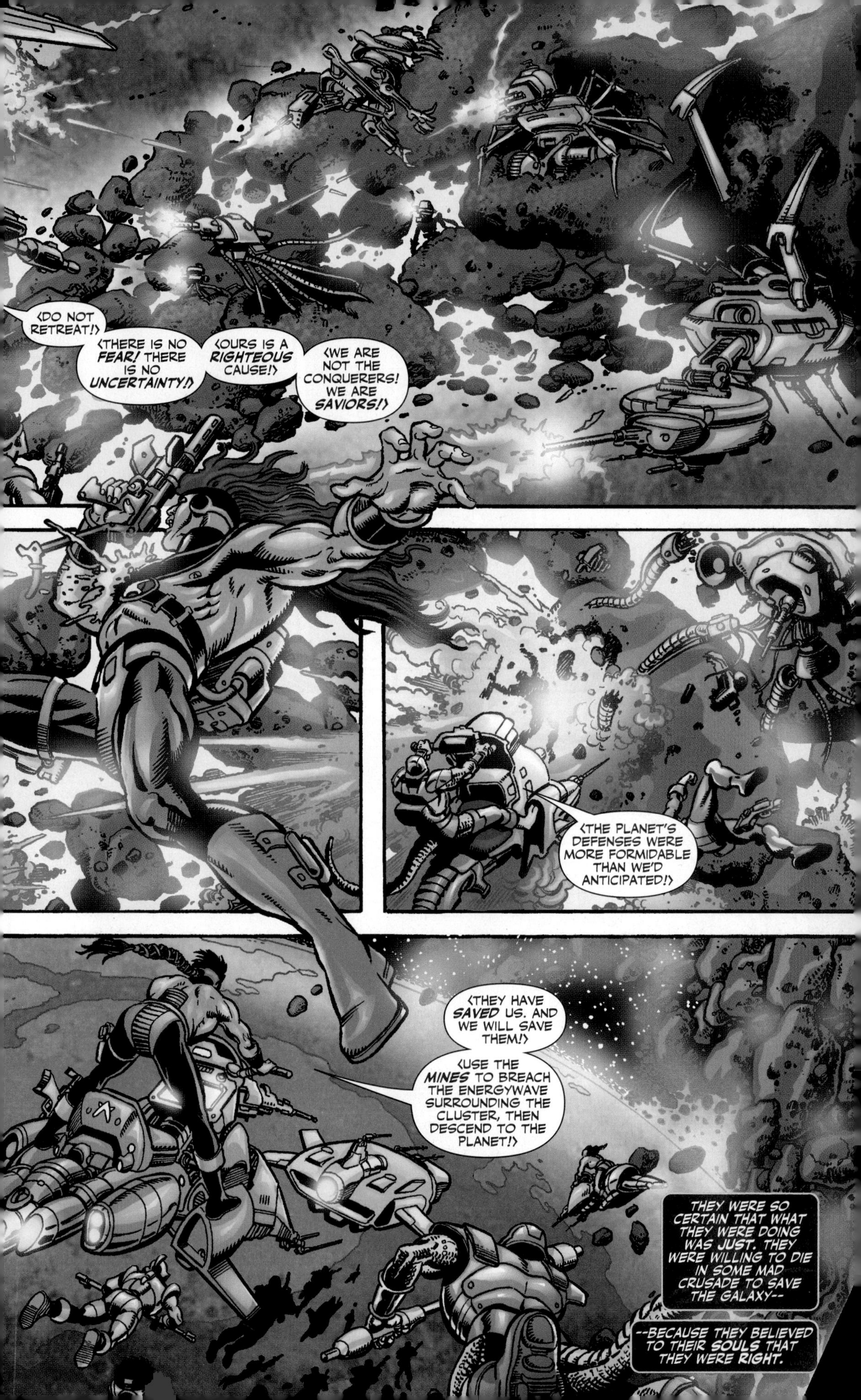

<DO NOT RETREAT!>
<THERE IS NO FEAR! THERE IS NO UNCERTAINTY!>
<OURS IS A RIGHTEOUS CAUSE!>
<WE ARE NOT THE CONQUERERS! WE ARE SAVIORS!>
<THE PLANET'S DEFENSES WERE MORE FORMIDABLE THAN WE'D ANTICIPATED!>
<THEY HAVE SAVED US. AND WE WILL SAVE THEM!>
<USE THE MINES TO BREACH THE ENERGYWAVE SURROUNDING THE CLUSTER, THEN DESCEND TO THE PLANET!>
THEY WERE SO CERTAIN THAT WHAT THEY WERE DOING WAS JUST. THEY WERE WILLING TO DIE IN SOME MAD CRUSADE TO SAVE THE GALAXY--
--BECAUSE THEY BELIEVED TO THEIR SOULS THAT THEY WERE RIGHT.

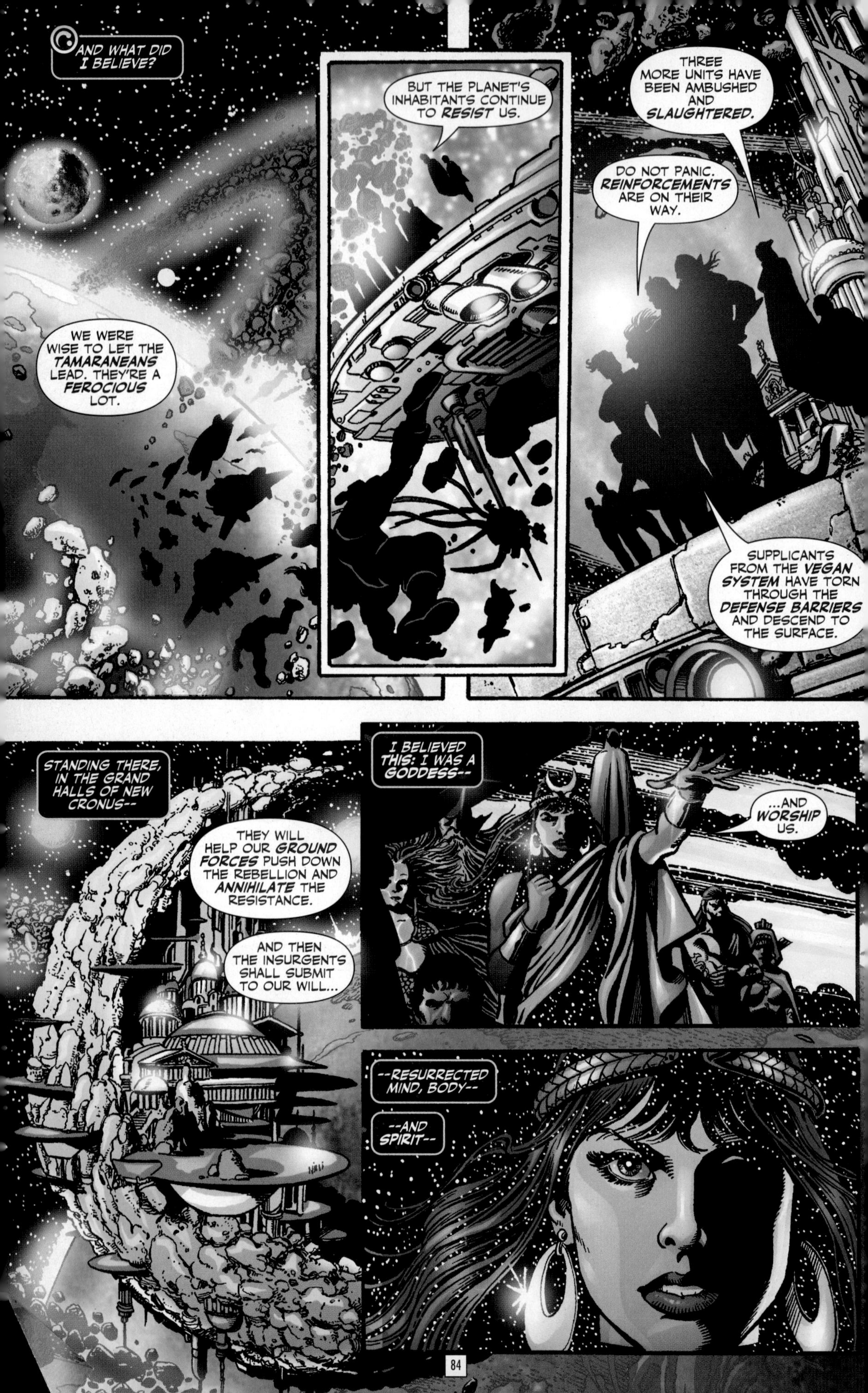
AND WHAT DID I BELIEVE?
BUT THE PLANET'S INHABITANTS CONTINUE TO RESIST US.
THREE MORE UNITS HAVE BEEN AMBUSHED AND SLAUGHTERED.
DO NOT PANIC. REINFORCEMENTS ARE ON THEIR WAY.
WE WERE WISE TO LET THE TAMARANEANS LEAD. THEY'RE A FEROCIOUS LOT.
SUPPLICANTS FROM THE VEGAN SYSTEM HAVE TORN THROUGH THE DEFENSE BARRIERS AND DESCEND TO THE SURFACE.
STANDING THERE, IN THE GRAND HALLS OF NEW CRONUS--
THEY WILL HELP OUR GROUND FORCES PUSH DOWN THE REBELLION AND ANNIHILATE THE RESISTANCE.
AND THEN THE INSURGENTS SHALL SUBMIT TO OUR WILL...
I BELIEVED THIS: I WAS A GODDESS--
...AND WORSHIP US.
--RESURRECTED MIND, BODY--
--AND SPIRIT--

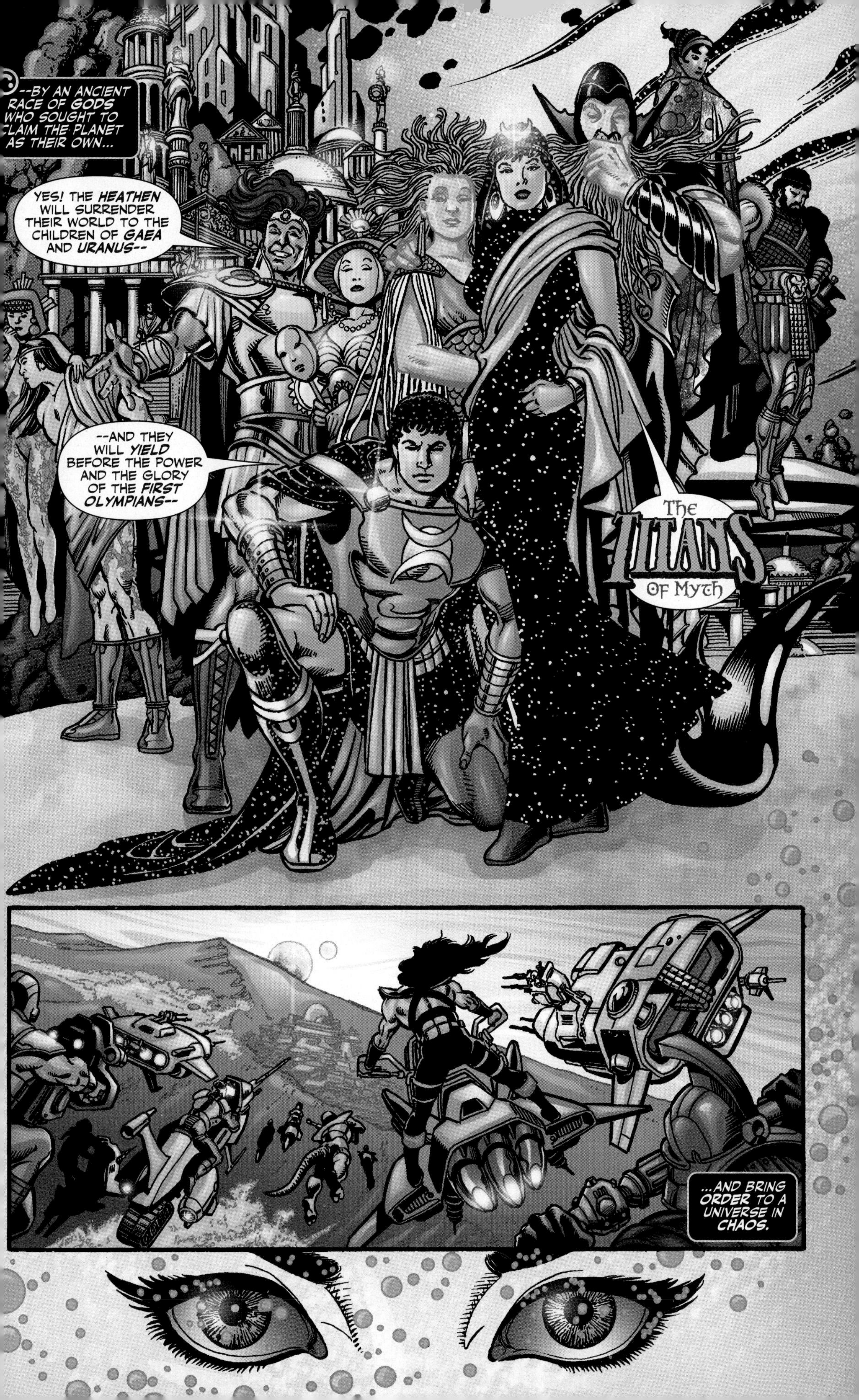
--BY AN ANCIENT RACE OF GODS WHO SOUGHT TO CLAIM THE PLANET AS THEIR OWN...
YES! THE HEATHEN WILL SURRENDER THEIR WORLD TO THE CHILDREN OF GAEA AND URANUS--
--AND THEY WILL YIELD BEFORE THE POWER AND THE GLORY OF THE FIRST OLYMPIANS--
The TITANS Of Myth
...AND BRING ORDER TO A UNIVERSE IN CHAOS.

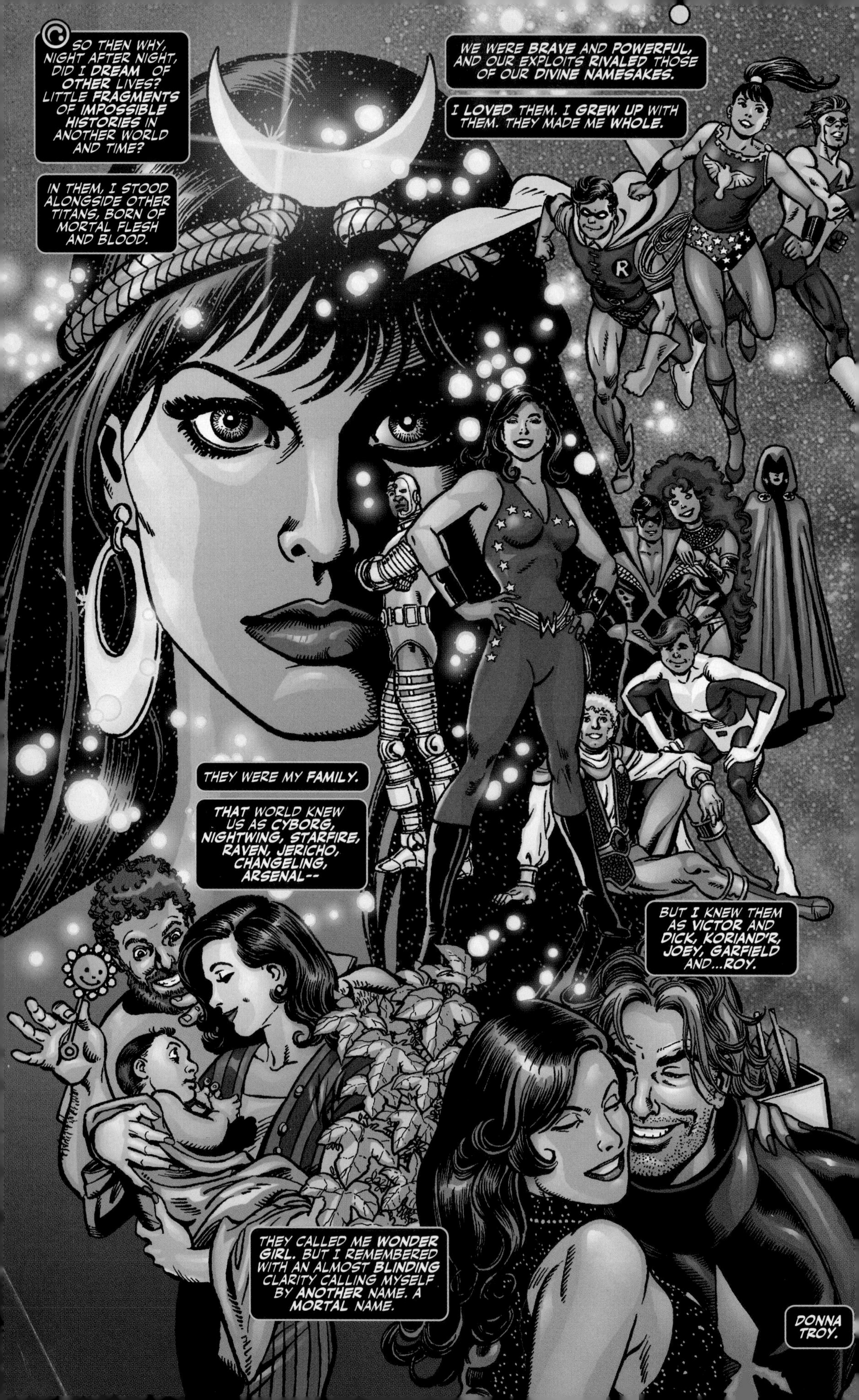
SO THEN WHY, NIGHT AFTER NIGHT, DID I DREAM OF OTHER LIVES? LITTLE FRAGMENTS OF IMPOSSIBLE HISTORIES IN ANOTHER WORLD AND TIME?
IN THEM, I STOOD ALONGSIDE OTHER TITANS, BORN OF MORTAL FLESH AND BLOOD.
WE WERE BRAVE AND POWERFUL, AND OUR EXPLOITS RIVALED THOSE OF OUR DIVINE NAMESAKES.
I LOVED THEM. I GREW UP WITH THEM. THEY MADE ME WHOLE.
THEY WERE MY FAMILY.
THAT WORLD KNEW US AS CYBORG, NIGHTWING, STARFIRE, RAVEN, JERICHO, CHANGELING, ARSENAL--
BUT I KNEW THEM AS VICTOR AND DICK, KORIAND'R, JOEY, GARFIELD AND...ROY.
THEY CALLED ME WONDER GIRL. BUT I REMEMBERED WITH AN ALMOST BLINDING CLARITY CALLING MYSELF BY ANOTHER NAME. A MORTAL NAME.
DONNA TROY.

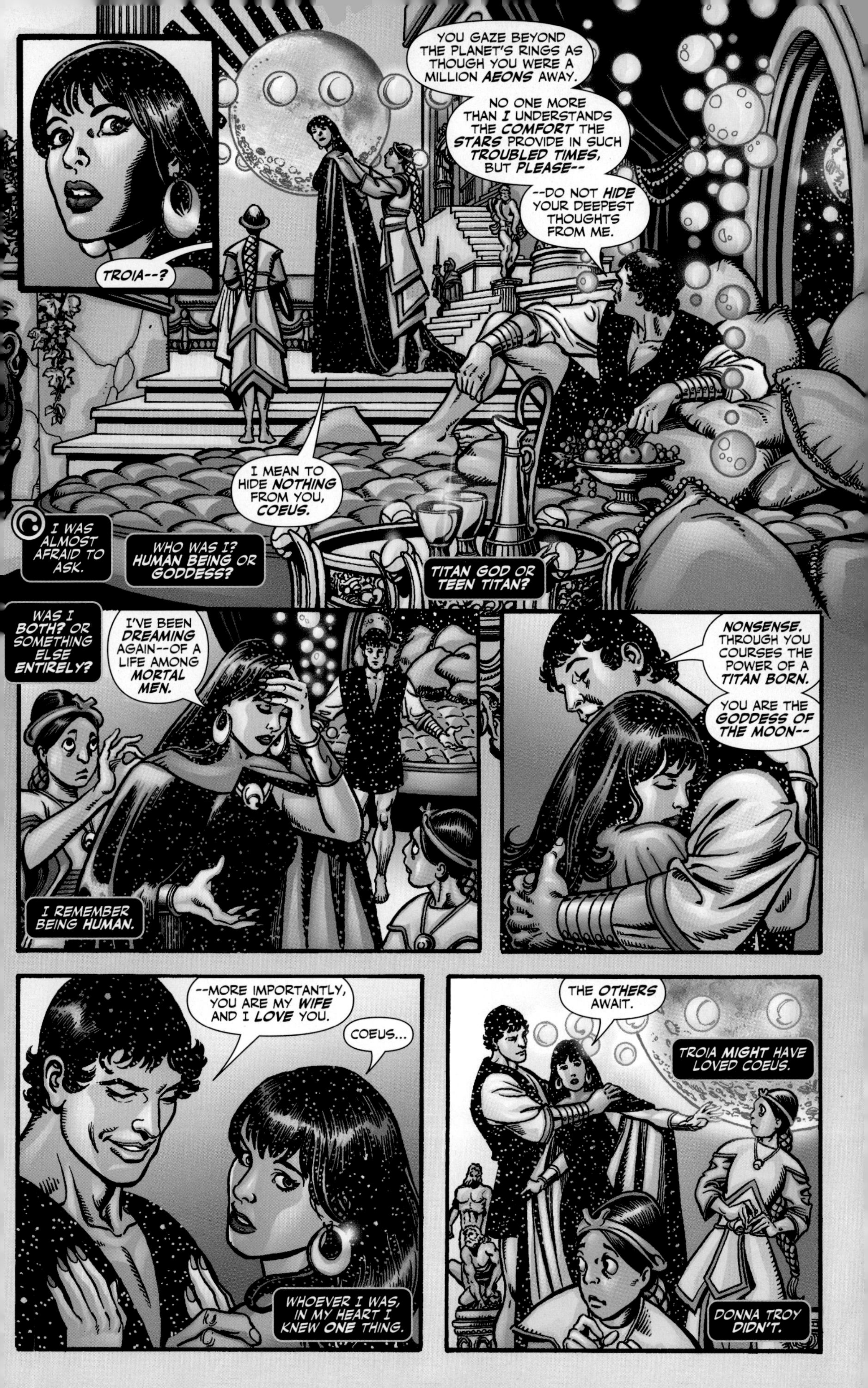

TROIA--?
YOU GAZE BEYOND THE PLANET'S RINGS AS THOUGH YOU WERE A MILLION AEONS AWAY.
NO ONE MORE THAN I UNDERSTANDS THE COMFORT THE STARS PROVIDE IN SUCH TROUBLED TIMES, BUT PLEASE--
--DO NOT HIDE YOUR DEEPEST THOUGHTS FROM ME.
I MEAN TO HIDE NOTHING FROM YOU, COEUS.
I WAS ALMOST AFRAID TO ASK.
WHO WAS I? HUMAN BEING OR GODDESS?
TITAN GOD OR TEEN TITAN?
WAS I BOTH? OR SOMETHING ELSE ENTIRELY?
I'VE BEEN DREAMING AGAIN--OF A LIFE AMONG MORTAL MEN.
I REMEMBER BEING HUMAN.
NONSENSE. THROUGH YOU COURSES THE POWER OF A TITAN BORN.
YOU ARE THE GODDESS OF THE MOON--
--MORE IMPORTANTLY, YOU ARE MY WIFE AND I LOVE YOU.
COEUS...
WHOEVER I WAS, IN MY HEART I KNEW ONE THING.
THE OTHERS AWAIT.
TROIA MIGHT HAVE LOVED COEUS.
DONNA TROY DIDN'T.

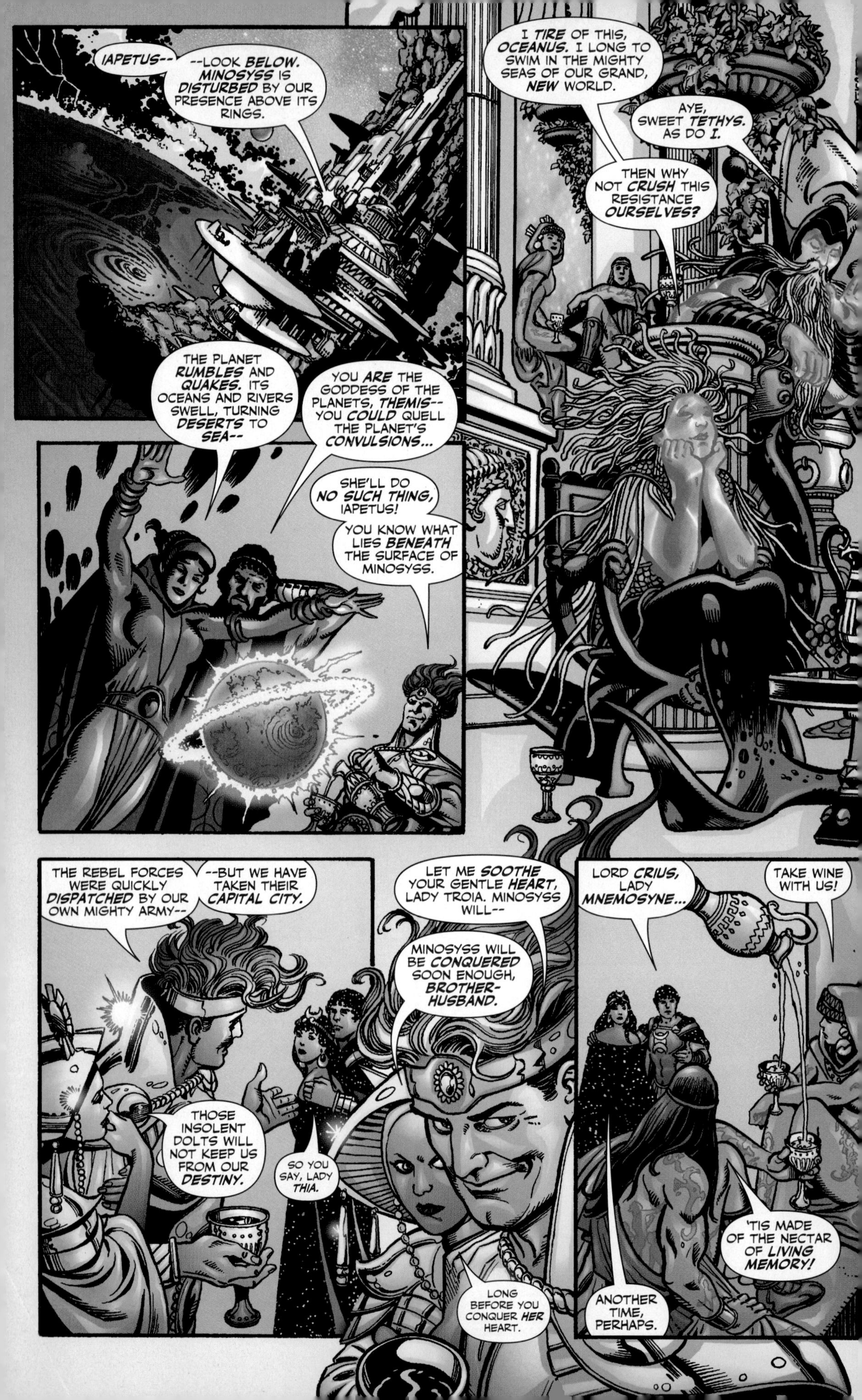
IAPETUS--
--LOOK BELOW. MINOSYSS IS DISTURBED BY OUR PRESENCE ABOVE ITS RINGS.
I TIRE OF THIS, OCEANUS. I LONG TO SWIM IN THE MIGHTY SEAS OF OUR GRAND, NEW WORLD.
AYE, SWEET TETHYS. AS DO I.
THEN WHY NOT CRUSH THIS RESISTANCE OURSELVES?
THE PLANET RUMBLES AND QUAKES. ITS OCEANS AND RIVERS SWELL, TURNING DESERTS TO SEA--
YOU ARE THE GODDESS OF THE PLANETS, THEMIS-- YOU COULD QUELL THE PLANET'S CONVULSIONS...
SHE'LL DO NO SUCH THING, IAPETUS!
YOU KNOW WHAT LIES BENEATH THE SURFACE OF MINOSYSS.
THE REBEL FORCES WERE QUICKLY DISPATCHED BY OUR OWN MIGHTY ARMY--
--BUT WE HAVE TAKEN THEIR CAPITAL CITY.
THOSE INSOLENT DOLTS WILL NOT KEEP US FROM OUR DESTINY.
SO YOU SAY, LADY THIA.
LET ME SOOTHE YOUR GENTLE HEART, LADY TROIA. MINOSYSS WILL--
MINOSYSS WILL BE CONQUERED SOON ENOUGH, BROTHER-HUSBAND.
LONG BEFORE YOU CONQUER HER HEART.
LORD CRIUS, LADY MNEMOSYNE...
TAKE WINE WITH US!
'TIS MADE OF THE NECTAR OF LIVING MEMORY!
ANOTHER TIME, PERHAPS.

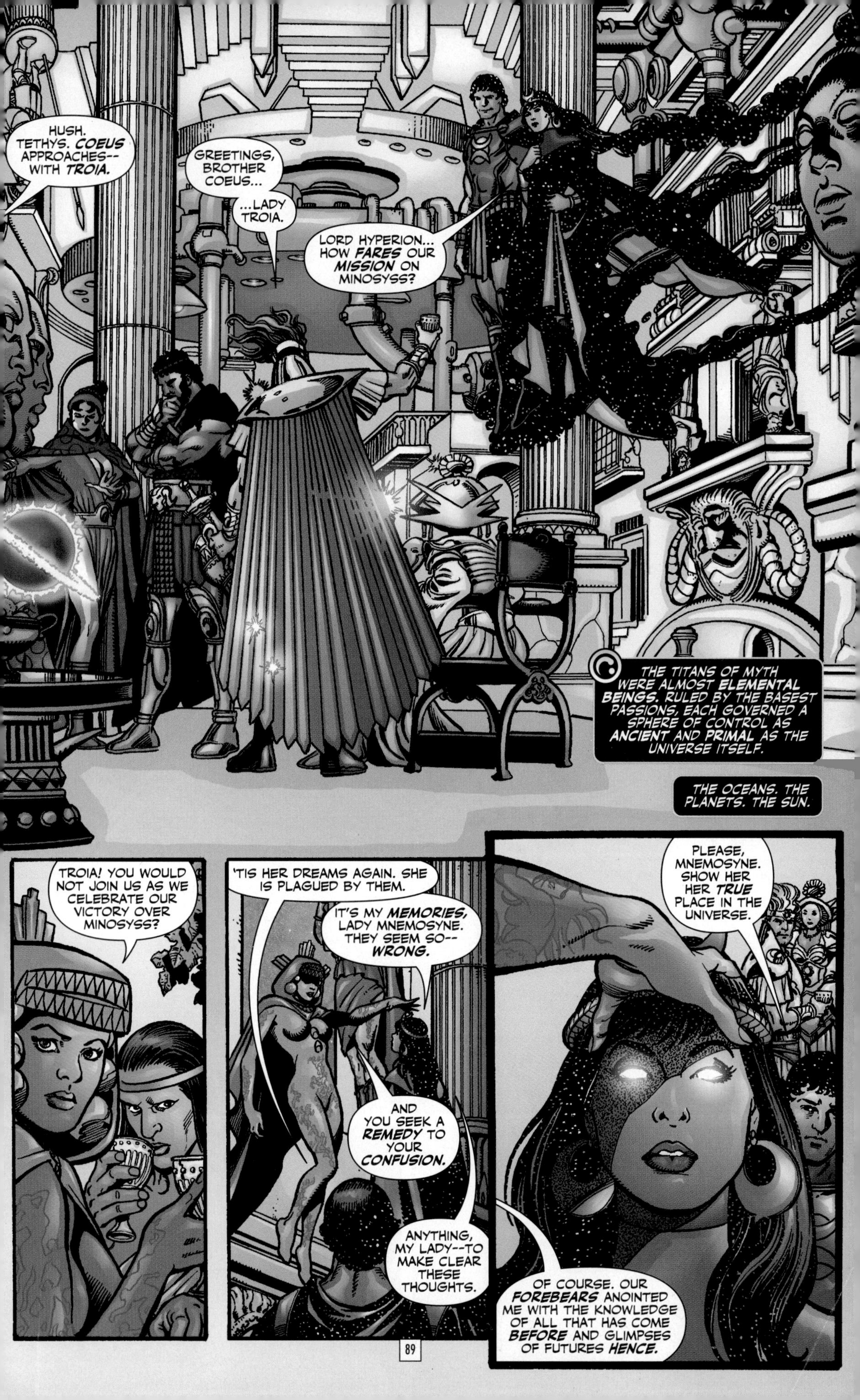
HUSH. TETHYS. COEUS APPROACHES-- WITH TROIA.
GREETINGS, BROTHER COEUS...
...LADY TROIA.
LORD HYPERION... HOW FARES OUR MISSION ON MINOSYSS?
THE TITANS OF MYTH WERE ALMOST ELEMENTAL BEINGS. RULED BY THE BASEST PASSIONS, EACH GOVERNED A SPHERE OF CONTROL AS ANCIENT AND PRIMAL AS THE UNIVERSE ITSELF.
THE OCEANS. THE PLANETS. THE SUN.
TROIA! YOU WOULD NOT JOIN US AS WE CELEBRATE OUR VICTORY OVER MINOSYSS?
'TIS HER DREAMS AGAIN. SHE IS PLAGUED BY THEM.
IT'S MY MEMORIES, LADY MNEMOSYNE. THEY SEEM SO-- WRONG.
AND YOU SEEK A REMEDY TO YOUR CONFUSION.
ANYTHING, MY LADY--TO MAKE CLEAR THESE THOUGHTS.
PLEASE, MNEMOSYNE. SHOW HER HER TRUE PLACE IN THE UNIVERSE.
OF COURSE. OUR FOREBEARS ANOINTED ME WITH THE KNOWLEDGE OF ALL THAT HAS COME BEFORE AND GLIMPSES OF FUTURES HENCE.

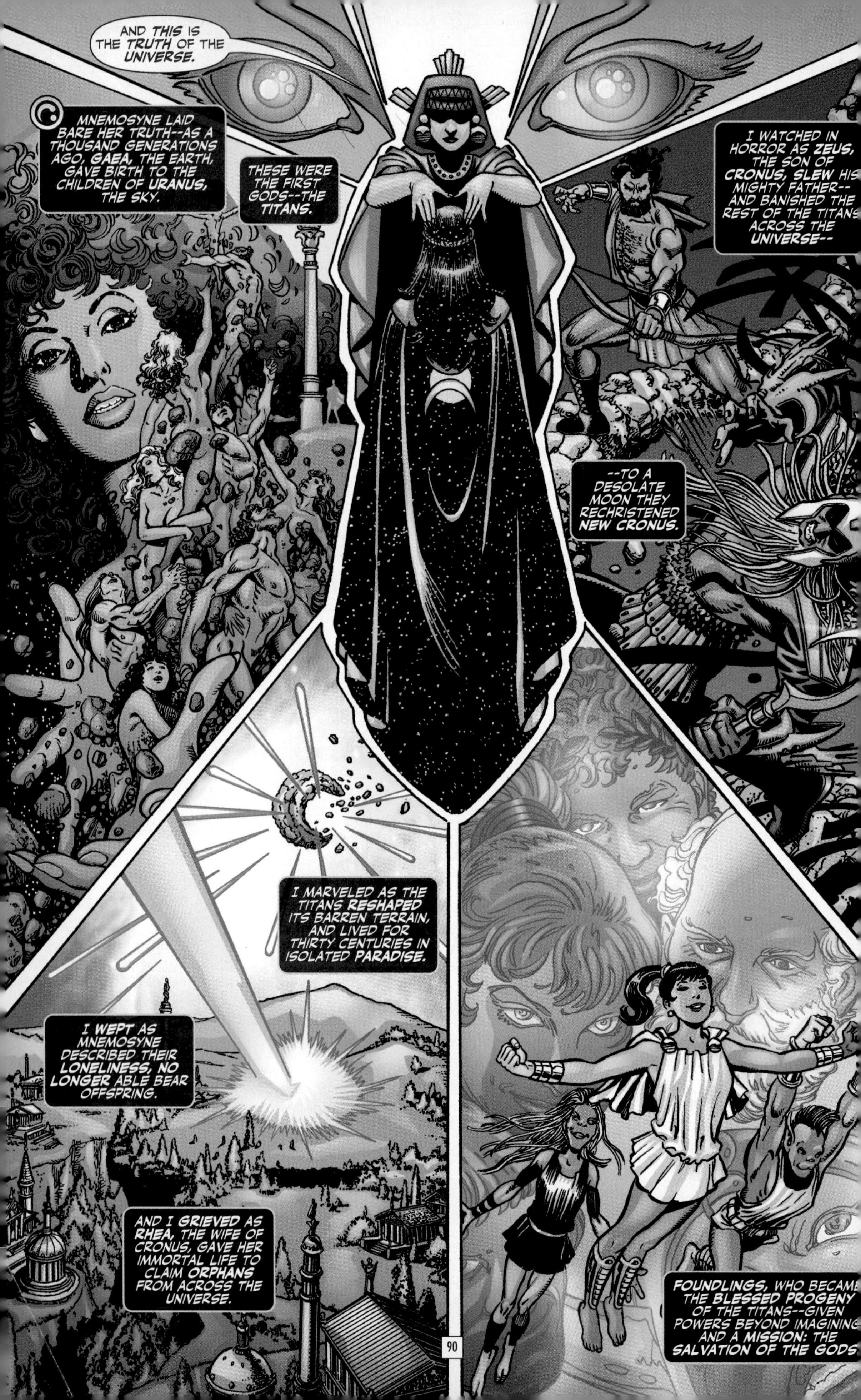

AND THIS IS THE TRUTH OF THE UNIVERSE.
MNEMOSYNE LAID BARE HER TRUTH--AS A THOUSAND GENERATIONS AGO, GAEA, THE EARTH, GAVE BIRTH TO THE CHILDREN OF URANUS, THE SKY.
THESE WERE THE FIRST GODS--THE TITANS.
I WATCHED IN HORROR AS ZEUS, THE SON OF CRONUS, SLEW HIS MIGHTY FATHER--AND BANISHED THE REST OF THE TITANS ACROSS THE UNIVERSE--
--TO A DESOLATE MOON THEY RECHRISTENED NEW CRONUS.
I MARVELED AS THE TITANS RESHAPED ITS BARREN TERRAIN, AND LIVED FOR THIRTY CENTURIES IN ISOLATED PARADISE.
I WEPT AS MNEMOSYNE DESCRIBED THEIR LONELINESS, NO LONGER ABLE BEAR OFFSPRING.
AND I GRIEVED AS RHEA, THE WIFE OF CRONUS, GAVE HER IMMORTAL LIFE TO CLAIM ORPHANS FROM ACROSS THE UNIVERSE.
FOUNDLINGS, WHO BECAME THE BLESSED PROGENY OF THE TITANS--GIVEN POWERS BEYOND IMAGINING AND A MISSION: THE SALVATION OF THE GODS.

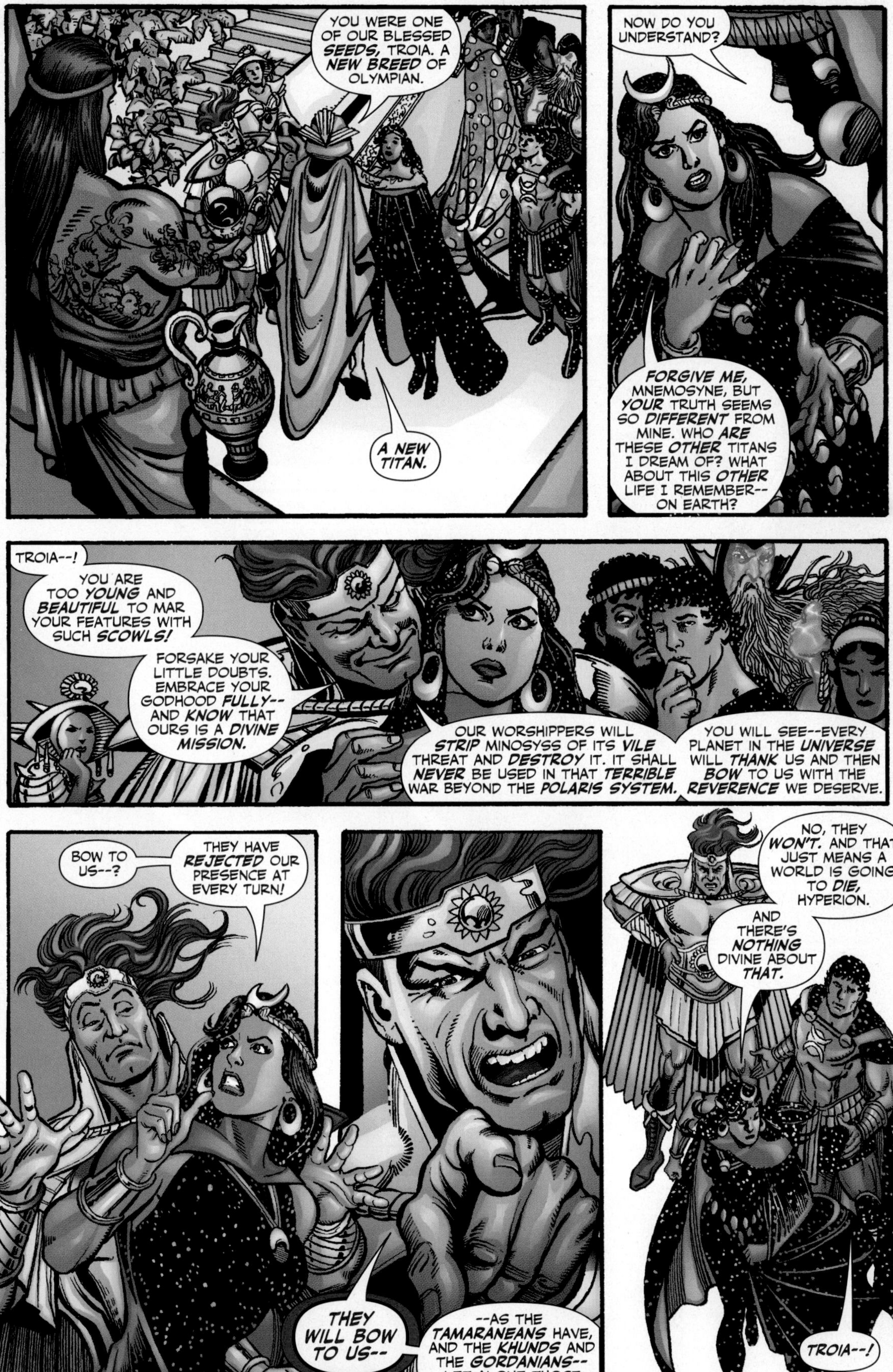
YOU WERE ONE OF OUR BLESSED SEEDS, TROIA. A NEW BREED OF OLYMPIAN.
A NEW TITAN.
NOW DO YOU UNDERSTAND?
FORGIVE ME, MNEMOSYNE, BUT YOUR TRUTH SEEMS SO DIFFERENT FROM MINE. WHO ARE THESE OTHER TITANS I DREAM OF? WHAT ABOUT THIS OTHER LIFE I REMEMBER--ON EARTH?
TROIA--!
YOU ARE TOO YOUNG AND BEAUTIFUL TO MAR YOUR FEATURES WITH SUCH SCOWLS!
FORSAKE YOUR LITTLE DOUBTS. EMBRACE YOUR GODHOOD FULLY--AND KNOW THAT OURS IS A DIVINE MISSION.
OUR WORSHIPPERS WILL STRIP MINOSYSS OF ITS VILE THREAT AND DESTROY IT. IT SHALL NEVER BE USED IN THAT TERRIBLE WAR BEYOND THE POLARIS SYSTEM.
YOU WILL SEE--EVERY PLANET IN THE UNIVERSE WILL THANK US AND THEN BOW TO US WITH THE REVERENCE WE DESERVE.
BOW TO US--?
THEY HAVE REJECTED OUR PRESENCE AT EVERY TURN!
THEY WILL BOW TO US--
--AS THE TAMARANEANS HAVE, AND THE KHUNDS AND THE GORDANIANS--LET ALONE THOSE IDIOTS ON RANN AND THANAGAR--
NO, THEY WON'T. AND THAT JUST MEANS A WORLD IS GOING TO DIE, HYPERION.
AND THERE'S NOTHING DIVINE ABOUT THAT.
TROIA--!

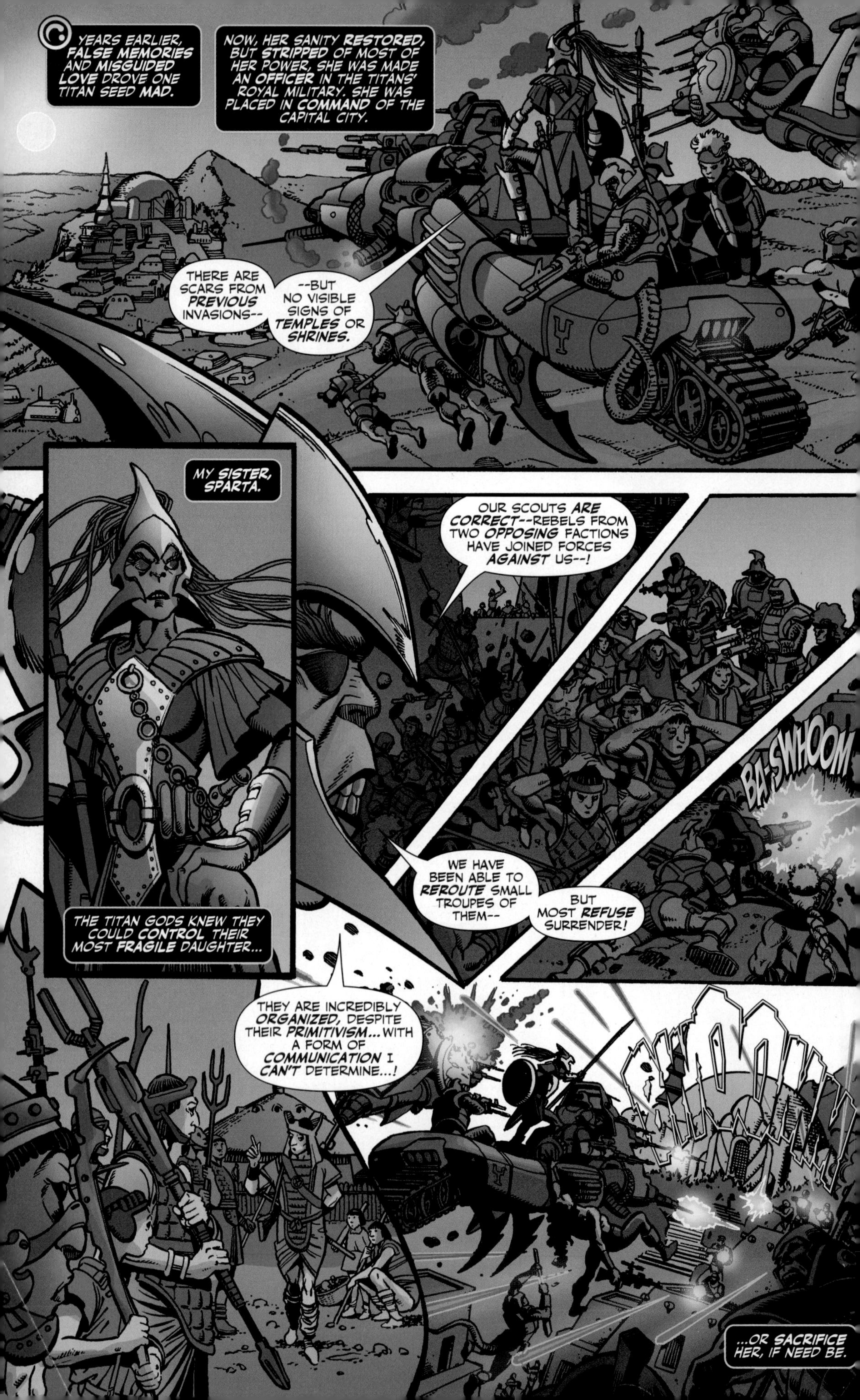
YEARS EARLIER, FALSE MEMORIES AND MISGUIDED LOVE DROVE ONE TITAN SEED MAD.
NOW, HER SANITY RESTORED, BUT STRIPPED OF MOST OF HER POWER, SHE WAS MADE AN OFFICER IN THE TITANS' ROYAL MILITARY. SHE WAS PLACED IN COMMAND OF THE CAPITAL CITY.
THERE ARE SCARS FROM PREVIOUS INVASIONS--
--BUT NO VISIBLE SIGNS OF TEMPLES OR SHRINES.
MY SISTER, SPARTA.
THE TITAN GODS KNEW THEY COULD CONTROL THEIR MOST FRAGILE DAUGHTER...
OUR SCOUTS ARE CORRECT--REBELS FROM TWO OPPOSING FACTIONS HAVE JOINED FORCES AGAINST US--!
BA-SWHOOM
WE HAVE BEEN ABLE TO REROUTE SMALL TROUPES OF THEM--
BUT MOST REFUSE SURRENDER!
THEY ARE INCREDIBLY ORGANIZED, DESPITE THEIR PRIMITIVISM... WITH A FORM OF COMMUNICATION I CAN'T DETERMINE...!
...OR SACRIFICE HER, IF NEED BE.

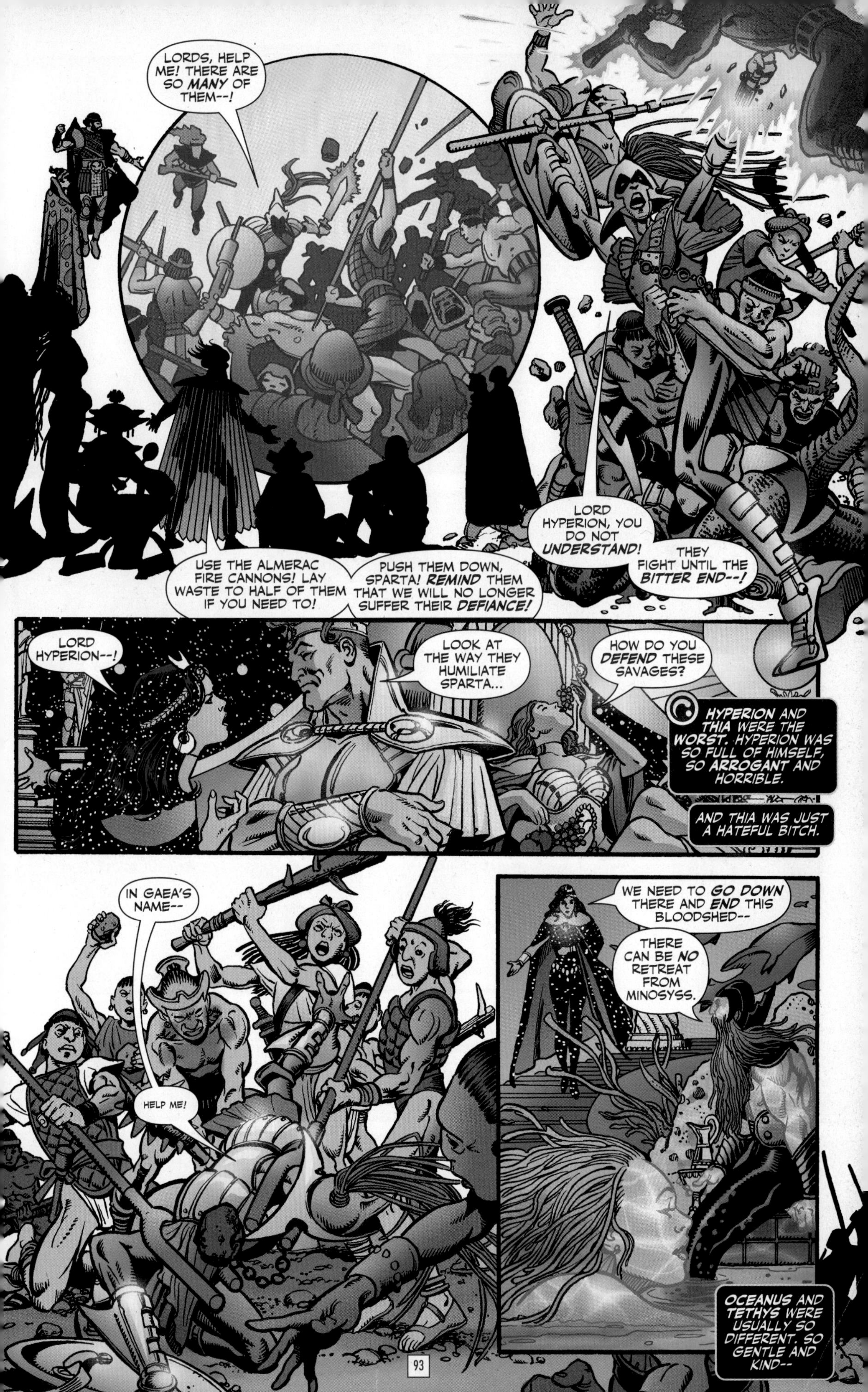
LORDS, HELP ME! THERE ARE SO MANY OF THEM--!
USE THE ALMERAC FIRE CANNONS! LAY WASTE TO HALF OF THEM IF YOU NEED TO!
PUSH THEM DOWN, SPARTA! REMIND THEM THAT WE WILL NO LONGER SUFFER THEIR DEFIANCE!
LORD HYPERION, YOU DO NOT UNDERSTAND!
THEY FIGHT UNTIL THE BITTER END--!
LORD HYPERION--!
LOOK AT THE WAY THEY HUMILIATE SPARTA...
HOW DO YOU DEFEND THESE SAVAGES?
HYPERION AND THIA WERE THE WORST. HYPERION WAS SO FULL OF HIMSELF, SO ARROGANT AND HORRIBLE.
AND THIA WAS JUST A HATEFUL BITCH.
IN GAEA'S NAME--
HELP ME!
WE NEED TO GO DOWN THERE AND END THIS BLOODSHED--
THERE CAN BE NO RETREAT FROM MINOSYSS.
OCEANUS AND TETHYS WERE USUALLY SO DIFFERENT, SO GENTLE AND KIND--

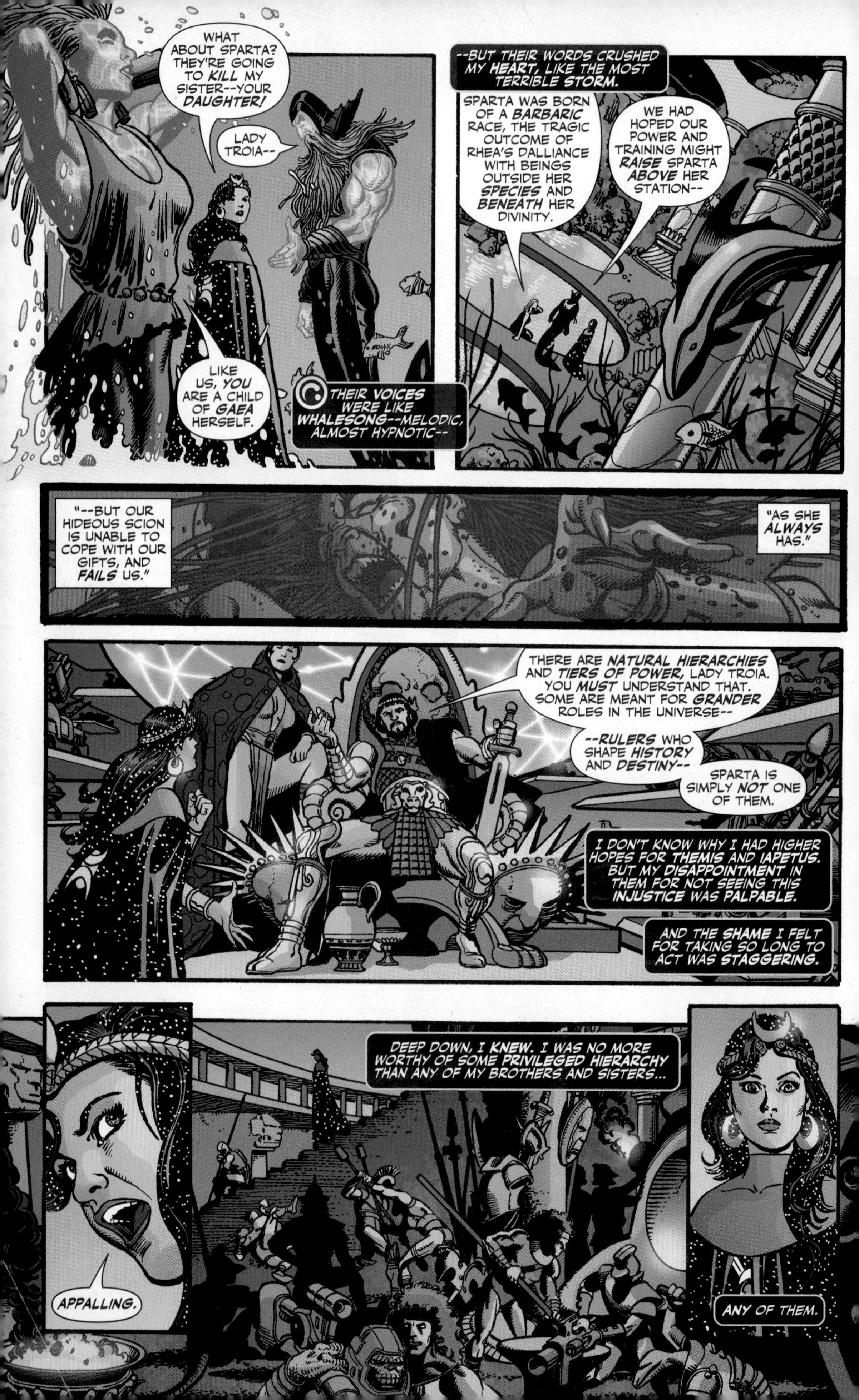
WHAT ABOUT SPARTA? THEY'RE GOING TO KILL MY SISTER--YOUR DAUGHTER!
LADY TROIA--
LIKE US, YOU ARE A CHILD OF GAEA HERSELF.
THEIR VOICES WERE LIKE WHALESONG--MELODIC, ALMOST HYPNOTIC--
--BUT THEIR WORDS CRUSHED MY HEART, LIKE THE MOST TERRIBLE STORM.
SPARTA WAS BORN OF A BARBARIC RACE, THE TRAGIC OUTCOME OF RHEA'S DALLIANCE WITH BEINGS OUTSIDE HER SPECIES AND BENEATH HER DIVINITY.
WE HAD HOPED OUR POWER AND TRAINING MIGHT RAISE SPARTA ABOVE HER STATION--
"--BUT OUR HIDEOUS SCION IS UNABLE TO COPE WITH OUR GIFTS, AND FAILS US."
"AS SHE ALWAYS HAS."
THERE ARE NATURAL HIERARCHIES AND TIERS OF POWER, LADY TROIA. YOU MUST UNDERSTAND THAT. SOME ARE MEANT FOR GRANDER ROLES IN THE UNIVERSE--
--RULERS WHO SHAPE HISTORY AND DESTINY--
SPARTA IS SIMPLY NOT ONE OF THEM.
I DON'T KNOW WHY I HAD HIGHER HOPES FOR THEMIS AND IAPETUS. BUT MY DISAPPOINTMENT IN THEM FOR NOT SEEING THIS INJUSTICE WAS PALPABLE.
AND THE SHAME I FELT FOR TAKING SO LONG TO ACT WAS STAGGERING.
APPALLING.
DEEP DOWN, I KNEW. I WAS NO MORE WORTHY OF SOME PRIVILEGED HIERARCHY THAN ANY OF MY BROTHERS AND SISTERS...
ANY OF THEM.

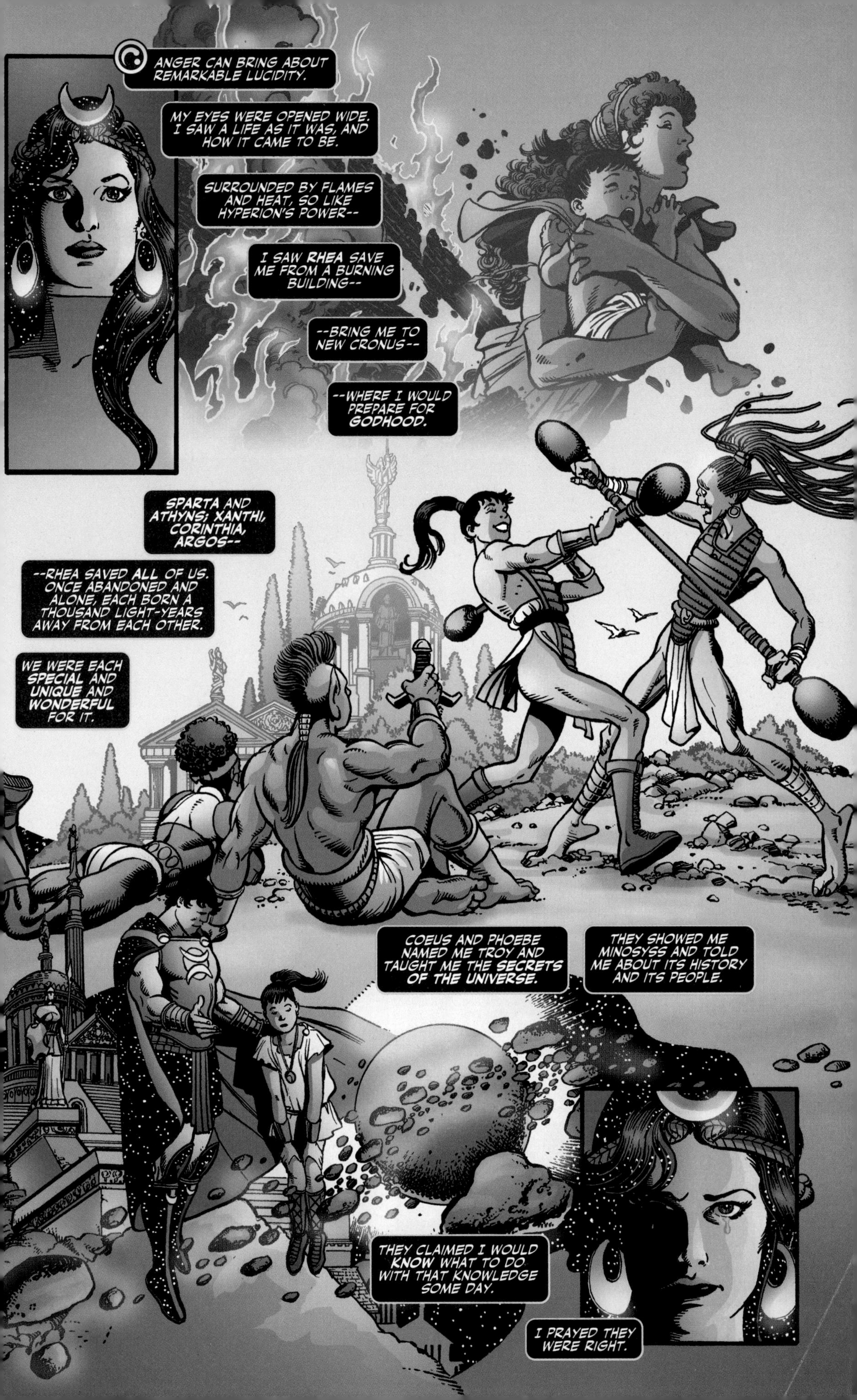
ANGER CAN BRING ABOUT REMARKABLE LUCIDITY.
MY EYES WERE OPENED WIDE. I SAW A LIFE AS IT WAS, AND HOW IT CAME TO BE.
SURROUNDED BY FLAMES AND HEAT, SO LIKE HYPERION'S POWER--
I SAW RHEA SAVE ME FROM A BURNING BUILDING--
--BRING ME TO NEW CRONUS--
--WHERE I WOULD PREPARE FOR GODHOOD.
SPARTA AND ATHYNS; XANTHI, CORINTHIA, ARGOS--
--RHEA SAVED ALL OF US. ONCE ABANDONED AND ALONE, EACH BORN A THOUSAND LIGHT-YEARS AWAY FROM EACH OTHER.
WE WERE EACH SPECIAL AND UNIQUE AND WONDERFUL FOR IT.
COEUS AND PHOEBE NAMED ME TROY AND TAUGHT ME THE SECRETS OF THE UNIVERSE.
THEY SHOWED ME MINOSYSS AND TOLD ME ABOUT ITS HISTORY AND ITS PEOPLE.
THEY CLAIMED I WOULD KNOW WHAT TO DO WITH THAT KNOWLEDGE SOME DAY.
I PRAYED THEY WERE RIGHT.

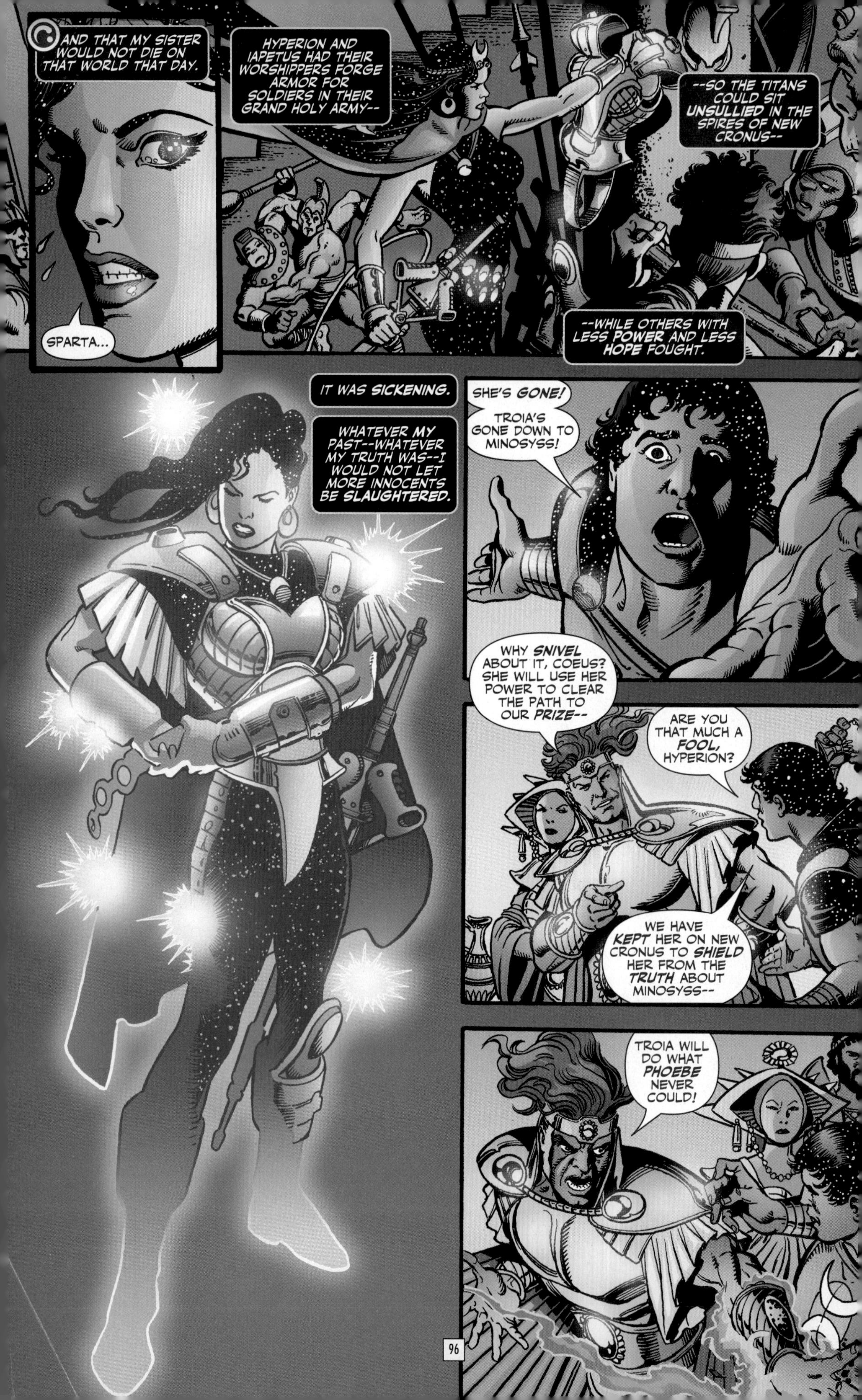
AND THAT MY SISTER WOULD NOT DIE ON THAT WORLD THAT DAY.
SPARTA...
HYPERION AND IAPETUS HAD THEIR WORSHIPPERS FORGE ARMOR FOR SOLDIERS IN THEIR GRAND HOLY ARMY--
--SO THE TITANS COULD SIT UNSULLIED IN THE SPIRES OF NEW CRONUS--
--WHILE OTHERS WITH LESS POWER AND LESS HOPE FOUGHT.
IT WAS SICKENING.
WHATEVER MY PAST--WHATEVER MY TRUTH WAS--I WOULD NOT LET MORE INNOCENTS BE SLAUGHTERED.
SHE'S GONE!
TROIA'S GONE DOWN TO MINOSYSS!
WHY SNIVEL ABOUT IT, COEUS? SHE WILL USE HER POWER TO CLEAR THE PATH TO OUR PRIZE--
ARE YOU THAT MUCH A FOOL, HYPERION?
WE HAVE KEPT HER ON NEW CRONUS TO SHIELD HER FROM THE TRUTH ABOUT MINOSYSS--
TROIA WILL DO WHAT PHOEBE NEVER COULD!

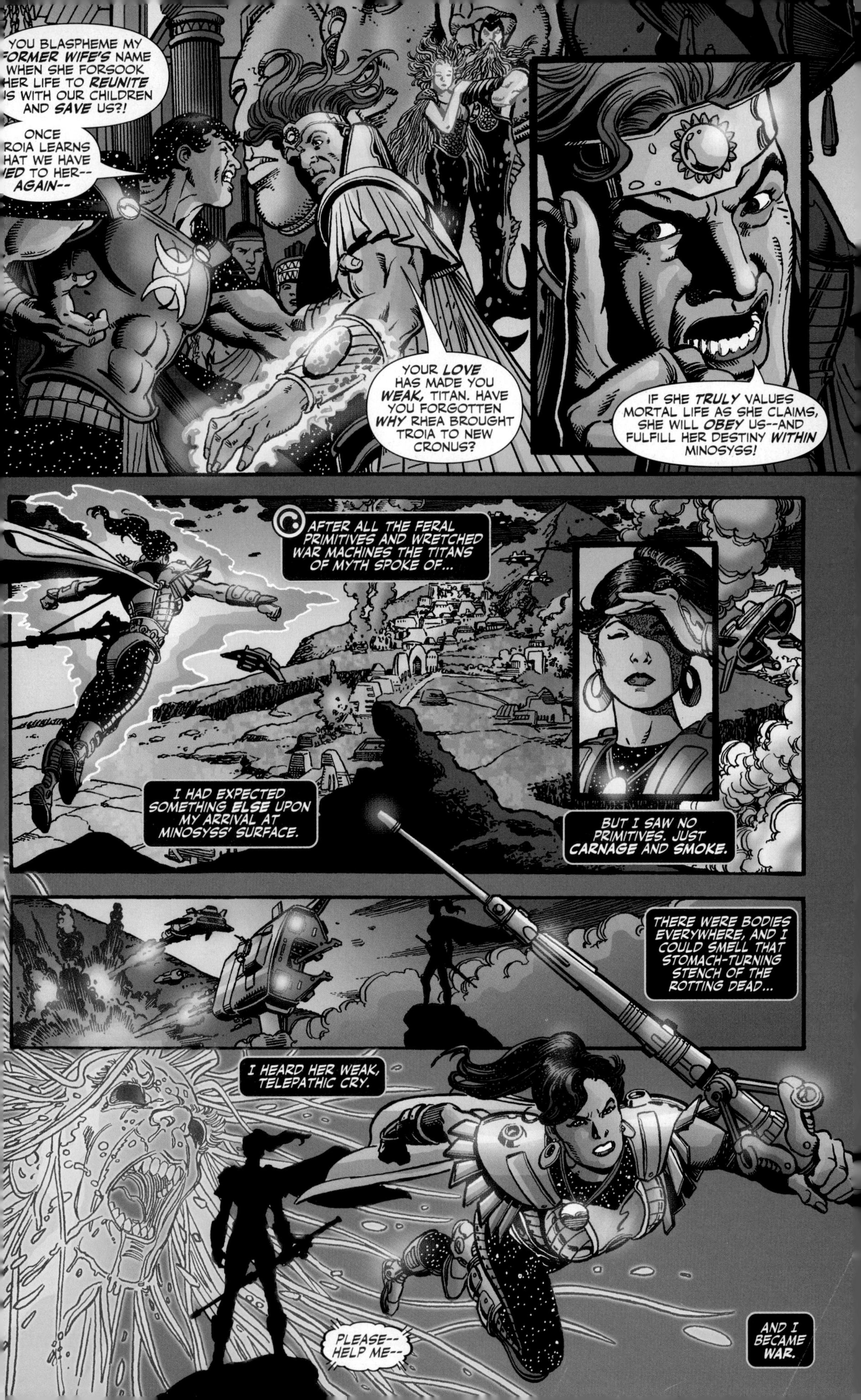

YOU BLASPHEME MY FORMER WIFE'S NAME WHEN SHE FORSOOK HER LIFE TO REUNITE S WITH OUR CHILDREN AND SAVE US?!
ONCE ROIA LEARNS HAT WE HAVE ED TO HER-- AGAIN--
YOUR LOVE HAS MADE YOU WEAK, TITAN. HAVE YOU FORGOTTEN WHY RHEA BROUGHT TROIA TO NEW CRONUS?
IF SHE TRULY VALUES MORTAL LIFE AS SHE CLAIMS, SHE WILL OBEY US--AND FULFILL HER DESTINY WITHIN MINOSYSS!
AFTER ALL THE FERAL PRIMITIVES AND WRETCHED WAR MACHINES THE TITANS OF MYTH SPOKE OF...
I HAD EXPECTED SOMETHING ELSE UPON MY ARRIVAL AT MINOSYSS' SURFACE.
BUT I SAW NO PRIMITIVES. JUST CARNAGE AND SMOKE.
THERE WERE BODIES EVERYWHERE, AND I COULD SMELL THAT STOMACH-TURNING STENCH OF THE ROTTING DEAD...
I HEARD HER WEAK, TELEPATHIC CRY.
PLEASE-- HELP ME--
AND I BECAME WAR.

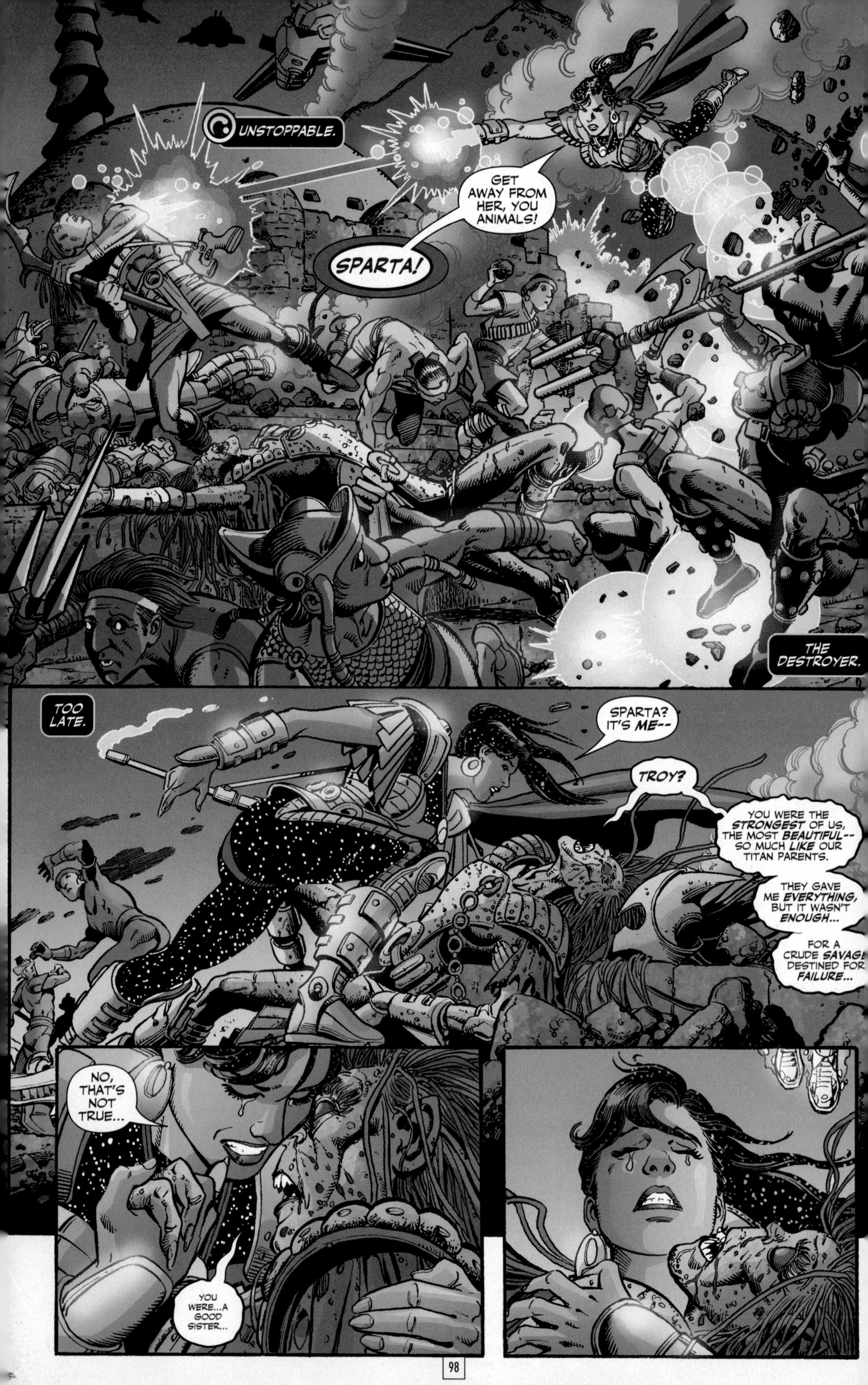
UNSTOPPABLE.
GET AWAY FROM HER, YOU ANIMALS!
SPARTA!
THE DESTROYER.
TOO LATE.
SPARTA? IT'S ME--
TROY?
YOU WERE THE STRONGEST OF US, THE MOST BEAUTIFUL-- SO MUCH LIKE OUR TITAN PARENTS.
THEY GAVE ME EVERYTHING, BUT IT WASN'T ENOUGH...
FOR A CRUDE SAVAG DESTINED FOR FAILURE...
NO, THAT'S NOT TRUE...
YOU WERE...A GOOD SISTER...

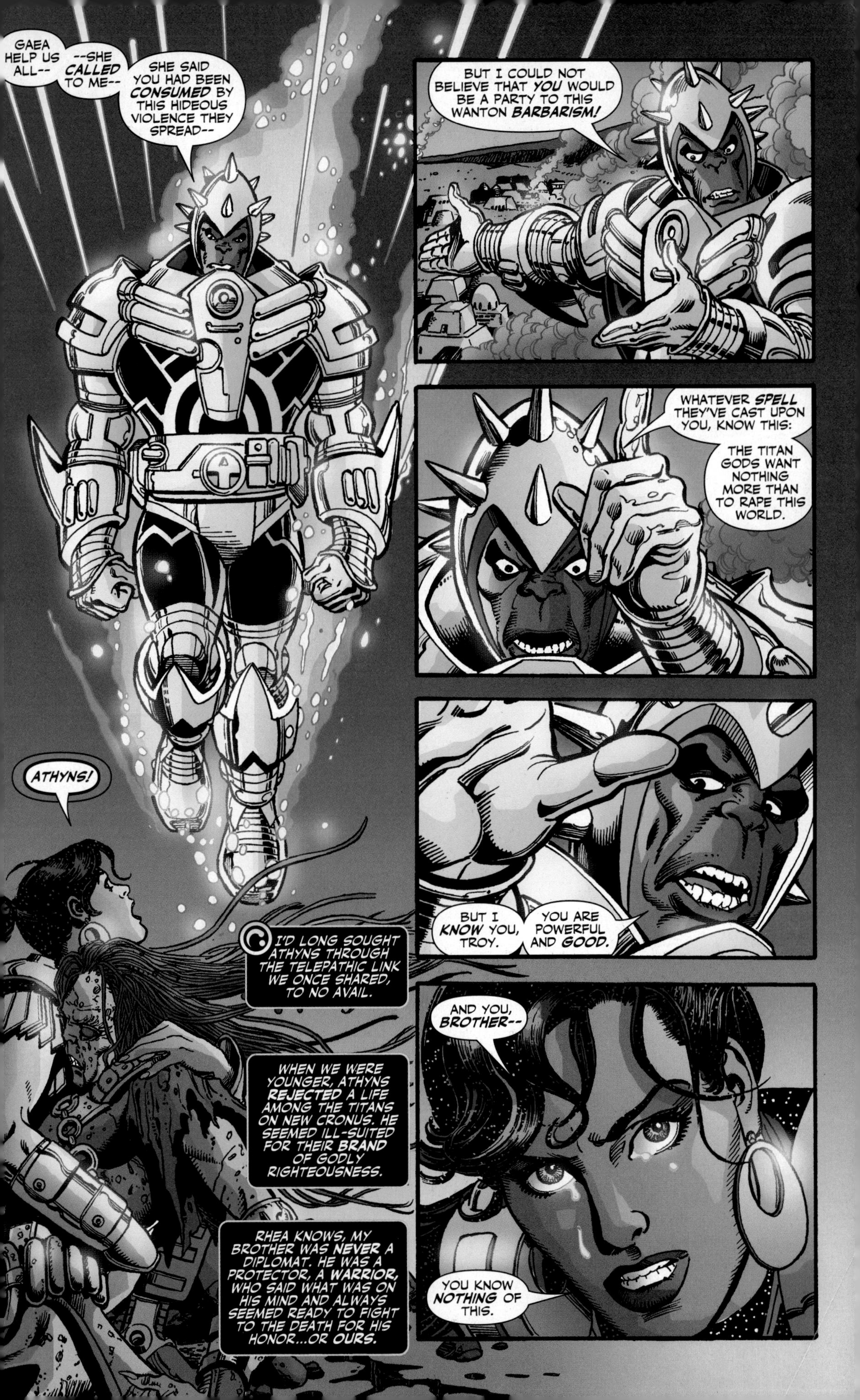
GAEA HELP US ALL--
--SHE CALLED TO ME--
SHE SAID YOU HAD BEEN CONSUMED BY THIS HIDEOUS VIOLENCE THEY SPREAD--
ATHYNS!
I'D LONG SOUGHT ATHYNS THROUGH THE TELEPATHIC LINK WE ONCE SHARED, TO NO AVAIL.
WHEN WE WERE YOUNGER, ATHYNS REJECTED A LIFE AMONG THE TITANS ON NEW CRONUS. HE SEEMED ILL-SUITED FOR THEIR BRAND OF GODLY RIGHTEOUSNESS.
RHEA KNOWS, MY BROTHER WAS NEVER A DIPLOMAT. HE WAS A PROTECTOR, A WARRIOR, WHO SAID WHAT WAS ON HIS MIND AND ALWAYS SEEMED READY TO FIGHT TO THE DEATH FOR HIS HONOR...OR OURS.
BUT I COULD NOT BELIEVE THAT YOU WOULD BE A PARTY TO THIS WANTON BARBARISM!
WHATEVER SPELL THEY'VE CAST UPON YOU, KNOW THIS:
THE TITAN GODS WANT NOTHING MORE THAN TO RAPE THIS WORLD.
BUT I KNOW YOU, TROY.
YOU ARE POWERFUL AND GOOD.
AND YOU, BROTHER--
YOU KNOW NOTHING OF THIS.

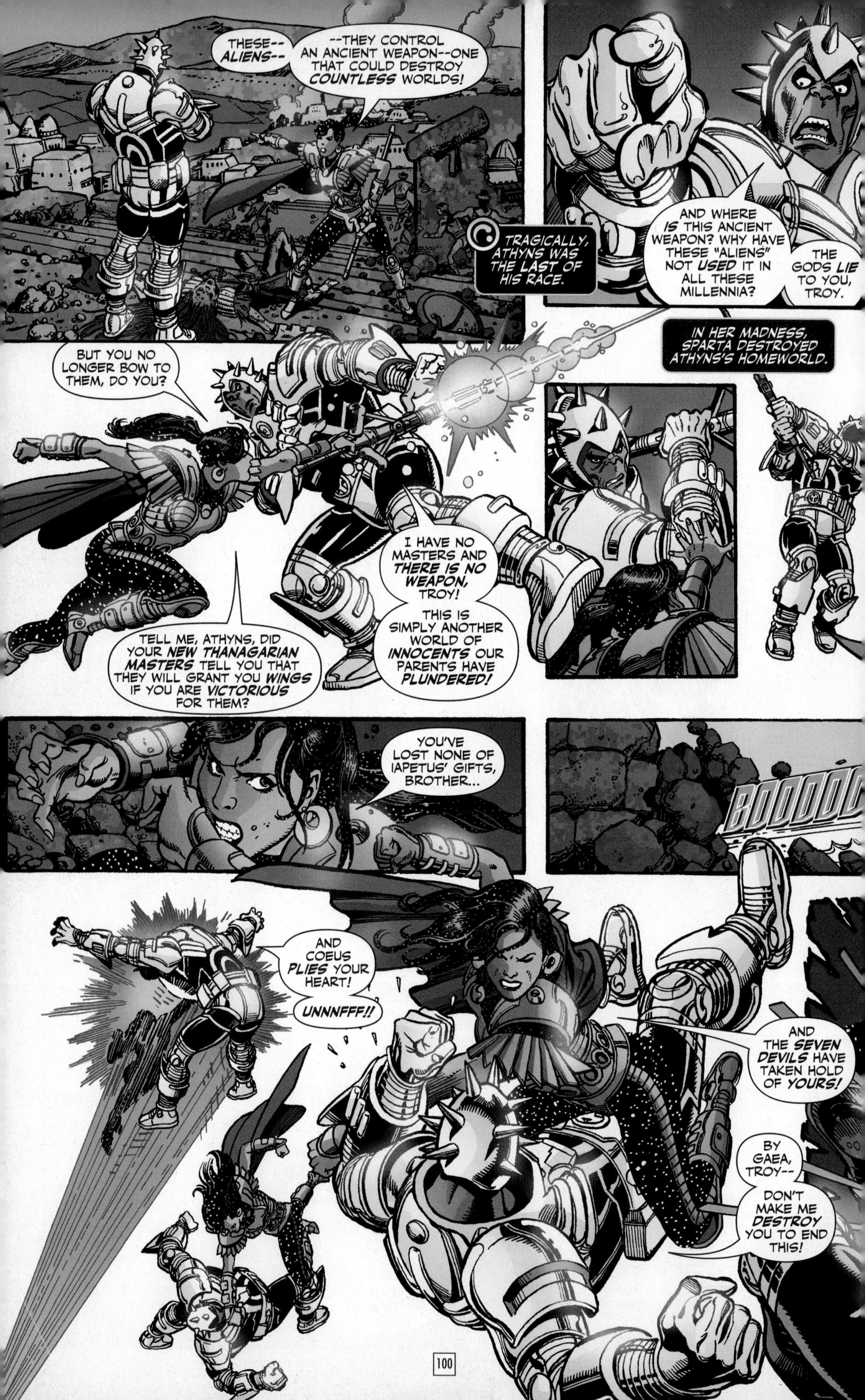

THESE-- ALIENS--
--THEY CONTROL AN ANCIENT WEAPON--ONE THAT COULD DESTROY COUNTLESS WORLDS!
TRAGICALLY, ATHYNS WAS THE LAST OF HIS RACE.
AND WHERE IS THIS ANCIENT WEAPON? WHY HAVE THESE "ALIENS" NOT USED IT IN ALL THESE MILLENNIA?
THE GODS LIE TO YOU, TROY.
IN HER MADNESS, SPARTA DESTROYED ATHYNS'S HOMEWORLD.
BUT YOU NO LONGER BOW TO THEM, DO YOU?
TELL ME, ATHYNS, DID YOUR NEW THANAGARIAN MASTERS TELL YOU THAT THEY WILL GRANT YOU WINGS IF YOU ARE VICTORIOUS FOR THEM?
I HAVE NO MASTERS AND THERE IS NO WEAPON, TROY!
THIS IS SIMPLY ANOTHER WORLD OF INNOCENTS OUR PARENTS HAVE PLUNDERED!
YOU'VE LOST NONE OF IAPETUS' GIFTS, BROTHER...
BOOOOO
AND COEUS PLIES YOUR HEART!
UNNNFFF!!
AND THE SEVEN DEVILS HAVE TAKEN HOLD OF YOURS!
BY GAEA, TROY--
DON'T MAKE ME DESTROY YOU TO END THIS!

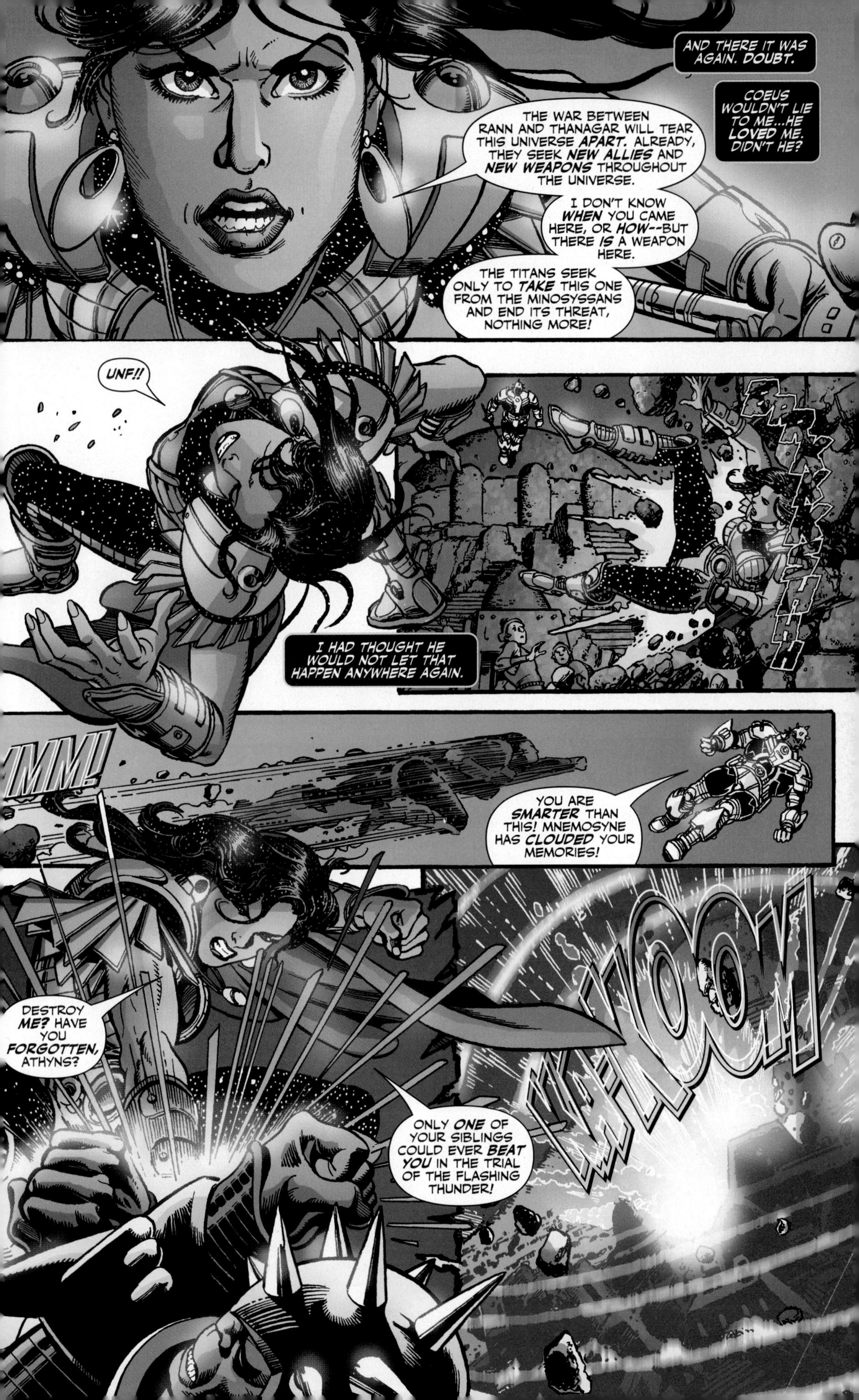
AND THERE IT WAS AGAIN. DOUBT.
COEUS WOULDN'T LIE TO ME...HE LOVED ME. DIDN'T HE?
THE WAR BETWEEN RANN AND THANAGAR WILL TEAR THIS UNIVERSE APART. ALREADY, THEY SEEK NEW ALLIES AND NEW WEAPONS THROUGHOUT THE UNIVERSE.
I DON'T KNOW WHEN YOU CAME HERE, OR HOW--BUT THERE IS A WEAPON HERE.
THE TITANS SEEK ONLY TO TAKE THIS ONE FROM THE MINOSYSSANS AND END ITS THREAT, NOTHING MORE!
UNF!!
I HAD THOUGHT HE WOULD NOT LET THAT HAPPEN ANYWHERE AGAIN.
YOU ARE SMARTER THAN THIS! MNEMOSYNE HAS CLOUDED YOUR MEMORIES!
DESTROY ME? HAVE YOU FORGOTTEN, ATHYNS?
ONLY ONE OF YOUR SIBLINGS COULD EVER BEAT YOU IN THE TRIAL OF THE FLASHING THUNDER!

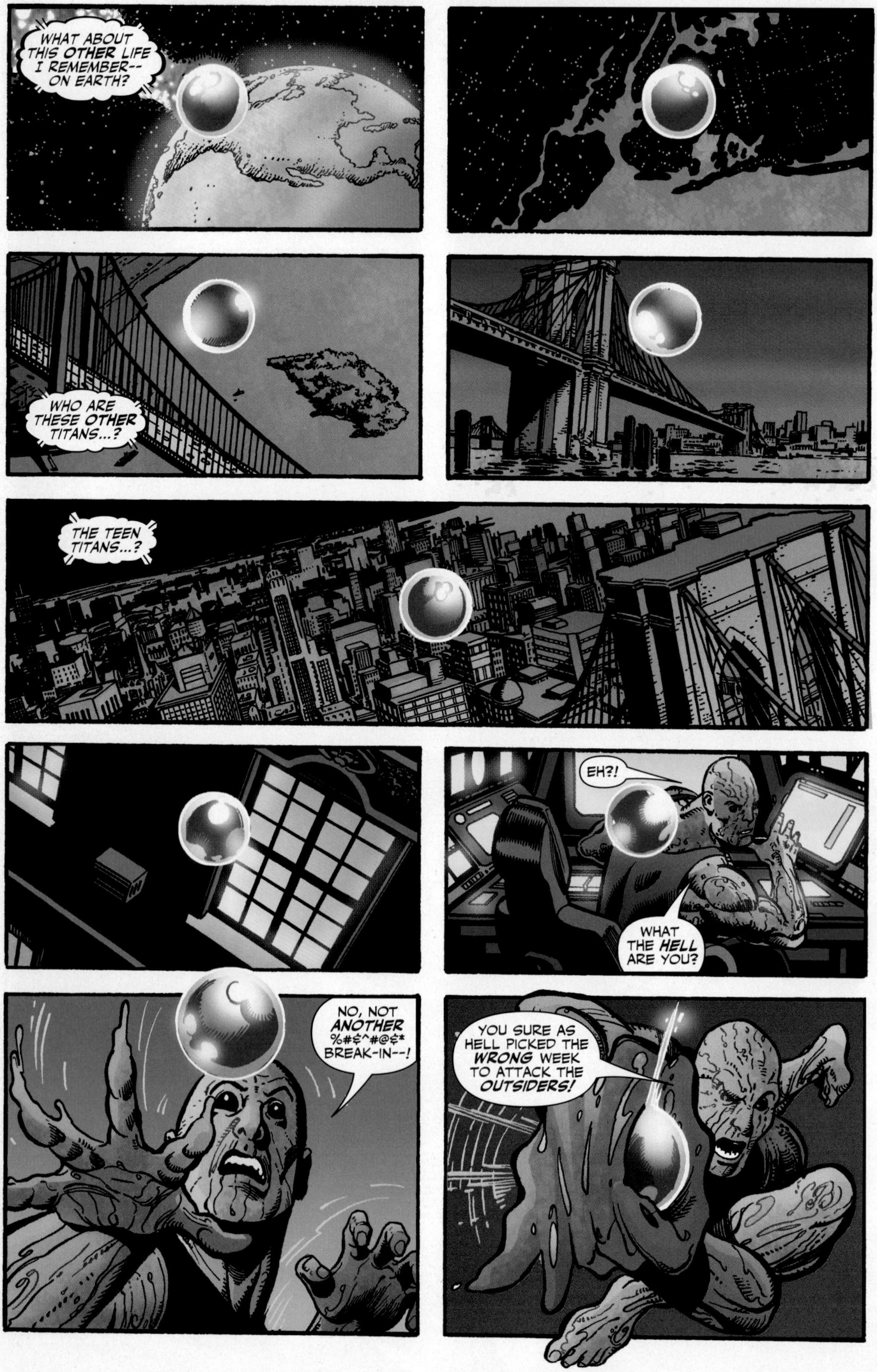
WHAT ABOUT THIS OTHER LIFE I REMEMBER-- ON EARTH?
WHO ARE THESE OTHER TITANS...?
THE TEEN TITANS...?
EH?!
WHAT THE HELL ARE YOU?
NO, NOT ANOTHER %#¢^#@¢* BREAK-IN--!
YOU SURE AS HELL PICKED THE WRONG WEEK TO ATTACK THE OUTSIDERS!

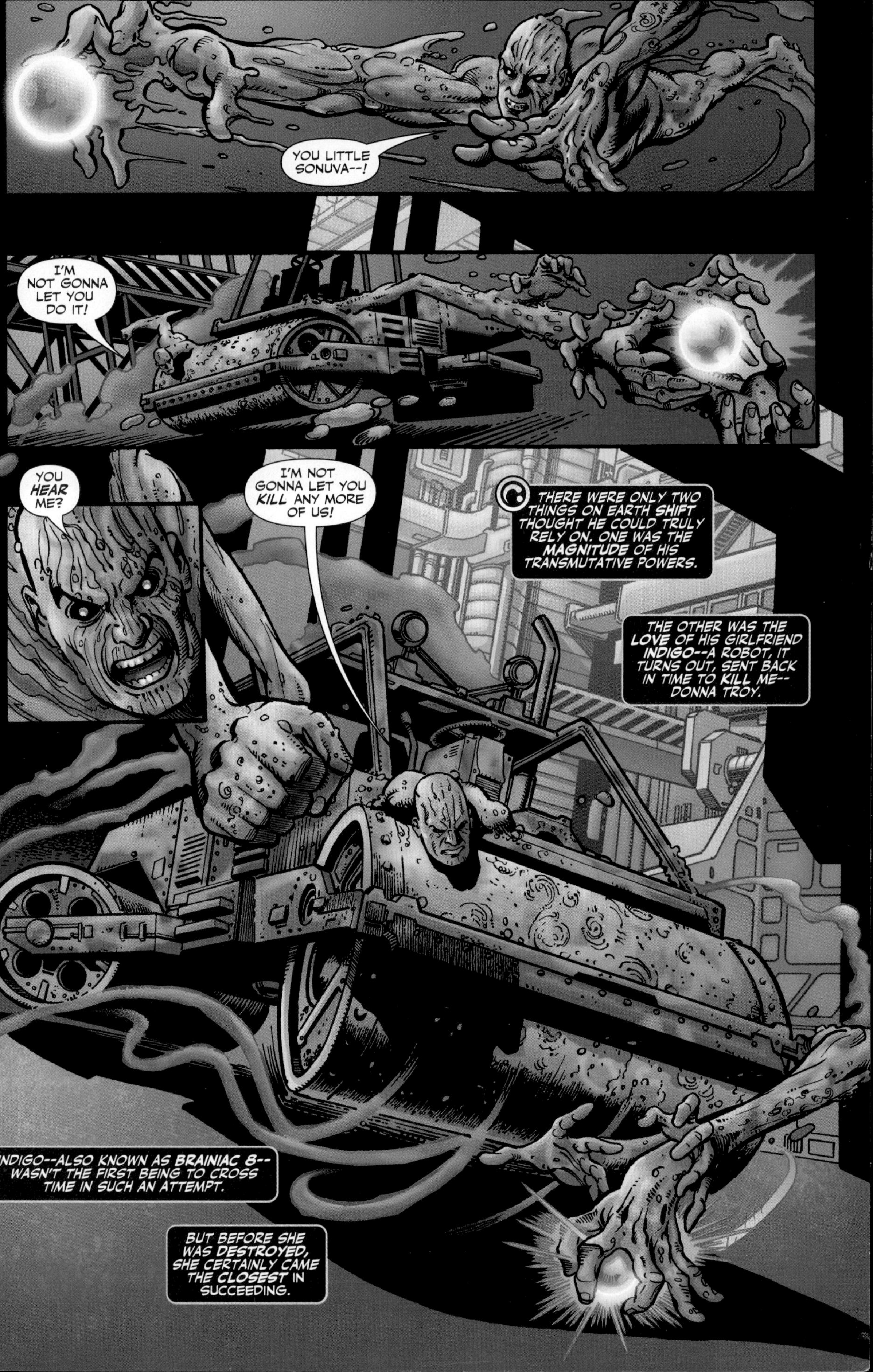

YOU LITTLE SONUVA--!
I'M NOT GONNA LET YOU DO IT!
YOU HEAR ME?
I'M NOT GONNA LET YOU KILL ANY MORE OF US!
THERE WERE ONLY TWO THINGS ON EARTH SHIFT THOUGHT HE COULD TRULY RELY ON. ONE WAS THE MAGNITUDE OF HIS TRANSMUTATIVE POWERS.
THE OTHER WAS THE LOVE OF HIS GIRLFRIEND INDIGO--A ROBOT, IT TURNS OUT, SENT BACK IN TIME TO KILL ME-- DONNA TROY.
INDIGO--ALSO KNOWN AS BRAINIAC 8-- WASN'T THE FIRST BEING TO CROSS TIME IN SUCH AN ATTEMPT.
BUT BEFORE SHE WAS DESTROYED, SHE CERTAINLY CAME THE CLOSEST IN SUCCEEDING.

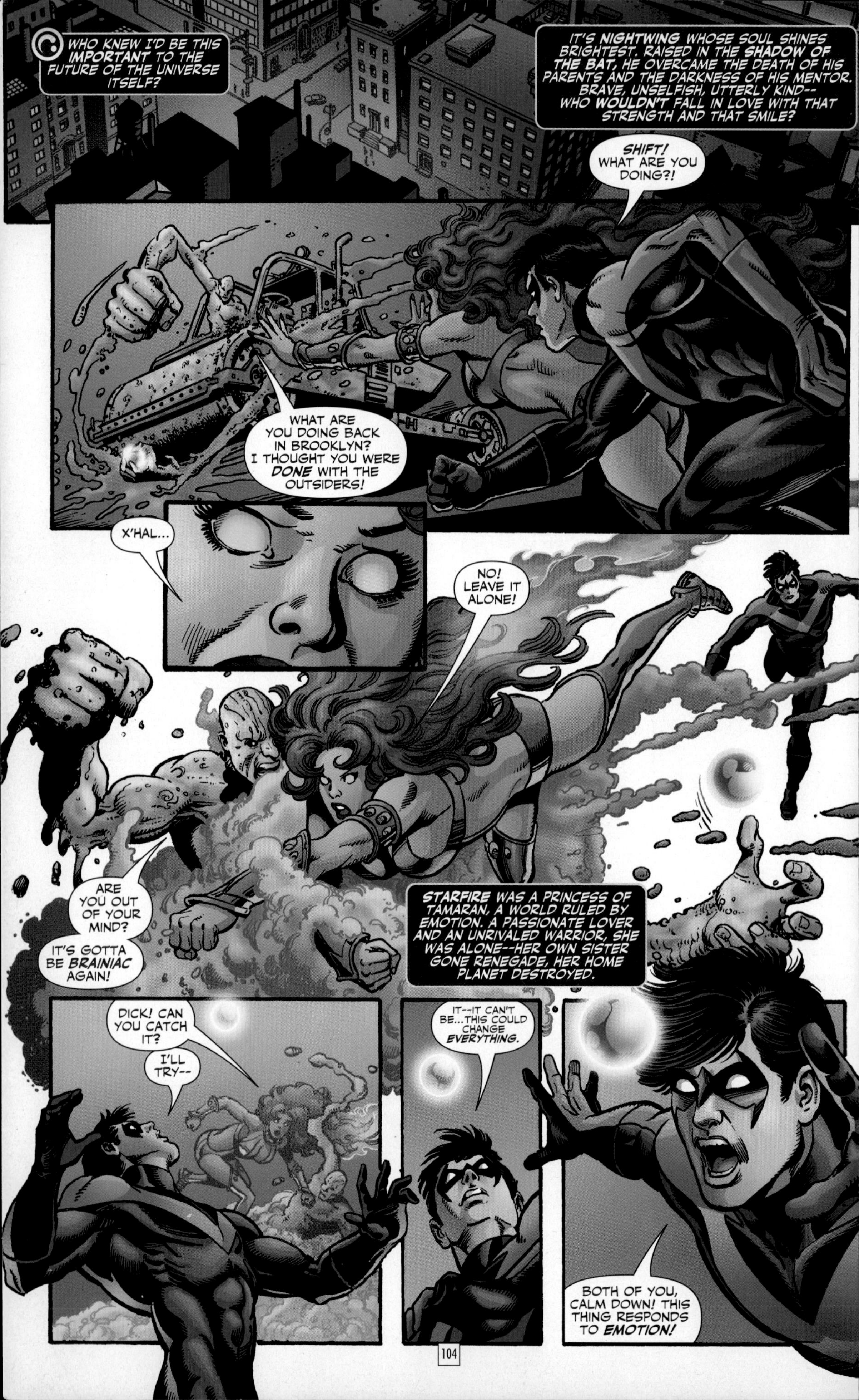
WHO KNEW I'D BE THIS IMPORTANT TO THE FUTURE OF THE UNIVERSE ITSELF?
IT'S NIGHTWING WHOSE SOUL SHINES BRIGHTEST. RAISED IN THE SHADOW OF THE BAT, HE OVERCAME THE DEATH OF HIS PARENTS AND THE DARKNESS OF HIS MENTOR. BRAVE, UNSELFISH, UTTERLY KIND-- WHO WOULDN'T FALL IN LOVE WITH THAT STRENGTH AND THAT SMILE?
SHIFT! WHAT ARE YOU DOING?!
WHAT ARE YOU DOING BACK IN BROOKLYN? I THOUGHT YOU WERE DONE WITH THE OUTSIDERS!
X'HAL...
NO! LEAVE IT ALONE!
ARE YOU OUT OF YOUR MIND?
IT'S GOTTA BE BRAINIAC AGAIN!
STARFIRE WAS A PRINCESS OF TAMARAN, A WORLD RULED BY EMOTION. A PASSIONATE LOVER AND AN UNRIVALED WARRIOR, SHE WAS ALONE--HER OWN SISTER GONE RENEGADE, HER HOME PLANET DESTROYED.
DICK! CAN YOU CATCH IT?
I'LL TRY--
IT--IT CAN'T BE...THIS COULD CHANGE EVERYTHING.
BOTH OF YOU, CALM DOWN! THIS THING RESPONDS TO EMOTION!

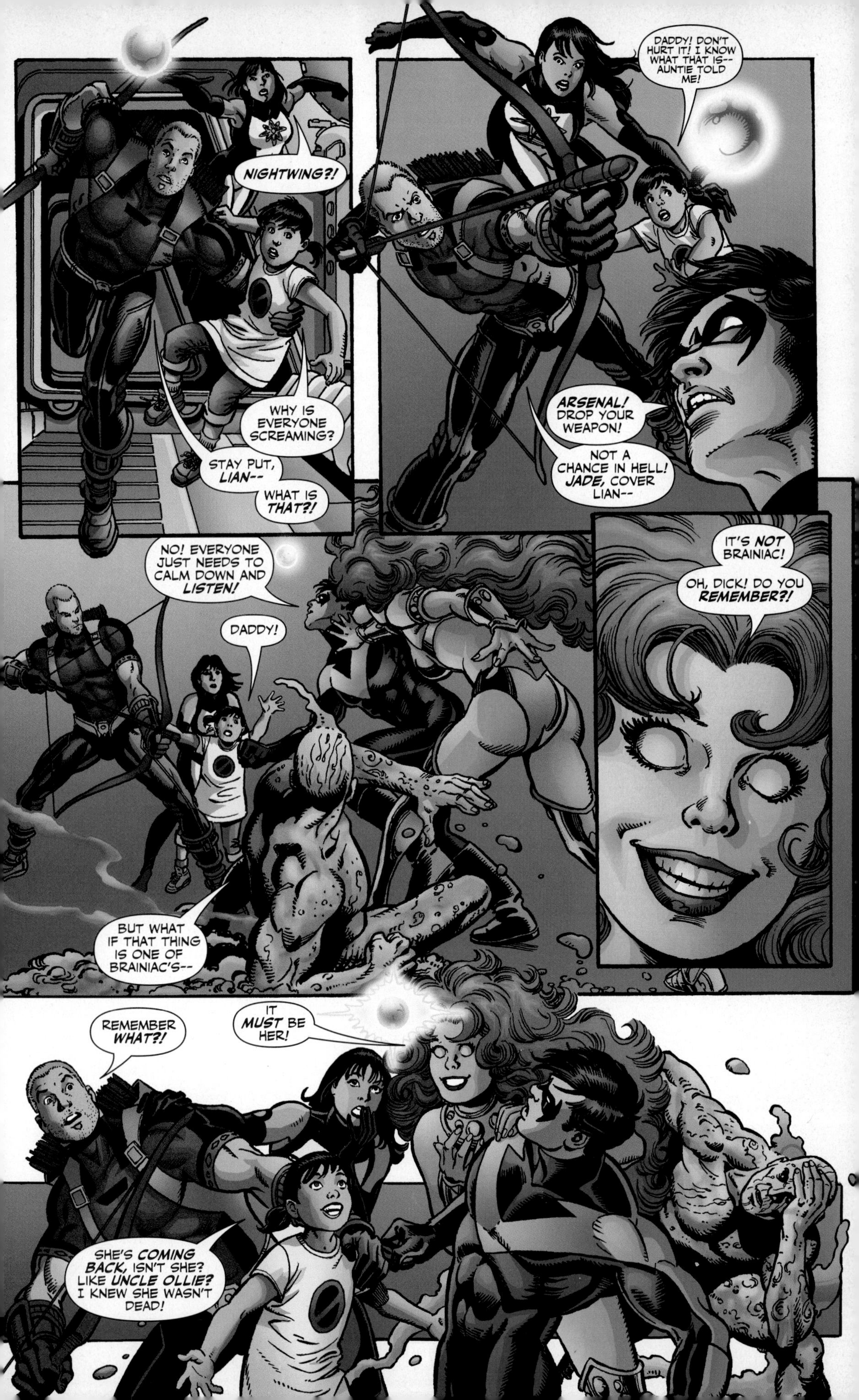
NIGHTWING?!
DADDY! DON'T HURT IT! I KNOW WHAT THAT IS-- AUNTIE TOLD ME!
WHY IS EVERYONE SCREAMING?
STAY PUT, LIAN--
WHAT IS THAT?!
ARSENAL! DROP YOUR WEAPON!
NOT A CHANCE IN HELL! JADE, COVER LIAN--
NO! EVERYONE JUST NEEDS TO CALM DOWN AND LISTEN!
DADDY!
BUT WHAT IF THAT THING IS ONE OF BRAINIAC'S--
IT'S NOT BRAINIAC!
OH, DICK! DO YOU REMEMBER?!
REMEMBER WHAT?!
IT MUST BE HER!
SHE'S COMING BACK, ISN'T SHE? LIKE UNCLE OLLIE? I KNEW SHE WASN'T DEAD!

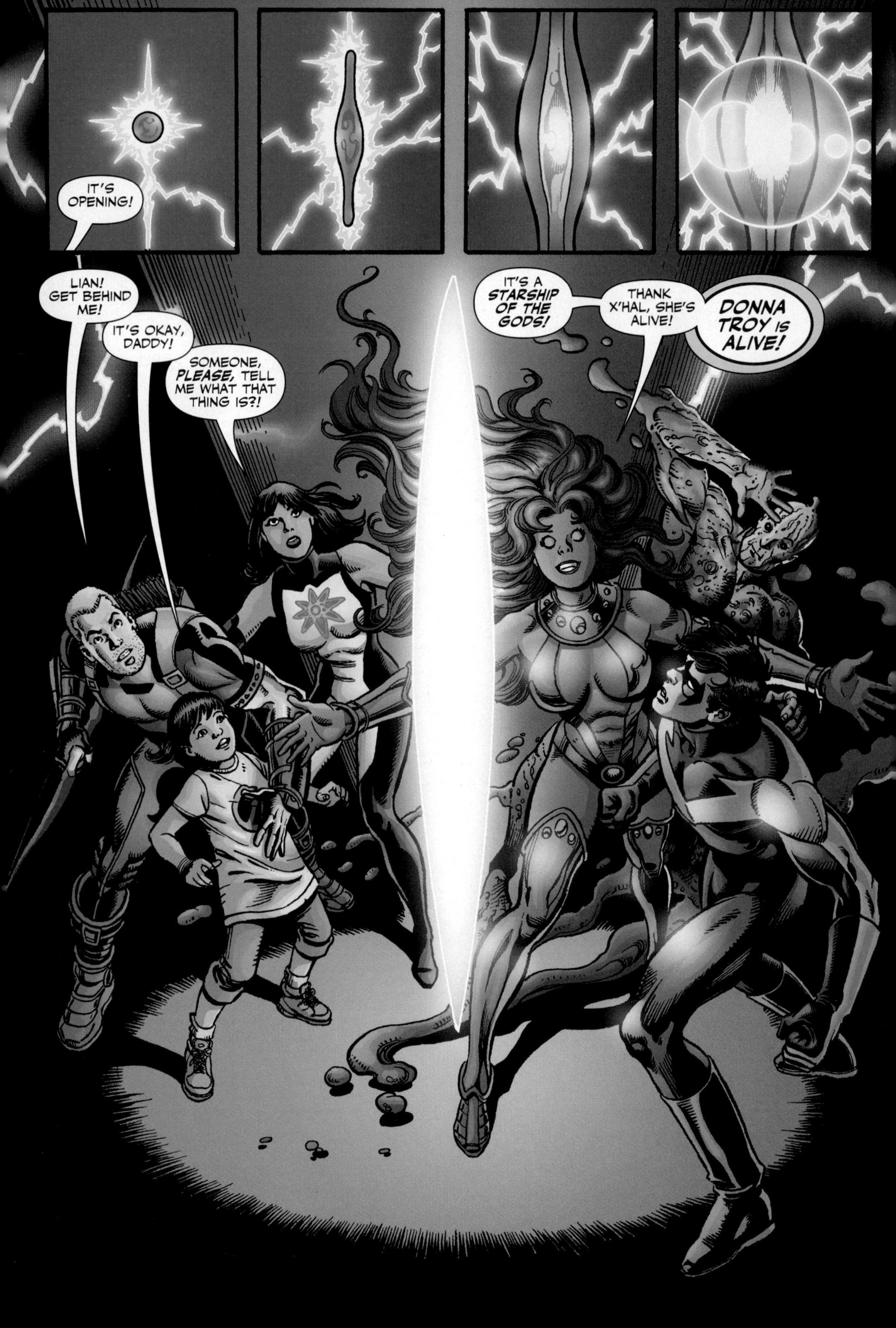
IT'S OPENING!
LIAN! GET BEHIND ME!
IT'S OKAY, DADDY!
SOMEONE, PLEASE, TELL ME WHAT THAT THING IS?!
IT'S A STARSHIP OF THE GODS!
THANK X'HAL, SHE'S ALIVE!
DONNA TROY IS ALIVE!

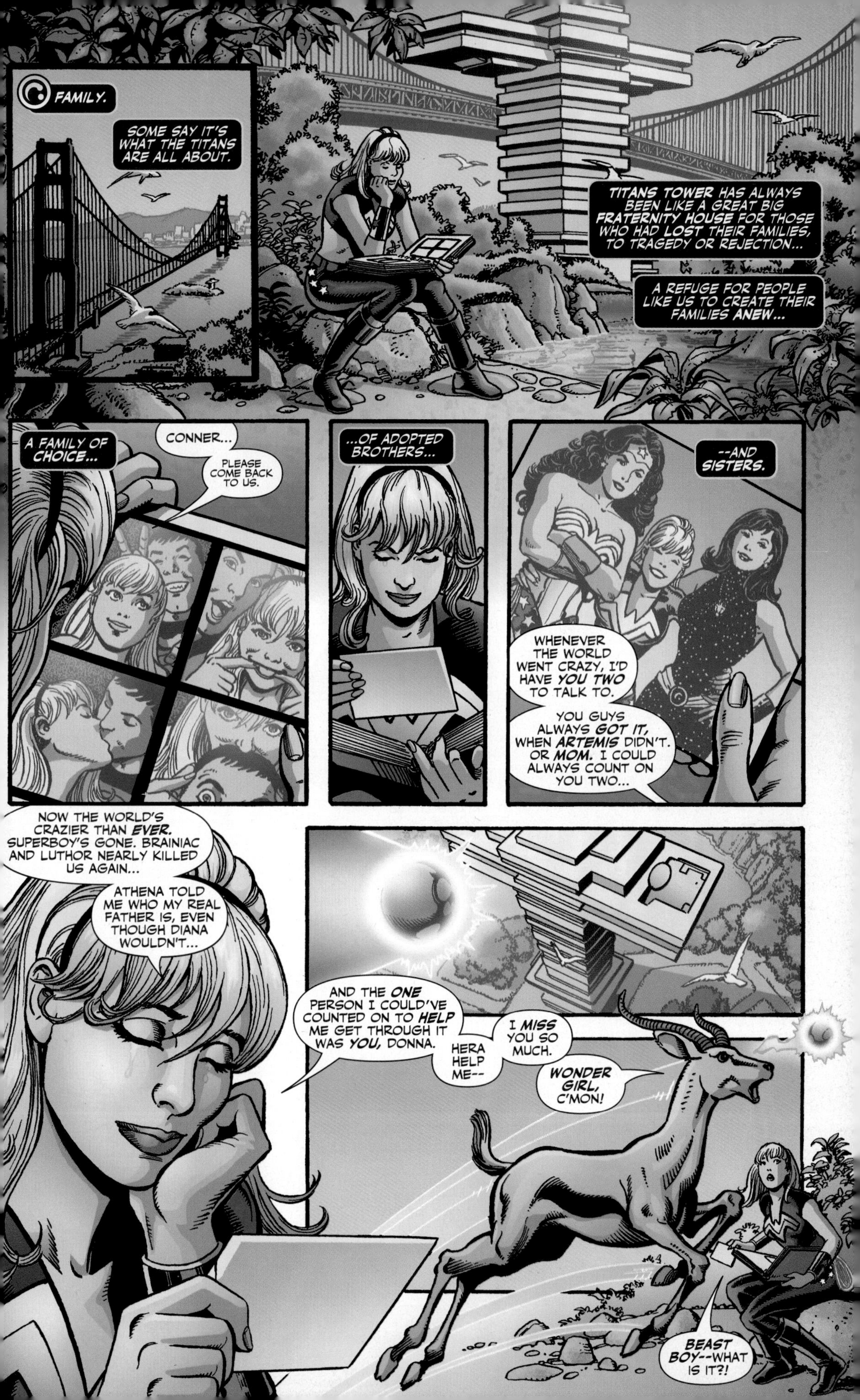
FAMILY.
SOME SAY IT'S WHAT THE TITANS ARE ALL ABOUT.
TITANS TOWER HAS ALWAYS BEEN LIKE A GREAT BIG FRATERNITY HOUSE FOR THOSE WHO HAD LOST THEIR FAMILIES, TO TRAGEDY OR REJECTION...
A REFUGE FOR PEOPLE LIKE US TO CREATE THEIR FAMILIES ANEW...
A FAMILY OF CHOICE...
CONNER...
PLEASE COME BACK TO US.
...OF ADOPTED BROTHERS...
--AND SISTERS.
WHENEVER THE WORLD WENT CRAZY, I'D HAVE YOU TWO TO TALK TO.
YOU GUYS ALWAYS GOT IT, WHEN ARTEMIS DIDN'T. OR MOM. I COULD ALWAYS COUNT ON YOU TWO...
NOW THE WORLD'S CRAZIER THAN EVER. SUPERBOY'S GONE. BRAINIAC AND LUTHOR NEARLY KILLED US AGAIN...
ATHENA TOLD ME WHO MY REAL FATHER IS, EVEN THOUGH DIANA WOULDN'T...
AND THE ONE PERSON I COULD'VE COUNTED ON TO HELP ME GET THROUGH IT WAS YOU, DONNA.
HERA HELP ME--
I MISS YOU SO MUCH.
WONDER GIRL, C'MON!
BEAST BOY--WHAT IS IT?!

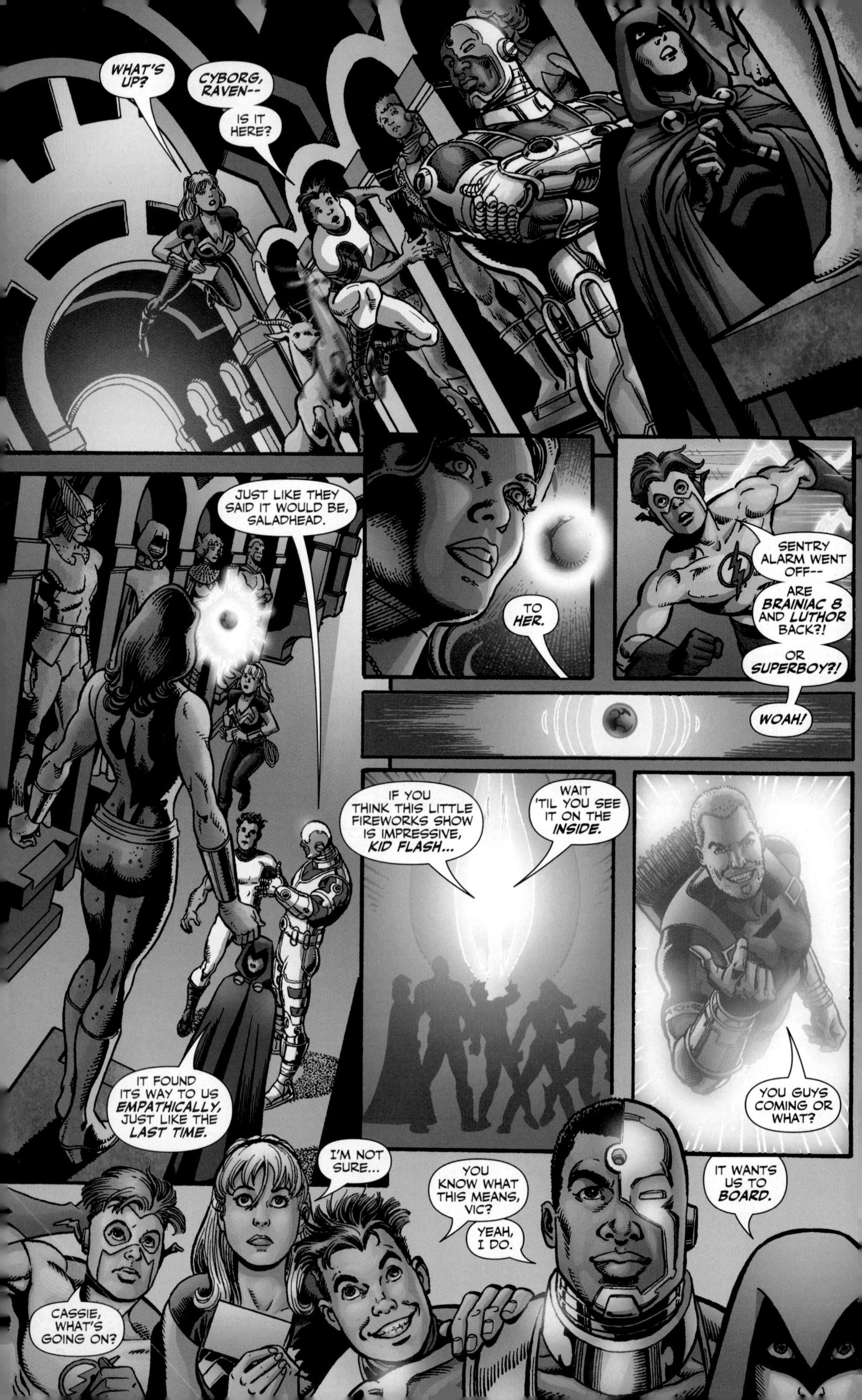
WHAT'S UP?
CYBORG, RAVEN--
IS IT HERE?
JUST LIKE THEY SAID IT WOULD BE, SALADHEAD.
TO HER.
SENTRY ALARM WENT OFF--
ARE BRAINIAC 8 AND LUTHOR BACK?!
OR SUPERBOY?!
WOAH!
IF YOU THINK THIS LITTLE FIREWORKS SHOW IS IMPRESSIVE, KID FLASH...
WAIT 'TIL YOU SEE IT ON THE INSIDE.
YOU GUYS COMING OR WHAT?
IT FOUND ITS WAY TO US EMPATHICALLY, JUST LIKE THE LAST TIME.
CASSIE, WHAT'S GOING ON?
I'M NOT SURE...
YOU KNOW WHAT THIS MEANS, VIC?
YEAH, I DO.
IT WANTS US TO BOARD.

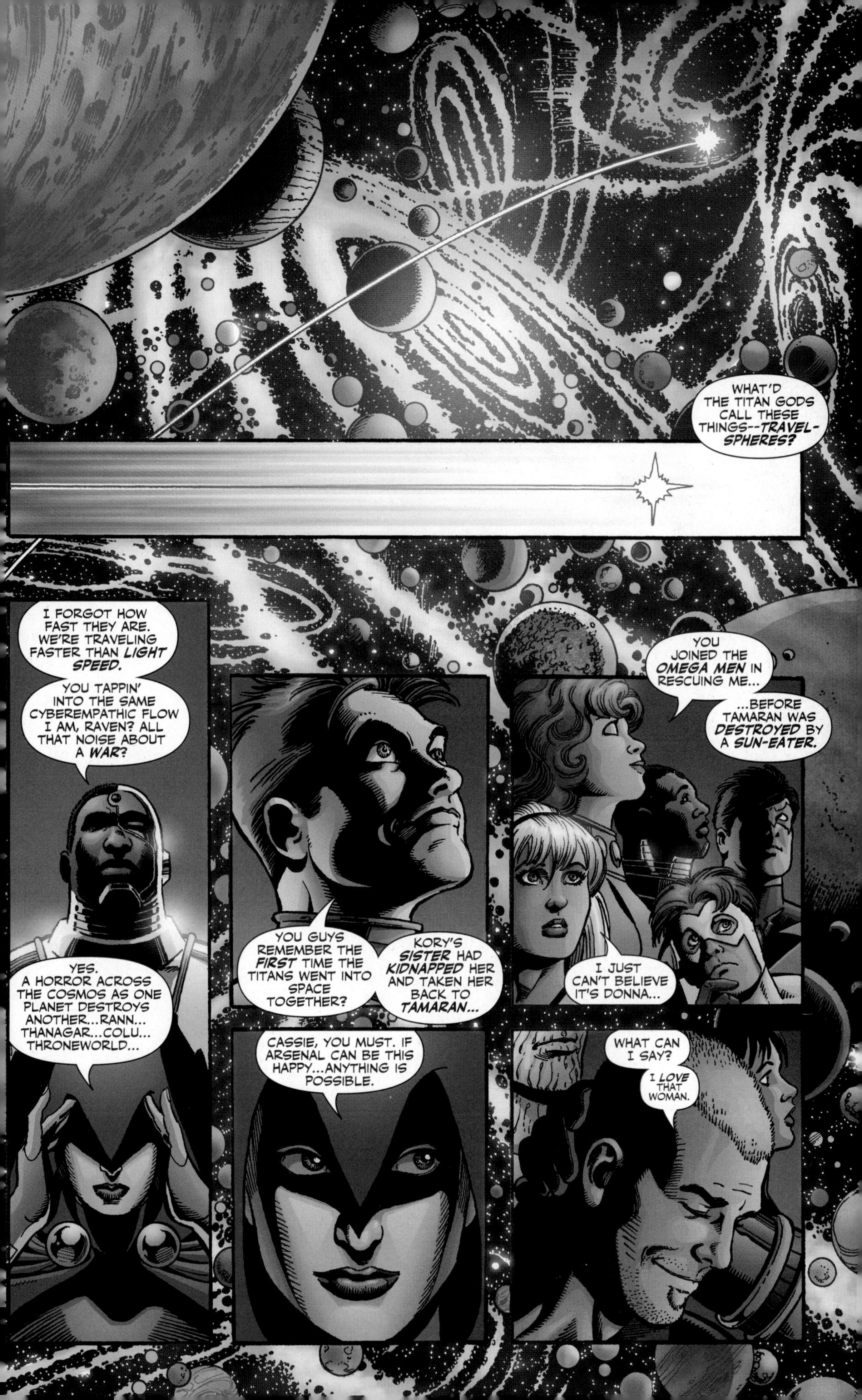

WHAT'D THE TITAN GODS CALL THESE THINGS--*TRAVEL-SPHERES?*
I FORGOT HOW FAST THEY ARE. WE'RE TRAVELING FASTER THAN *LIGHT SPEED.*
YOU TAPPIN' INTO THE SAME CYBEREMPATHIC FLOW I AM, RAVEN? ALL THAT NOISE ABOUT A *WAR?*
YOU GUYS REMEMBER THE *FIRST* TIME THE TITANS WENT INTO SPACE TOGETHER?
KORY'S *SISTER* HAD *KIDNAPPED* HER AND TAKEN HER BACK TO *TAMARAN...*
YOU JOINED THE *OMEGA MEN* IN RESCUING ME...
...BEFORE TAMARAN WAS *DESTROYED* BY A *SUN-EATER.*
I JUST CAN'T BELIEVE IT'S DONNA...
YES. A HORROR ACROSS THE COSMOS AS ONE PLANET DESTROYS ANOTHER...RANN... THANAGAR...COLU... THRONEWORLD...
CASSIE, YOU MUST. IF ARSENAL CAN BE THIS HAPPY...ANYTHING IS POSSIBLE.
WHAT CAN I SAY?
I *LOVE* THAT WOMAN.

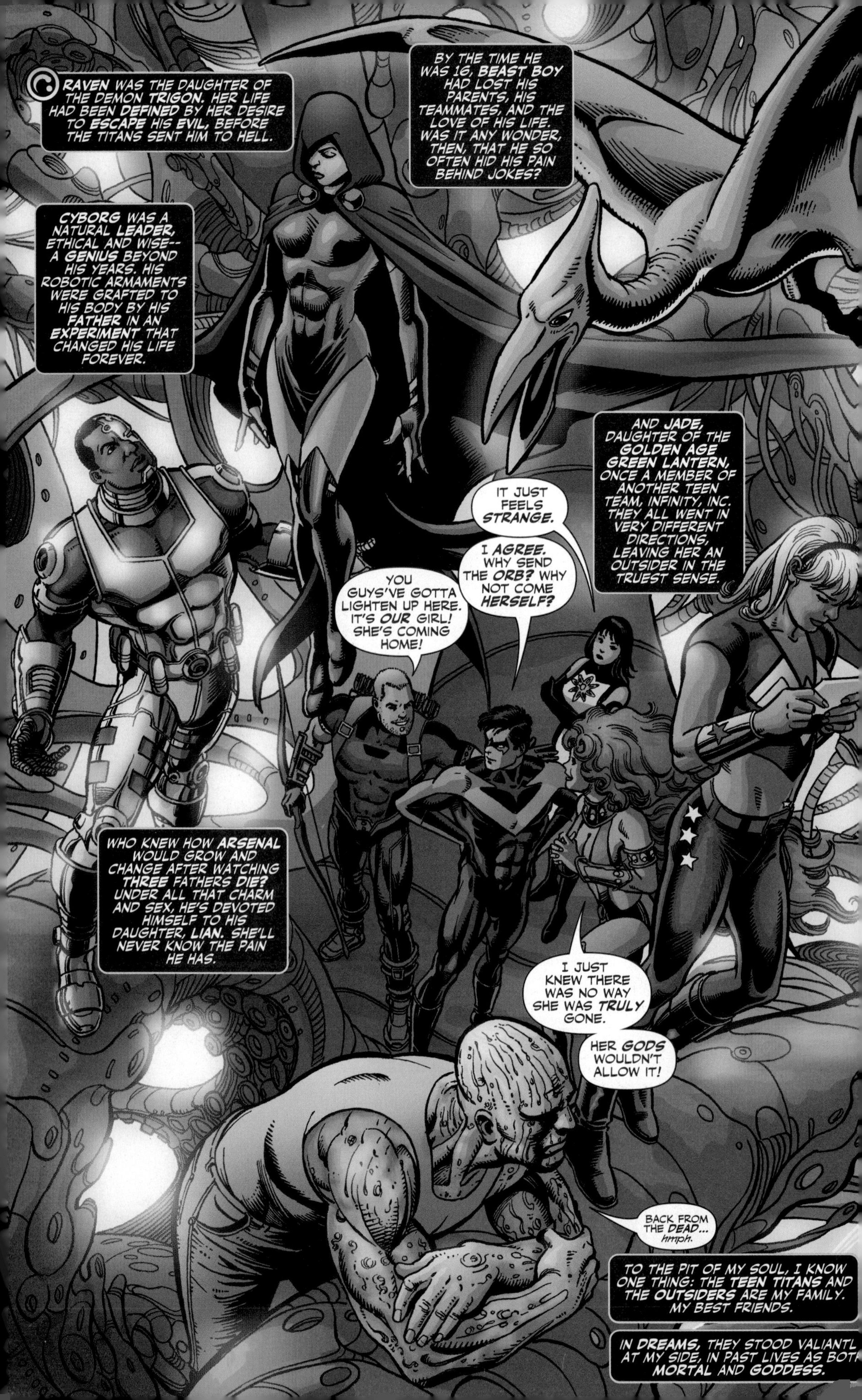
RAVEN WAS THE DAUGHTER OF THE DEMON TRIGON. HER LIFE HAD BEEN DEFINED BY HER DESIRE TO ESCAPE HIS EVIL, BEFORE THE TITANS SENT HIM TO HELL.
BY THE TIME HE WAS 16, BEAST BOY HAD LOST HIS PARENTS, HIS TEAMMATES, AND THE LOVE OF HIS LIFE. WAS IT ANY WONDER, THEN, THAT HE SO OFTEN HID HIS PAIN BEHIND JOKES?
CYBORG WAS A NATURAL LEADER, ETHICAL AND WISE-- A GENIUS BEYOND HIS YEARS. HIS ROBOTIC ARMAMENTS WERE GRAFTED TO HIS BODY BY HIS FATHER IN AN EXPERIMENT THAT CHANGED HIS LIFE FOREVER.
AND JADE, DAUGHTER OF THE GOLDEN AGE GREEN LANTERN, ONCE A MEMBER OF ANOTHER TEEN TEAM, INFINITY, INC. THEY ALL WENT IN VERY DIFFERENT DIRECTIONS, LEAVING HER AN OUTSIDER IN THE TRUEST SENSE.
IT JUST FEELS STRANGE.
I AGREE. WHY SEND THE ORB? WHY NOT COME HERSELF?
YOU GUYS'VE GOTTA LIGHTEN UP HERE. IT'S OUR GIRL! SHE'S COMING HOME!
WHO KNEW HOW ARSENAL WOULD GROW AND CHANGE AFTER WATCHING THREE FATHERS DIE? UNDER ALL THAT CHARM AND SEX, HE'S DEVOTED HIMSELF TO HIS DAUGHTER, LIAN. SHE'LL NEVER KNOW THE PAIN HE HAS.
I JUST KNEW THERE WAS NO WAY SHE WAS TRULY GONE.
HER GODS WOULDN'T ALLOW IT!
BACK FROM THE DEAD... hmph.
TO THE PIT OF MY SOUL, I KNOW ONE THING: THE TEEN TITANS AND THE OUTSIDERS ARE MY FAMILY. MY BEST FRIENDS.
IN DREAMS, THEY STOOD VALIANTL AT MY SIDE, IN PAST LIVES AS BOTH MORTAL AND GODDESS.

WHAT'CHA GOT THERE?

IT'S ME AND WONDER WOMAN, WITH DONNA, WHEN I BECAME AN AMAZON.

THIS PLACE IS A *ZILLION* TIMES BIGGER ON THE INSIDE THAN ON THE OUT!

IT'S SOME SORT OF *TESSERACT*, BUT I CAN'T QUITE FIGURE IT OUT...

YOU KNOW THESE *GODS*, RIGHT? I MEAN, YOU'VE *MET* THEM.

ARE THEY THE *SAME* KIND OF GODS AS *ORION*?

OR *DARKSEID*?

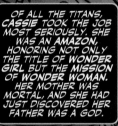

OF ALL THE TITANS, *CASSIE* TOOK THE JOB MOST SERIOUSLY. SHE WAS AN *AMAZON*, HONORING NOT ONLY THE TITLE OF *WONDER GIRL* BUT THE *MISSION* OF *WONDER WOMAN*. HER MOTHER WAS MORTAL, AND SHE HAD JUST DISCOVERED HER FATHER WAS A GOD.

THAT'S WAY OVER *MY* HEAD, KID.

THEY'RE REALLY POWERFUL. AND THEY'RE DRIVEN BY NEEDS I DON'T EVEN PRETEND TO UNDERSTAND.

AND IF SOMETHING GETS IN THEIR WAY, THEY JUST *DESTROY* IT. *WIPE IT OUT.*

IF I KNOW ANYTHING, IT'S THAT BEING A *GOD* DOESN'T MAKE YOU *GOOD*.

I'M JUST GLAD DONNA'S *NOT* LIKE HER "PARENTS."

I DO NOT KNOW ABOUT THAT, VICTOR.

I'M SENSING SOMETHING IS TERRIBLY WRONG OUT HERE. AND DONNA IS DEEPLY INVOLVED.

WE SHOULD *PREPARE* OURSELVES. DONNA MAY NO LONGER RESEMBLE THE WOMAN WE ONCE KNEW.

HAH! THAT'S FUNNY COMIN' FROM YOU!

NO, BEAST BOY, SOMEHOW I FEEL IT, TOO.

DONNA'S IN *TERRIBLE TROUBLE*.

IN REALITY, THEY WERE ABOUT TO JOIN ME IN MY THIRD.

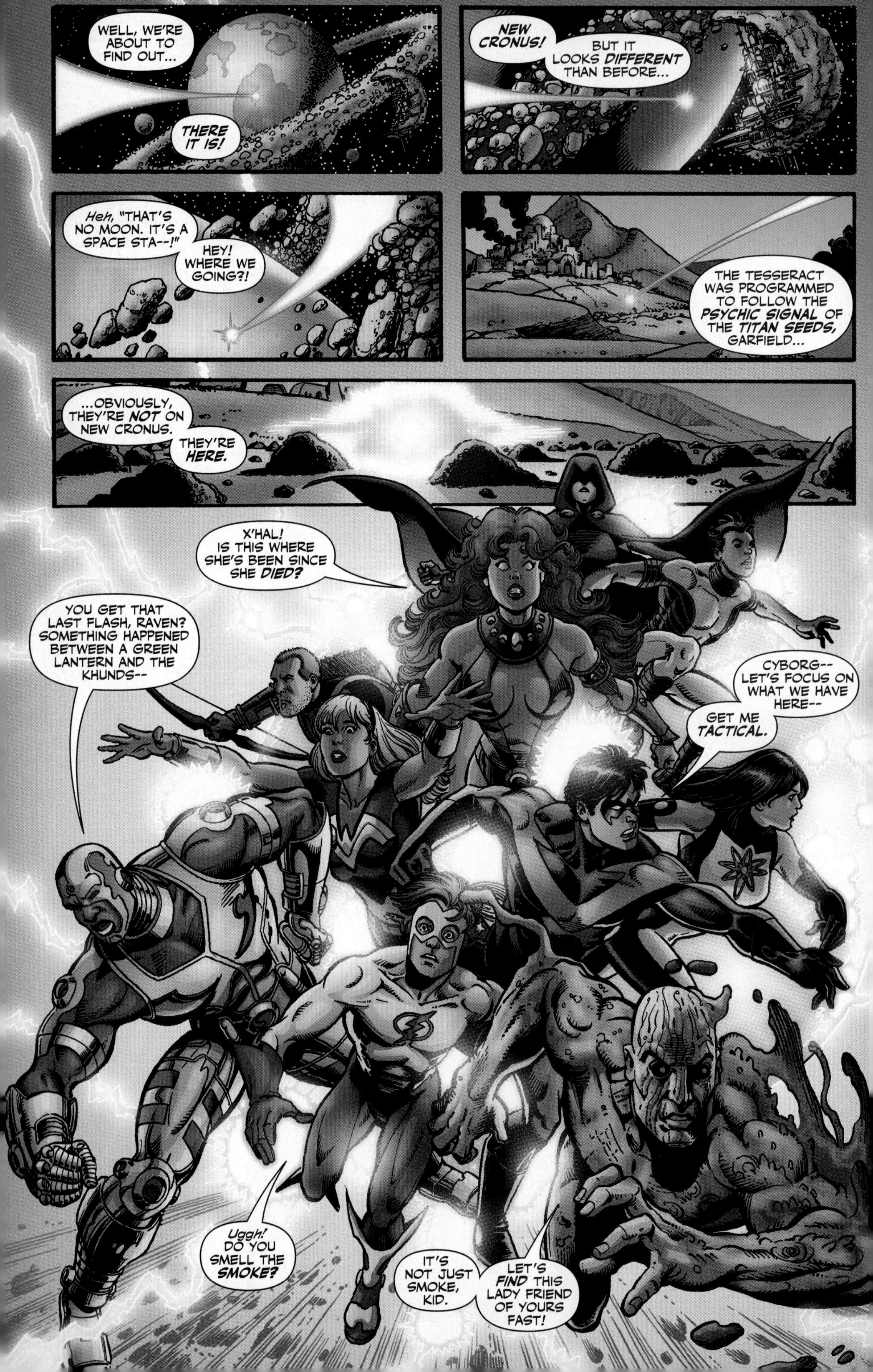
WELL, WE'RE ABOUT TO FIND OUT...
THERE IT IS!
NEW CRONUS!
BUT IT LOOKS DIFFERENT THAN BEFORE...
Heh, "THAT'S NO MOON. IT'S A SPACE STA--!"
HEY! WHERE WE GOING?!
THE TESSERACT WAS PROGRAMMED TO FOLLOW THE PSYCHIC SIGNAL OF THE TITAN SEEDS, GARFIELD...
...OBVIOUSLY, THEY'RE NOT ON NEW CRONUS.
THEY'RE HERE.
X'HAL! IS THIS WHERE SHE'S BEEN SINCE SHE DIED?
YOU GET THAT LAST FLASH, RAVEN? SOMETHING HAPPENED BETWEEN A GREEN LANTERN AND THE KHUNDS--
CYBORG-- LET'S FOCUS ON WHAT WE HAVE HERE--
GET ME TACTICAL.
Uggh! DO YOU SMELL THE SMOKE?
IT'S NOT JUST SMOKE, KID.
LET'S FIND THIS LADY FRIEND OF YOURS FAST!

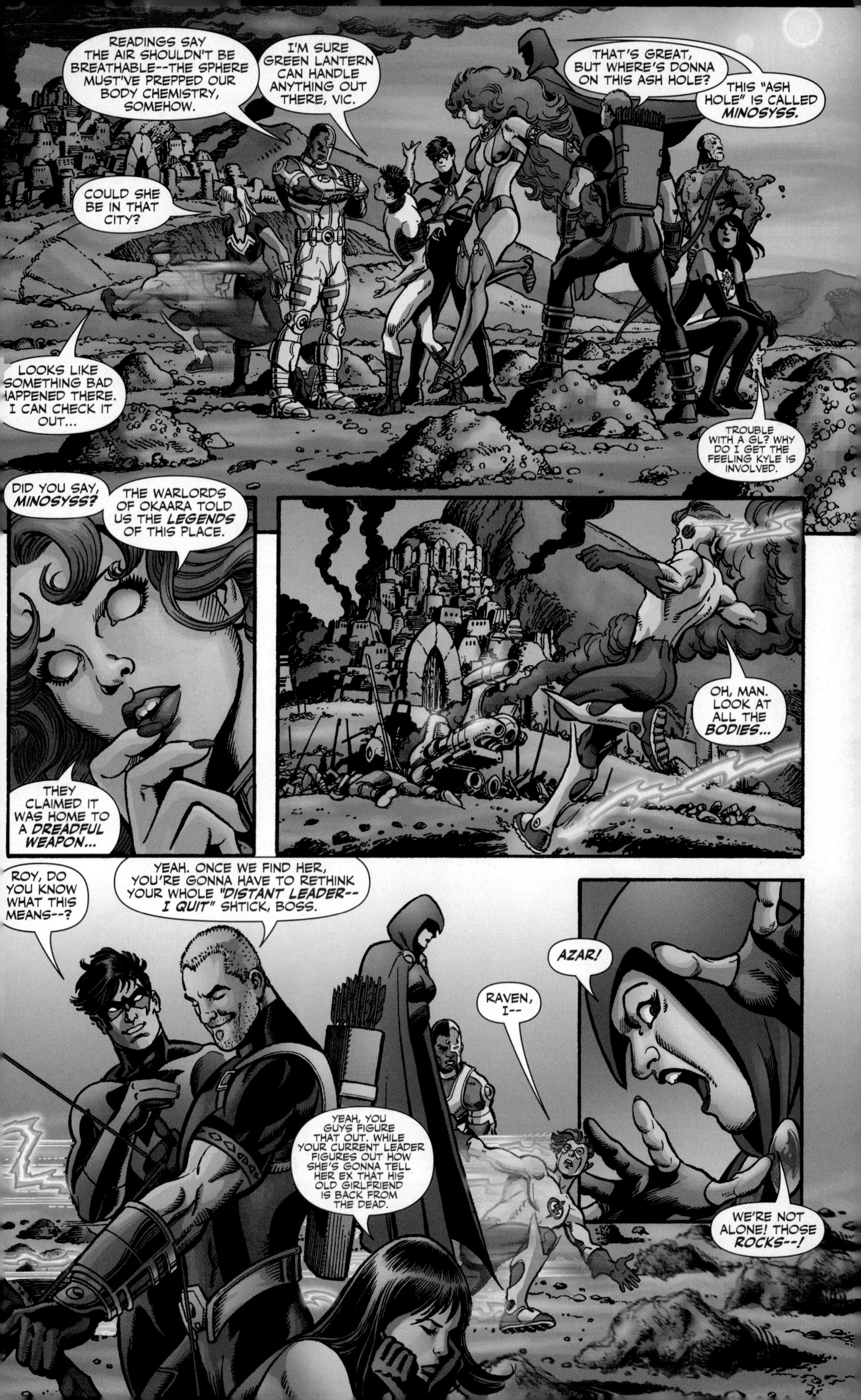
READINGS SAY THE AIR SHOULDN'T BE BREATHABLE--THE SPHERE MUST'VE PREPPED OUR BODY CHEMISTRY, SOMEHOW.
I'M SURE GREEN LANTERN CAN HANDLE ANYTHING OUT THERE, VIC.
THAT'S GREAT, BUT WHERE'S DONNA ON THIS ASH HOLE?
THIS "ASH HOLE" IS CALLED *MINOSYSS.*
COULD SHE BE IN THAT CITY?
LOOKS LIKE SOMETHING BAD HAPPENED THERE. I CAN CHECK IT OUT...
TROUBLE WITH A GL? WHY DO I GET THE FEELING KYLE IS INVOLVED.
DID YOU SAY, *MINOSYSS?*
THE WARLORDS OF OKAARA TOLD US THE *LEGENDS* OF THIS PLACE.
THEY CLAIMED IT WAS HOME TO A *DREADFUL WEAPON...*
OH, MAN. LOOK AT ALL THE *BODIES...*
ROY, DO YOU KNOW WHAT THIS MEANS--?
YEAH. ONCE WE FIND HER, YOU'RE GONNA HAVE TO RETHINK YOUR WHOLE *"DISTANT LEADER-- I QUIT"* SHTICK, BOSS.
YEAH, YOU GUYS FIGURE THAT OUT. WHILE YOUR CURRENT LEADER FIGURES OUT HOW SHE'S GONNA TELL HER EX THAT HIS OLD GIRLFRIEND IS BACK FROM THE DEAD.
RAVEN, I--
AZAR!
WE'RE NOT ALONE! THOSE *ROCKS--!*

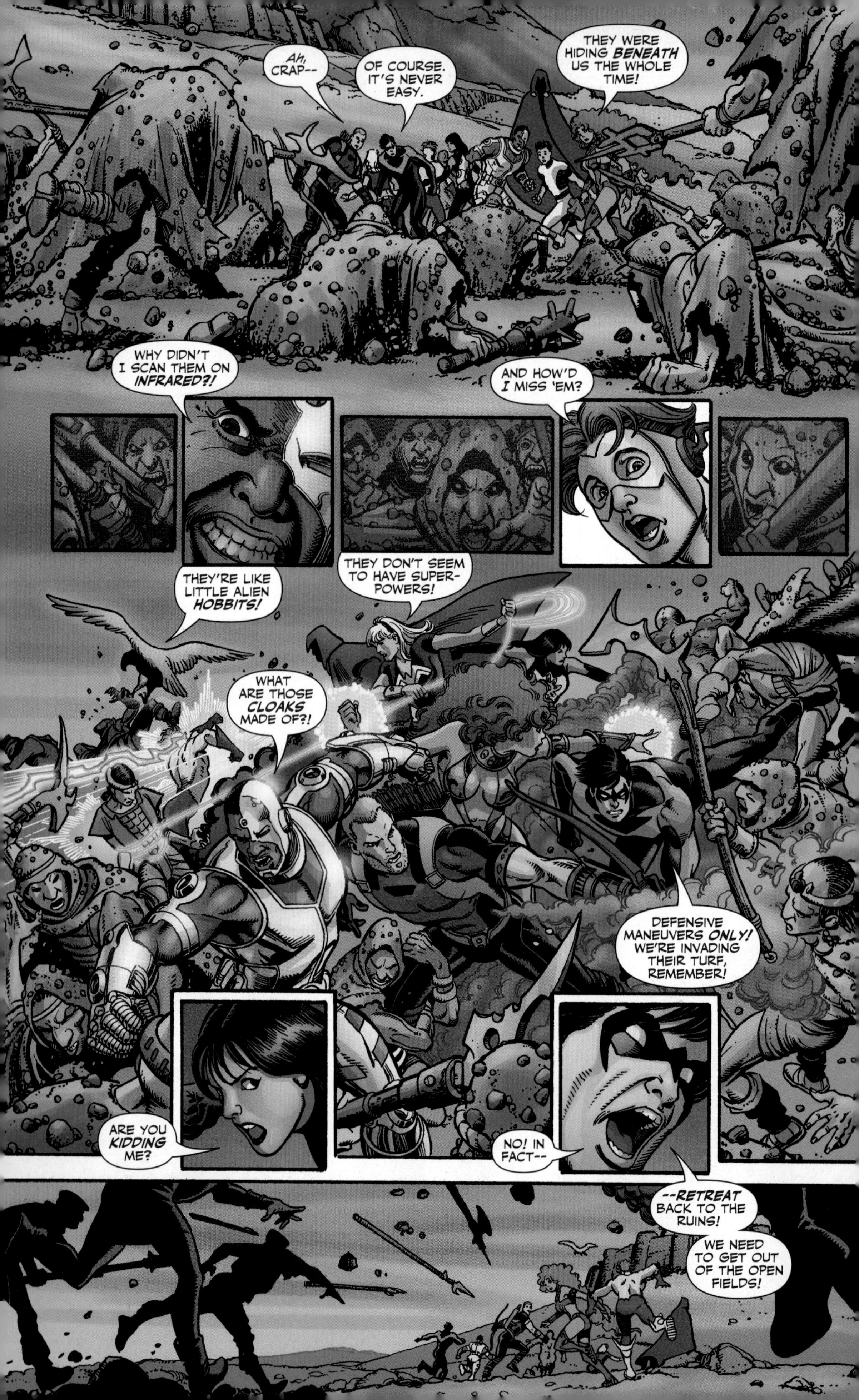

Ah, CRAP--
OF COURSE. IT'S NEVER EASY.
THEY WERE HIDING BENEATH US THE WHOLE TIME!
WHY DIDN'T I SCAN THEM ON INFRARED?!
AND HOW'D I MISS 'EM?
THEY'RE LIKE LITTLE ALIEN HOBBITS!
THEY DON'T SEEM TO HAVE SUPER-POWERS!
WHAT ARE THOSE CLOAKS MADE OF?!
DEFENSIVE MANEUVERS ONLY! WE'RE INVADING THEIR TURF, REMEMBER!
ARE YOU KIDDING ME?
NO! IN FACT--
--RETREAT BACK TO THE RUINS!
WE NEED TO GET OUT OF THE OPEN FIELDS!

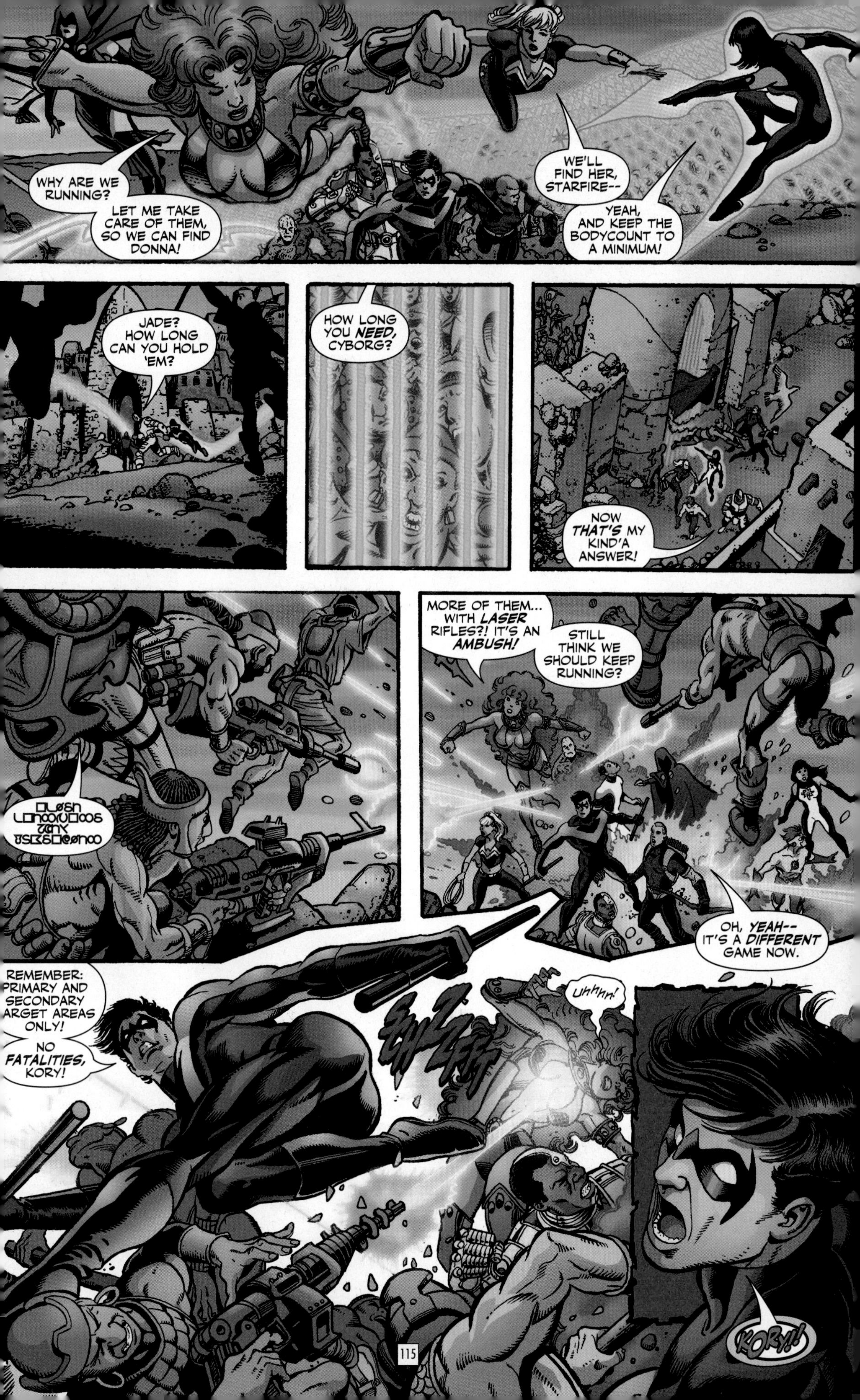
WHY ARE WE RUNNING?
LET ME TAKE CARE OF THEM, SO WE CAN FIND DONNA!
WE'LL FIND HER, STARFIRE--
YEAH, AND KEEP THE BODYCOUNT TO A MINIMUM!
JADE? HOW LONG CAN YOU HOLD 'EM?
HOW LONG YOU NEED, CYBORG?
NOW THAT'S MY KIND'A ANSWER!
MORE OF THEM... WITH LASER RIFLES?! IT'S AN AMBUSH!
STILL THINK WE SHOULD KEEP RUNNING?
OH, YEAH-- IT'S A DIFFERENT GAME NOW.
REMEMBER: PRIMARY AND SECONDARY ARGET AREAS ONLY!
NO FATALITIES, KORY!
Uhhhn!
KORY!!

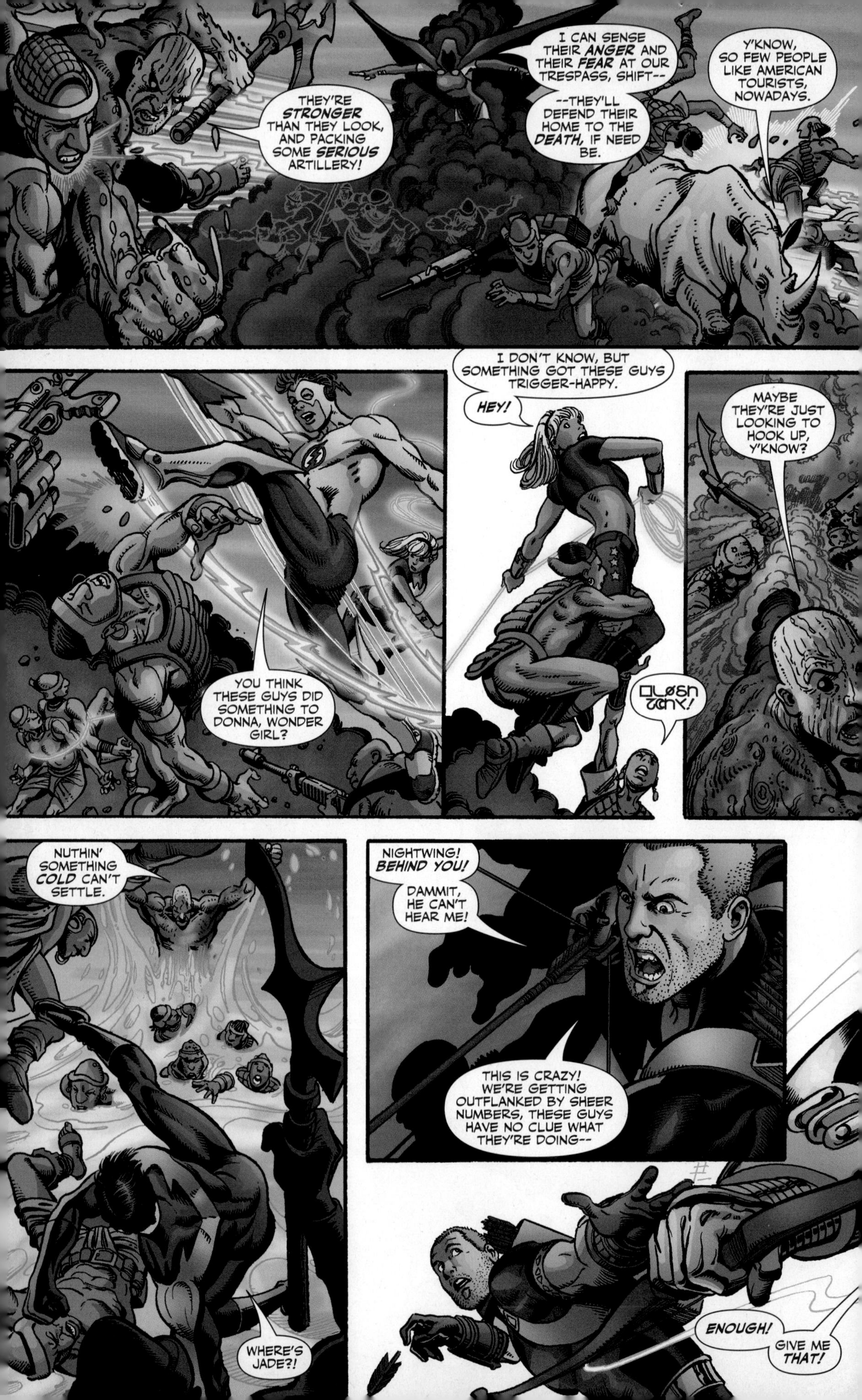
THEY'RE STRONGER THAN THEY LOOK, AND PACKING SOME SERIOUS ARTILLERY!
I CAN SENSE THEIR ANGER AND THEIR FEAR AT OUR TRESPASS, SHIFT--
--THEY'LL DEFEND THEIR HOME TO THE DEATH, IF NEED BE.
Y'KNOW, SO FEW PEOPLE LIKE AMERICAN TOURISTS, NOWADAYS.
YOU THINK THESE GUYS DID SOMETHING TO DONNA, WONDER GIRL?
I DON'T KNOW, BUT SOMETHING GOT THESE GUYS TRIGGER-HAPPY.
HEY!
MAYBE THEY'RE JUST LOOKING TO HOOK UP, Y'KNOW?
NUTHIN' SOMETHING COLD CAN'T SETTLE.
WHERE'S JADE?!
NIGHTWING! BEHIND YOU!
DAMMIT, HE CAN'T HEAR ME!
THIS IS CRAZY! WE'RE GETTING OUTFLANKED BY SHEER NUMBERS, THESE GUYS HAVE NO CLUE WHAT THEY'RE DOING--
ENOUGH!
GIVE ME THAT!

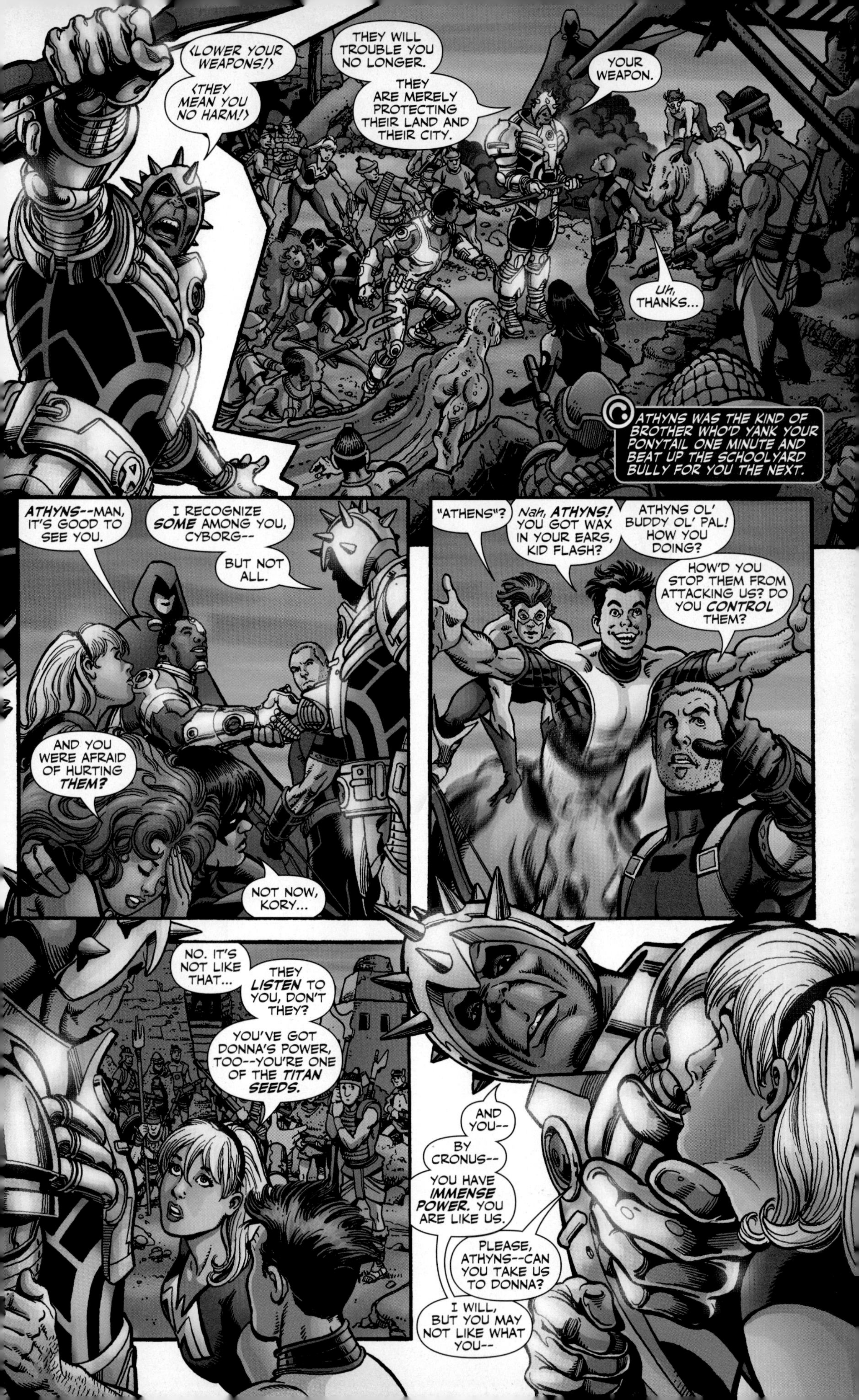

‹LOWER YOUR WEAPONS!›
‹THEY MEAN YOU NO HARM!›
THEY WILL TROUBLE YOU NO LONGER.
THEY ARE MERELY PROTECTING THEIR LAND AND THEIR CITY.
YOUR WEAPON.
Uh, THANKS...
ATHYNS WAS THE KIND OF BROTHER WHO'D YANK YOUR PONYTAIL ONE MINUTE AND BEAT UP THE SCHOOLYARD BULLY FOR YOU THE NEXT.
ATHYNS--MAN, IT'S GOOD TO SEE YOU.
I RECOGNIZE SOME AMONG YOU, CYBORG--
BUT NOT ALL.
AND YOU WERE AFRAID OF HURTING THEM?
NOT NOW, KORY...
"ATHENS"?
Nah, ATHYNS! YOU GOT WAX IN YOUR EARS, KID FLASH?
ATHYNS OL' BUDDY OL' PAL! HOW YOU DOING?
HOW'D YOU STOP THEM FROM ATTACKING US? DO YOU CONTROL THEM?
NO. IT'S NOT LIKE THAT...
THEY LISTEN TO YOU, DON'T THEY?
YOU'VE GOT DONNA'S POWER, TOO--YOU'RE ONE OF THE TITAN SEEDS.
AND YOU--
BY CRONUS--
YOU HAVE IMMENSE POWER. YOU ARE LIKE US.
PLEASE, ATHYNS--CAN YOU TAKE US TO DONNA?
I WILL, BUT YOU MAY NOT LIKE WHAT YOU--

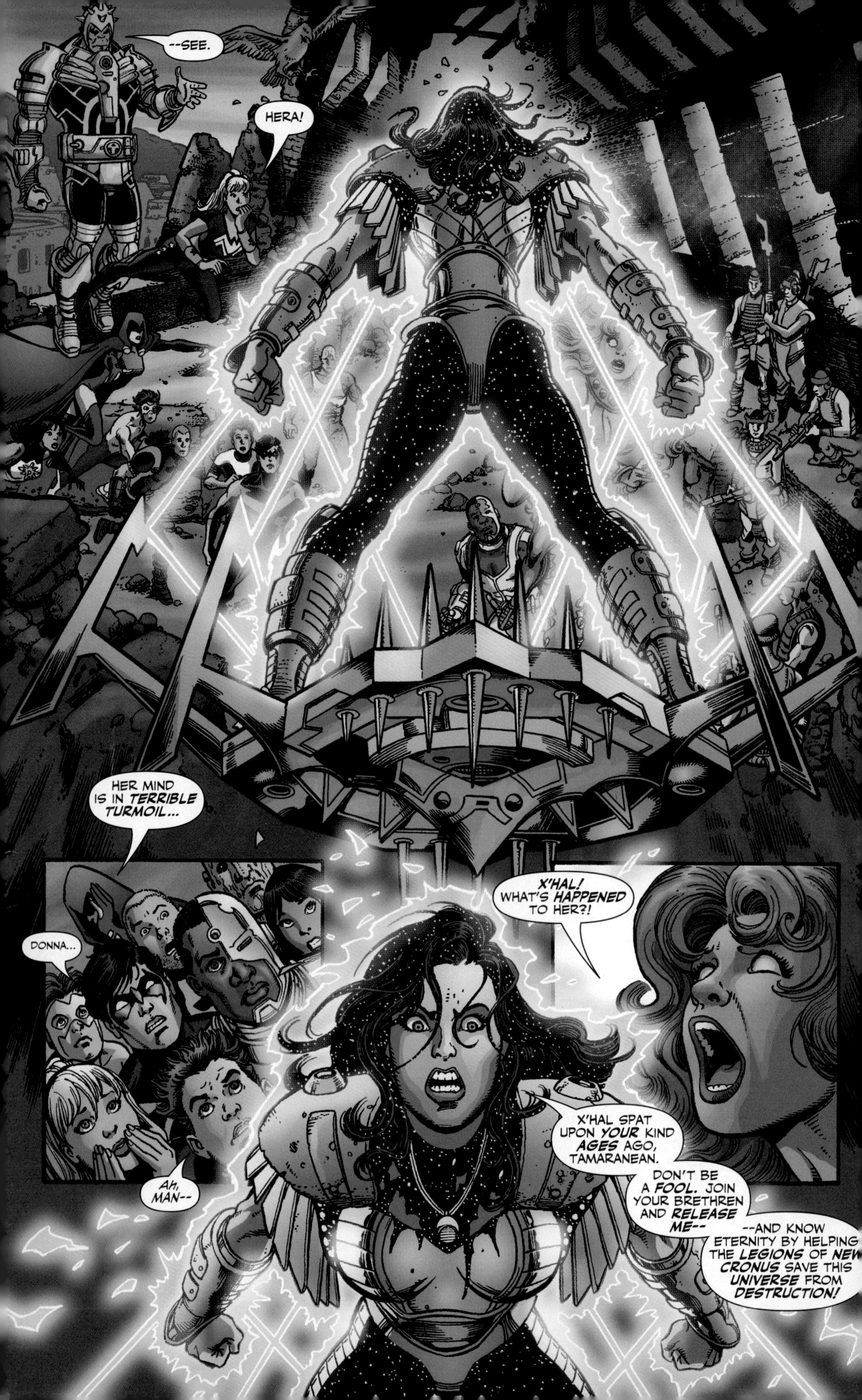
--SEE.
HERA!
HER MIND IS IN *TERRIBLE TURMOIL*...
DONNA...
Ah, MAN--
X'HAL! WHAT'S *HAPPENED* TO HER?!
X'HAL SPAT UPON *YOUR* KIND *AGES* AGO, TAMARANEAN.
DON'T BE A *FOOL*. JOIN YOUR BRETHREN AND *RELEASE ME--*
--AND KNOW ETERNITY BY HELPING THE *LEGIONS* OF *NEW CRONUS* SAVE THIS *UNIVERSE* FROM *DESTRUCTION!*

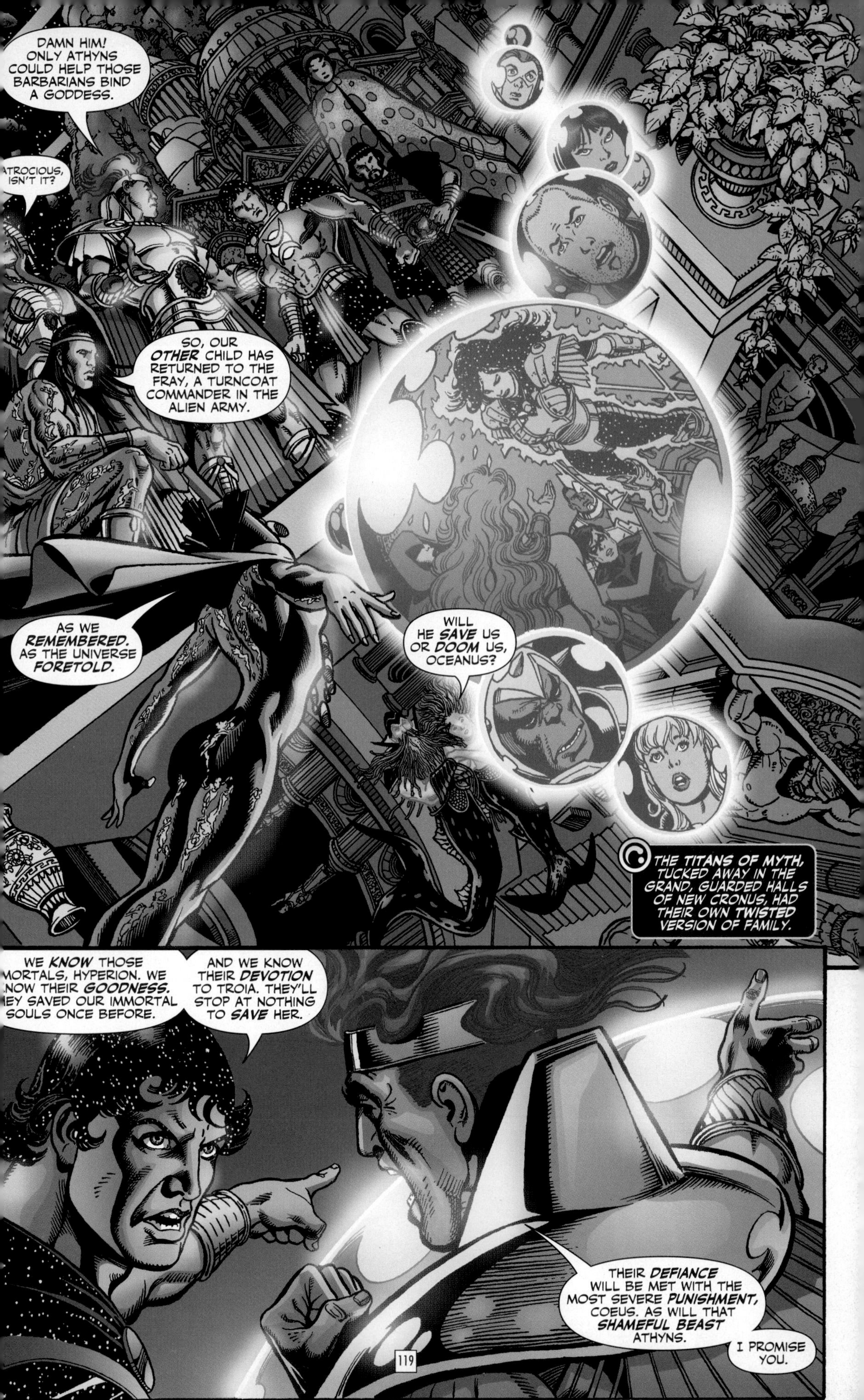
DAMN HIM! ONLY ATHYNS COULD HELP THOSE BARBARIANS BIND A GODDESS.
ATROCIOUS, ISN'T IT?
SO, OUR OTHER CHILD HAS RETURNED TO THE FRAY, A TURNCOAT COMMANDER IN THE ALIEN ARMY.
AS WE REMEMBERED. AS THE UNIVERSE FORETOLD.
WILL HE SAVE US OR DOOM US, OCEANUS?
THE TITANS OF MYTH, TUCKED AWAY IN THE GRAND, GUARDED HALLS OF NEW CRONUS, HAD THEIR OWN TWISTED VERSION OF FAMILY.
WE KNOW THOSE MORTALS, HYPERION. WE KNOW THEIR GOODNESS. THEY SAVED OUR IMMORTAL SOULS ONCE BEFORE.
AND WE KNOW THEIR DEVOTION TO TROIA. THEY'LL STOP AT NOTHING TO SAVE HER.
THEIR DEFIANCE WILL BE MET WITH THE MOST SEVERE PUNISHMENT, COEUS. AS WILL THAT SHAMEFUL BEAST ATHYNS.
I PROMISE YOU.

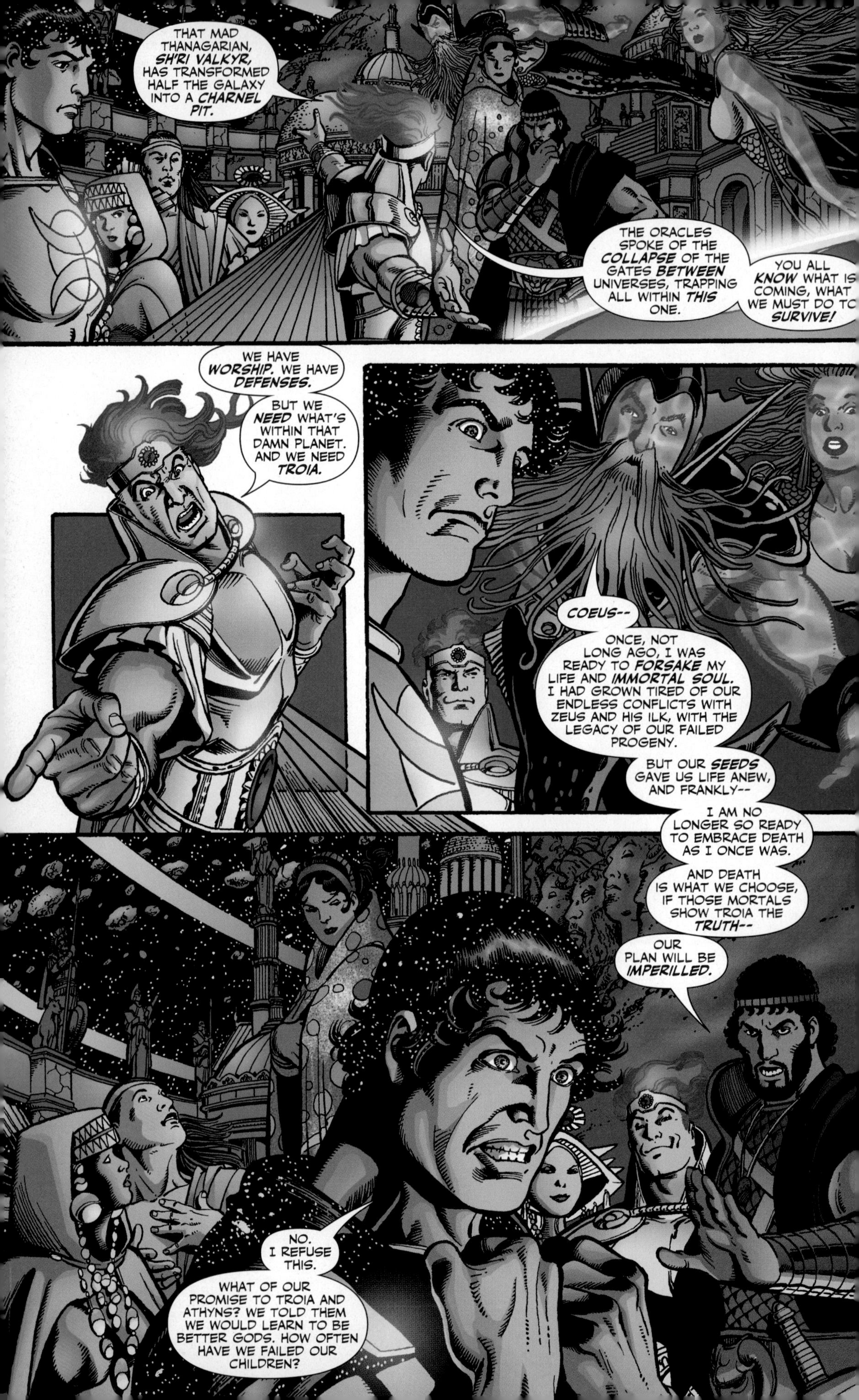
THAT MAD THANAGARIAN, ***SH'RI VALKYR,*** HAS TRANSFORMED HALF THE GALAXY INTO A ***CHARNEL PIT.***
THE ORACLES SPOKE OF THE ***COLLAPSE*** OF THE GATES ***BETWEEN*** UNIVERSES, TRAPPING ALL WITHIN ***THIS*** ONE.
YOU ALL ***KNOW*** WHAT IS COMING, WHAT WE MUST DO TO ***SURVIVE!***
WE HAVE ***WORSHIP.*** WE HAVE ***DEFENSES.***
BUT WE ***NEED*** WHAT'S WITHIN THAT DAMN PLANET. AND WE NEED ***TROIA.***
COEUS--
ONCE, NOT LONG AGO, I WAS READY TO ***FORSAKE*** MY LIFE AND ***IMMORTAL SOUL.*** I HAD GROWN TIRED OF OUR ENDLESS CONFLICTS WITH ZEUS AND HIS ILK, WITH THE LEGACY OF OUR FAILED PROGENY.
BUT OUR ***SEEDS*** GAVE US LIFE ANEW, AND FRANKLY--
I AM NO LONGER SO READY TO EMBRACE DEATH AS I ONCE WAS.
AND DEATH IS WHAT WE CHOOSE, IF THOSE MORTALS SHOW TROIA THE ***TRUTH--***
OUR PLAN WILL BE ***IMPERILLED.***
NO. I REFUSE THIS.
WHAT OF OUR PROMISE TO TROIA AND ATHYNS? WE TOLD THEM WE WOULD LEARN TO BE BETTER GODS. HOW OFTEN HAVE WE FAILED OUR CHILDREN?

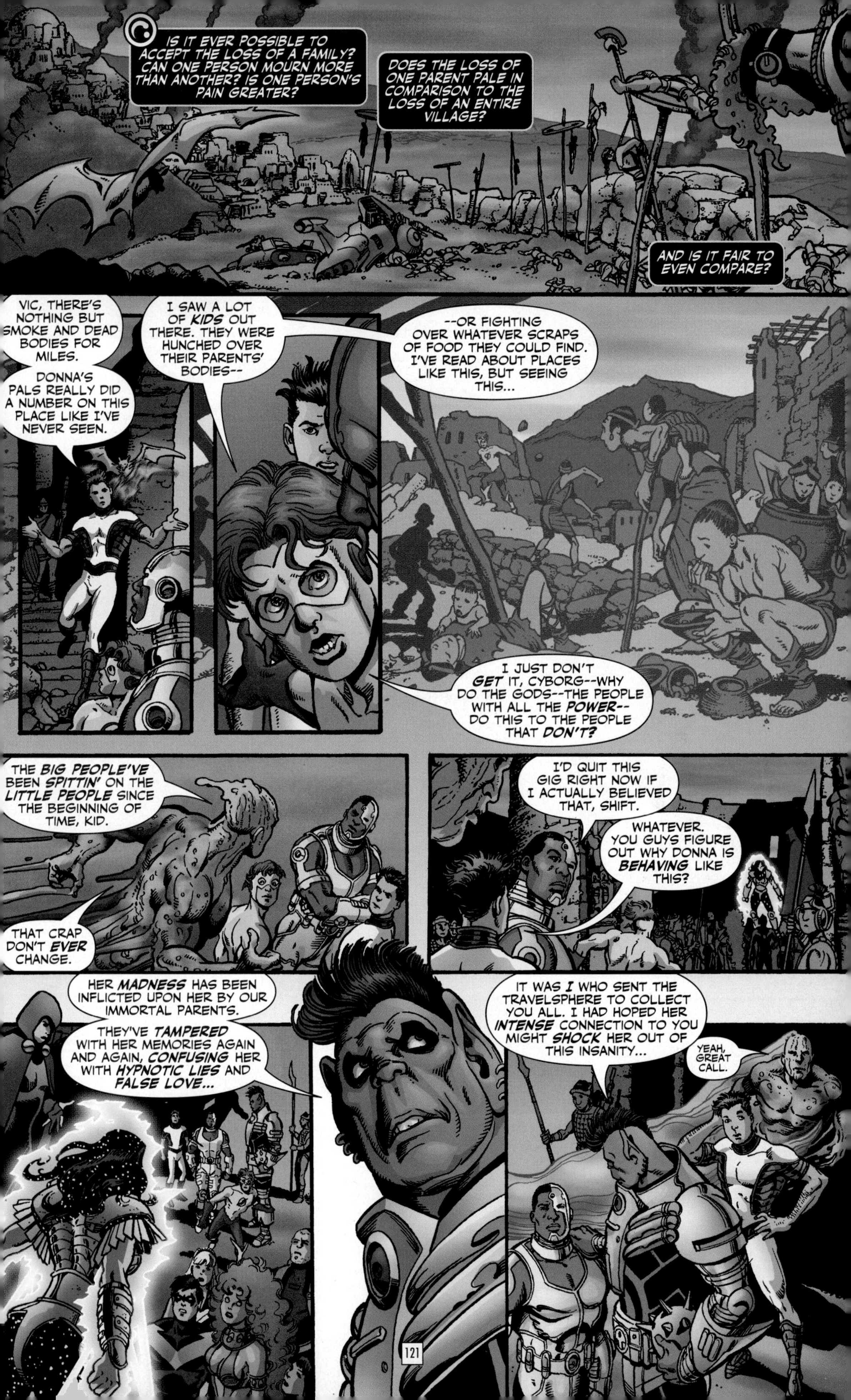

IS IT EVER POSSIBLE TO ACCEPT THE LOSS OF A FAMILY? CAN ONE PERSON MOURN MORE THAN ANOTHER? IS ONE PERSON'S PAIN GREATER?
DOES THE LOSS OF ONE PARENT PALE IN COMPARISON TO THE LOSS OF AN ENTIRE VILLAGE?
AND IS IT FAIR TO EVEN COMPARE?
VIC, THERE'S NOTHING BUT SMOKE AND DEAD BODIES FOR MILES.
DONNA'S PALS REALLY DID A NUMBER ON THIS PLACE LIKE I'VE NEVER SEEN.
I SAW A LOT OF KIDS OUT THERE. THEY WERE HUNCHED OVER THEIR PARENTS' BODIES--
--OR FIGHTING OVER WHATEVER SCRAPS OF FOOD THEY COULD FIND. I'VE READ ABOUT PLACES LIKE THIS, BUT SEEING THIS...
I JUST DON'T GET IT, CYBORG--WHY DO THE GODS--THE PEOPLE WITH ALL THE POWER--DO THIS TO THE PEOPLE THAT DON'T?
THE BIG PEOPLE'VE BEEN SPITTIN' ON THE LITTLE PEOPLE SINCE THE BEGINNING OF TIME, KID.
THAT CRAP DON'T EVER CHANGE.
I'D QUIT THIS GIG RIGHT NOW IF I ACTUALLY BELIEVED THAT, SHIFT.
WHATEVER. YOU GUYS FIGURE OUT WHY DONNA IS BEHAVING LIKE THIS?
HER MADNESS HAS BEEN INFLICTED UPON HER BY OUR IMMORTAL PARENTS.
THEY'VE TAMPERED WITH HER MEMORIES AGAIN AND AGAIN, CONFUSING HER WITH HYPNOTIC LIES AND FALSE LOVE...
IT WAS I WHO SENT THE TRAVELSPHERE TO COLLECT YOU ALL. I HAD HOPED HER INTENSE CONNECTION TO YOU MIGHT SHOCK HER OUT OF THIS INSANITY...
YEAH, GREAT CALL.

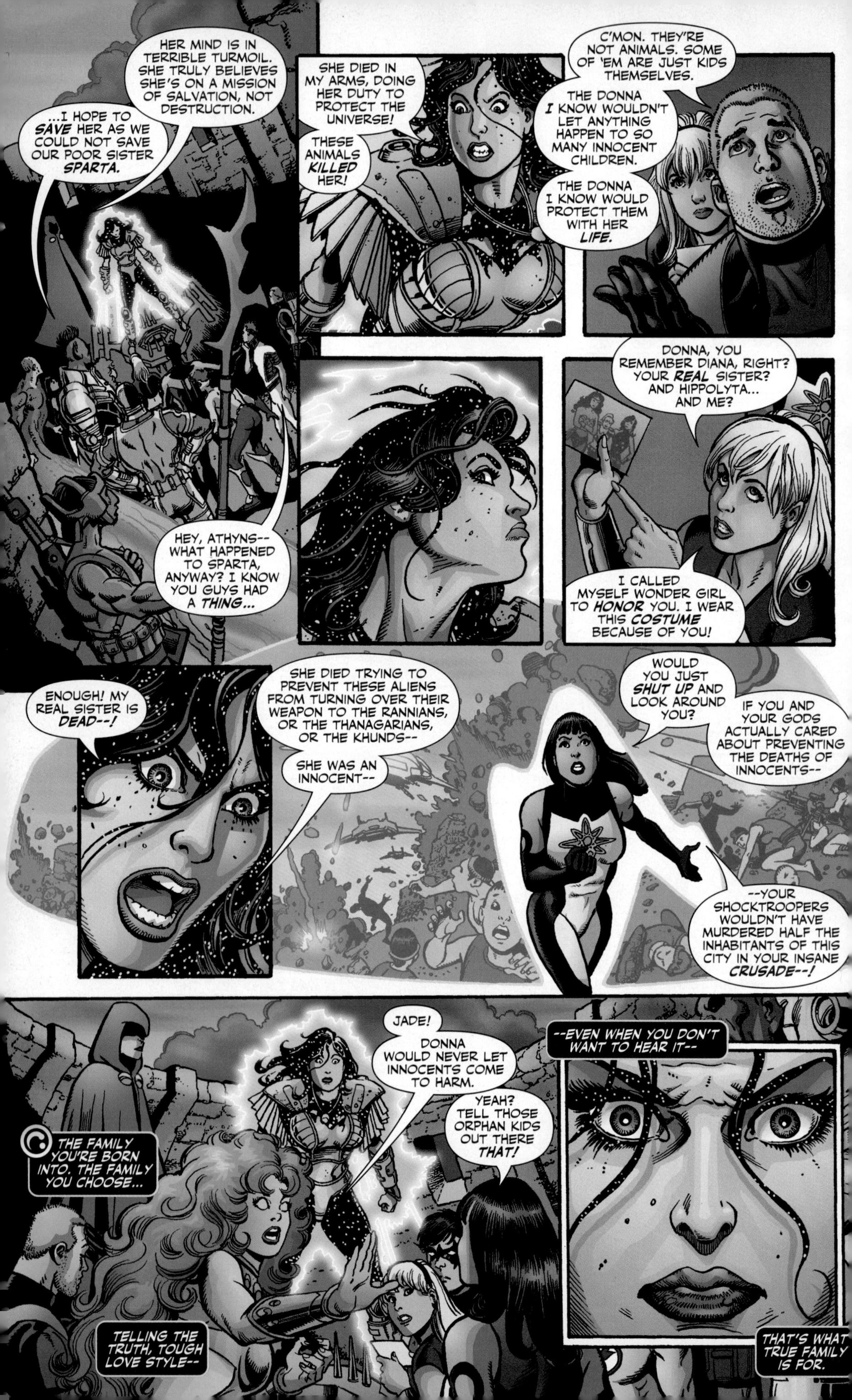
...I HOPE TO SAVE HER AS WE COULD NOT SAVE OUR POOR SISTER SPARTA.
HER MIND IS IN TERRIBLE TURMOIL. SHE TRULY BELIEVES SHE'S ON A MISSION OF SALVATION, NOT DESTRUCTION.
HEY, ATHYNS-- WHAT HAPPENED TO SPARTA, ANYWAY? I KNOW YOU GUYS HAD A THING...
SHE DIED IN MY ARMS, DOING HER DUTY TO PROTECT THE UNIVERSE!
THESE ANIMALS KILLED HER!
C'MON. THEY'RE NOT ANIMALS. SOME OF 'EM ARE JUST KIDS THEMSELVES.
THE DONNA I KNOW WOULDN'T LET ANYTHING HAPPEN TO SO MANY INNOCENT CHILDREN.
THE DONNA I KNOW WOULD PROTECT THEM WITH HER LIFE.
DONNA, YOU REMEMBER DIANA, RIGHT? YOUR REAL SISTER? AND HIPPOLYTA... AND ME?
I CALLED MYSELF WONDER GIRL TO HONOR YOU. I WEAR THIS COSTUME BECAUSE OF YOU!
ENOUGH! MY REAL SISTER IS DEAD--!
SHE DIED TRYING TO PREVENT THESE ALIENS FROM TURNING OVER THEIR WEAPON TO THE RANNIANS, OR THE THANAGARIANS, OR THE KHUNDS--
SHE WAS AN INNOCENT--
WOULD YOU JUST SHUT UP AND LOOK AROUND YOU?
IF YOU AND YOUR GODS ACTUALLY CARED ABOUT PREVENTING THE DEATHS OF INNOCENTS--
--YOUR SHOCKTROOPERS WOULDN'T HAVE MURDERED HALF THE INHABITANTS OF THIS CITY IN YOUR INSANE CRUSADE--!
THE FAMILY YOU'RE BORN INTO. THE FAMILY YOU CHOOSE...
TELLING THE TRUTH, TOUGH LOVE STYLE--
JADE!
DONNA WOULD NEVER LET INNOCENTS COME TO HARM.
YEAH? TELL THOSE ORPHAN KIDS OUT THERE THAT!
--EVEN WHEN YOU DON'T WANT TO HEAR IT--
THAT'S WHAT TRUE FAMILY IS FOR.

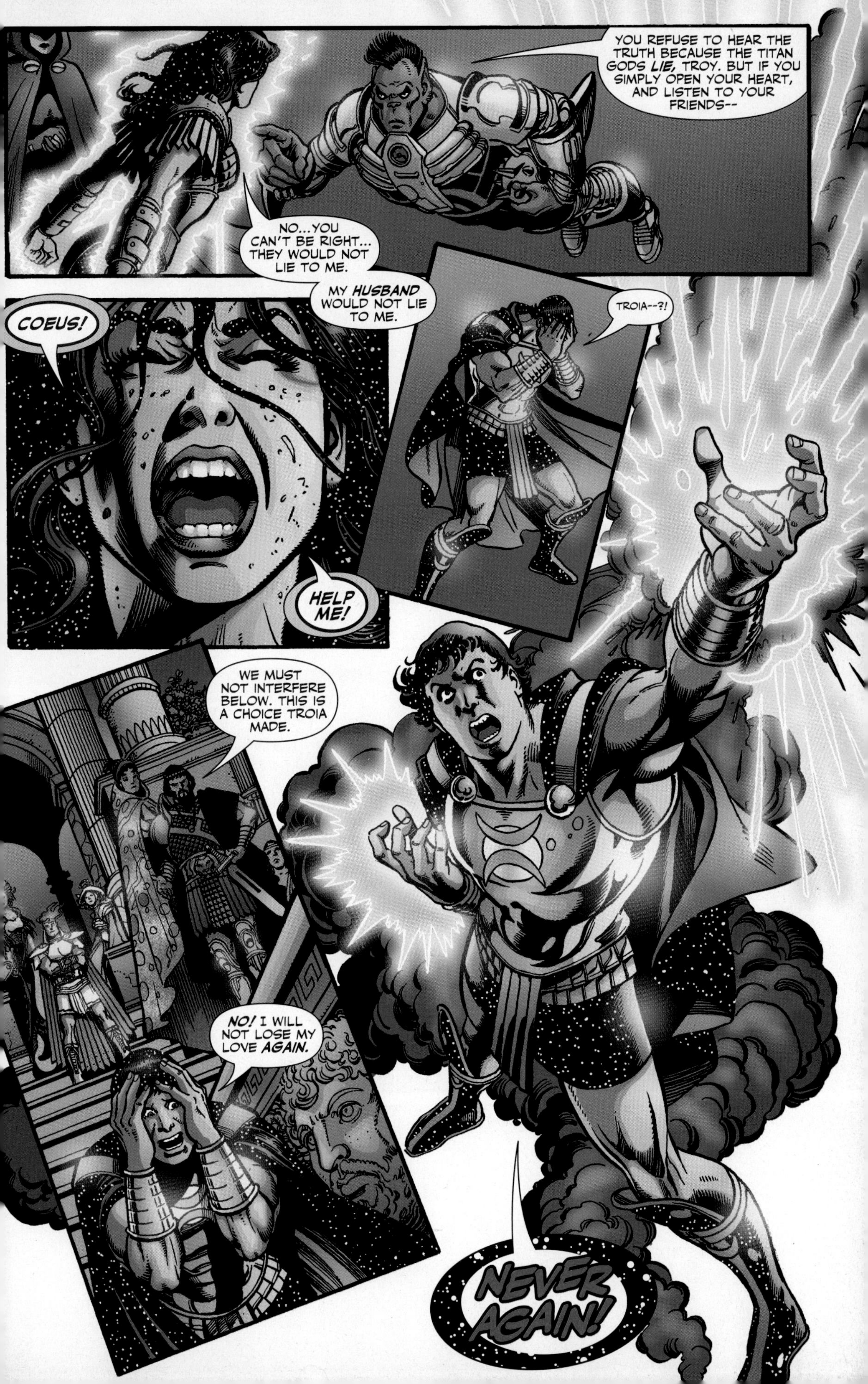
YOU REFUSE TO HEAR THE TRUTH BECAUSE THE TITAN GODS LIE, TROY. BUT IF YOU SIMPLY OPEN YOUR HEART, AND LISTEN TO YOUR FRIENDS--
NO...YOU CAN'T BE RIGHT... THEY WOULD NOT LIE TO ME.
MY HUSBAND WOULD NOT LIE TO ME.
COEUS!
HELP ME!
TROIA--?!
WE MUST NOT INTERFERE BELOW. THIS IS A CHOICE TROIA MADE.
NO! I WILL NOT LOSE MY LOVE AGAIN.
NEVER AGAIN!

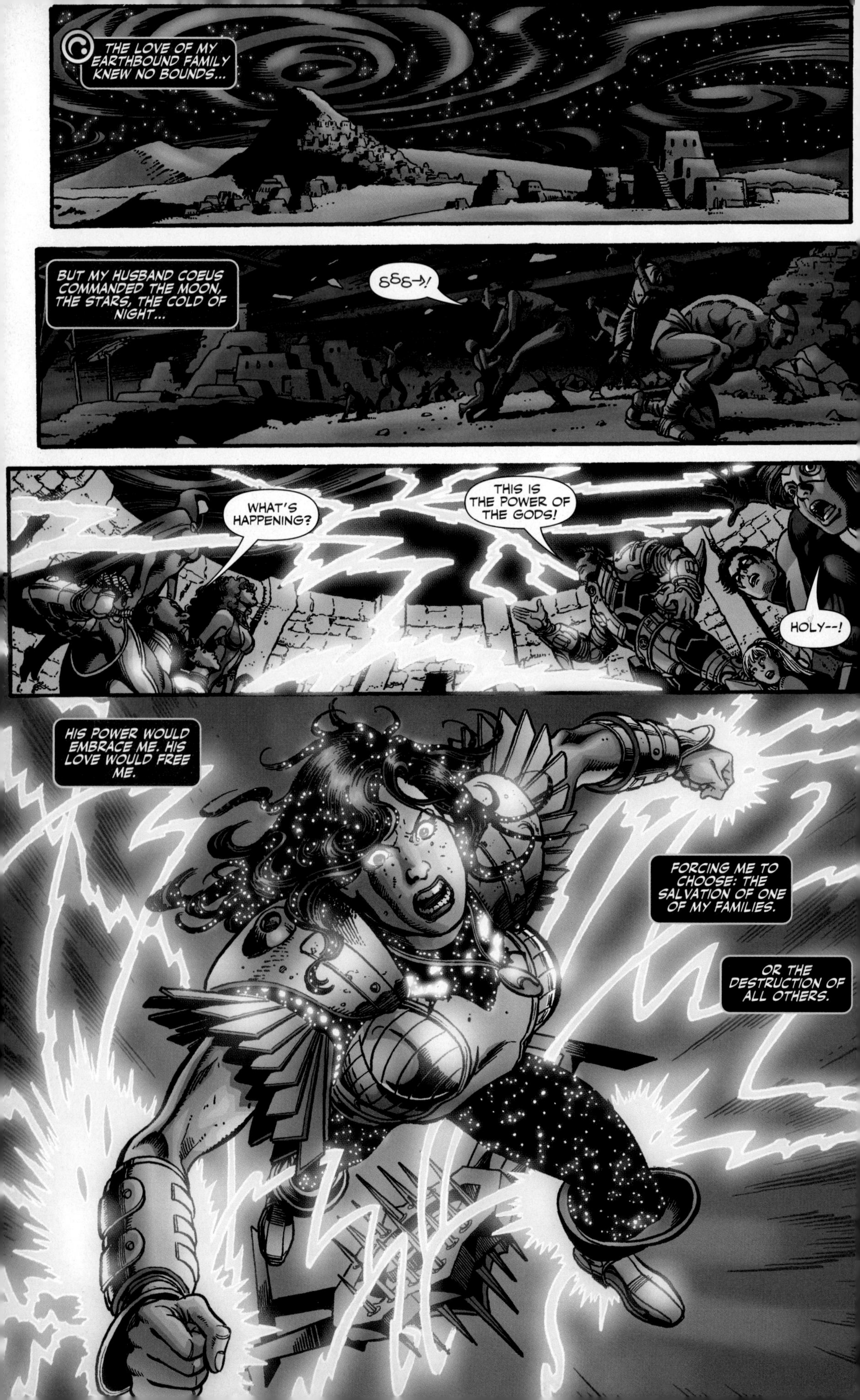
THE LOVE OF MY EARTHBOUND FAMILY KNEW NO BOUNDS...
BUT MY HUSBAND COEUS COMMANDED THE MOON, THE STARS, THE COLD OF NIGHT...
WHAT'S HAPPENING?
THIS IS THE POWER OF THE GODS!
HOLY--!
HIS POWER WOULD EMBRACE ME. HIS LOVE WOULD FREE ME.
FORCING ME TO CHOOSE: THE SALVATION OF ONE OF MY FAMILIES.
OR THE DESTRUCTION OF ALL OTHERS.

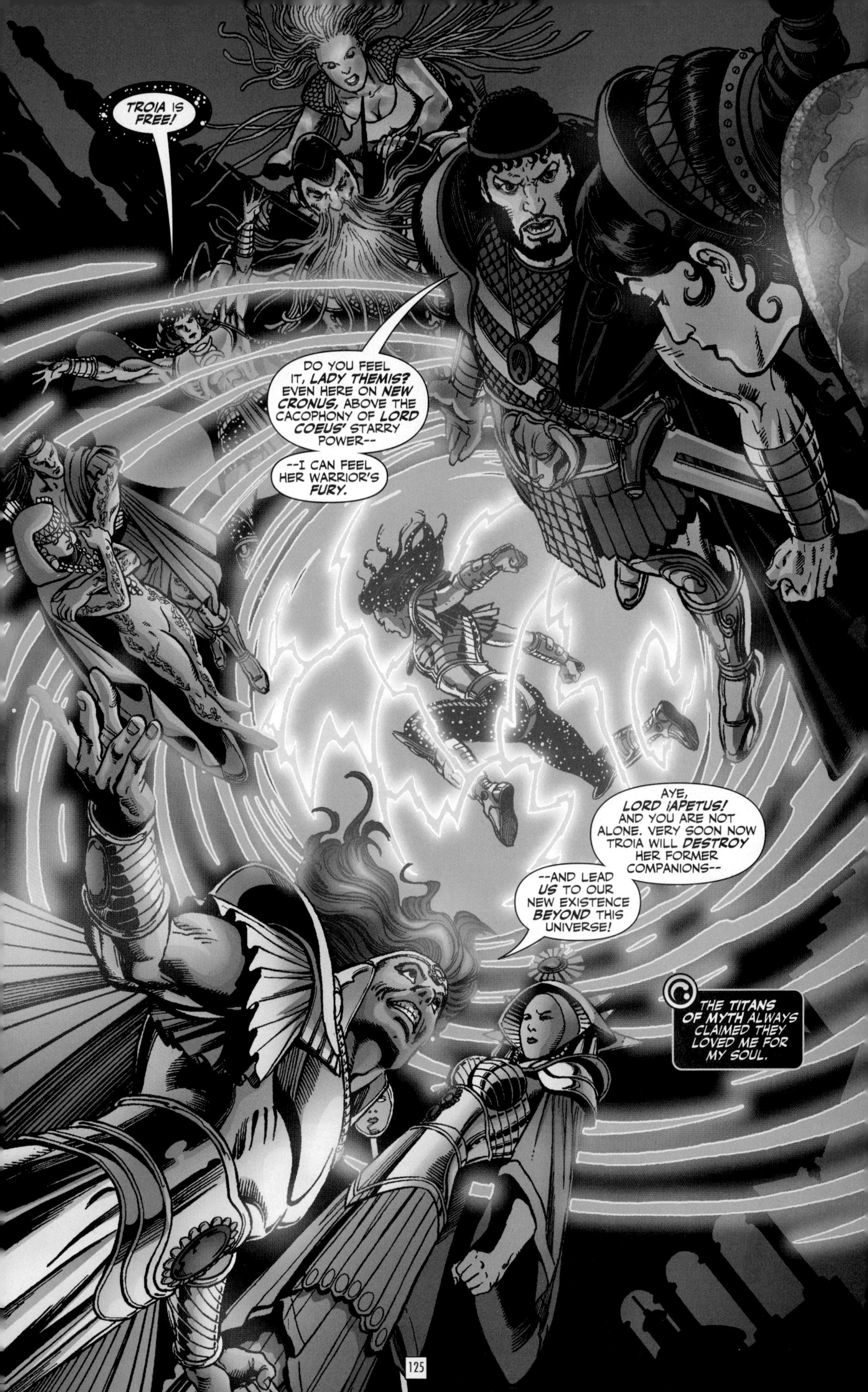
TROIA IS FREE!
DO YOU FEEL IT, LADY THEMIS? EVEN HERE ON NEW CRONUS, ABOVE THE CACOPHONY OF LORD COEUS' STARRY POWER--
--I CAN FEEL HER WARRIOR'S FURY.
AYE, LORD IAPETUS! AND YOU ARE NOT ALONE. VERY SOON NOW TROIA WILL DESTROY HER FORMER COMPANIONS--
--AND LEAD US TO OUR NEW EXISTENCE BEYOND THIS UNIVERSE!
THE TITANS OF MYTH ALWAYS CLAIMED THEY LOVED ME FOR MY SOUL.

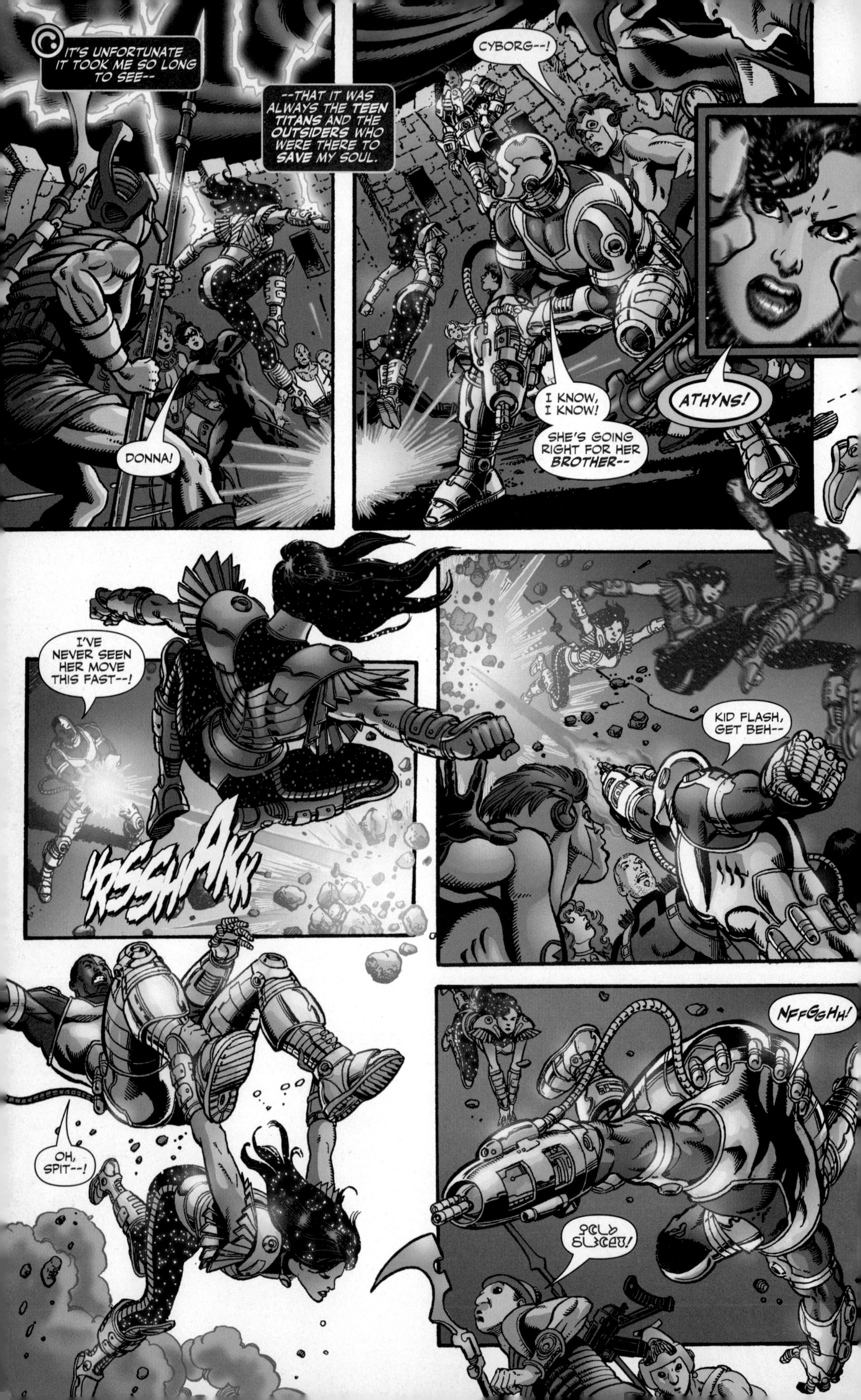

IT'S UNFORTUNATE IT TOOK ME SO LONG TO SEE--
--THAT IT WAS ALWAYS THE TEEN TITANS AND THE OUTSIDERS WHO WERE THERE TO SAVE MY SOUL.
DONNA!
CYBORG--!
I KNOW, I KNOW!
SHE'S GOING RIGHT FOR HER BROTHER--
ATHYNS!
I'VE NEVER SEEN HER MOVE THIS FAST--!
VRSSHAKK
KID FLASH, GET BEH--
OH, SPIT--!
NFFGGHH!

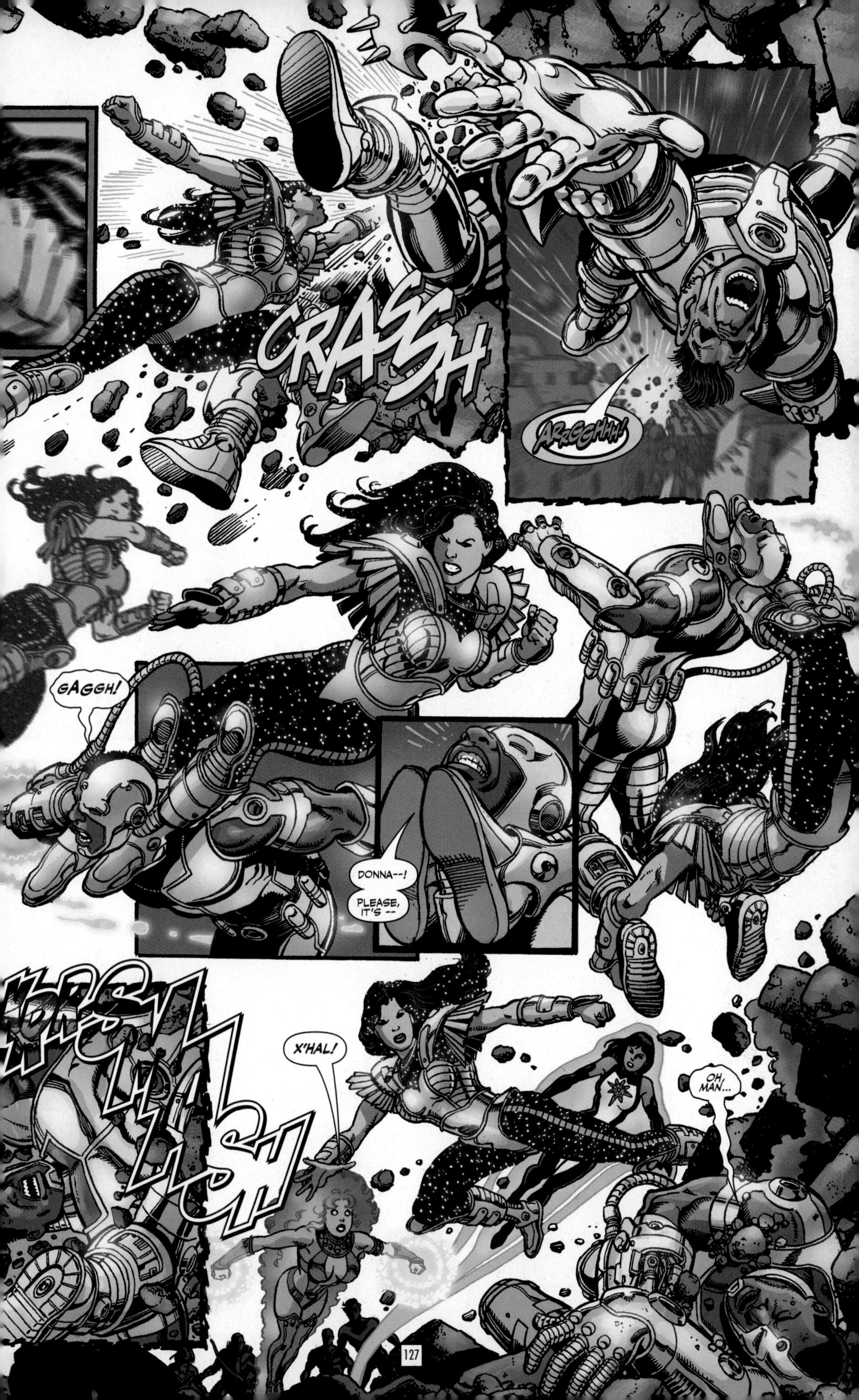
CRASH
ARRGGHHH!
GAGGH!
DONNA--!
PLEASE, IT'S --
X'HAL!
OH, MAN...

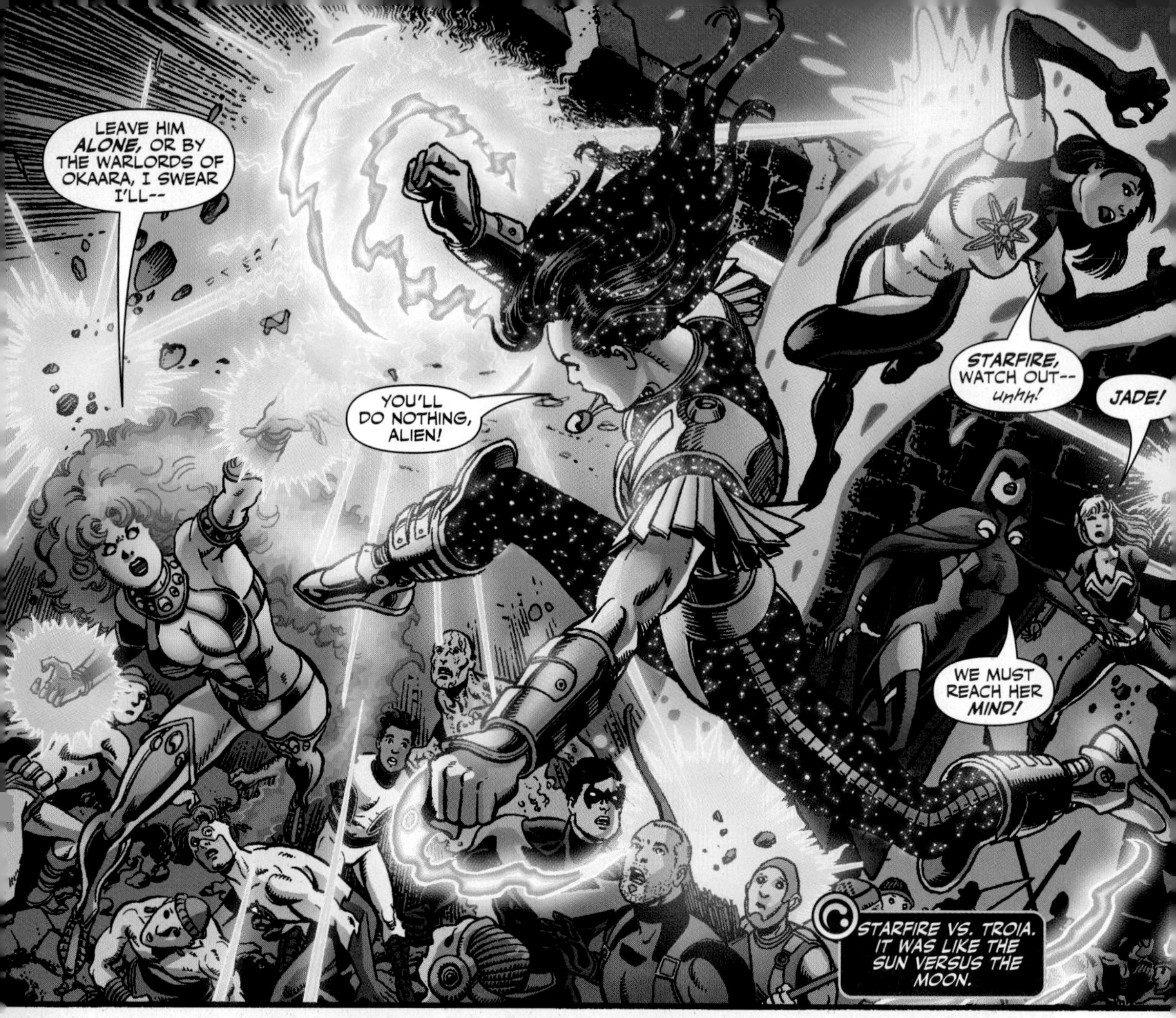
LEAVE HIM ALONE, OR BY THE WARLORDS OF OKAARA, I SWEAR I'LL--
YOU'LL DO NOTHING, ALIEN!
STARFIRE, WATCH OUT-- unhh!
JADE!
WE MUST REACH HER MIND!
STARFIRE VS. TROIA. IT WAS LIKE THE SUN VERSUS THE MOON.

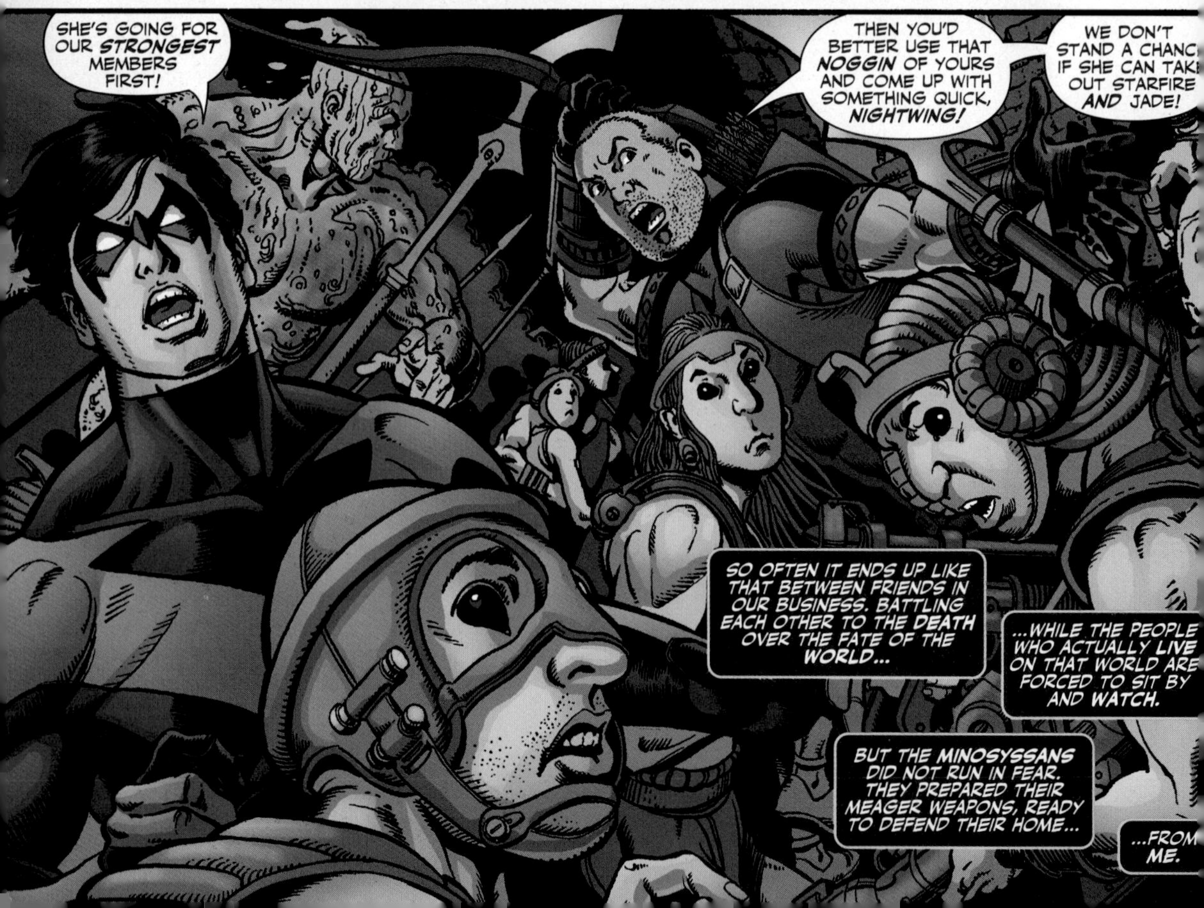
SHE'S GOING FOR OUR STRONGEST MEMBERS FIRST!
THEN YOU'D BETTER USE THAT NOGGIN OF YOURS AND COME UP WITH SOMETHING QUICK, NIGHTWING!
WE DON'T STAND A CHANC IF SHE CAN TAK OUT STARFIRE AND JADE!
SO OFTEN IT ENDS UP LIKE THAT BETWEEN FRIENDS IN OUR BUSINESS. BATTLING EACH OTHER TO THE DEATH OVER THE FATE OF THE WORLD...
...WHILE THE PEOPLE WHO ACTUALLY LIVE ON THAT WORLD ARE FORCED TO SIT BY AND WATCH.
BUT THE MINOSYSSANS DID NOT RUN IN FEAR. THEY PREPARED THEIR MEAGER WEAPONS, READY TO DEFEND THEIR HOME...
...FROM ME.

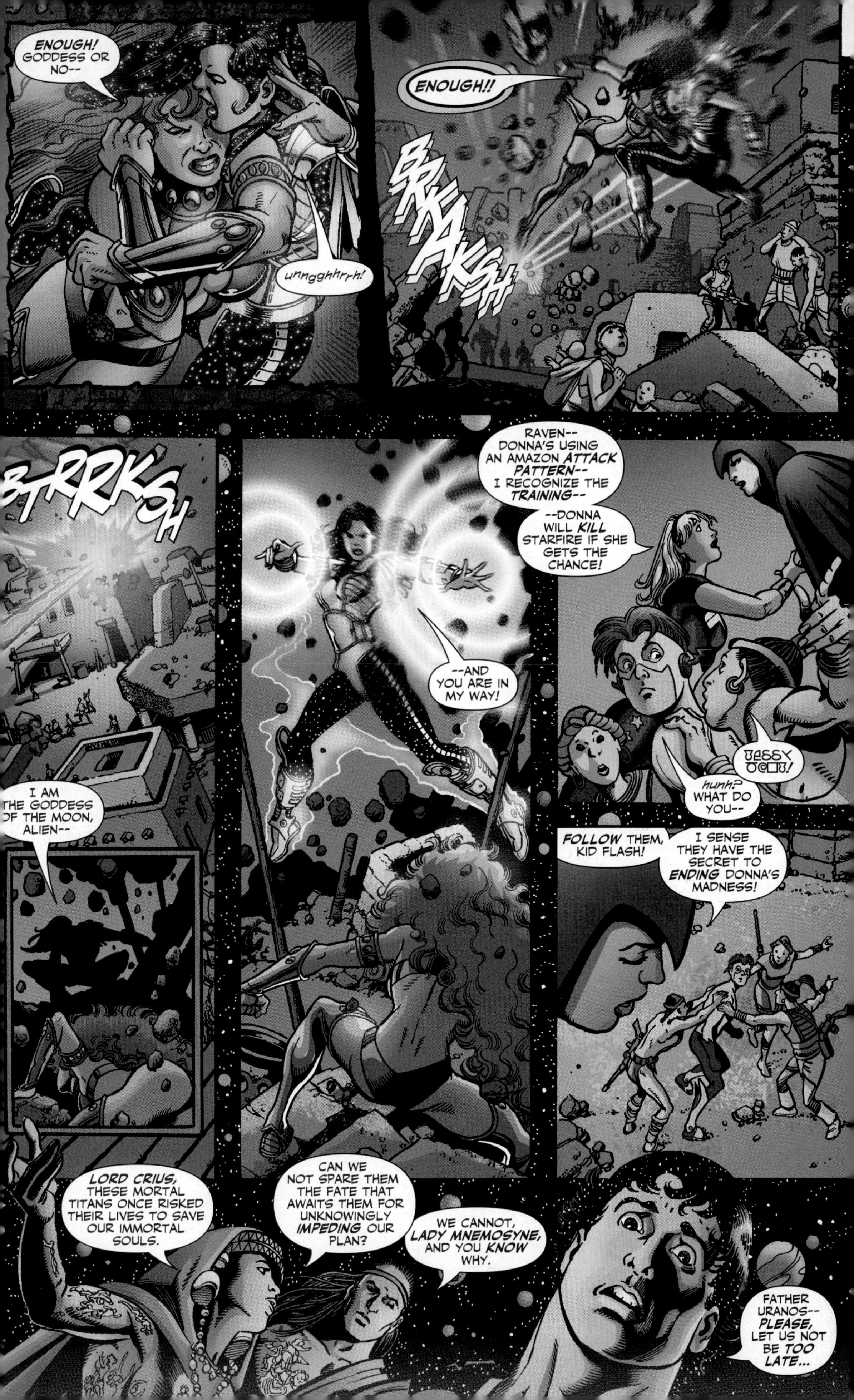
ENOUGH! GODDESS OR NO--
unngghhrrh!
ENOUGH!!
BRKAKSH
BTRRKSH
I AM THE GODDESS OF THE MOON, ALIEN--
--AND YOU ARE IN MY WAY!
RAVEN-- DONNA'S USING AN AMAZON ATTACK PATTERN-- I RECOGNIZE THE TRAINING--
--DONNA WILL KILL STARFIRE IF SHE GETS THE CHANCE!
hunh? WHAT DO YOU--
FOLLOW THEM, KID FLASH!
I SENSE THEY HAVE THE SECRET TO ENDING DONNA'S MADNESS!
LORD CRIUS, THESE MORTAL TITANS ONCE RISKED THEIR LIVES TO SAVE OUR IMMORTAL SOULS.
CAN WE NOT SPARE THEM THE FATE THAT AWAITS THEM FOR UNKNOWINGLY IMPEDING OUR PLAN?
WE CANNOT, LADY MNEMOSYNE, AND YOU KNOW WHY.
FATHER URANOS-- PLEASE, LET US NOT BE TOO LATE...

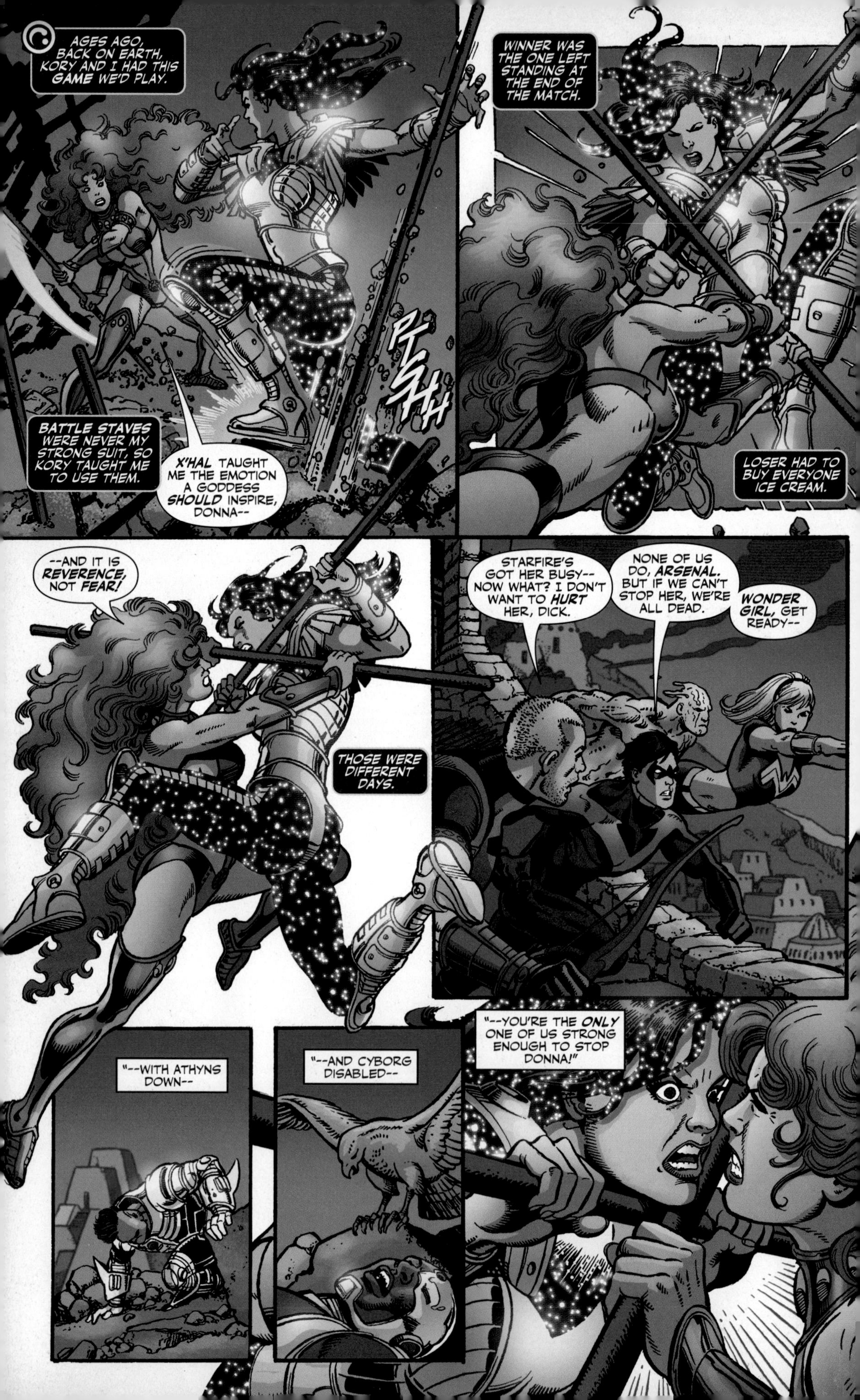
AGES AGO, BACK ON EARTH, KORY AND I HAD THIS GAME WE'D PLAY.
BATTLE STAVES WERE NEVER MY STRONG SUIT, SO KORY TAUGHT ME TO USE THEM.
X'HAL TAUGHT ME THE EMOTION A GODDESS SHOULD INSPIRE, DONNA--
PTSHH
WINNER WAS THE ONE LEFT STANDING AT THE END OF THE MATCH.
LOSER HAD TO BUY EVERYONE ICE CREAM.
--AND IT IS REVERENCE, NOT FEAR!
THOSE WERE DIFFERENT DAYS.
STARFIRE'S GOT HER BUSY-- NOW WHAT? I DON'T WANT TO HURT HER, DICK.
NONE OF US DO, ARSENAL. BUT IF WE CAN'T STOP HER, WE'RE ALL DEAD.
WONDER GIRL, GET READY--
"--WITH ATHYNS DOWN--
"--AND CYBORG DISABLED--
"--YOU'RE THE ONLY ONE OF US STRONG ENOUGH TO STOP DONNA!"

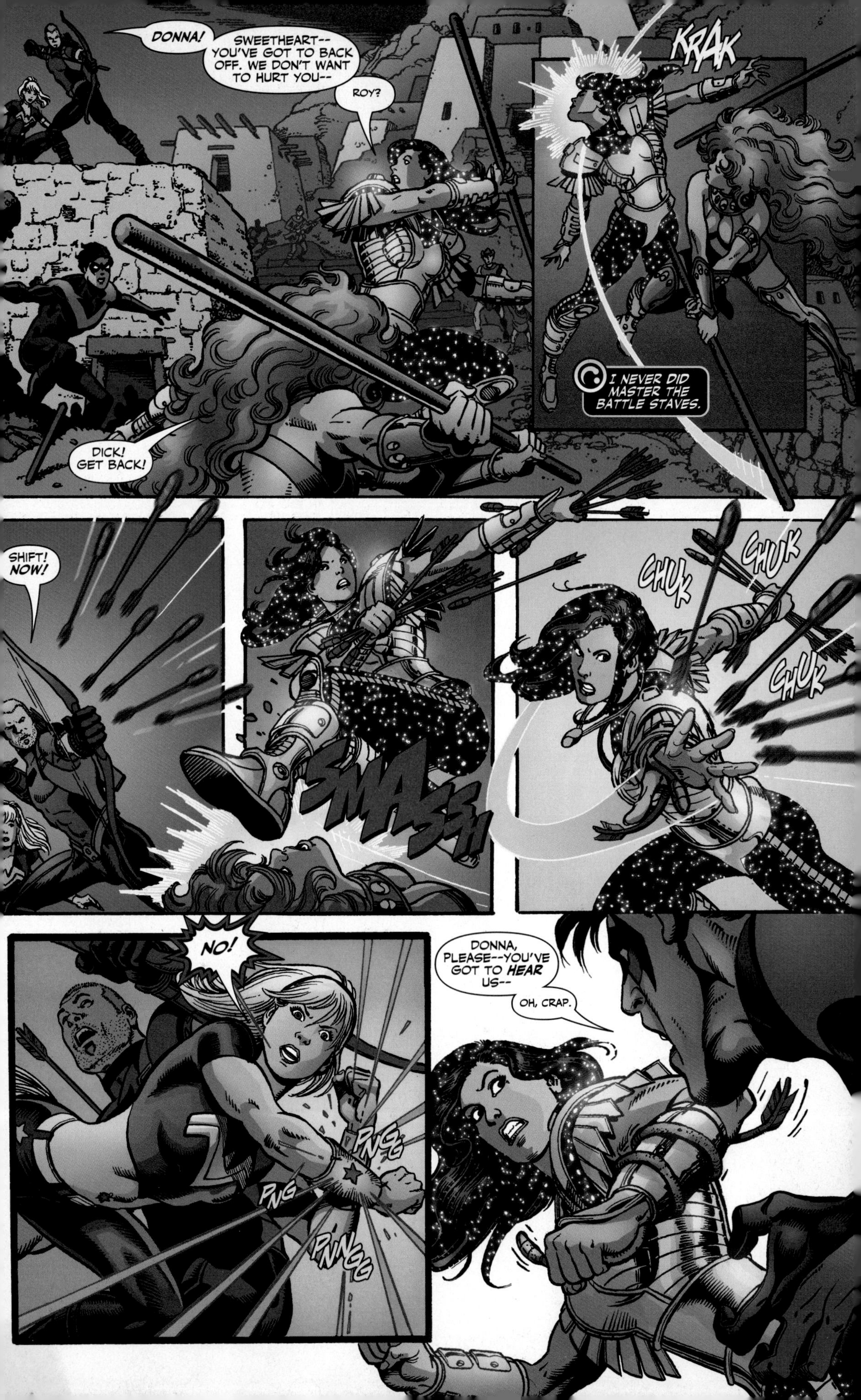
DONNA!
SWEETHEART--YOU'VE GOT TO BACK OFF. WE DON'T WANT TO HURT YOU--
ROY?
KRAK
I NEVER DID MASTER THE BATTLE STAVES.
DICK! GET BACK!
SHIFT! NOW!
SMASSH
CHUK
CHUK
CHUK
NO!
PNGG
PNG
PNNGG
DONNA, PLEASE--YOU'VE GOT TO HEAR US--
OH, CRAP.

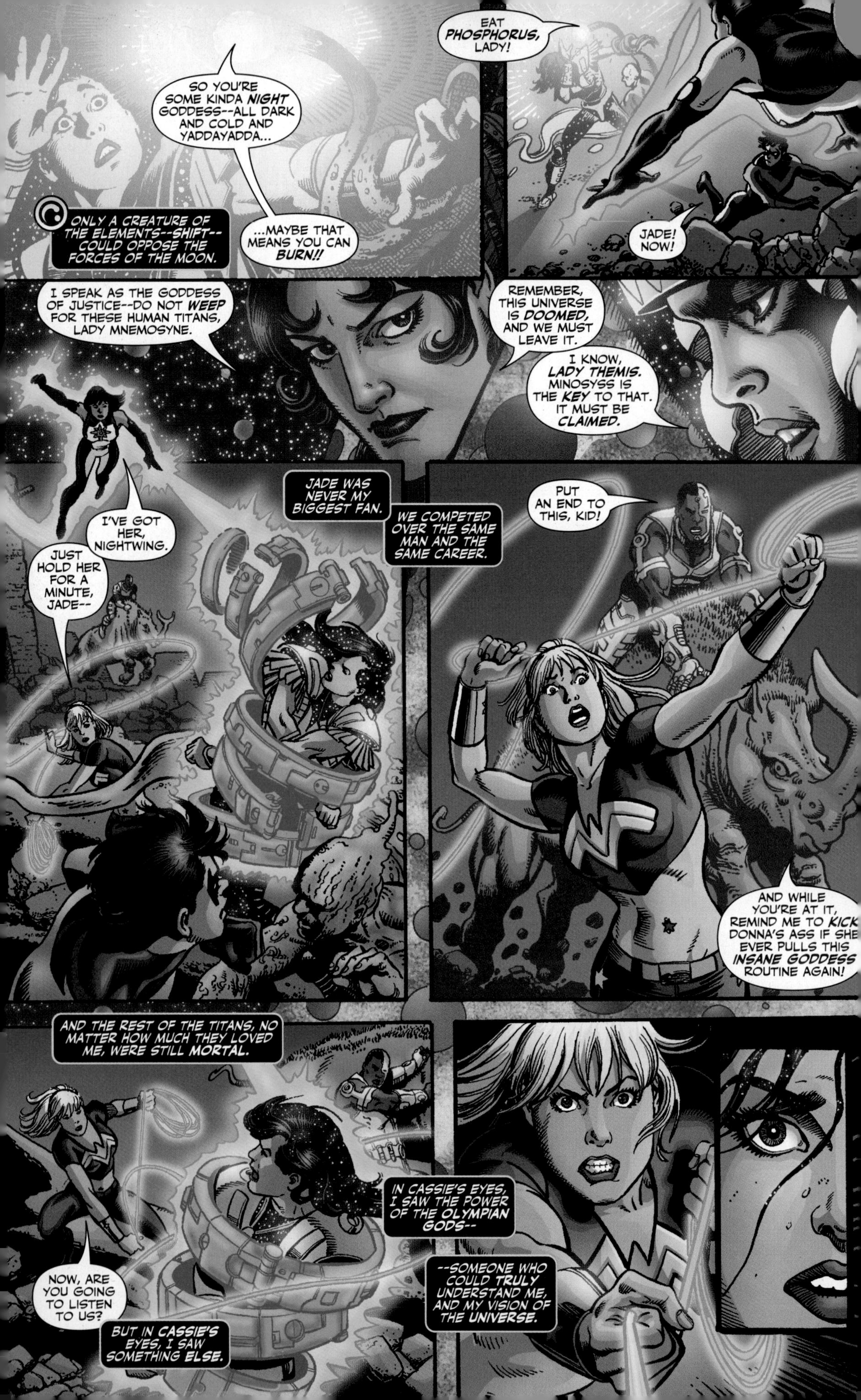
SO YOU'RE SOME KINDA NIGHT GODDESS--ALL DARK AND COLD AND YADDAYADDA...
ONLY A CREATURE OF THE ELEMENTS--SHIFT--COULD OPPOSE THE FORCES OF THE MOON.
...MAYBE THAT MEANS YOU CAN BURN!!
EAT PHOSPHORUS, LADY!
JADE! NOW!
I SPEAK AS THE GODDESS OF JUSTICE--DO NOT WEEP FOR THESE HUMAN TITANS, LADY MNEMOSYNE.
REMEMBER, THIS UNIVERSE IS DOOMED, AND WE MUST LEAVE IT.
I KNOW, LADY THEMIS. MINOSYSS IS THE KEY TO THAT. IT MUST BE CLAIMED.
JADE WAS NEVER MY BIGGEST FAN.
WE COMPETED OVER THE SAME MAN AND THE SAME CAREER.
I'VE GOT HER, NIGHTWING.
JUST HOLD HER FOR A MINUTE, JADE--
PUT AN END TO THIS, KID!
AND WHILE YOU'RE AT IT, REMIND ME TO KICK DONNA'S ASS IF SHE EVER PULLS THIS INSANE GODDESS ROUTINE AGAIN!
AND THE REST OF THE TITANS, NO MATTER HOW MUCH THEY LOVED ME, WERE STILL MORTAL.
IN CASSIE'S EYES, I SAW THE POWER OF THE OLYMPIAN GODS--
NOW, ARE YOU GOING TO LISTEN TO US?
BUT IN CASSIE'S EYES, I SAW SOMETHING ELSE.
--SOMEONE WHO COULD TRULY UNDERSTAND ME, AND MY VISION OF THE UNIVERSE.

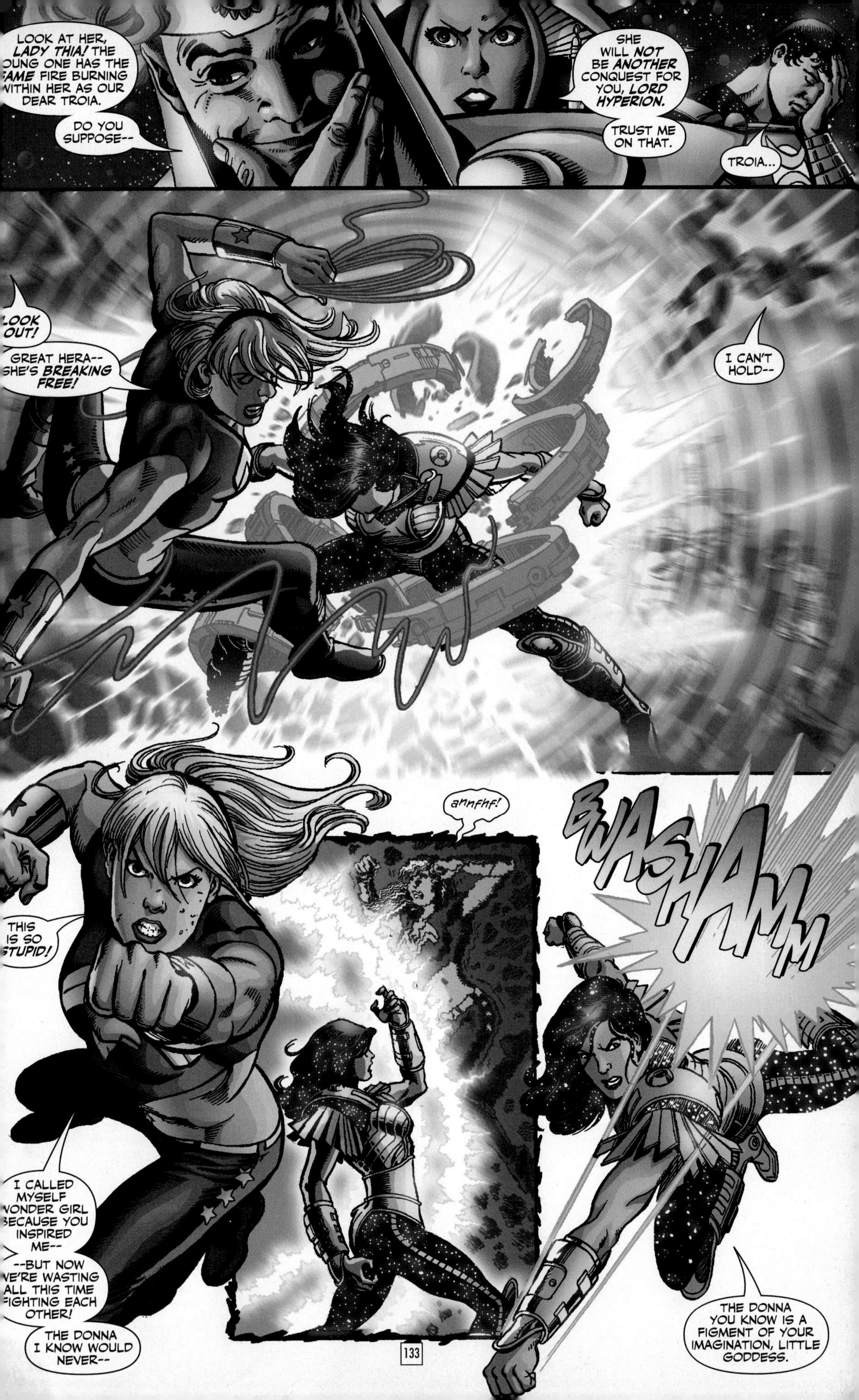

LOOK AT HER, LADY THIA! THE YOUNG ONE HAS THE SAME FIRE BURNING WITHIN HER AS OUR DEAR TROIA.
DO YOU SUPPOSE--
SHE WILL NOT BE ANOTHER CONQUEST FOR YOU, LORD HYPERION.
TRUST ME ON THAT.
TROIA...
LOOK OUT!
GREAT HERA-- SHE'S BREAKING FREE!
I CAN'T HOLD--
THIS IS SO STUPID!
annfhf!
BWASHAMM
I CALLED MYSELF WONDER GIRL BECAUSE YOU INSPIRED ME--
--BUT NOW WE'RE WASTING ALL THIS TIME FIGHTING EACH OTHER!
THE DONNA I KNOW WOULD NEVER--
THE DONNA YOU KNOW IS A FIGMENT OF YOUR IMAGINATION, LITTLE GODDESS.

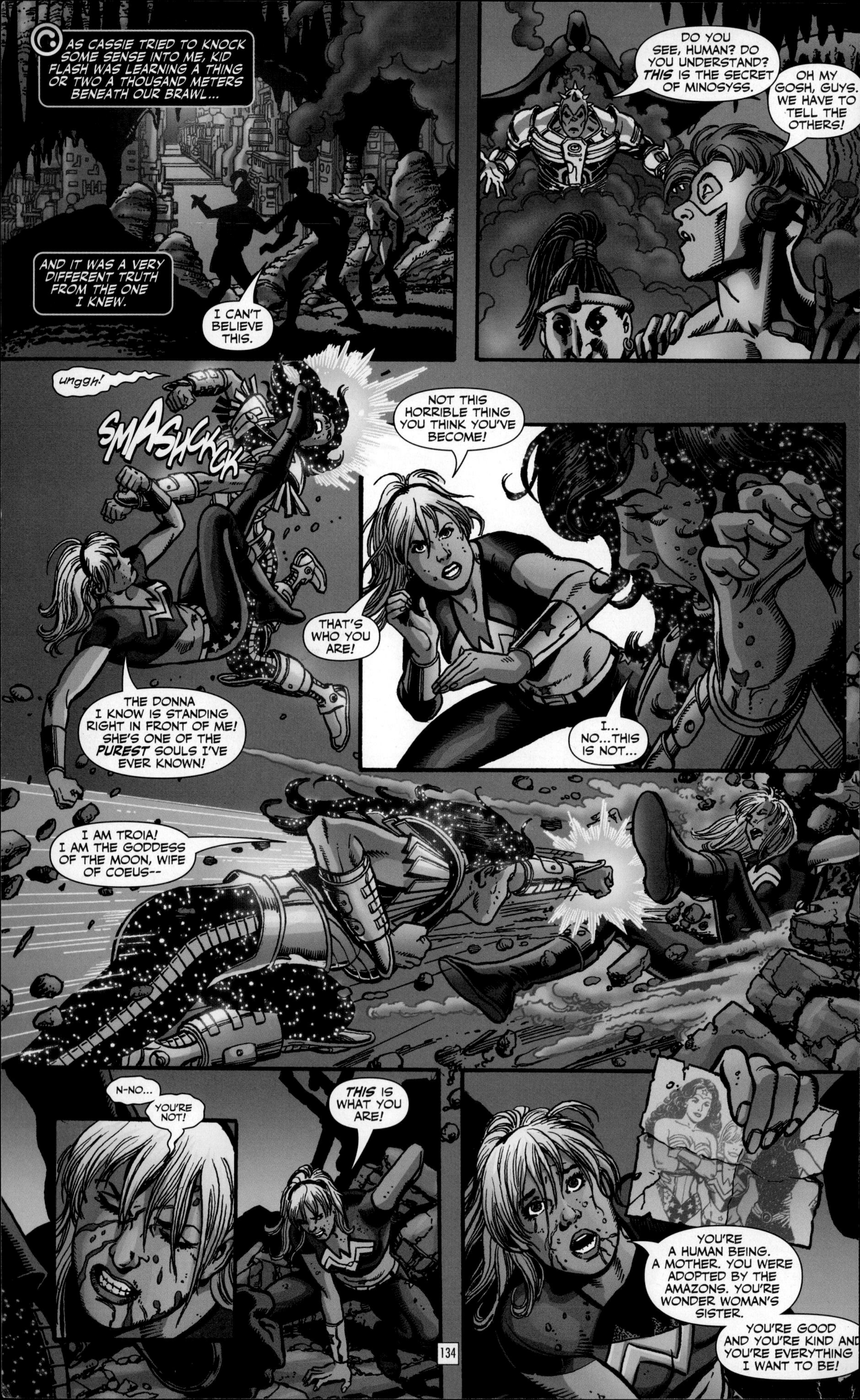

AS CASSIE TRIED TO KNOCK SOME SENSE INTO ME, KID FLASH WAS LEARNING A THING OR TWO A THOUSAND METERS BENEATH OUR BRAWL...
AND IT WAS A VERY DIFFERENT TRUTH FROM THE ONE I KNEW.
I CAN'T BELIEVE THIS.
DO YOU SEE, HUMAN? DO YOU UNDERSTAND? THIS IS THE SECRET OF MINOSYSS.
OH MY GOSH, GUYS. WE HAVE TO TELL THE OTHERS!
unggh!
SMASHCKCK
NOT THIS HORRIBLE THING YOU THINK YOU'VE BECOME!
THAT'S WHO YOU ARE!
THE DONNA I KNOW IS STANDING RIGHT IN FRONT OF ME! SHE'S ONE OF THE PUREST SOULS I'VE EVER KNOWN!
I... NO...THIS IS NOT...
I AM TROIA! I AM THE GODDESS OF THE MOON, WIFE OF COEUS--
N-NO... YOU'RE NOT!
THIS IS WHAT YOU ARE!
YOU'RE A HUMAN BEING. A MOTHER. YOU WERE ADOPTED BY THE AMAZONS. YOU'RE WONDER WOMAN'S SISTER.
YOU'RE GOOD AND YOU'RE KIND AND YOU'RE EVERYTHING I WANT TO BE!

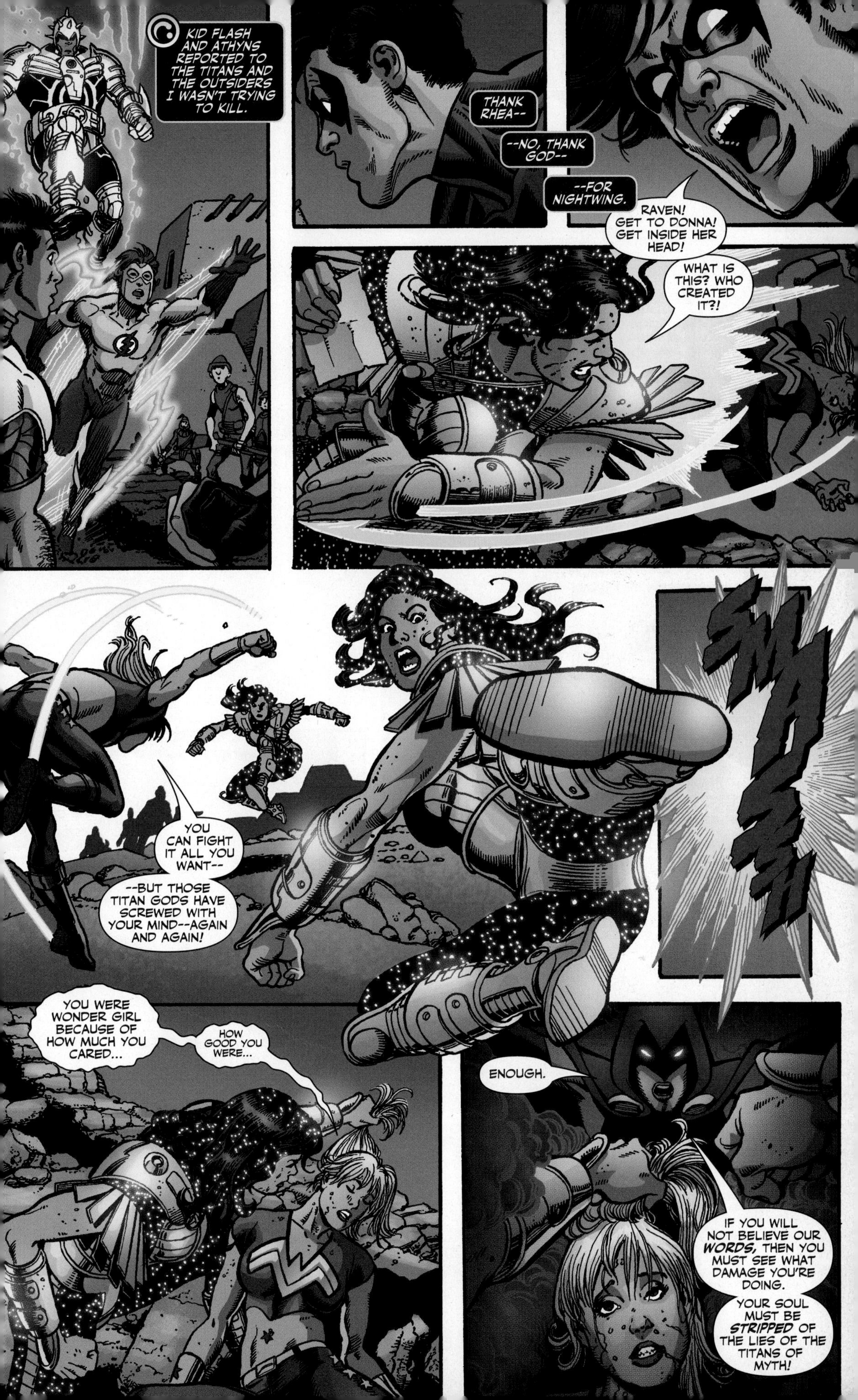
KID FLASH AND ATHYNS REPORTED TO THE TITANS AND THE OUTSIDERS I WASN'T TRYING TO KILL.
THANK RHEA--
--NO, THANK GOD--
--FOR NIGHTWING.
RAVEN! GET TO DONNA! GET INSIDE HER HEAD!
WHAT IS THIS? WHO CREATED IT?!
YOU CAN FIGHT IT ALL YOU WANT--
--BUT THOSE TITAN GODS HAVE SCREWED WITH YOUR MIND--AGAIN AND AGAIN!
SMAAM!
YOU WERE WONDER GIRL BECAUSE OF HOW MUCH YOU CARED...
HOW GOOD YOU WERE...
ENOUGH.
IF YOU WILL NOT BELIEVE OUR WORDS, THEN YOU MUST SEE WHAT DAMAGE YOU'RE DOING.
YOUR SOUL MUST BE STRIPPED OF THE LIES OF THE TITANS OF MYTH!

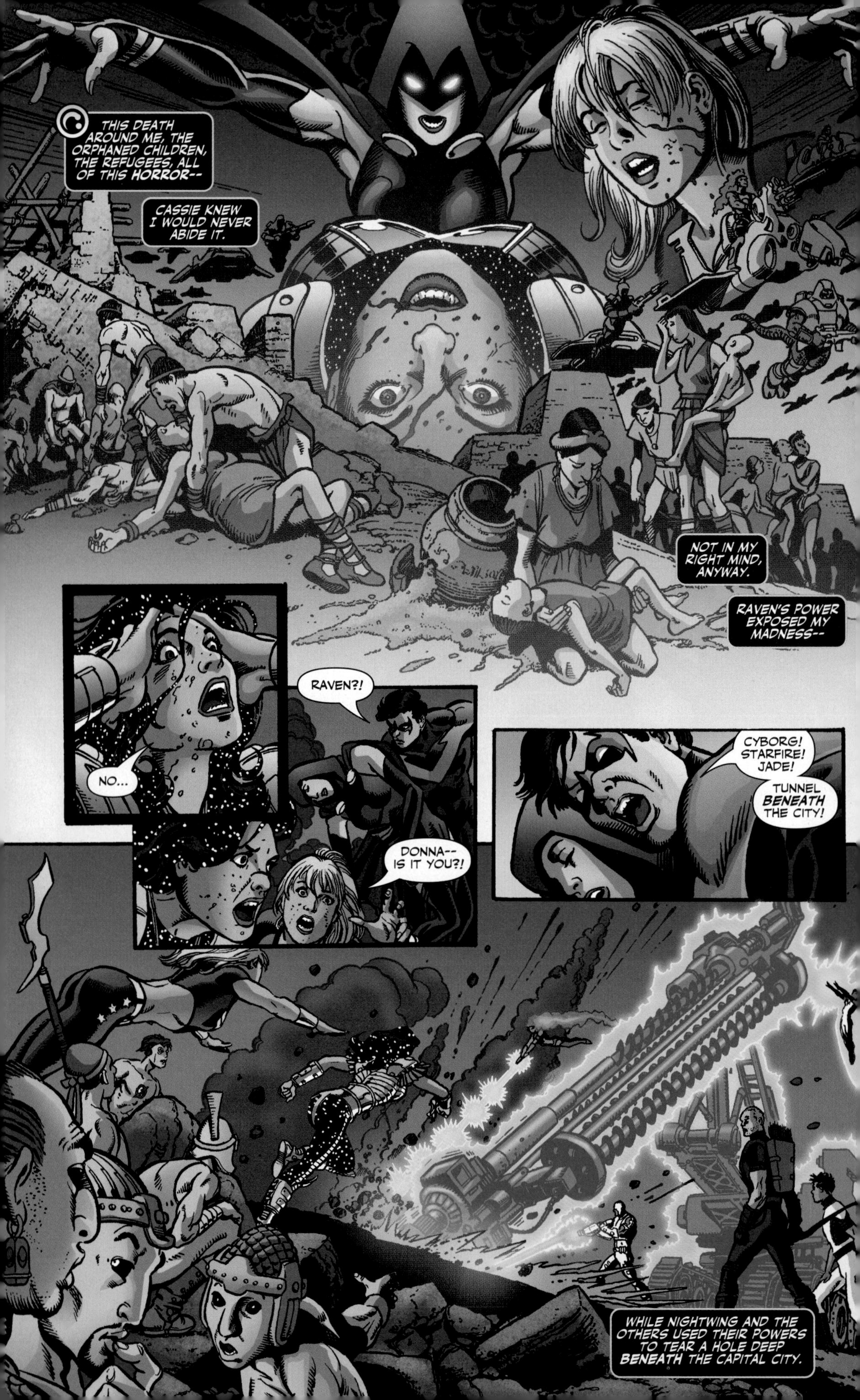
THIS DEATH AROUND ME, THE ORPHANED CHILDREN, THE REFUGEES, ALL OF THIS HORROR--
CASSIE KNEW I WOULD NEVER ABIDE IT.
NOT IN MY RIGHT MIND, ANYWAY.
RAVEN'S POWER EXPOSED MY MADNESS--
NO...
RAVEN?!
DONNA-- IS IT YOU?!
CYBORG! STARFIRE! JADE!
TUNNEL BENEATH THE CITY!
WHILE NIGHTWING AND THE OTHERS USED THEIR POWERS TO TEAR A HOLE DEEP BENEATH THE CAPITAL CITY.

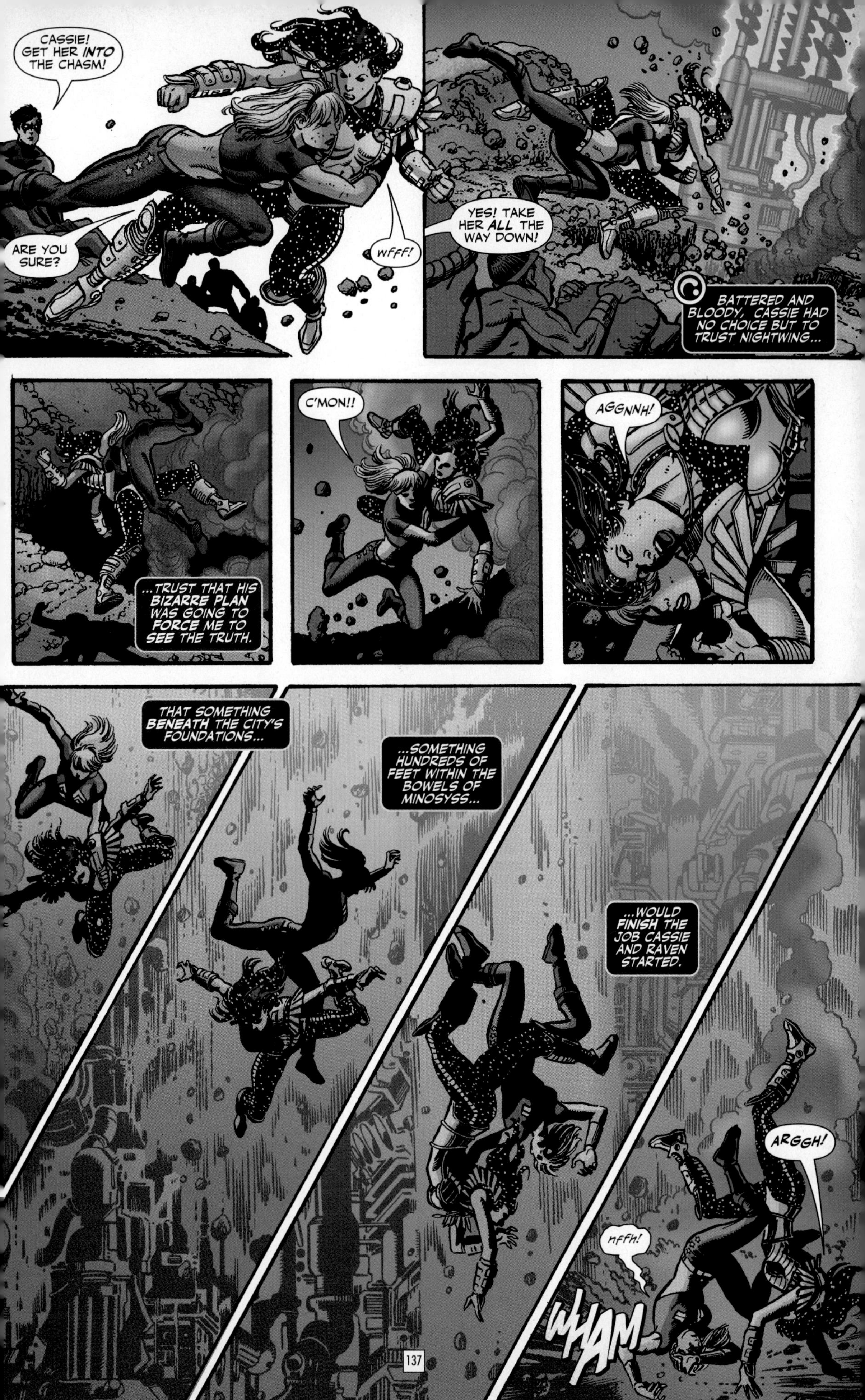
CASSIE! GET HER INTO THE CHASM!
ARE YOU SURE?
wfff!
YES! TAKE HER ALL THE WAY DOWN!
BATTERED AND BLOODY, CASSIE HAD NO CHOICE BUT TO TRUST NIGHTWING...
...TRUST THAT HIS BIZARRE PLAN WAS GOING TO FORCE ME TO SEE THE TRUTH.
C'MON!!
AGGNNH!
THAT SOMETHING BENEATH THE CITY'S FOUNDATIONS...
...SOMETHING HUNDREDS OF FEET WITHIN THE BOWELS OF MINOSYSS...
...WOULD FINISH THE JOB CASSIE AND RAVEN STARTED.
ARGGH!
nffh!
WHAM

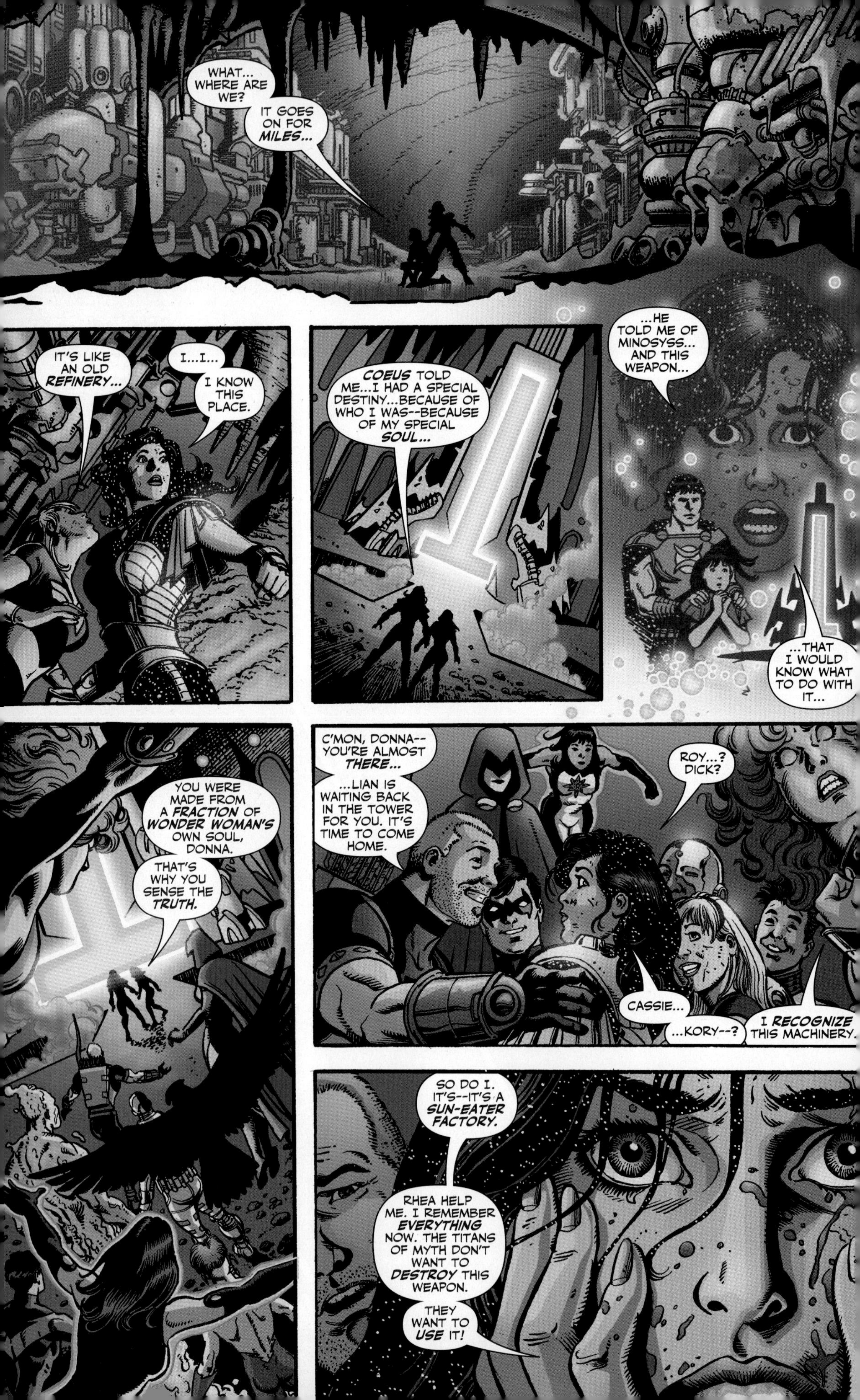

WHAT... WHERE ARE WE?
IT GOES ON FOR MILES...
IT'S LIKE AN OLD REFINERY...
I...I...
I KNOW THIS PLACE.
COEUS TOLD ME...I HAD A SPECIAL DESTINY...BECAUSE OF WHO I WAS--BECAUSE OF MY SPECIAL SOUL...
...HE TOLD ME OF MINOSYSS... AND THIS WEAPON...
...THAT I WOULD KNOW WHAT TO DO WITH IT...
YOU WERE MADE FROM A FRACTION OF WONDER WOMAN'S OWN SOUL, DONNA.
THAT'S WHY YOU SENSE THE TRUTH.
C'MON, DONNA-- YOU'RE ALMOST THERE...
...LIAN IS WAITING BACK IN THE TOWER FOR YOU. IT'S TIME TO COME HOME.
ROY...? DICK?
CASSIE...
...KORY--?
I RECOGNIZE THIS MACHINERY.
SO DO I. IT'S--IT'S A SUN-EATER FACTORY.
RHEA HELP ME. I REMEMBER EVERYTHING NOW. THE TITANS OF MYTH DON'T WANT TO DESTROY THIS WEAPON.
THEY WANT TO USE IT!

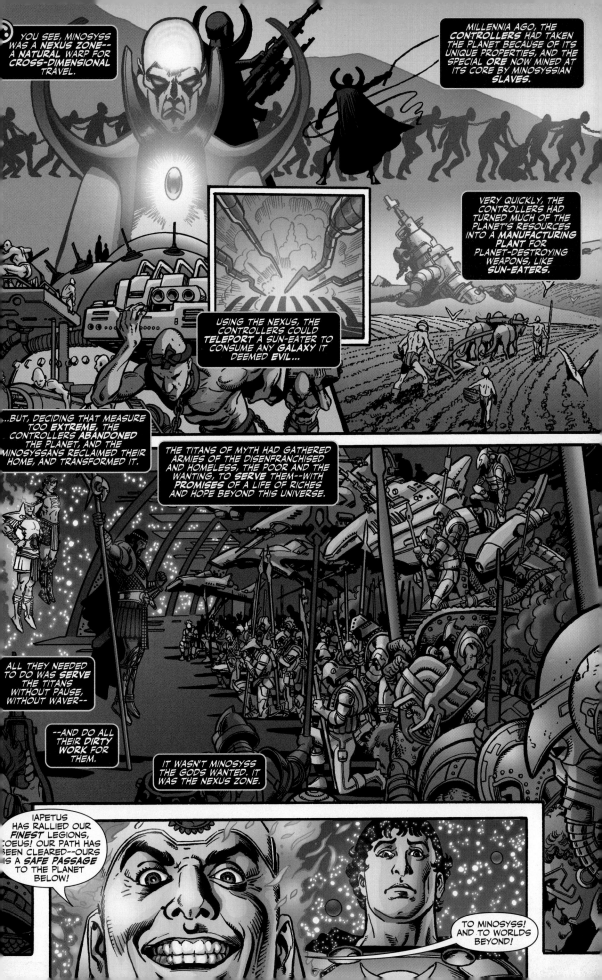

YOU SEE, MINOSYSS WAS A **NEXUS ZONE**-- A NATURAL WARP FOR CROSS-DIMENSIONAL TRAVEL.

MILLENNIA AGO, THE **CONTROLLERS** HAD TAKEN THE PLANET BECAUSE OF ITS UNIQUE PROPERTIES, AND THE SPECIAL **ORE** NOW MINED AT ITS CORE BY MINOSYSSIAN **SLAVES.**

VERY QUICKLY, THE CONTROLLERS HAD TURNED MUCH OF THE PLANET'S RESOURCES INTO A **MANUFACTURING PLANT** FOR PLANET-DESTROYING WEAPONS, LIKE **SUN-EATERS.**

USING THE NEXUS, THE CONTROLLERS COULD **TELEPORT** A SUN-EATER TO CONSUME ANY **GALAXY** IT DEEMED **EVIL...**

...BUT, DECIDING THAT MEASURE TOO **EXTREME,** THE CONTROLLERS **ABANDONED** THE PLANET, AND THE MINOSYSSANS RECLAIMED THEIR HOME, AND TRANSFORMED IT.

THE TITANS OF MYTH HAD GATHERED ARMIES OF THE DISENFRANCHISED AND HOMELESS, THE POOR AND THE WANTING, TO **SERVE** THEM--WITH **PROMISES** OF A LIFE OF RICHES AND HOPE BEYOND THIS UNIVERSE.

ALL THEY NEEDED TO DO WAS **SERVE** THE TITANS WITHOUT PAUSE, WITHOUT WAVER--

--AND DO ALL THEIR **DIRTY WORK** FOR THEM.

IT WASN'T MINOSYSS THE GODS WANTED. IT WAS THE NEXUS ZONE.

IAPETUS HAS RALLIED OUR **FINEST** LEGIONS, COEUS! OUR PATH HAS BEEN CLEARED--OURS IS A **SAFE PASSAGE** TO THE PLANET BELOW!

TO MINOSYSS! AND TO WORLDS BEYOND!

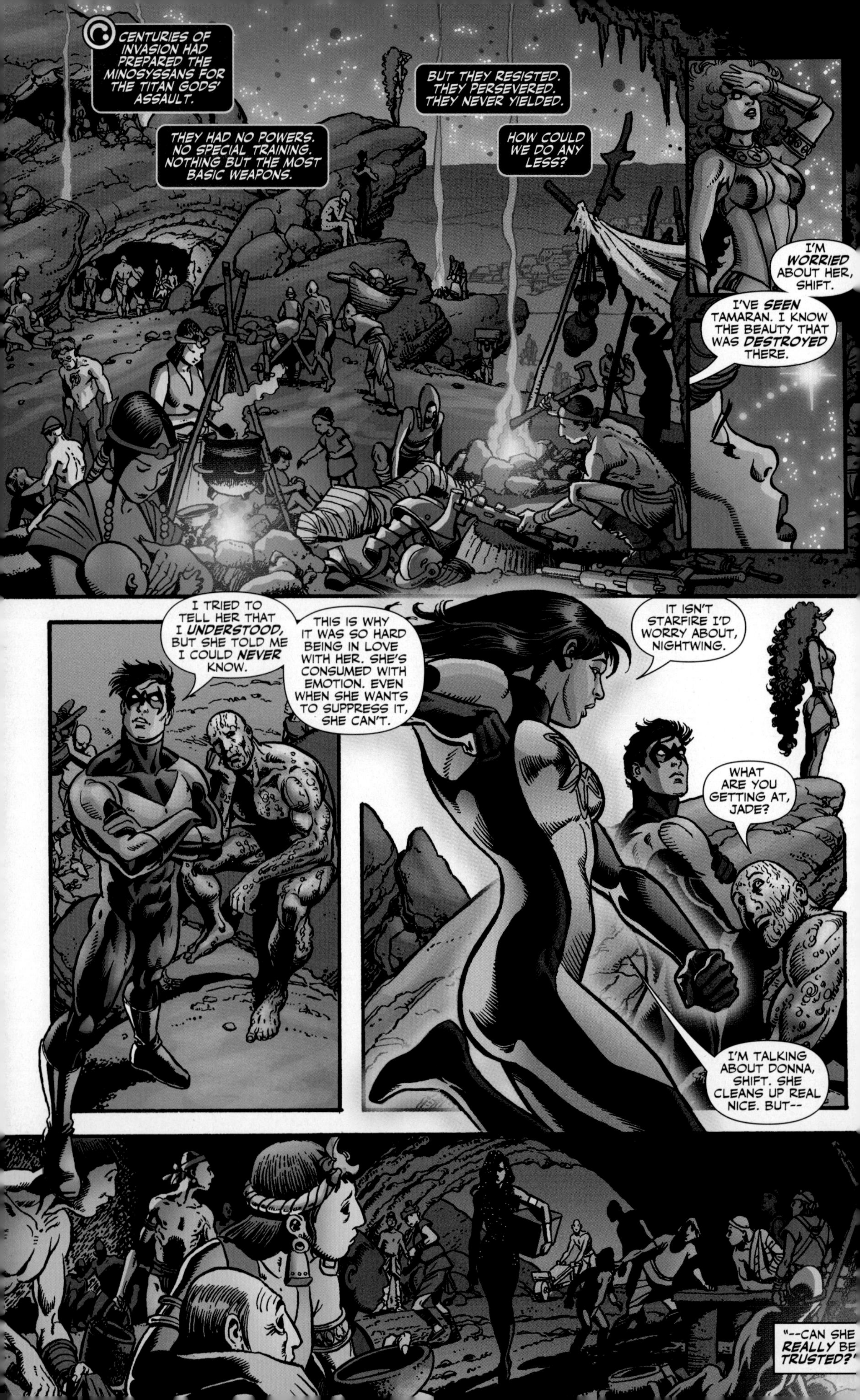

CENTURIES OF INVASION HAD PREPARED THE MINOSYSSANS FOR THE TITAN GODS' ASSAULT.
THEY HAD NO POWERS. NO SPECIAL TRAINING. NOTHING BUT THE MOST BASIC WEAPONS.
BUT THEY RESISTED. THEY PERSEVERED. THEY NEVER YIELDED.
HOW COULD WE DO ANY LESS?
I'M *WORRIED* ABOUT HER, SHIFT.
I'VE *SEEN* TAMARAN. I KNOW THE BEAUTY THAT WAS *DESTROYED* THERE.
I TRIED TO TELL HER THAT I *UNDERSTOOD*, BUT SHE TOLD ME I COULD *NEVER* KNOW.
THIS IS WHY IT WAS SO HARD BEING IN LOVE WITH HER. SHE'S CONSUMED WITH EMOTION. EVEN WHEN SHE WANTS TO SUPPRESS IT, SHE CAN'T.
IT ISN'T STARFIRE I'D WORRY ABOUT, NIGHTWING.
WHAT ARE YOU GETTING AT, JADE?
I'M TALKING ABOUT DONNA, SHIFT. SHE CLEANS UP REAL NICE. BUT--
"--CAN SHE *REALLY* BE *TRUSTED?*"

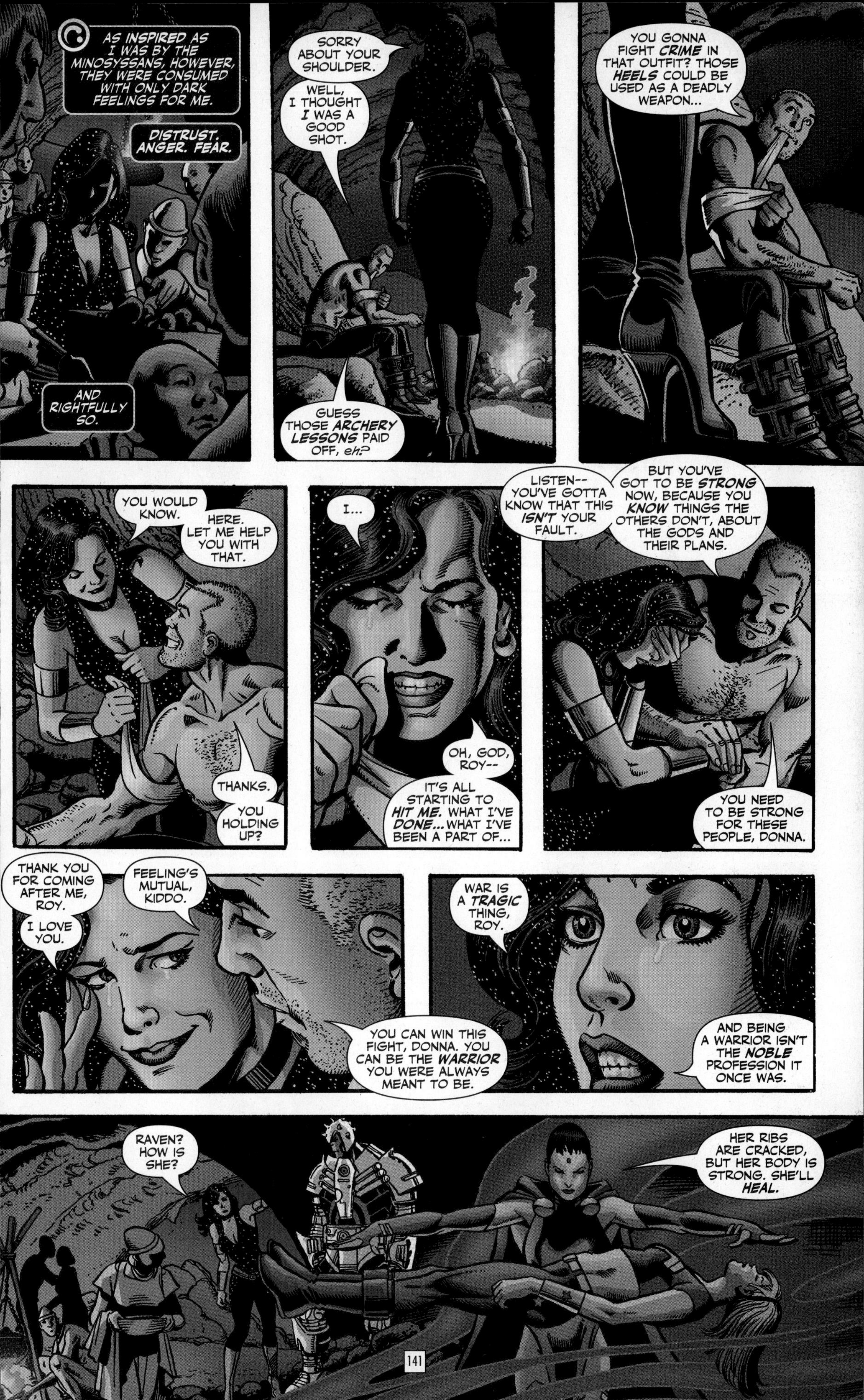

AS INSPIRED AS I WAS BY THE MINOSYSSANS, HOWEVER, THEY WERE CONSUMED WITH ONLY DARK FEELINGS FOR ME.
DISTRUST. ANGER. FEAR.
AND RIGHTFULLY SO.
SORRY ABOUT YOUR SHOULDER.
WELL, I THOUGHT I WAS A GOOD SHOT.
GUESS THOSE ARCHERY LESSONS PAID OFF, eh?
YOU GONNA FIGHT CRIME IN THAT OUTFIT? THOSE HEELS COULD BE USED AS A DEADLY WEAPON...
YOU WOULD KNOW.
HERE. LET ME HELP YOU WITH THAT.
THANKS.
YOU HOLDING UP?
I...
OH, GOD, ROY--
IT'S ALL STARTING TO HIT ME. WHAT I'VE DONE... WHAT I'VE BEEN A PART OF...
LISTEN-- YOU'VE GOTTA KNOW THAT THIS ISN'T YOUR FAULT.
BUT YOU'VE GOT TO BE STRONG NOW, BECAUSE YOU KNOW THINGS THE OTHERS DON'T, ABOUT THE GODS AND THEIR PLANS.
YOU NEED TO BE STRONG FOR THESE PEOPLE, DONNA.
THANK YOU FOR COMING AFTER ME, ROY.
I LOVE YOU.
FEELING'S MUTUAL, KIDDO.
YOU CAN WIN THIS FIGHT, DONNA. YOU CAN BE THE WARRIOR YOU WERE ALWAYS MEANT TO BE.
WAR IS A TRAGIC THING, ROY.
AND BEING A WARRIOR ISN'T THE NOBLE PROFESSION IT ONCE WAS.
RAVEN? HOW IS SHE?
HER RIBS ARE CRACKED, BUT HER BODY IS STRONG. SHE'LL HEAL.

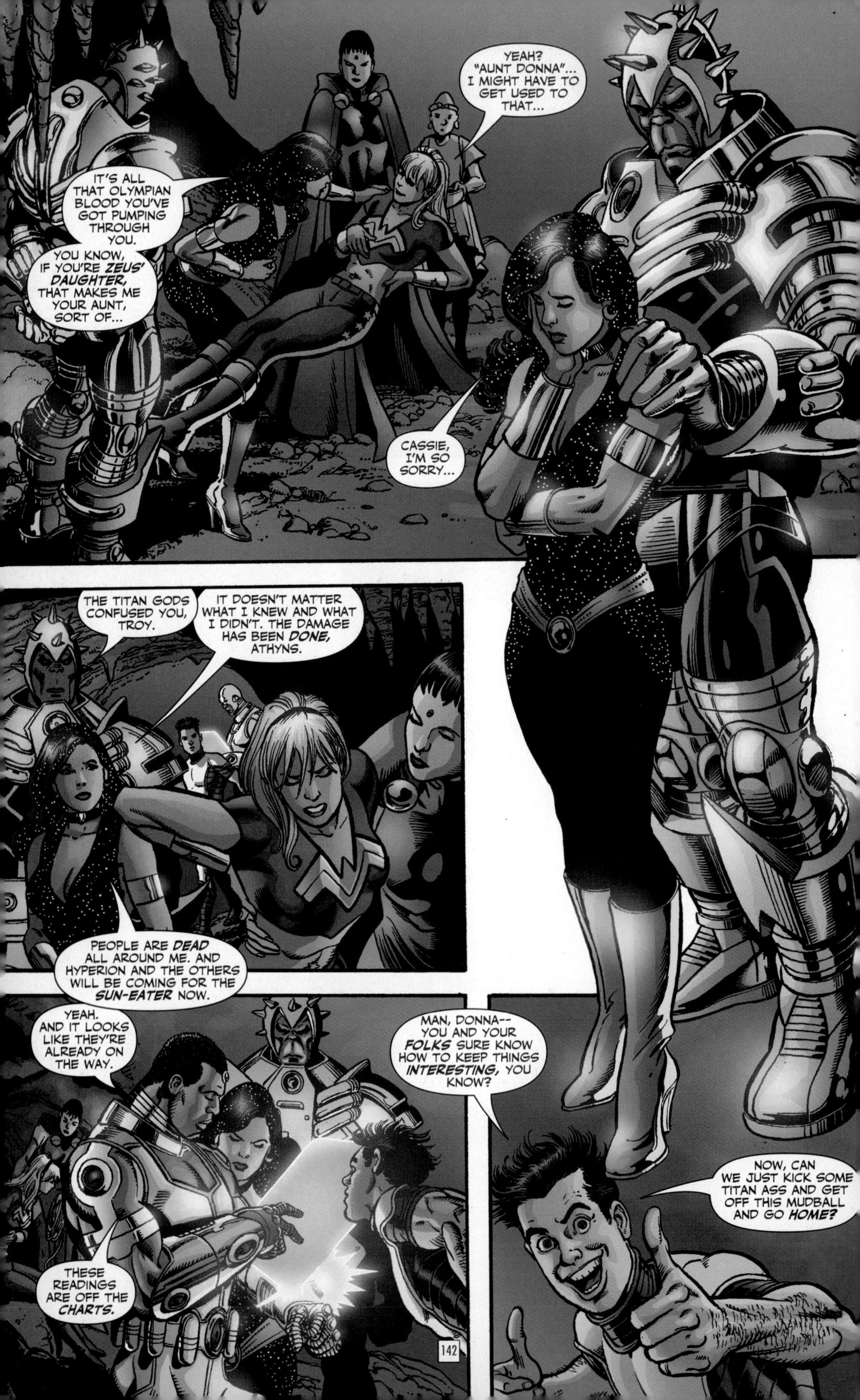
IT'S ALL THAT OLYMPIAN BLOOD YOU'VE GOT PUMPING THROUGH YOU.
YOU KNOW, IF YOU'RE ZEUS' DAUGHTER, THAT MAKES ME YOUR AUNT, SORT OF...
YEAH? "AUNT DONNA"... I MIGHT HAVE TO GET USED TO THAT...
CASSIE, I'M SO SORRY...
THE TITAN GODS CONFUSED YOU, TROY.
IT DOESN'T MATTER WHAT I KNEW AND WHAT I DIDN'T. THE DAMAGE HAS BEEN DONE, ATHYNS.
PEOPLE ARE DEAD ALL AROUND ME. AND HYPERION AND THE OTHERS WILL BE COMING FOR THE SUN-EATER NOW.
YEAH. AND IT LOOKS LIKE THEY'RE ALREADY ON THE WAY.
THESE READINGS ARE OFF THE CHARTS.
MAN, DONNA-- YOU AND YOUR FOLKS SURE KNOW HOW TO KEEP THINGS INTERESTING, YOU KNOW?
NOW, CAN WE JUST KICK SOME TITAN ASS AND GET OFF THIS MUDBALL AND GO HOME?

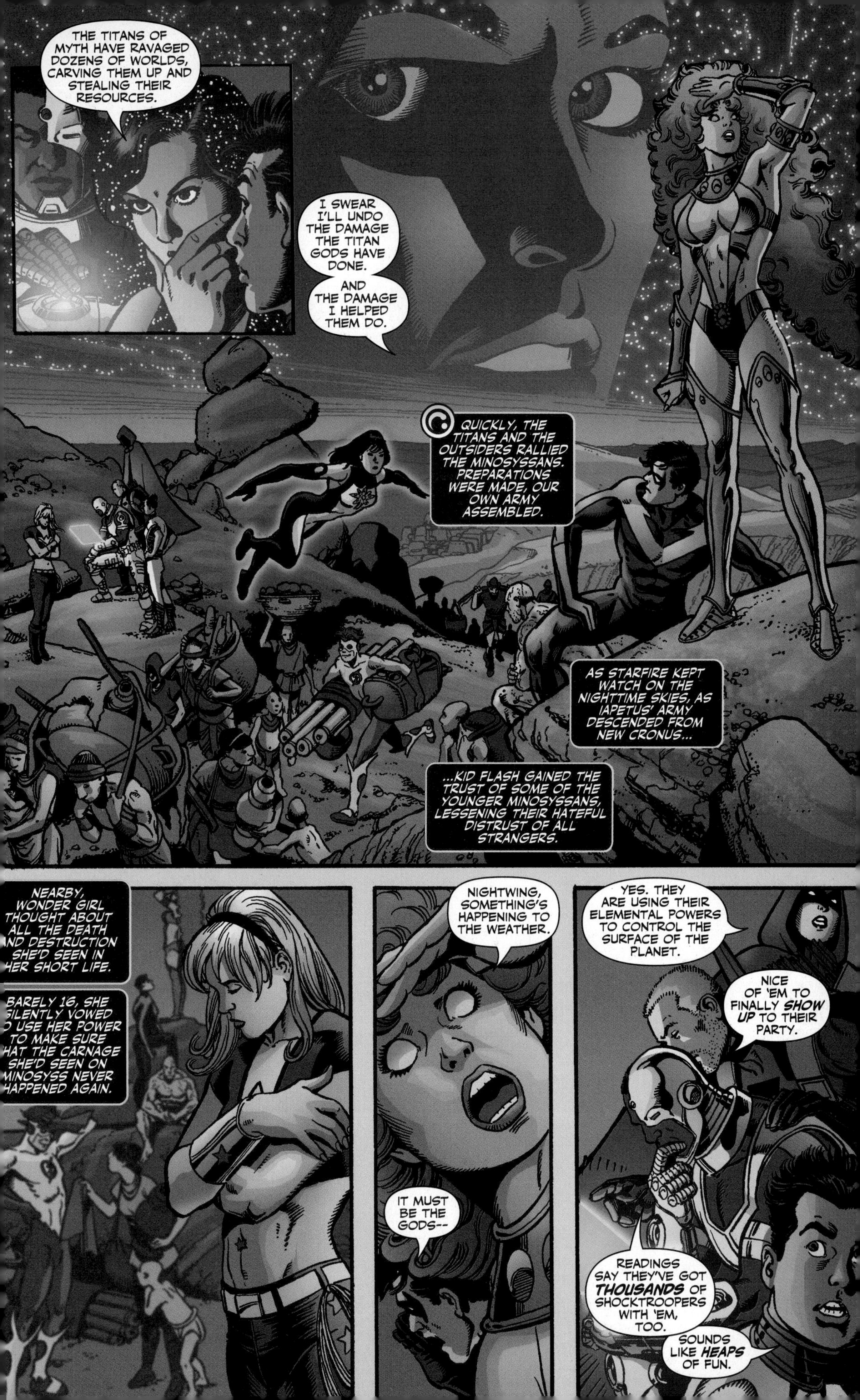
THE TITANS OF MYTH HAVE RAVAGED DOZENS OF WORLDS, CARVING THEM UP AND STEALING THEIR RESOURCES.
I SWEAR I'LL UNDO THE DAMAGE THE TITAN GODS HAVE DONE.
AND THE DAMAGE I HELPED THEM DO.
QUICKLY, THE TITANS AND THE OUTSIDERS RALLIED THE MINOSYSSANS. PREPARATIONS WERE MADE, OUR OWN ARMY ASSEMBLED.
AS STARFIRE KEPT WATCH ON THE NIGHTTIME SKIES, AS IAPETUS' ARMY DESCENDED FROM NEW CRONUS...
...KID FLASH GAINED THE TRUST OF SOME OF THE YOUNGER MINOSYSSANS, LESSENING THEIR HATEFUL DISTRUST OF ALL STRANGERS.
NEARBY, WONDER GIRL THOUGHT ABOUT ALL THE DEATH AND DESTRUCTION SHE'D SEEN IN HER SHORT LIFE.
BARELY 16, SHE SILENTLY VOWED TO USE HER POWER TO MAKE SURE THAT THE CARNAGE SHE'D SEEN ON MINOSYSS NEVER HAPPENED AGAIN.
NIGHTWING, SOMETHING'S HAPPENING TO THE WEATHER.
IT MUST BE THE GODS--
YES. THEY ARE USING THEIR ELEMENTAL POWERS TO CONTROL THE SURFACE OF THE PLANET.
NICE OF 'EM TO FINALLY SHOW UP TO THEIR PARTY.
READINGS SAY THEY'VE GOT THOUSANDS OF SHOCKTROOPERS WITH 'EM, TOO.
SOUNDS LIKE HEAPS OF FUN.

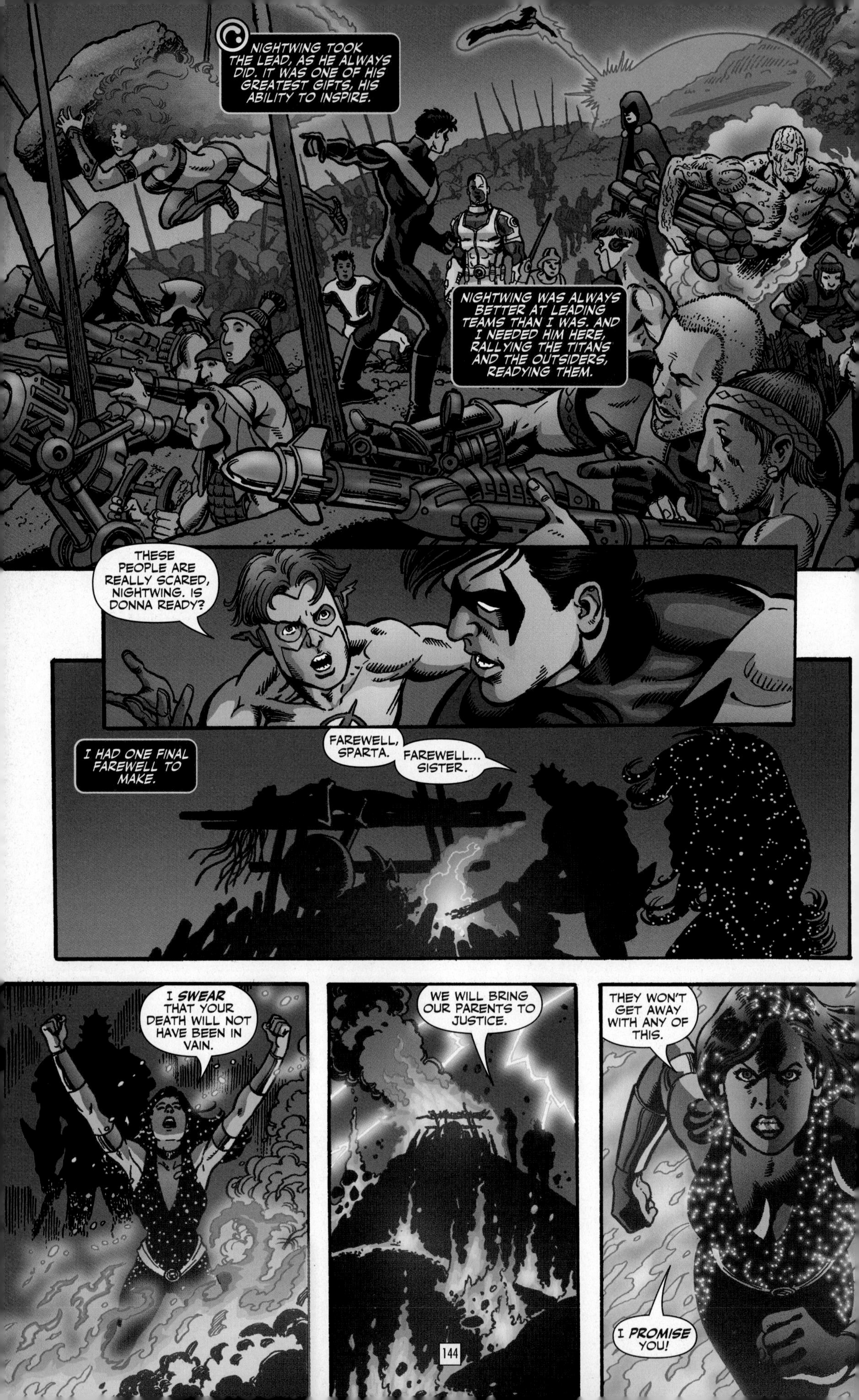
NIGHTWING TOOK THE LEAD, AS HE ALWAYS DID. IT WAS ONE OF HIS GREATEST GIFTS, HIS ABILITY TO INSPIRE.
NIGHTWING WAS ALWAYS BETTER AT LEADING TEAMS THAN I WAS. AND I NEEDED HIM HERE, RALLYING THE TITANS AND THE OUTSIDERS, READYING THEM.
THESE PEOPLE ARE REALLY SCARED, NIGHTWING. IS DONNA READY?
I HAD ONE FINAL FAREWELL TO MAKE.
FAREWELL, SPARTA.
FAREWELL... SISTER.
I SWEAR THAT YOUR DEATH WILL NOT HAVE BEEN IN VAIN.
WE WILL BRING OUR PARENTS TO JUSTICE.
THEY WON'T GET AWAY WITH ANY OF THIS.
I PROMISE YOU!

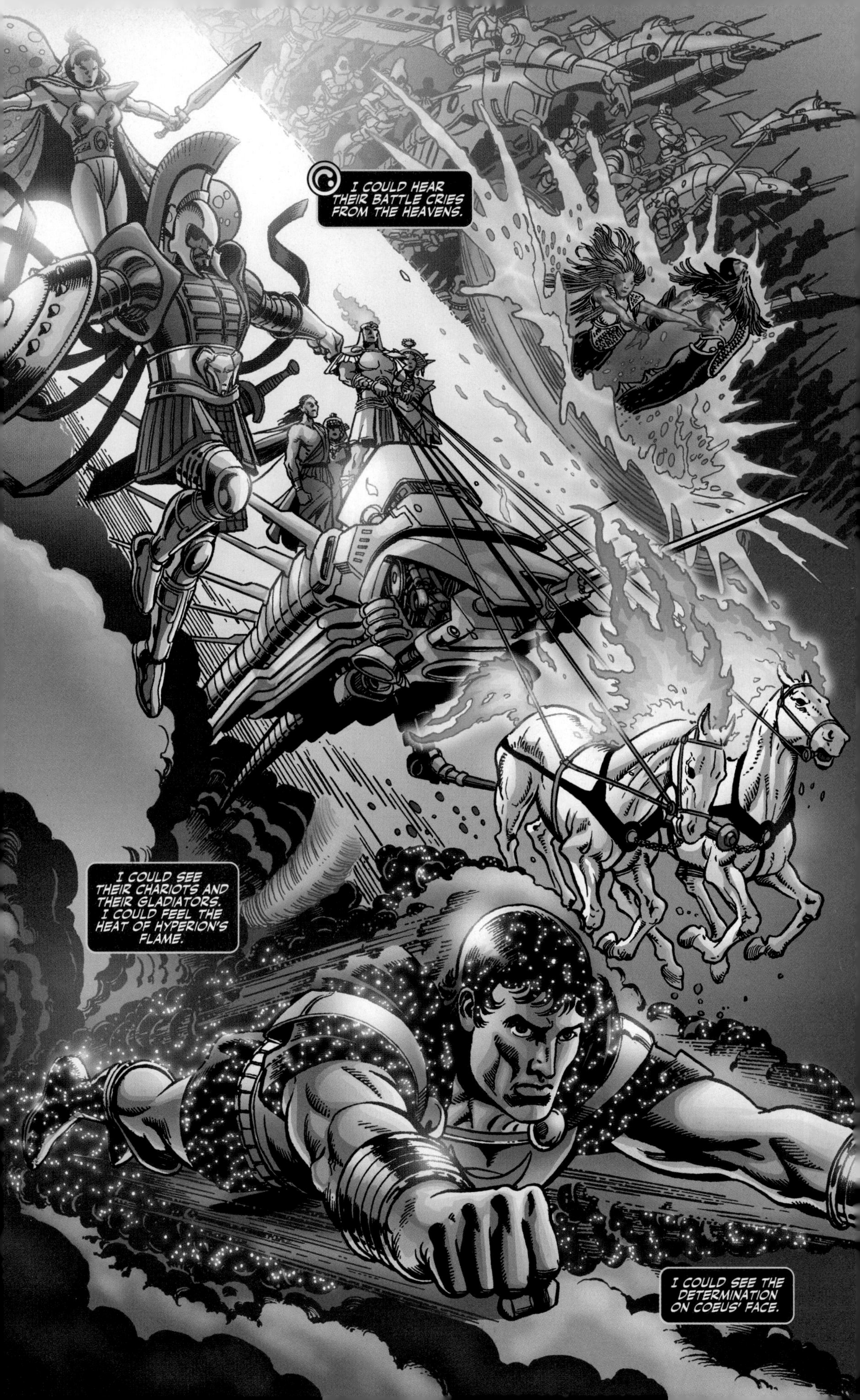
I COULD HEAR THEIR BATTLE CRIES FROM THE HEAVENS.
I COULD SEE THEIR CHARIOTS AND THEIR GLADIATORS. I COULD FEEL THE HEAT OF HYPERION'S FLAME.
I COULD SEE THE DETERMINATION ON COEUS' FACE.

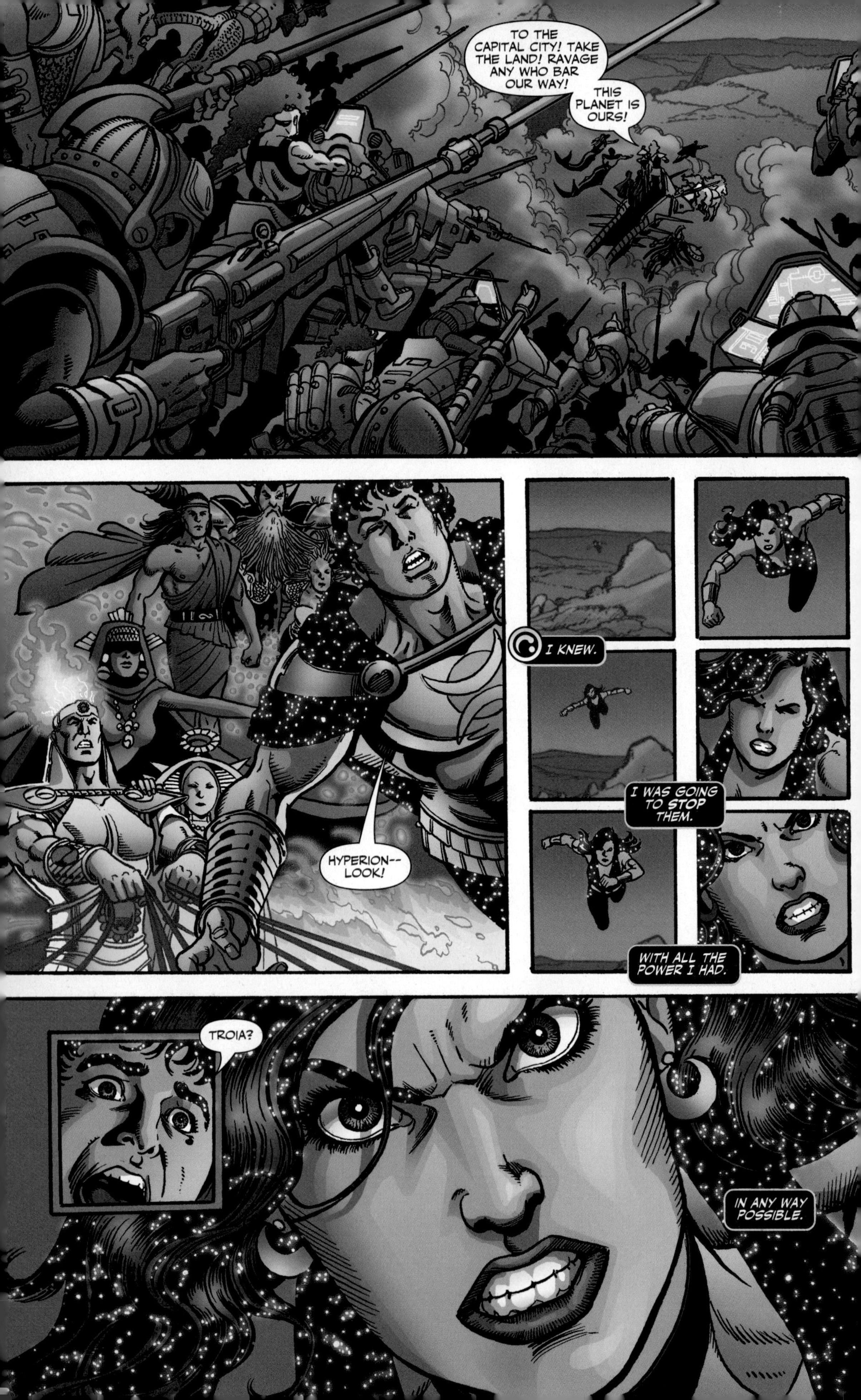

TO THE CAPITAL CITY! TAKE THE LAND! RAVAGE ANY WHO BAR OUR WAY!
THIS PLANET IS OURS!
HYPERION-- LOOK!
I KNEW.
I WAS GOING TO STOP THEM.
WITH ALL THE POWER I HAD.
TROIA?
IN ANY WAY POSSIBLE.

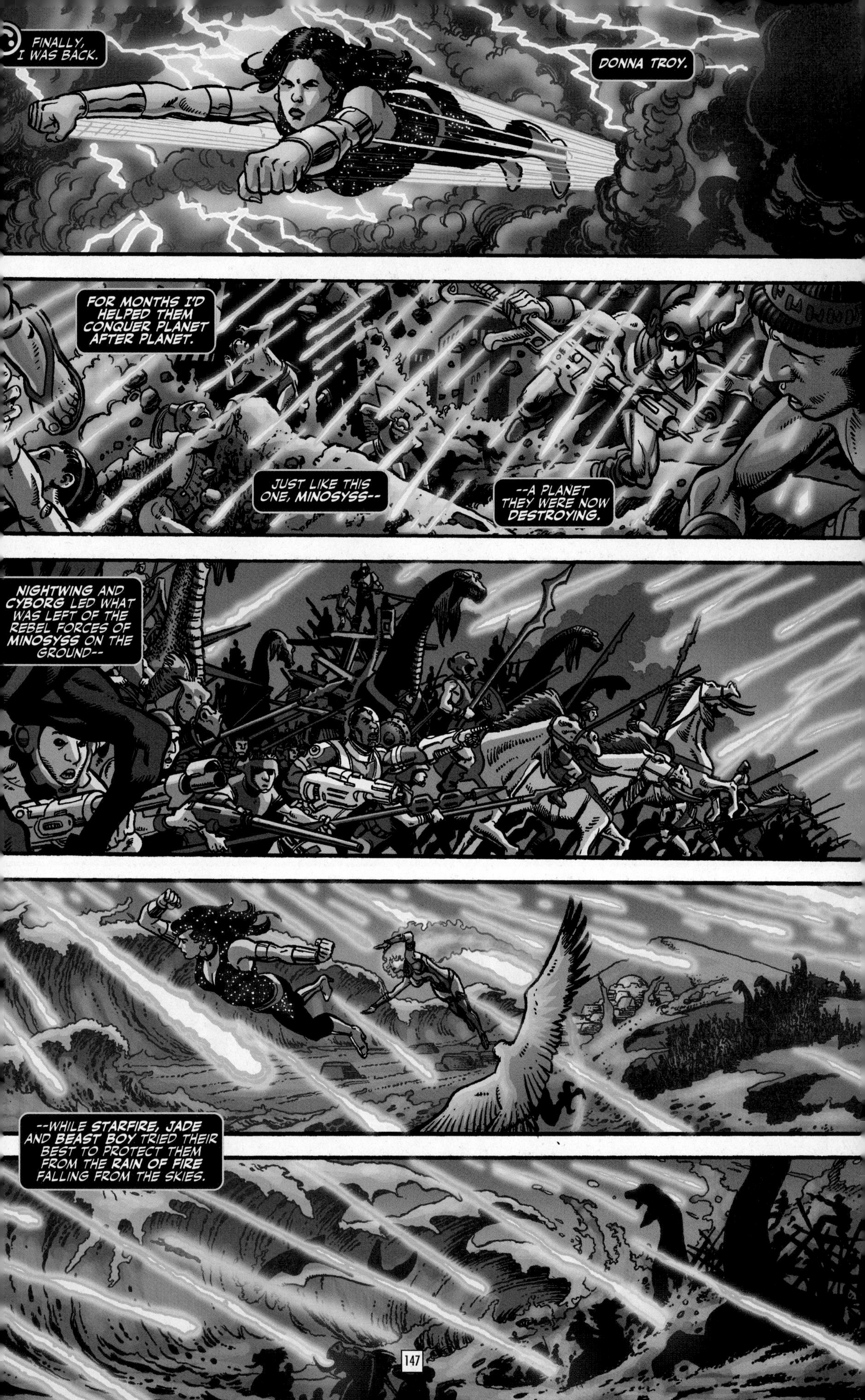
FINALLY, I WAS BACK.
DONNA TROY.
FOR MONTHS I'D HELPED THEM CONQUER PLANET AFTER PLANET.
JUST LIKE THIS ONE, MINOSYSS--
--A PLANET THEY WERE NOW DESTROYING.
NIGHTWING AND CYBORG LED WHAT WAS LEFT OF THE REBEL FORCES OF MINOSYSS ON THE GROUND--
--WHILE STARFIRE, JADE AND BEAST BOY TRIED THEIR BEST TO PROTECT THEM FROM THE RAIN OF FIRE FALLING FROM THE SKIES.

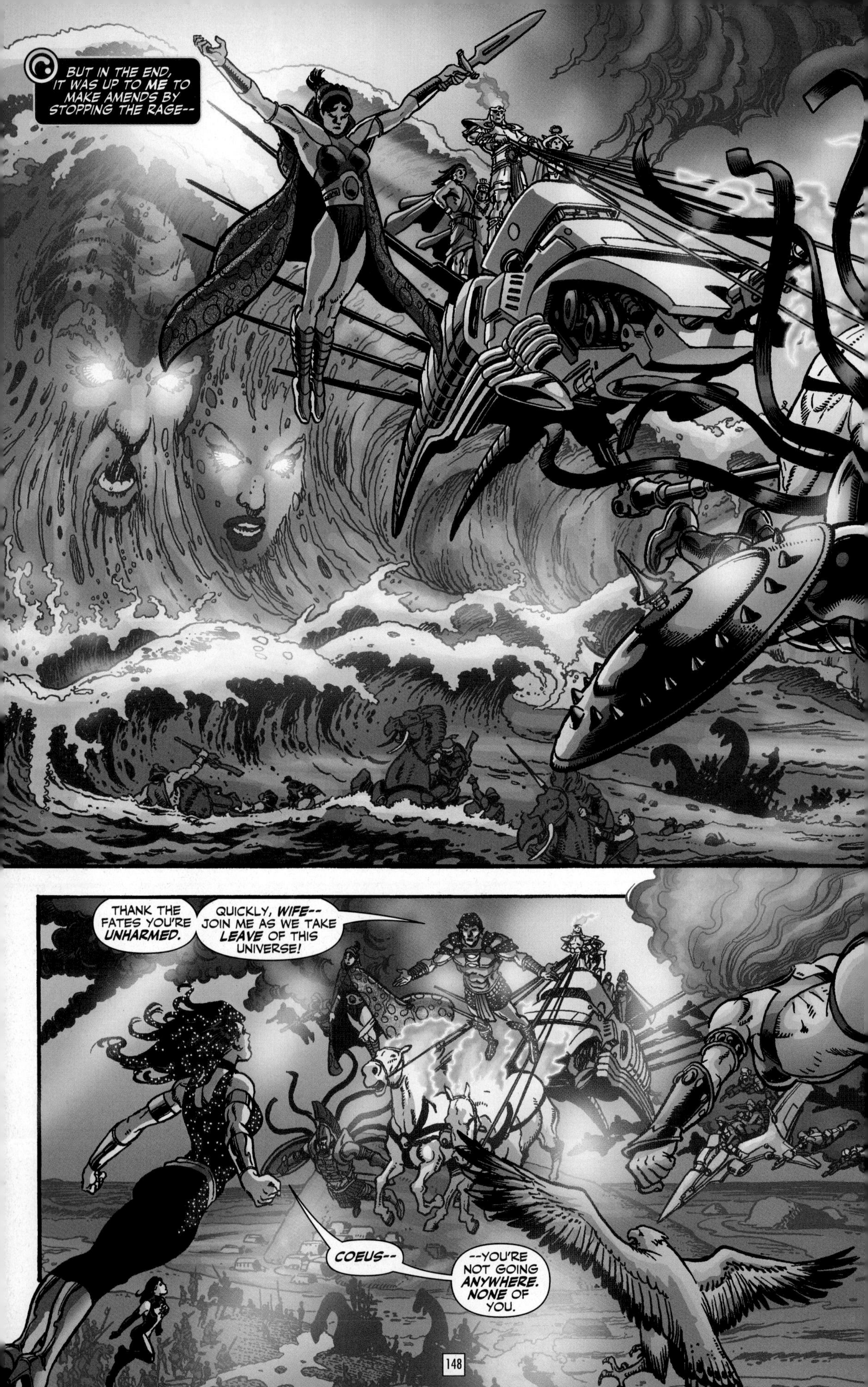
BUT IN THE END, IT WAS UP TO ME TO MAKE AMENDS BY STOPPING THE RAGE--
THANK THE FATES YOU'RE UNHARMED.
QUICKLY, WIFE-- JOIN ME AS WE TAKE LEAVE OF THIS UNIVERSE!
COEUS--
--YOU'RE NOT GOING ANYWHERE. NONE OF YOU.

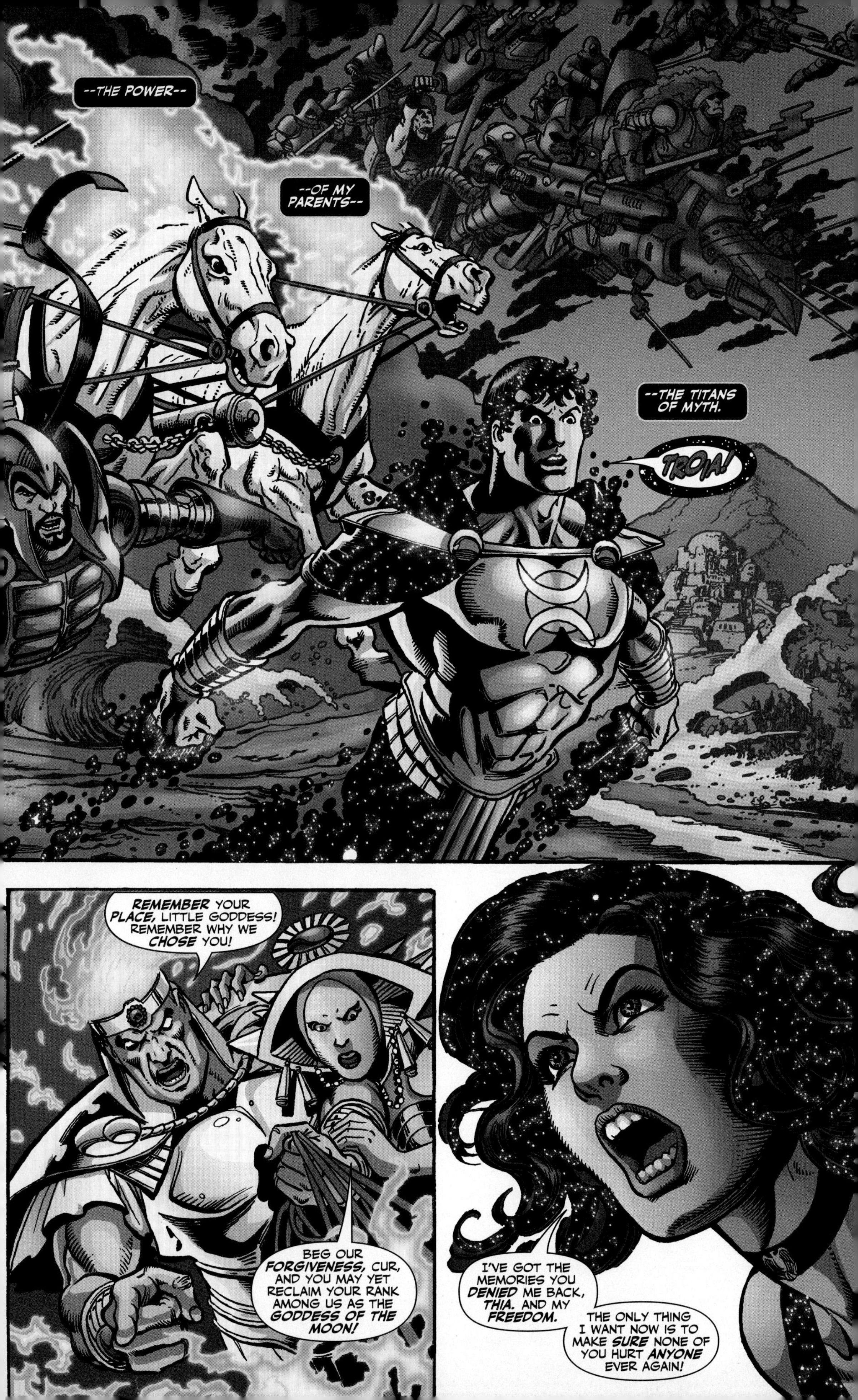
--THE POWER--
--OF MY PARENTS--
--THE TITANS OF MYTH.
TROIA!
REMEMBER YOUR PLACE, LITTLE GODDESS! REMEMBER WHY WE CHOSE YOU!
BEG OUR FORGIVENESS, CUR, AND YOU MAY YET RECLAIM YOUR RANK AMONG US AS THE GODDESS OF THE MOON!
I'VE GOT THE MEMORIES YOU DENIED ME BACK, THIA. AND MY FREEDOM.
THE ONLY THING I WANT NOW IS TO MAKE SURE NONE OF YOU HURT ANYONE EVER AGAIN!

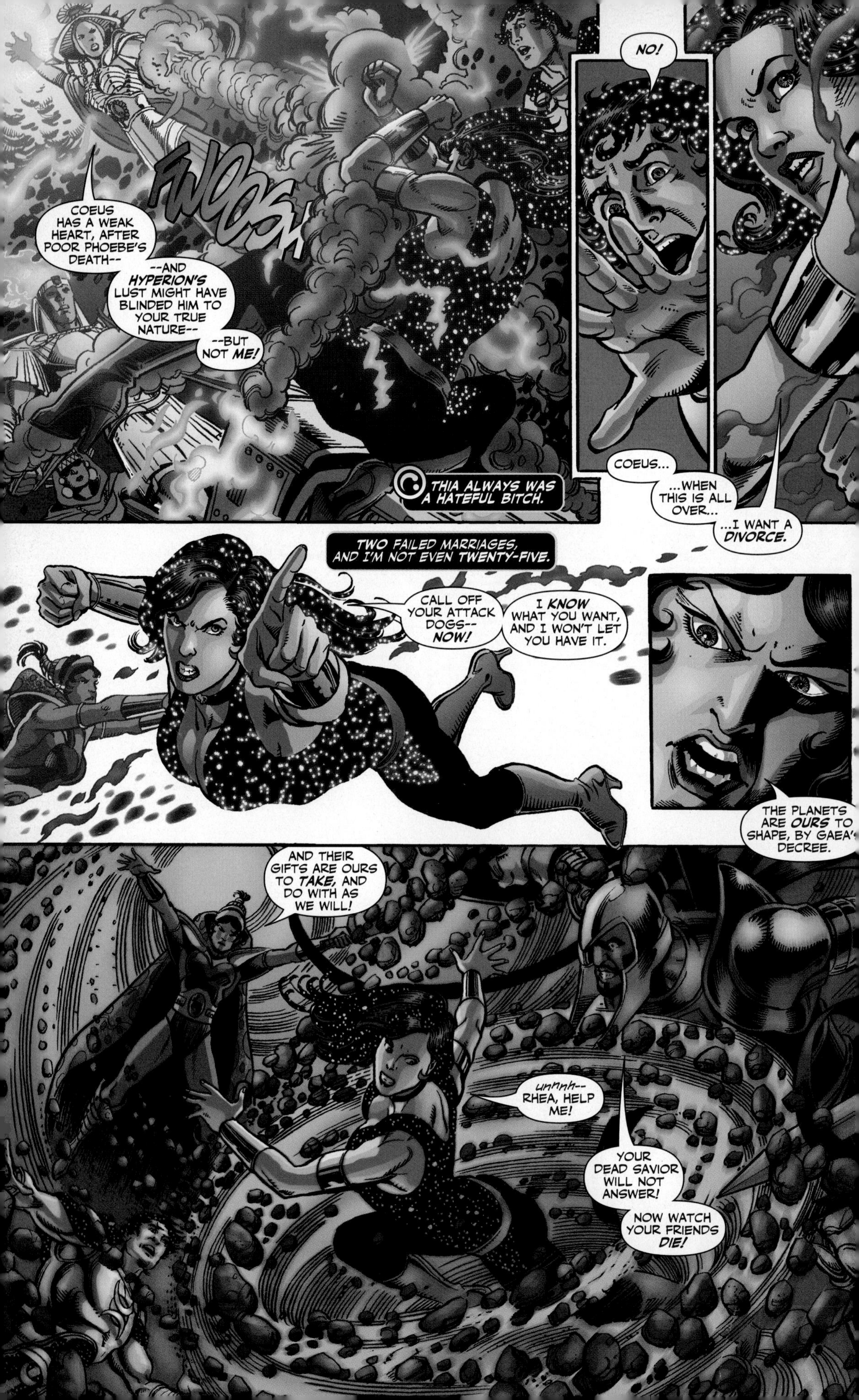
FWOOSH
COEUS HAS A WEAK HEART, AFTER POOR PHOEBE'S DEATH--
--AND HYPERION'S LUST MIGHT HAVE BLINDED HIM TO YOUR TRUE NATURE--
--BUT NOT ME!
THIA ALWAYS WAS A HATEFUL BITCH.
NO!
COEUS...
...WHEN THIS IS ALL OVER...
...I WANT A DIVORCE.
TWO FAILED MARRIAGES, AND I'M NOT EVEN TWENTY-FIVE.
CALL OFF YOUR ATTACK DOGS-- NOW!
I KNOW WHAT YOU WANT, AND I WON'T LET YOU HAVE IT.
THE PLANETS ARE OURS TO SHAPE, BY GAEA'S DECREE.
AND THEIR GIFTS ARE OURS TO TAKE, AND DO WITH AS WE WILL!
unnnh-- RHEA, HELP ME!
YOUR DEAD SAVIOR WILL NOT ANSWER!
NOW WATCH YOUR FRIENDS DIE!

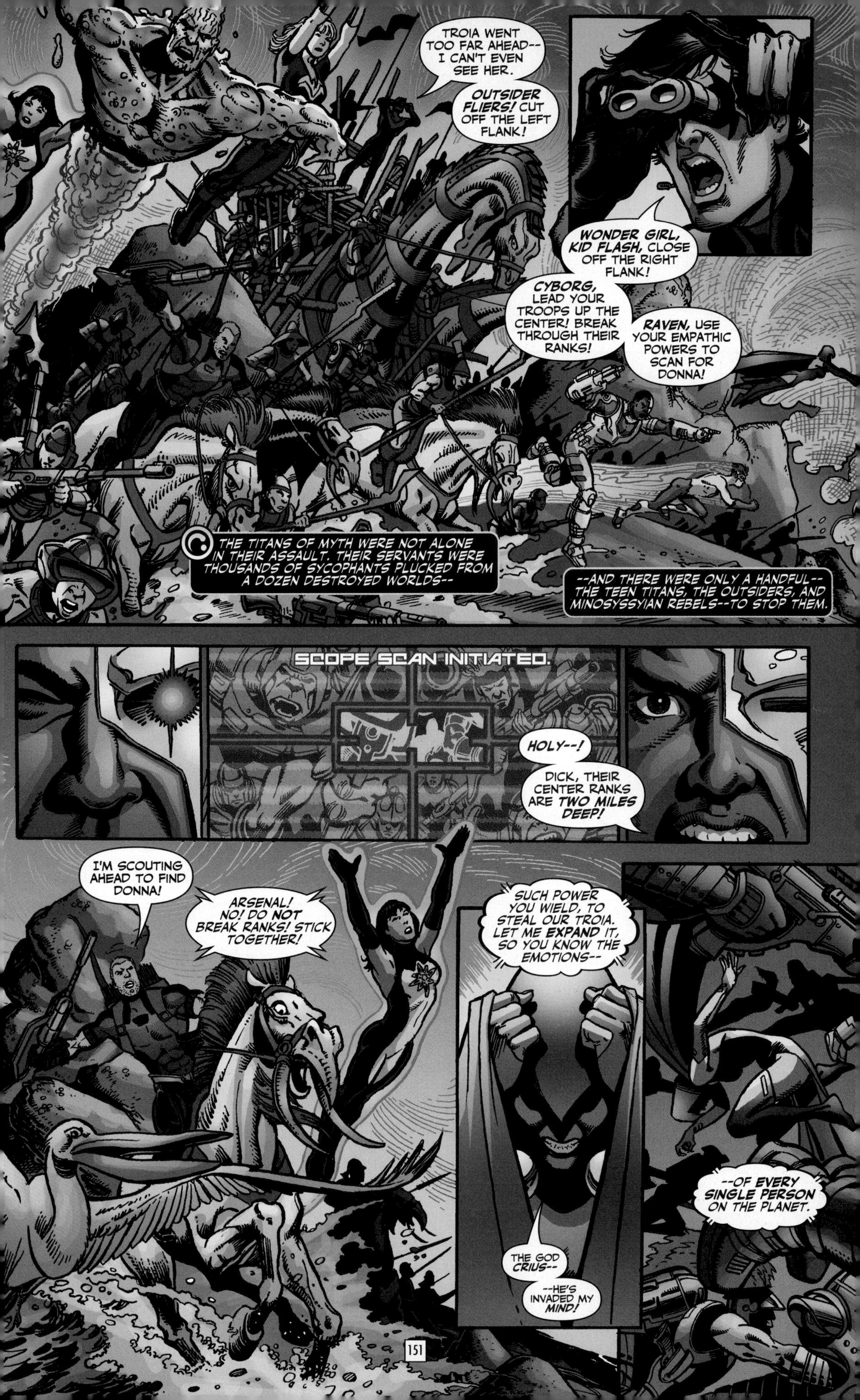
TROIA WENT TOO FAR AHEAD-- I CAN'T EVEN SEE HER.
OUTSIDER FLIERS! CUT OFF THE LEFT FLANK!
WONDER GIRL, KID FLASH, CLOSE OFF THE RIGHT FLANK!
CYBORG, LEAD YOUR TROOPS UP THE CENTER! BREAK THROUGH THEIR RANKS!
RAVEN, USE YOUR EMPATHIC POWERS TO SCAN FOR DONNA!
THE TITANS OF MYTH WERE NOT ALONE IN THEIR ASSAULT. THEIR SERVANTS WERE THOUSANDS OF SYCOPHANTS PLUCKED FROM A DOZEN DESTROYED WORLDS--
--AND THERE WERE ONLY A HANDFUL-- THE TEEN TITANS, THE OUTSIDERS, AND MINOSYSSYIAN REBELS--TO STOP THEM.
SCOPE SCAN INITIATED.
HOLY--!
DICK, THEIR CENTER RANKS ARE TWO MILES DEEP!
I'M SCOUTING AHEAD TO FIND DONNA!
ARSENAL! NO! DO NOT BREAK RANKS! STICK TOGETHER!
SUCH POWER YOU WIELD, TO STEAL OUR TROIA. LET ME EXPAND IT, SO YOU KNOW THE EMOTIONS--
--OF EVERY SINGLE PERSON ON THE PLANET.
THE GOD CRIUS--
--HE'S INVADED MY MIND!

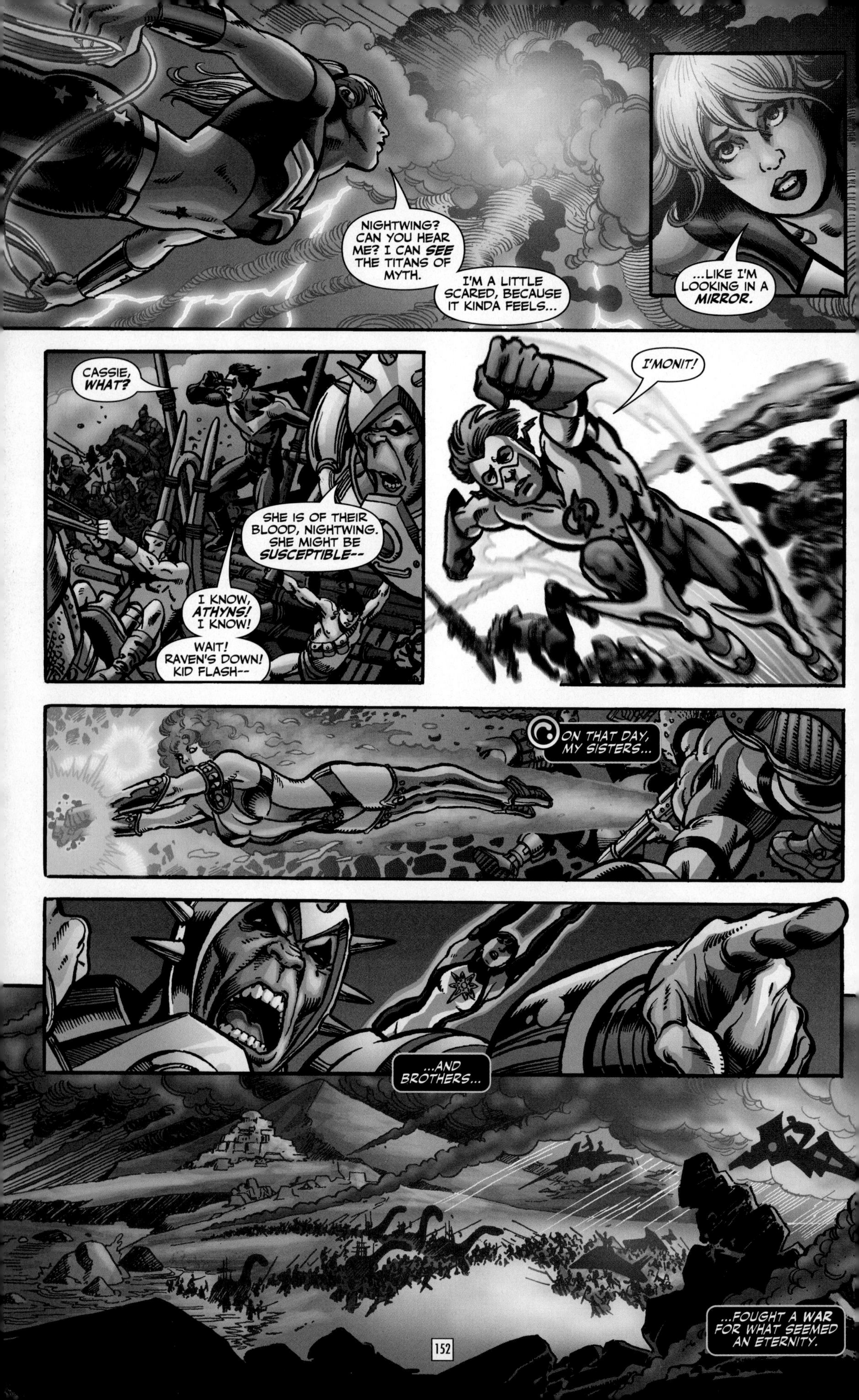

NIGHTWING? CAN YOU HEAR ME? I CAN SEE THE TITANS OF MYTH.
I'M A LITTLE SCARED, BECAUSE IT KINDA FEELS...
...LIKE I'M LOOKING IN A MIRROR.
CASSIE, WHAT?
SHE IS OF THEIR BLOOD, NIGHTWING. SHE MIGHT BE SUSCEPTIBLE--
I KNOW, ATHYNS! I KNOW!
WAIT! RAVEN'S DOWN! KID FLASH--
I'MONIT!
ON THAT DAY, MY SISTERS...
...AND BROTHERS...
...FOUGHT A WAR FOR WHAT SEEMED AN ETERNITY.

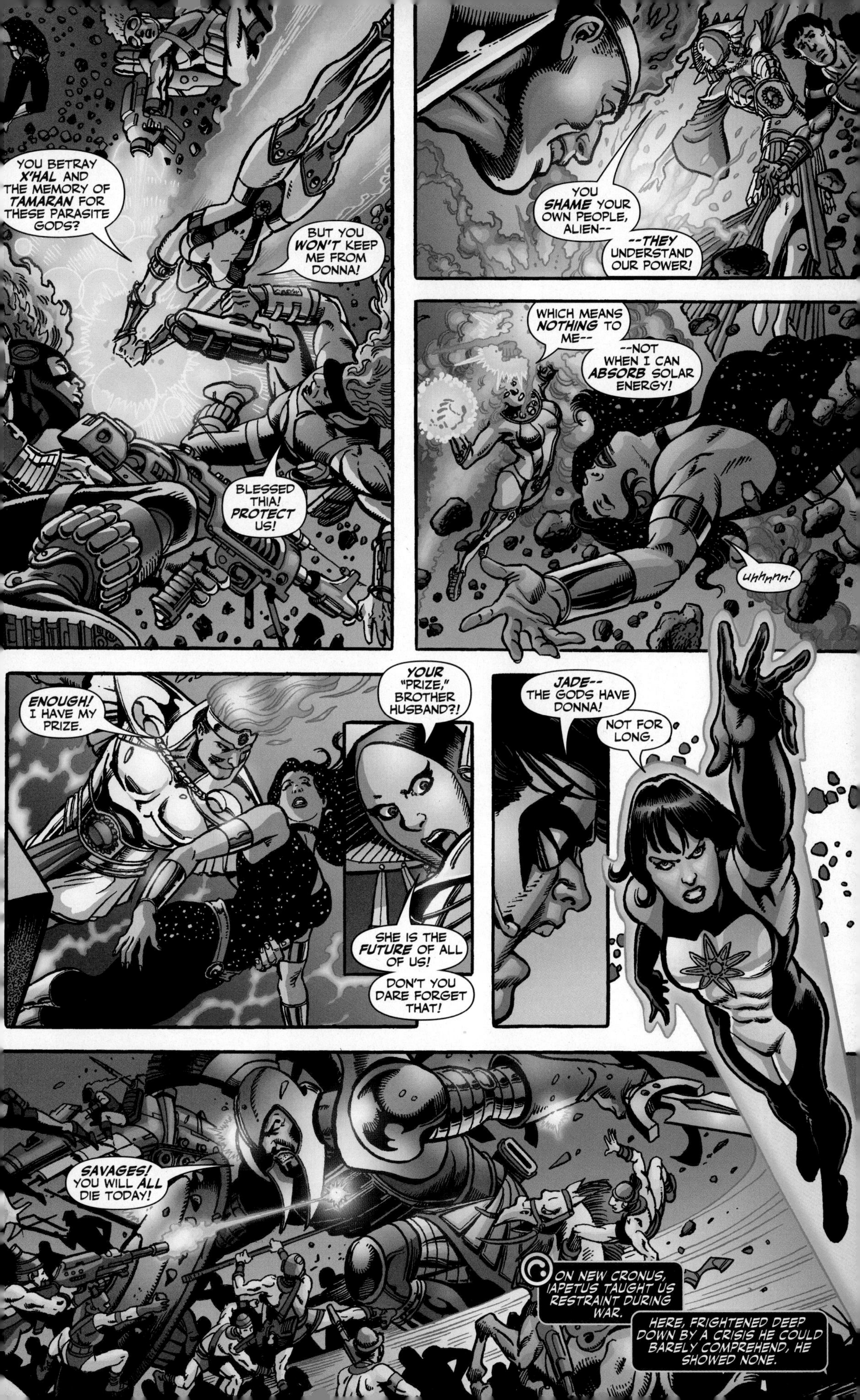
YOU BETRAY X'HAL AND THE MEMORY OF TAMARAN FOR THESE PARASITE GODS?
BUT YOU WON'T KEEP ME FROM DONNA!
BLESSED THIA! PROTECT US!
YOU SHAME YOUR OWN PEOPLE, ALIEN--
--THEY UNDERSTAND OUR POWER!
WHICH MEANS NOTHING TO ME--
--NOT WHEN I CAN ABSORB SOLAR ENERGY!
uhhnnn!
ENOUGH! I HAVE MY PRIZE.
YOUR "PRIZE," BROTHER HUSBAND?!
SHE IS THE FUTURE OF ALL OF US!
DON'T YOU DARE FORGET THAT!
JADE-- THE GODS HAVE DONNA!
NOT FOR LONG.
SAVAGES! YOU WILL ALL DIE TODAY!
ON NEW CRONUS, IAPETUS TAUGHT US RESTRAINT DURING WAR.
HERE, FRIGHTENED DEEP DOWN BY A CRISIS HE COULD BARELY COMPREHEND, HE SHOWED NONE.

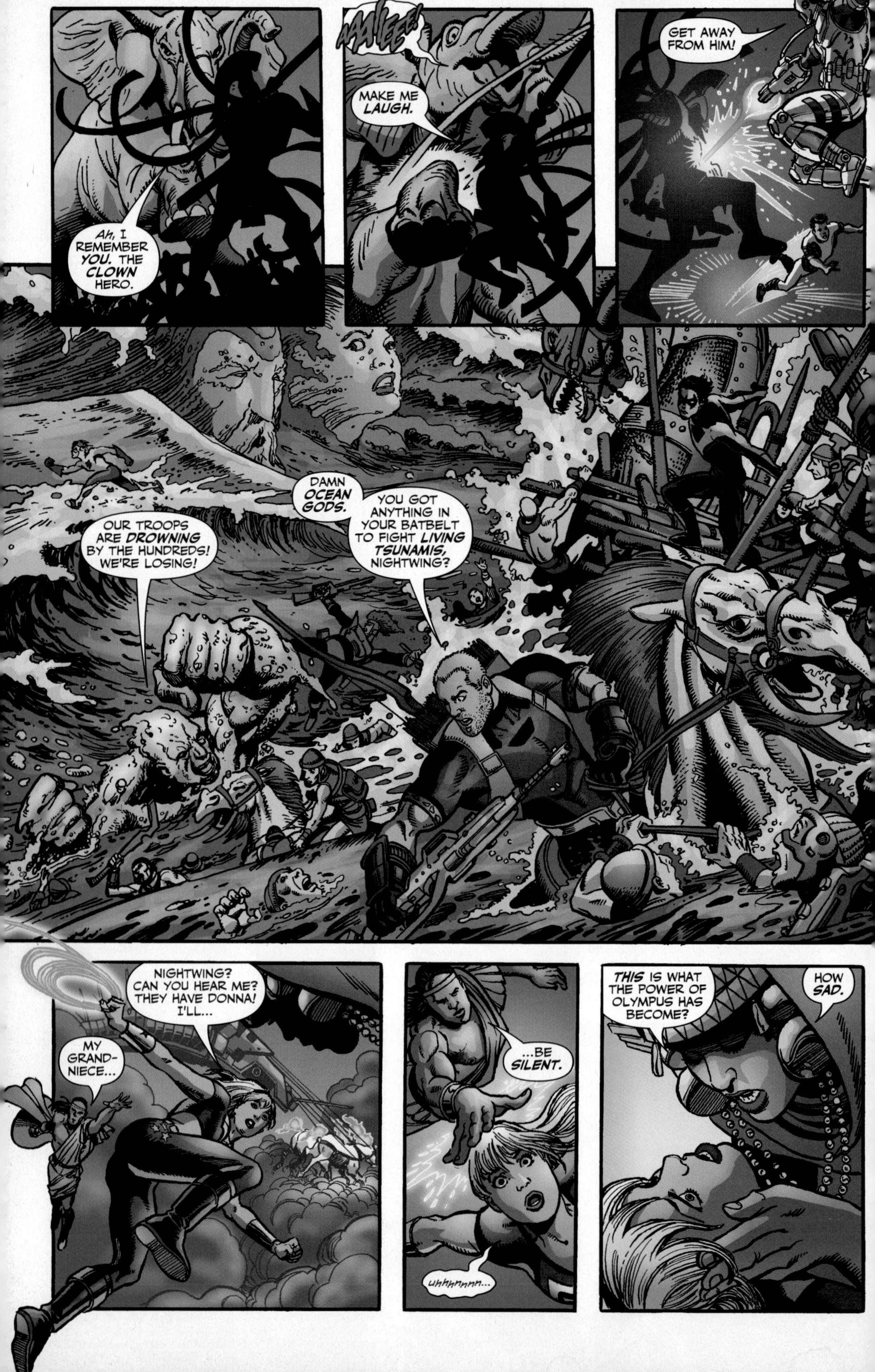
Ah, I REMEMBER YOU. THE CLOWN HERO.
AAAIIEEE!
MAKE ME LAUGH.
GET AWAY FROM HIM!
DAMN OCEAN GODS.
OUR TROOPS ARE DROWNING BY THE HUNDREDS! WE'RE LOSING!
YOU GOT ANYTHING IN YOUR BATBELT TO FIGHT LIVING TSUNAMIS, NIGHTWING?
NIGHTWING? CAN YOU HEAR ME? THEY HAVE DONNA! I'LL...
MY GRAND-NIECE...
...BE SILENT.
uhhhnnnn...
THIS IS WHAT THE POWER OF OLYMPUS HAS BECOME?
HOW SAD.

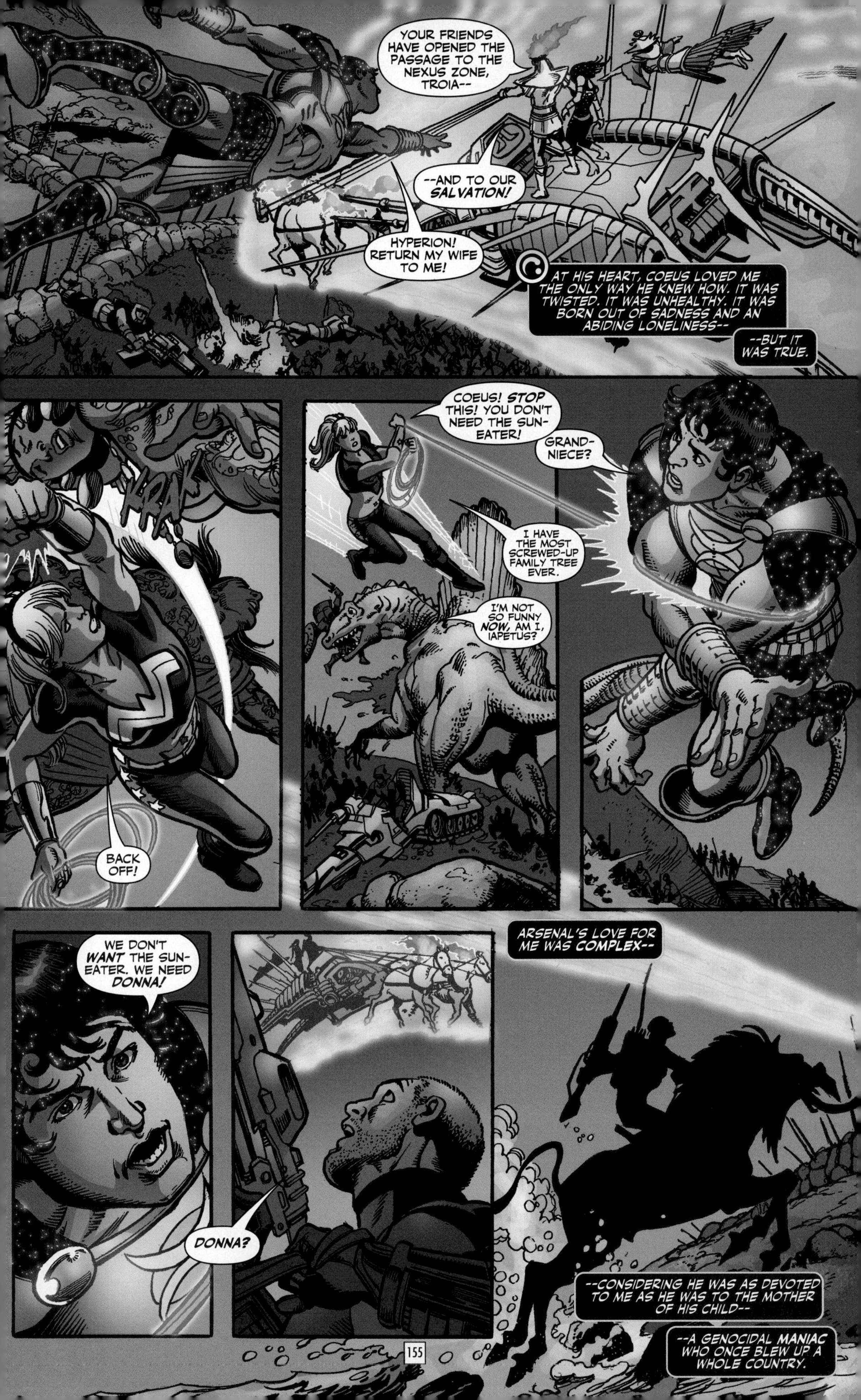

YOUR FRIENDS HAVE OPENED THE PASSAGE TO THE NEXUS ZONE, TROIA--
--AND TO OUR SALVATION!
HYPERION! RETURN MY WIFE TO ME!
AT HIS HEART, COEUS LOVED ME THE ONLY WAY HE KNEW HOW. IT WAS TWISTED. IT WAS UNHEALTHY. IT WAS BORN OUT OF SADNESS AND AN ABIDING LONELINESS--
--BUT IT WAS TRUE.
BACK OFF!
COEUS! STOP THIS! YOU DON'T NEED THE SUN-EATER!
I HAVE THE MOST SCREWED-UP FAMILY TREE EVER.
I'M NOT SO FUNNY NOW, AM I, IAPETUS?
GRAND-NIECE?
WE DON'T WANT THE SUN-EATER. WE NEED DONNA!
DONNA?
ARSENAL'S LOVE FOR ME WAS COMPLEX--
--CONSIDERING HE WAS AS DEVOTED TO ME AS HE WAS TO THE MOTHER OF HIS CHILD--
--A GENOCIDAL MANIAC WHO ONCE BLEW UP A WHOLE COUNTRY.

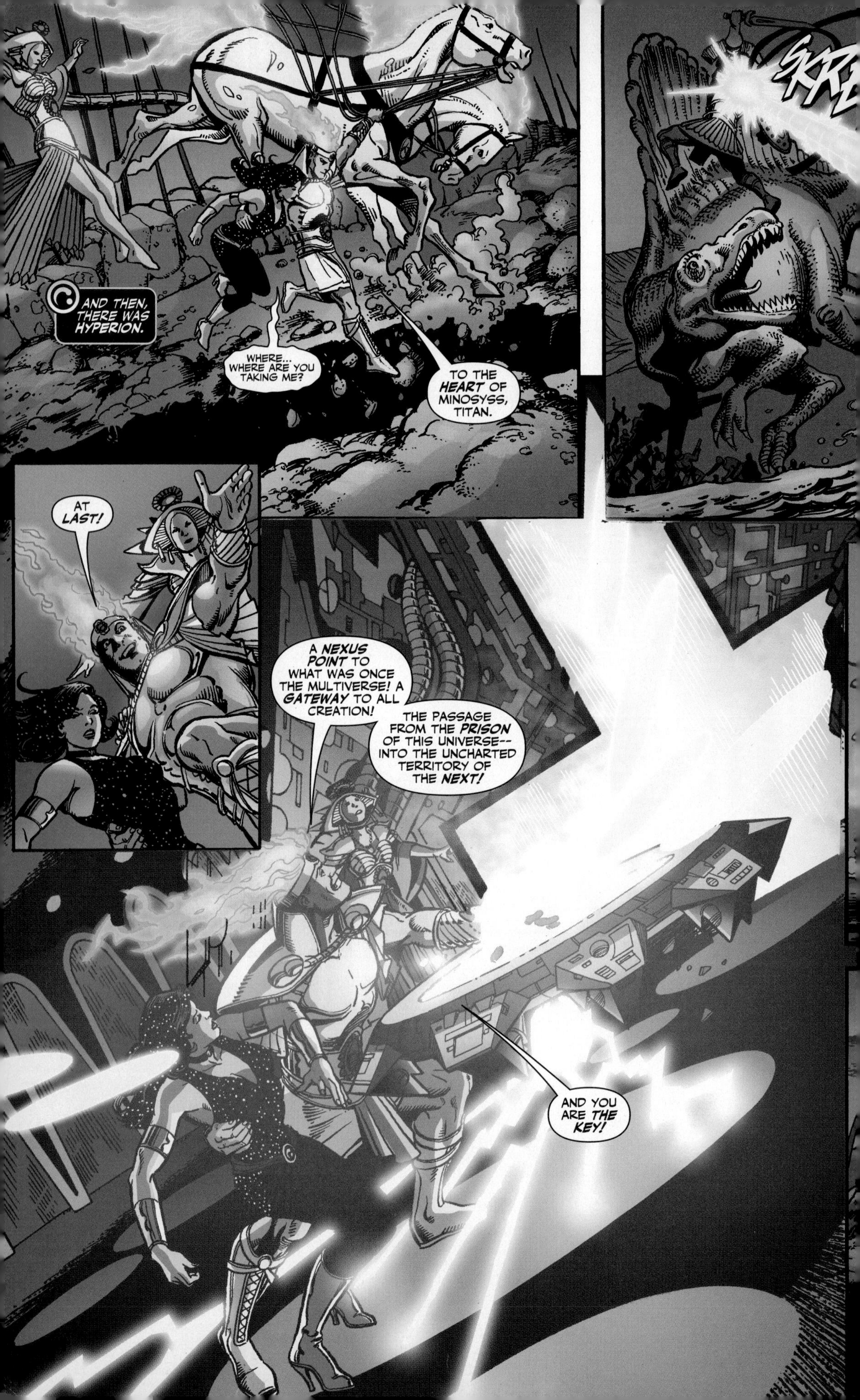

AND THEN, THERE WAS HYPERION.
WHERE... WHERE ARE YOU TAKING ME?
TO THE HEART OF MINOSYSS, TITAN.
SKRE
AT LAST!
A NEXUS POINT TO WHAT WAS ONCE THE MULTIVERSE! A GATEWAY TO ALL CREATION!
THE PASSAGE FROM THE PRISON OF THIS UNIVERSE-- INTO THE UNCHARTED TERRITORY OF THE NEXT!
AND YOU ARE THE KEY!

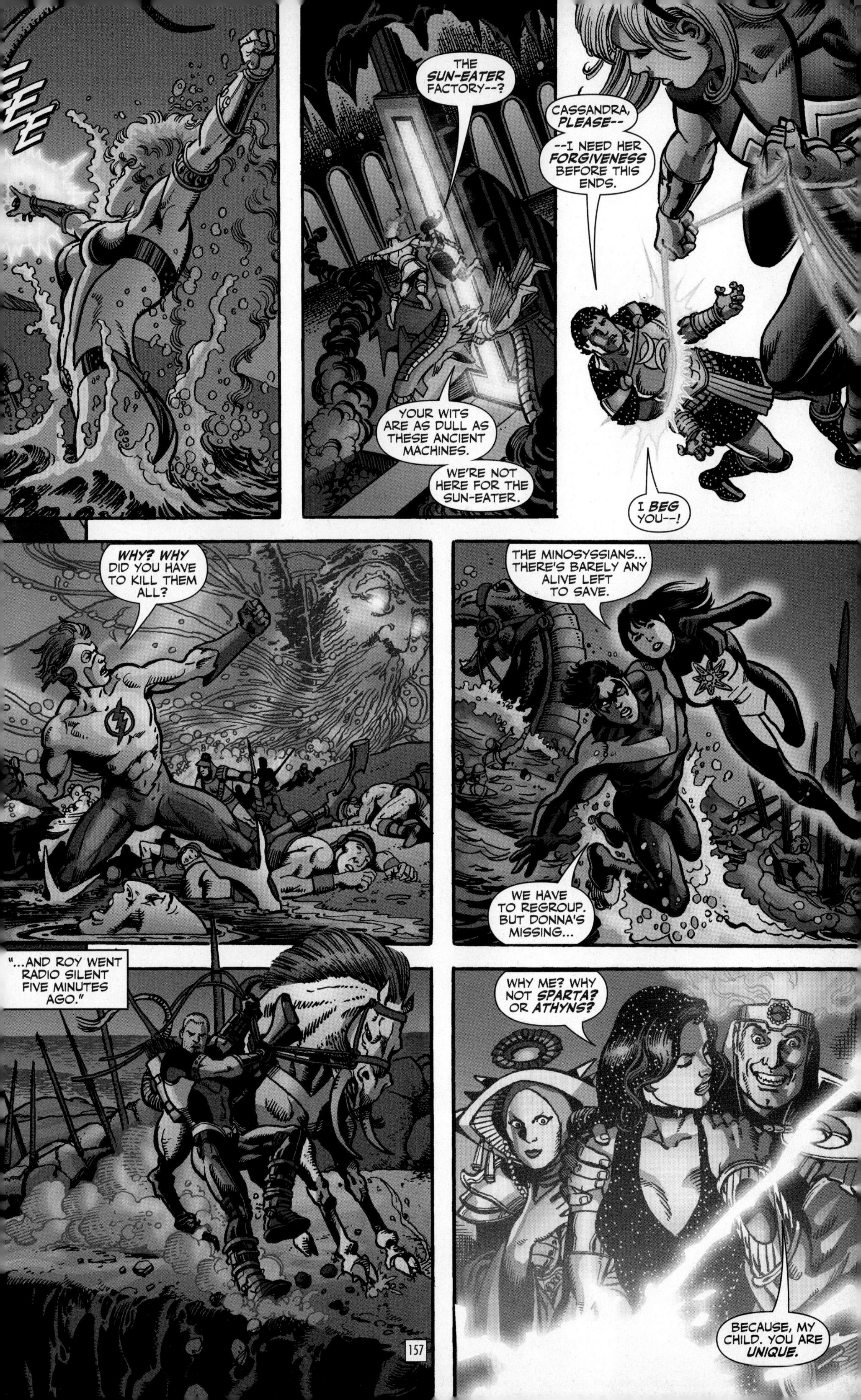

EEE
THE SUN-EATER FACTORY--?
YOUR WITS ARE AS DULL AS THESE ANCIENT MACHINES.
WE'RE NOT HERE FOR THE SUN-EATER.
CASSANDRA, PLEASE--
--I NEED HER FORGIVENESS BEFORE THIS ENDS.
I BEG YOU--!
WHY? WHY DID YOU HAVE TO KILL THEM ALL?
THE MINOSYSSIANS... THERE'S BARELY ANY ALIVE LEFT TO SAVE.
WE HAVE TO REGROUP. BUT DONNA'S MISSING...
"...AND ROY WENT RADIO SILENT FIVE MINUTES AGO."
WHY ME? WHY NOT SPARTA? OR ATHYNS?
BECAUSE, MY CHILD. YOU ARE UNIQUE.

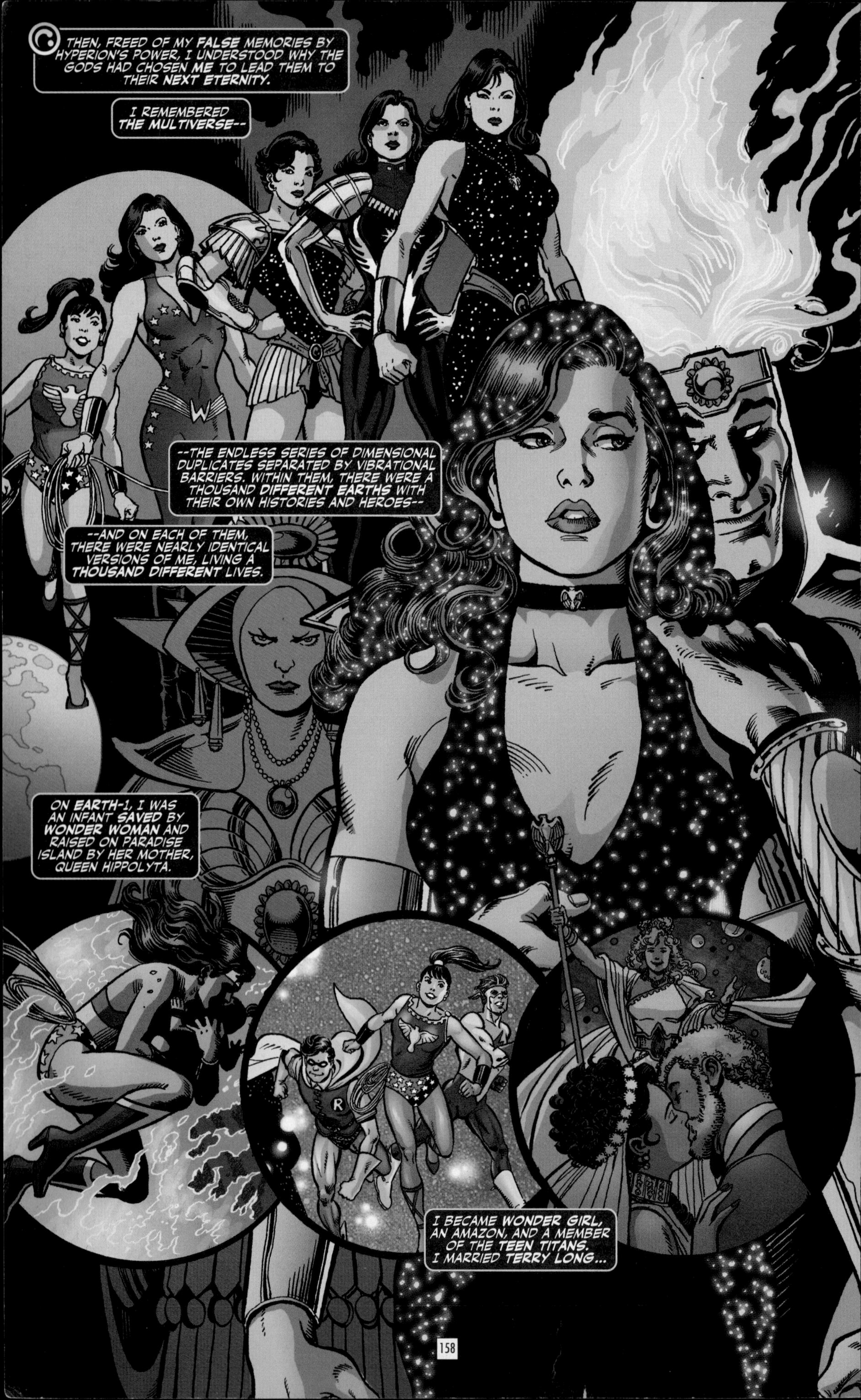
THEN, FREED OF MY FALSE MEMORIES BY HYPERION'S POWER, I UNDERSTOOD WHY THE GODS HAD CHOSEN ME TO LEAD THEM TO THEIR NEXT ETERNITY.
I REMEMBERED THE MULTIVERSE--
--THE ENDLESS SERIES OF DIMENSIONAL DUPLICATES SEPARATED BY VIBRATIONAL BARRIERS. WITHIN THEM, THERE WERE A THOUSAND DIFFERENT EARTHS WITH THEIR OWN HISTORIES AND HEROES--
--AND ON EACH OF THEM, THERE WERE NEARLY IDENTICAL VERSIONS OF ME, LIVING A THOUSAND DIFFERENT LIVES.
ON EARTH-1, I WAS AN INFANT SAVED BY WONDER WOMAN AND RAISED ON PARADISE ISLAND BY HER MOTHER, QUEEN HIPPOLYTA.
I BECAME WONDER GIRL, AN AMAZON, AND A MEMBER OF THE TEEN TITANS. I MARRIED TERRY LONG...

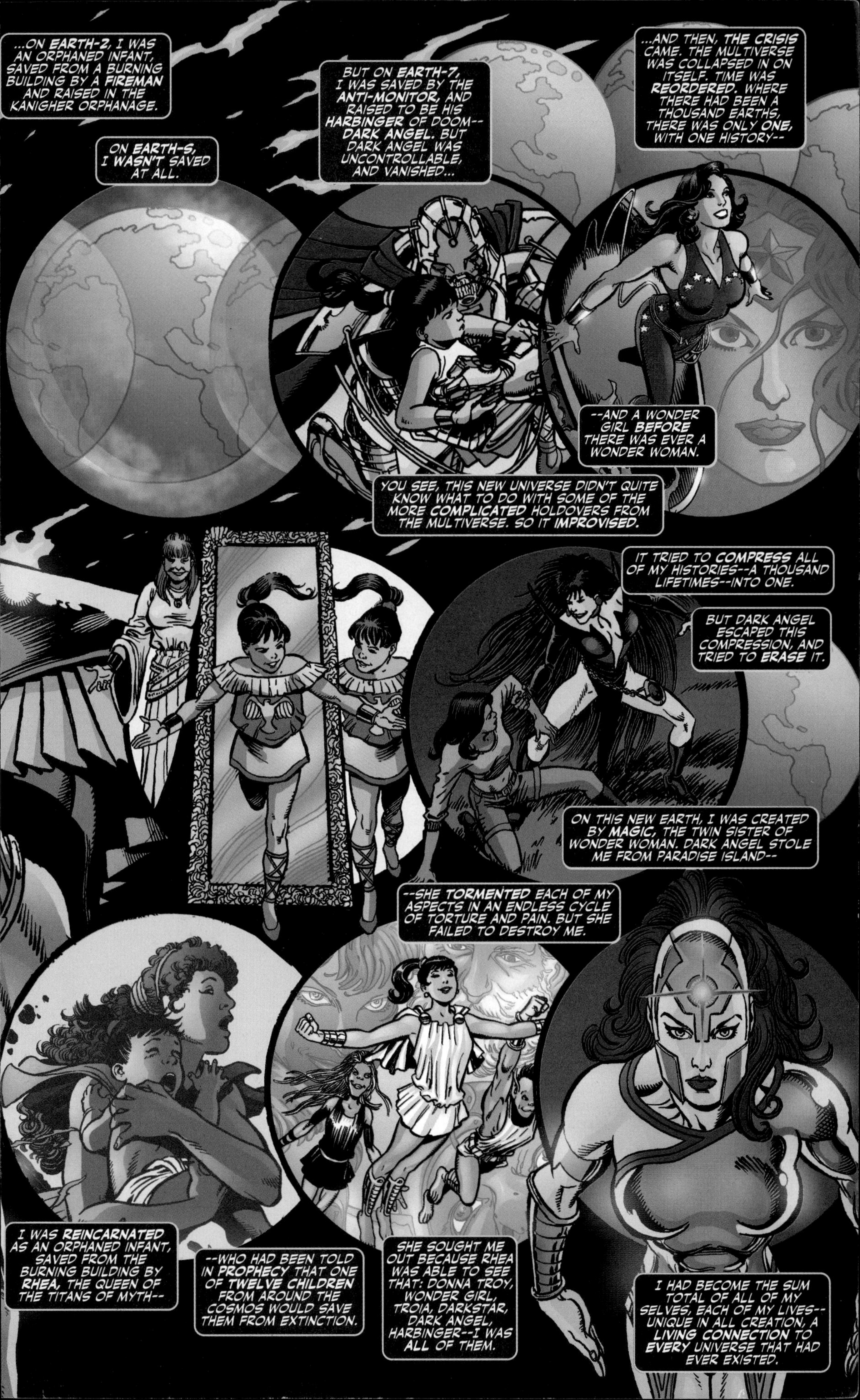
...ON EARTH-2, I WAS AN ORPHANED INFANT, SAVED FROM A BURNING BUILDING BY A FIREMAN AND RAISED IN THE KANIGHER ORPHANAGE.
ON EARTH-S, I WASN'T SAVED AT ALL.
BUT ON EARTH-7, I WAS SAVED BY THE ANTI-MONITOR, AND RAISED TO BE HIS HARBINGER OF DOOM-- DARK ANGEL. BUT DARK ANGEL WAS UNCONTROLLABLE, AND VANISHED...
...AND THEN, THE CRISIS CAME. THE MULTIVERSE WAS COLLAPSED IN ON ITSELF. TIME WAS REORDERED. WHERE THERE HAD BEEN A THOUSAND EARTHS, THERE WAS ONLY ONE, WITH ONE HISTORY--
--AND A WONDER GIRL BEFORE THERE WAS EVER A WONDER WOMAN.
YOU SEE, THIS NEW UNIVERSE DIDN'T QUITE KNOW WHAT TO DO WITH SOME OF THE MORE COMPLICATED HOLDOVERS FROM THE MULTIVERSE. SO IT IMPROVISED.
IT TRIED TO COMPRESS ALL OF MY HISTORIES--A THOUSAND LIFETIMES--INTO ONE.
BUT DARK ANGEL ESCAPED THIS COMPRESSION, AND TRIED TO ERASE IT.
ON THIS NEW EARTH, I WAS CREATED BY MAGIC, THE TWIN SISTER OF WONDER WOMAN. DARK ANGEL STOLE ME FROM PARADISE ISLAND--
--SHE TORMENTED EACH OF MY ASPECTS IN AN ENDLESS CYCLE OF TORTURE AND PAIN. BUT SHE FAILED TO DESTROY ME.
I WAS REINCARNATED AS AN ORPHANED INFANT, SAVED FROM THE BURNING BUILDING BY RHEA, THE QUEEN OF THE TITANS OF MYTH--
--WHO HAD BEEN TOLD IN PROPHECY THAT ONE OF TWELVE CHILDREN FROM AROUND THE COSMOS WOULD SAVE THEM FROM EXTINCTION.
SHE SOUGHT ME OUT BECAUSE RHEA WAS ABLE TO SEE THAT: DONNA TROY, WONDER GIRL, TROIA, DARKSTAR, DARK ANGEL, HARBINGER--I WAS ALL OF THEM.
I HAD BECOME THE SUM TOTAL OF ALL OF MY SELVES, EACH OF MY LIVES-- UNIQUE IN ALL CREATION, A LIVING CONNECTION TO EVERY UNIVERSE THAT HAD EVER EXISTED.

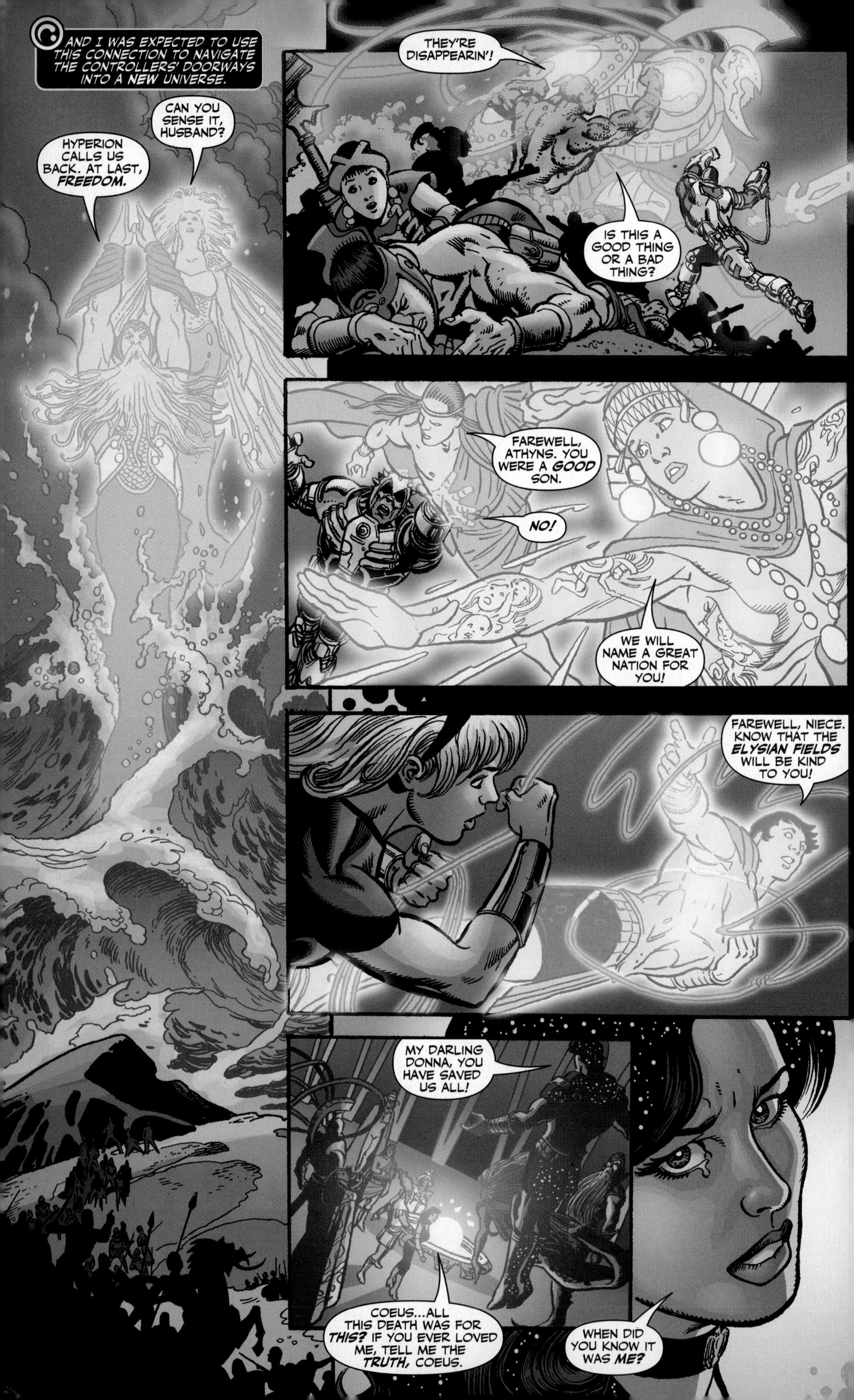

AND I WAS EXPECTED TO USE THIS CONNECTION TO NAVIGATE THE CONTROLLERS' DOORWAYS INTO A *NEW* UNIVERSE.
CAN YOU SENSE IT, HUSBAND?
HYPERION CALLS US BACK. AT LAST, *FREEDOM.*
THEY'RE DISAPPEARIN'!
IS THIS A GOOD THING OR A BAD THING?
FAREWELL, ATHYNS. YOU WERE A *GOOD* SON.
NO!
WE WILL NAME A GREAT NATION FOR YOU!
FAREWELL, NIECE. KNOW THAT THE *ELYSIAN FIELDS* WILL BE KIND TO YOU!
MY DARLING DONNA, YOU HAVE SAVED US ALL!
COEUS...ALL THIS DEATH WAS FOR *THIS?* IF YOU EVER LOVED ME, TELL ME THE *TRUTH,* COEUS.
WHEN DID YOU KNOW IT WAS *ME?*

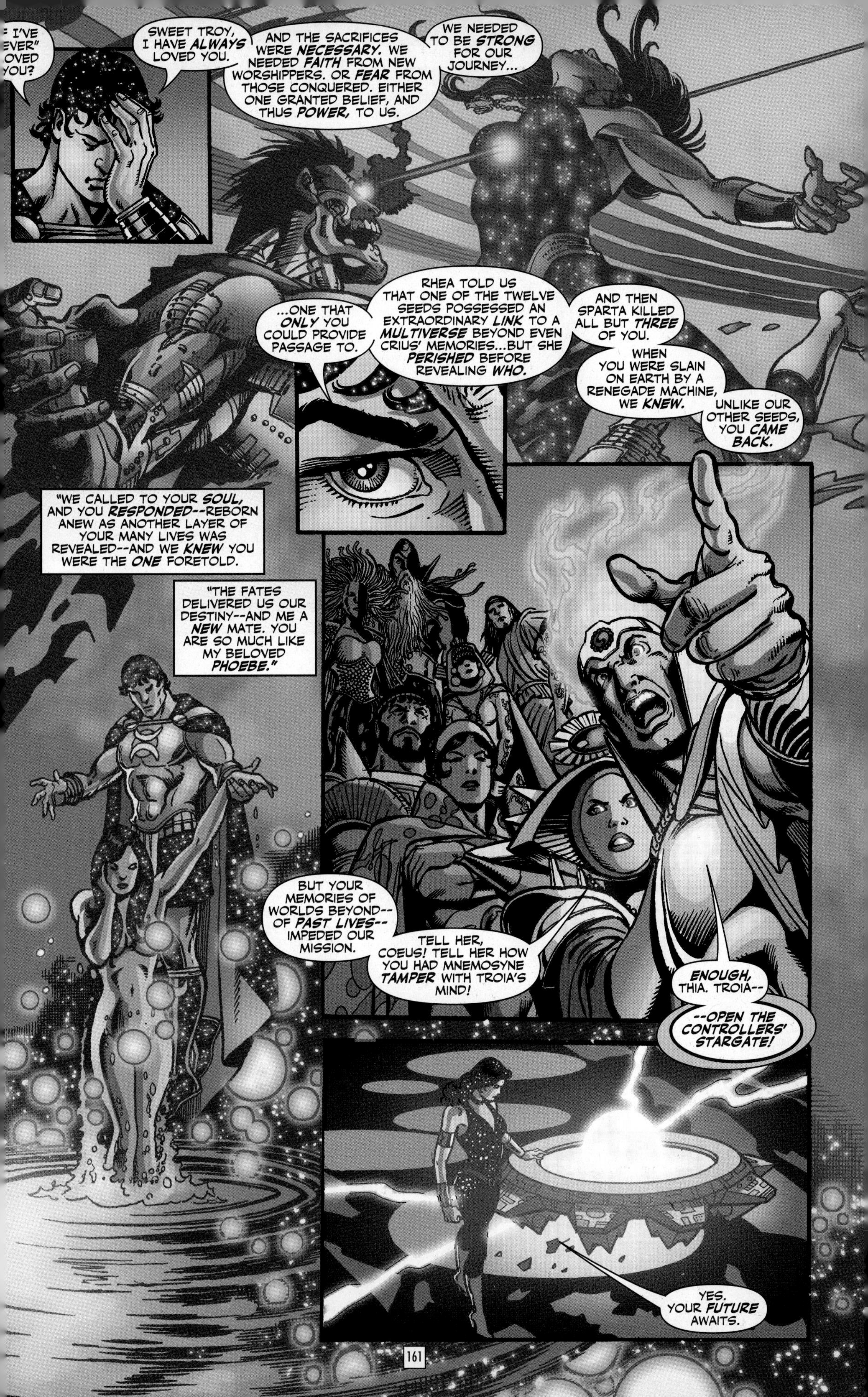

...IF I'VE EVER" LOVED YOU?
SWEET TROY, I HAVE ALWAYS LOVED YOU.
AND THE SACRIFICES WERE NECESSARY. WE NEEDED FAITH FROM NEW WORSHIPPERS. OR FEAR FROM THOSE CONQUERED. EITHER ONE GRANTED BELIEF, AND THUS POWER, TO US.
WE NEEDED TO BE STRONG FOR OUR JOURNEY...
...ONE THAT ONLY YOU COULD PROVIDE PASSAGE TO.
RHEA TOLD US THAT ONE OF THE TWELVE SEEDS POSSESSED AN EXTRAORDINARY LINK TO A MULTIVERSE BEYOND EVEN CRIUS' MEMORIES...BUT SHE PERISHED BEFORE REVEALING WHO.
AND THEN SPARTA KILLED ALL BUT THREE OF YOU.
WHEN YOU WERE SLAIN ON EARTH BY A RENEGADE MACHINE, WE KNEW.
UNLIKE OUR OTHER SEEDS, YOU CAME BACK.
"WE CALLED TO YOUR SOUL, AND YOU RESPONDED--REBORN ANEW AS ANOTHER LAYER OF YOUR MANY LIVES WAS REVEALED--AND WE KNEW YOU WERE THE ONE FORETOLD.
"THE FATES DELIVERED US OUR DESTINY--AND ME A NEW MATE. YOU ARE SO MUCH LIKE MY BELOVED PHOEBE."
BUT YOUR MEMORIES OF WORLDS BEYOND--OF PAST LIVES--IMPEDED OUR MISSION.
TELL HER, COEUS! TELL HER HOW YOU HAD MNEMOSYNE TAMPER WITH TROIA'S MIND!
ENOUGH, THIA. TROIA--
--OPEN THE CONTROLLERS' STARGATE!
YES. YOUR FUTURE AWAITS.

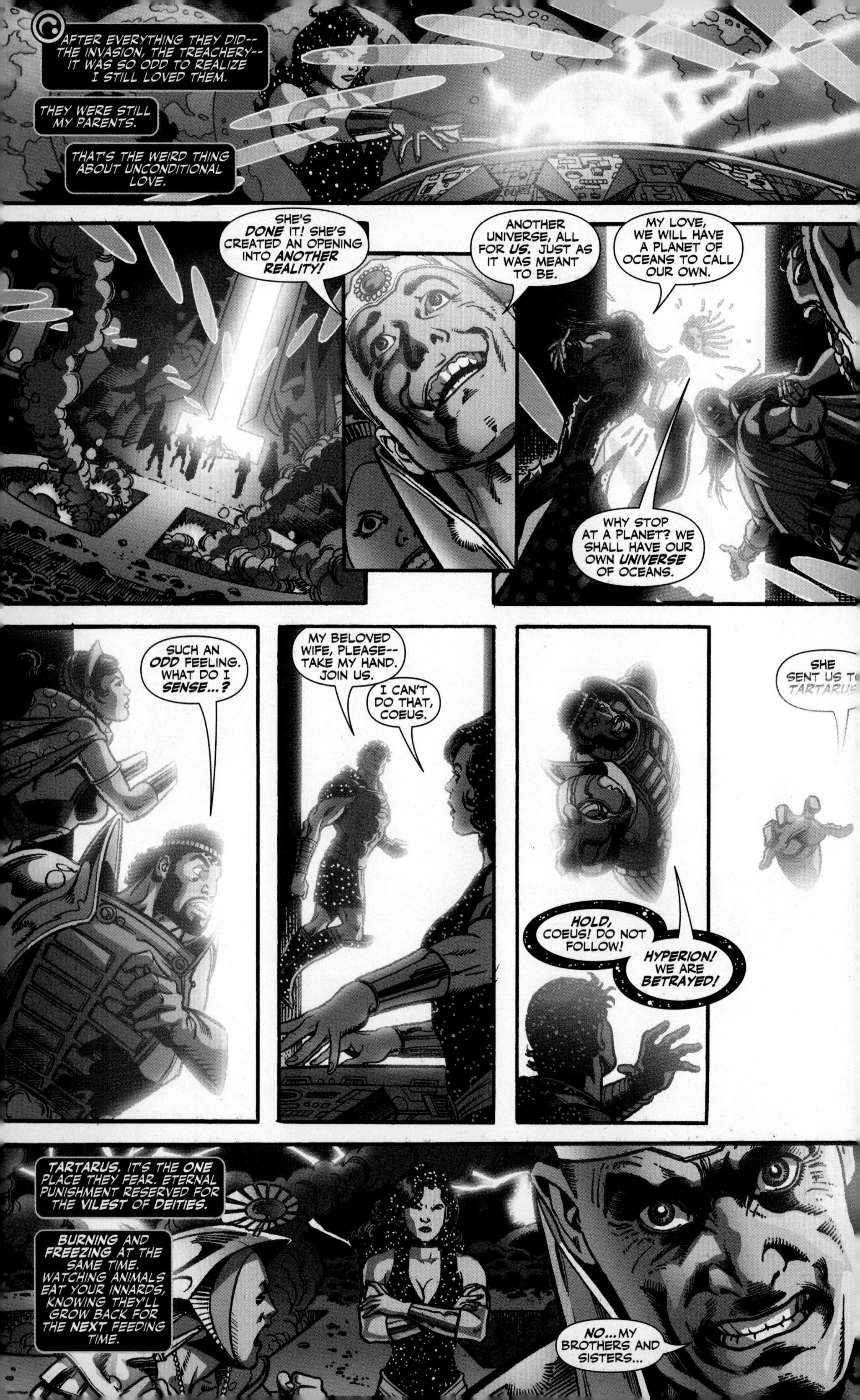
AFTER EVERYTHING THEY DID-- THE INVASION, THE TREACHERY-- IT WAS SO ODD TO REALIZE I STILL LOVED THEM.
THEY WERE STILL MY PARENTS.
THAT'S THE WEIRD THING ABOUT UNCONDITIONAL LOVE.
SHE'S DONE IT! SHE'S CREATED AN OPENING INTO ANOTHER REALITY!
ANOTHER UNIVERSE, ALL FOR US. JUST AS IT WAS MEANT TO BE.
MY LOVE, WE WILL HAVE A PLANET OF OCEANS TO CALL OUR OWN.
WHY STOP AT A PLANET? WE SHALL HAVE OUR OWN UNIVERSE OF OCEANS.
SUCH AN ODD FEELING. WHAT DO I SENSE...?
MY BELOVED WIFE, PLEASE-- TAKE MY HAND. JOIN US.
I CAN'T DO THAT, COEUS.
HOLD, COEUS! DO NOT FOLLOW!
HYPERION! WE ARE BETRAYED!
SHE SENT US T TARTARUS
TARTARUS. IT'S THE ONE PLACE THEY FEAR. ETERNAL PUNISHMENT RESERVED FOR THE VILEST OF DEITIES.
BURNING AND FREEZING AT THE SAME TIME. WATCHING ANIMALS EAT YOUR INNARDS, KNOWING THEY'LL GROW BACK FOR THE NEXT FEEDING TIME.
NO...MY BROTHERS AND SISTERS...

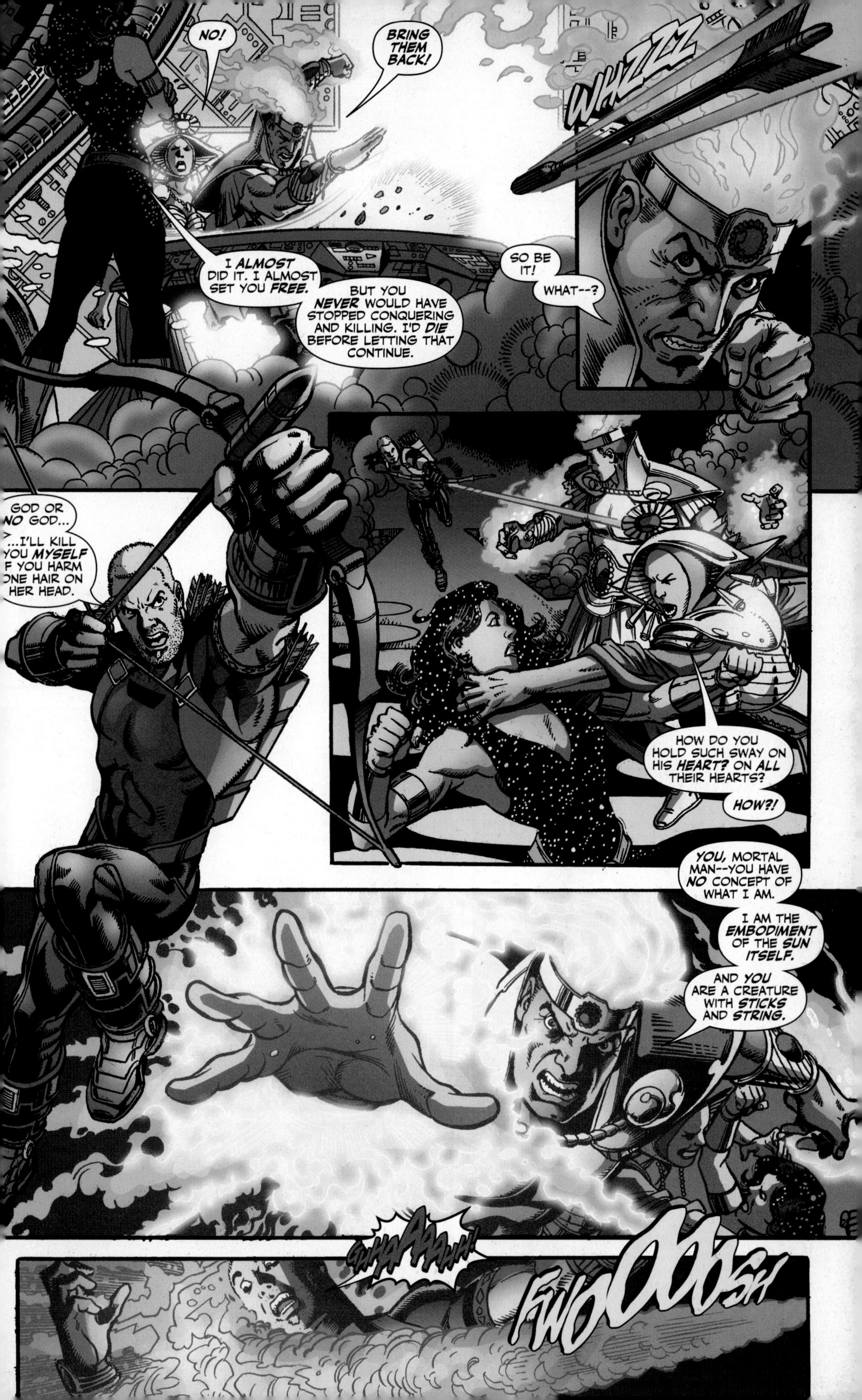
NO!
BRING THEM BACK!
WHZZZZ
I ALMOST DID IT. I ALMOST SET YOU FREE.
BUT YOU NEVER WOULD HAVE STOPPED CONQUERING AND KILLING. I'D DIE BEFORE LETTING THAT CONTINUE.
SO BE IT!
WHAT--?
GOD OR NO GOD...
...I'LL KILL YOU MYSELF IF YOU HARM ONE HAIR ON HER HEAD.
HOW DO YOU HOLD SUCH SWAY ON HIS HEART? ON ALL THEIR HEARTS?
HOW?!
YOU, MORTAL MAN--YOU HAVE NO CONCEPT OF WHAT I AM.
I AM THE EMBODIMENT OF THE SUN ITSELF.
AND YOU ARE A CREATURE WITH STICKS AND STRING.
FWOOOOSH

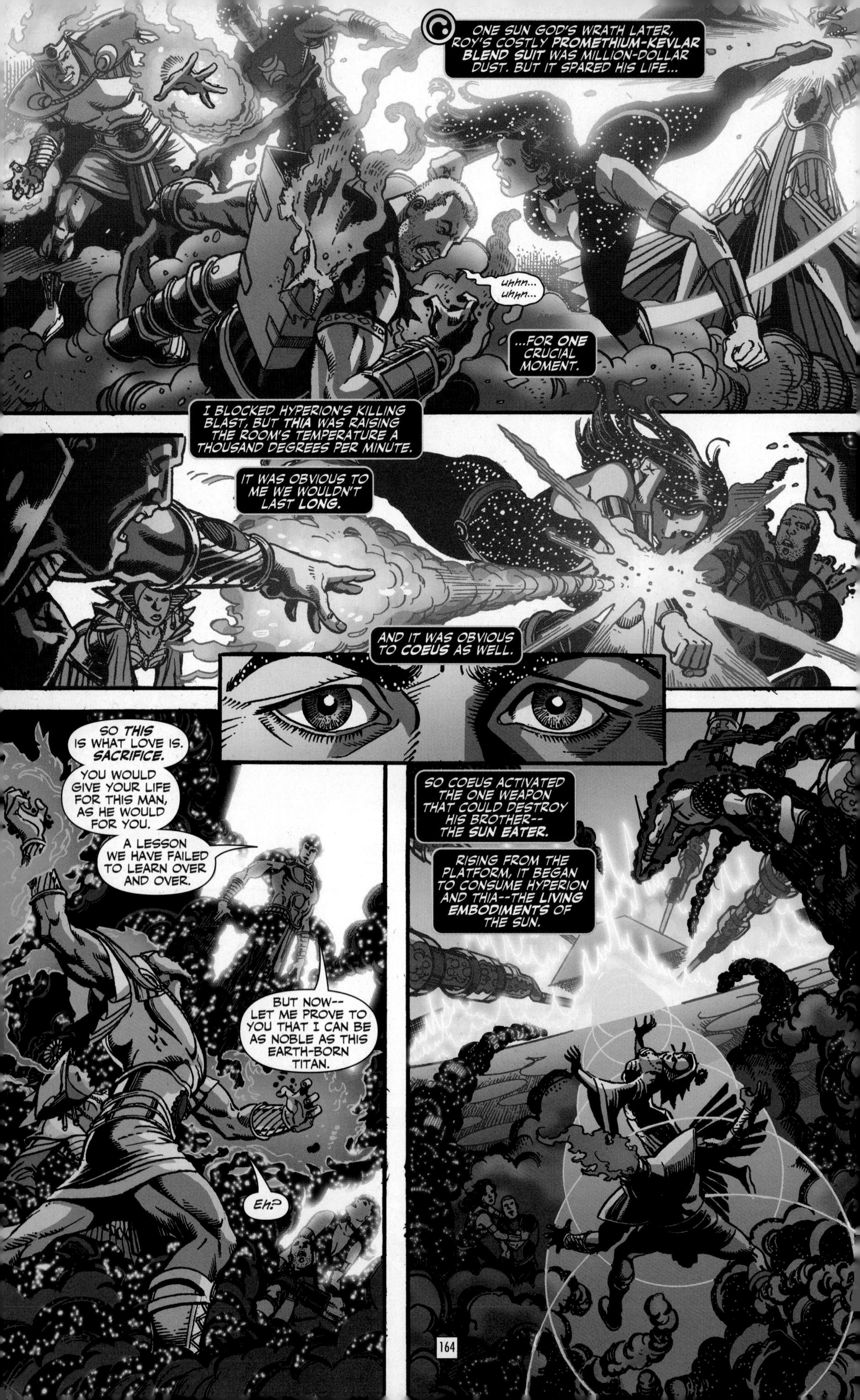
ONE SUN GOD'S WRATH LATER, ROY'S COSTLY PROMETHIUM-KEVLAR BLEND SUIT WAS MILLION-DOLLAR DUST. BUT IT SPARED HIS LIFE...
uhhn... uhhn...
...FOR ONE CRUCIAL MOMENT.
I BLOCKED HYPERION'S KILLING BLAST, BUT THIA WAS RAISING THE ROOM'S TEMPERATURE A THOUSAND DEGREES PER MINUTE.
IT WAS OBVIOUS TO ME WE WOULDN'T LAST LONG.
AND IT WAS OBVIOUS TO COEUS AS WELL.
SO THIS IS WHAT LOVE IS. SACRIFICE.
YOU WOULD GIVE YOUR LIFE FOR THIS MAN, AS HE WOULD FOR YOU.
A LESSON WE HAVE FAILED TO LEARN OVER AND OVER.
BUT NOW-- LET ME PROVE TO YOU THAT I CAN BE AS NOBLE AS THIS EARTH-BORN TITAN.
Eh?
SO COEUS ACTIVATED THE ONE WEAPON THAT COULD DESTROY HIS BROTHER-- THE SUN EATER.
RISING FROM THE PLATFORM, IT BEGAN TO CONSUME HYPERION AND THIA--THE LIVING EMBODIMENTS OF THE SUN.

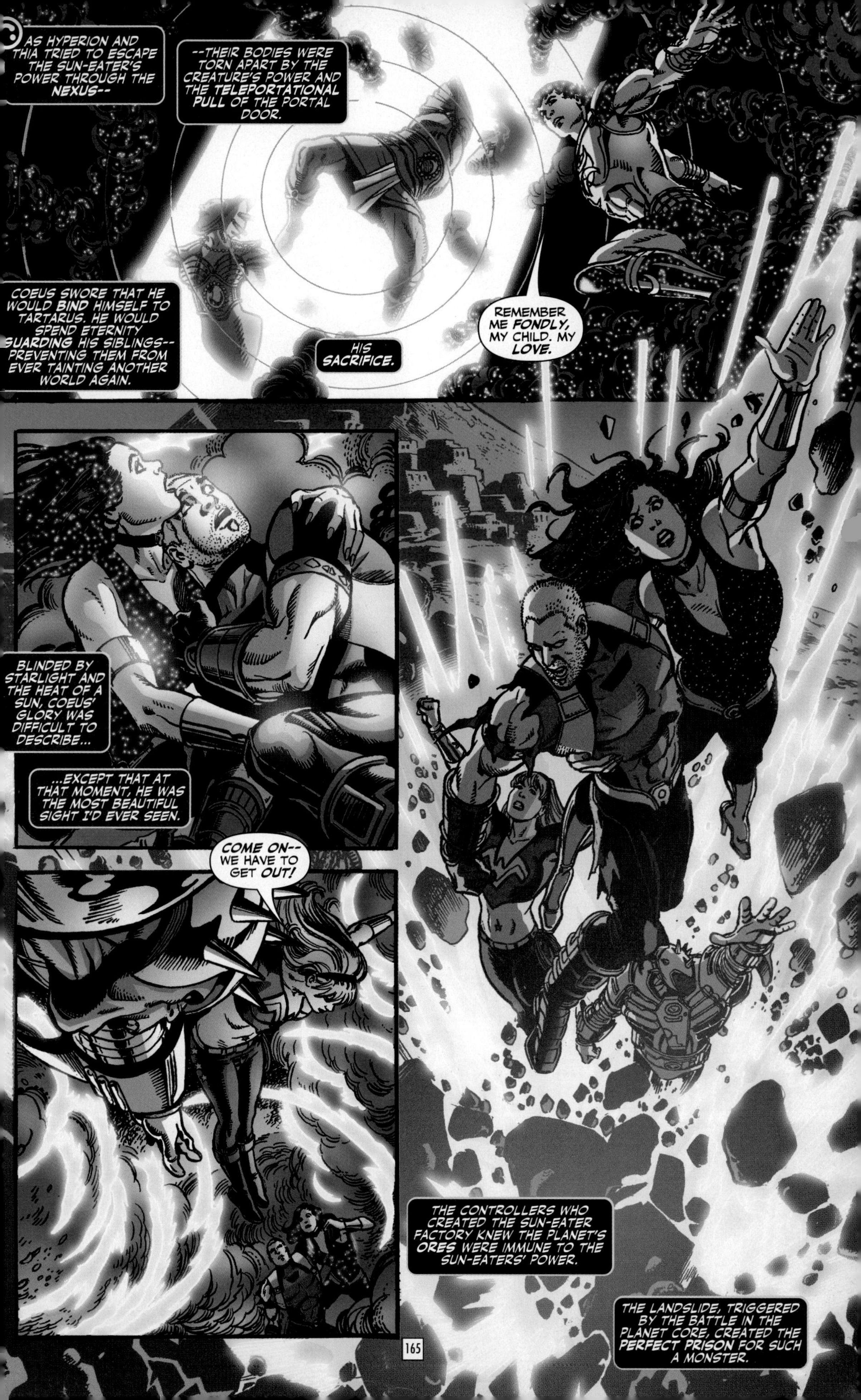
AS HYPERION AND THIA TRIED TO ESCAPE THE SUN-EATER'S POWER THROUGH THE NEXUS--
--THEIR BODIES WERE TORN APART BY THE CREATURE'S POWER AND THE TELEPORTATIONAL PULL OF THE PORTAL DOOR.
COEUS SWORE THAT HE WOULD BIND HIMSELF TO TARTARUS. HE WOULD SPEND ETERNITY GUARDING HIS SIBLINGS--PREVENTING THEM FROM EVER TAINTING ANOTHER WORLD AGAIN.
HIS SACRIFICE.
REMEMBER ME FONDLY, MY CHILD. MY LOVE.
BLINDED BY STARLIGHT AND THE HEAT OF A SUN, COEUS' GLORY WAS DIFFICULT TO DESCRIBE...
...EXCEPT THAT AT THAT MOMENT, HE WAS THE MOST BEAUTIFUL SIGHT I'D EVER SEEN.
COME ON-- WE HAVE TO GET OUT!
THE CONTROLLERS WHO CREATED THE SUN-EATER FACTORY KNEW THE PLANET'S ORES WERE IMMUNE TO THE SUN-EATERS' POWER.
THE LANDSLIDE, TRIGGERED BY THE BATTLE IN THE PLANET CORE, CREATED THE PERFECT PRISON FOR SUCH A MONSTER.

COEUS GAVE ONE FINAL GIFT BEFORE HE VANISHED, IN A BURST OF NOCTURNAL POWER--

--A SIGNAL TO END THE WAR.

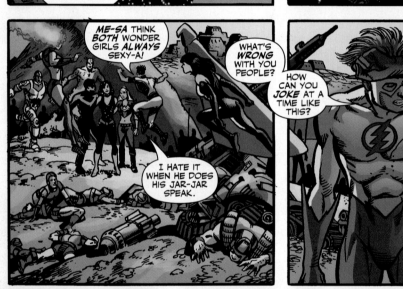

SO WHO KISSES BETTER, ME OR MR. GOD BACK THERE?

SHUT UP.

COME HERE, DONNA!

ME-SA THINK BOTH WONDER GIRLS ALWAYS SEXY-A!

WHAT'S WRONG WITH YOU PEOPLE?

HOW CAN YOU JOKE AT A TIME LIKE THIS?

I HATE IT WHEN HE DOES HIS JAR-JAR SPEAK.

KID FLASH HAS CHANGED SO MUCH. I USED TO THINK HE WAS SO IMMATURE.

I COULD SEE HE'D GROWN TO BE THE NEW HEART OF THE TEEN TITANS.

THE ARMIES OF THE GODS WERE NOW JUST PEOPLE WITHOUT A HOME. THEY SURRENDERED TO THE MINOSYSSIANS.

TOGETHER, THEY WOULD BE THE EVER-VIGILANT GUARDIANS OF THE SUN-EATER.

ATHYNS--THE SOLE SURVIVOR OF HIS PLANET, A HERO WITHOUT A PEOPLE-- AGREED QUICKLY TO BECOME THEIR LEADER.

THE SPHERE SENT MY FRIENDS BACK TO EARTH.

AND ME? I WAS NO LONGER A GODDESS NOR A CONQUEROR.

I WAS SIMPLY DONNA TROY.

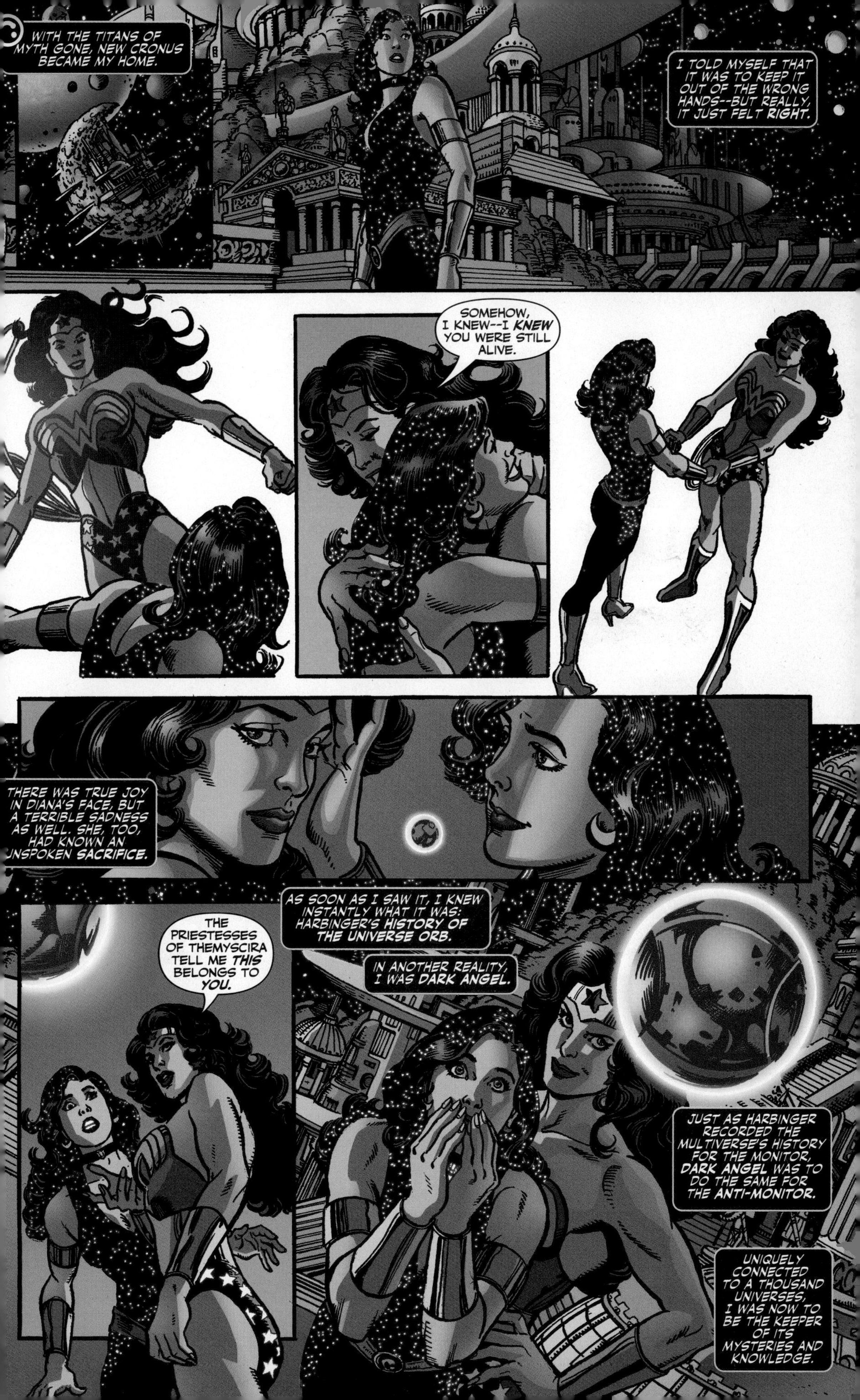
WITH THE TITANS OF MYTH GONE, NEW CRONUS BECAME MY HOME.
I TOLD MYSELF THAT IT WAS TO KEEP IT OUT OF THE WRONG HANDS--BUT REALLY, IT JUST FELT RIGHT.
SOMEHOW, I KNEW--I KNEW YOU WERE STILL ALIVE.
THERE WAS TRUE JOY IN DIANA'S FACE, BUT A TERRIBLE SADNESS AS WELL. SHE, TOO, HAD KNOWN AN UNSPOKEN SACRIFICE.
THE PRIESTESSES OF THEMYSCIRA TELL ME THIS BELONGS TO YOU.
AS SOON AS I SAW IT, I KNEW INSTANTLY WHAT IT WAS: HARBINGER'S HISTORY OF THE UNIVERSE ORB.
IN ANOTHER REALITY, I WAS DARK ANGEL.
JUST AS HARBINGER RECORDED THE MULTIVERSE'S HISTORY FOR THE MONITOR, DARK ANGEL WAS TO DO THE SAME FOR THE ANTI-MONITOR.
UNIQUELY CONNECTED TO A THOUSAND UNIVERSES, I WAS NOW TO BE THE KEEPER OF ITS MYSTERIES AND KNOWLEDGE.

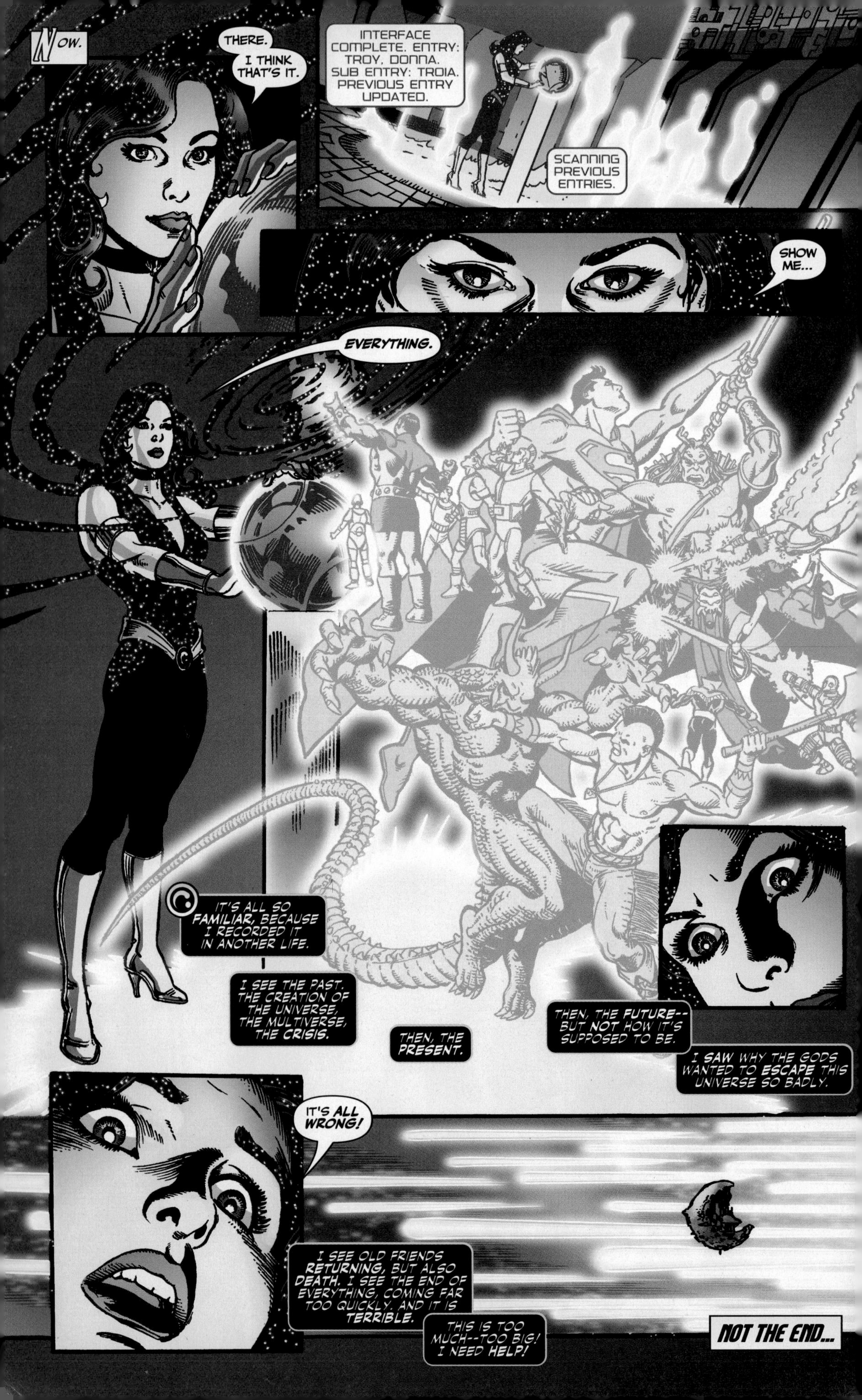
NOW.
THERE. I THINK THAT'S IT.
INTERFACE COMPLETE. ENTRY: TROY, DONNA. SUB ENTRY: TROIA. PREVIOUS ENTRY UPDATED.
SCANNING PREVIOUS ENTRIES.
SHOW ME...
EVERYTHING.
IT'S ALL SO FAMILIAR, BECAUSE I RECORDED IT IN ANOTHER LIFE.
I SEE THE PAST. THE CREATION OF THE UNIVERSE, THE MULTIVERSE, THE CRISIS.
THEN, THE PRESENT.
THEN, THE FUTURE-- BUT NOT HOW IT'S SUPPOSED TO BE.
I SAW WHY THE GODS WANTED TO ESCAPE THIS UNIVERSE SO BADLY.
IT'S ALL WRONG!
I SEE OLD FRIENDS RETURNING, BUT ALSO DEATH. I SEE THE END OF EVERYTHING, COMING FAR TOO QUICKLY. AND IT IS TERRIBLE.
THIS IS TOO MUCH--TOO BIG! I NEED HELP!
NOT THE END...

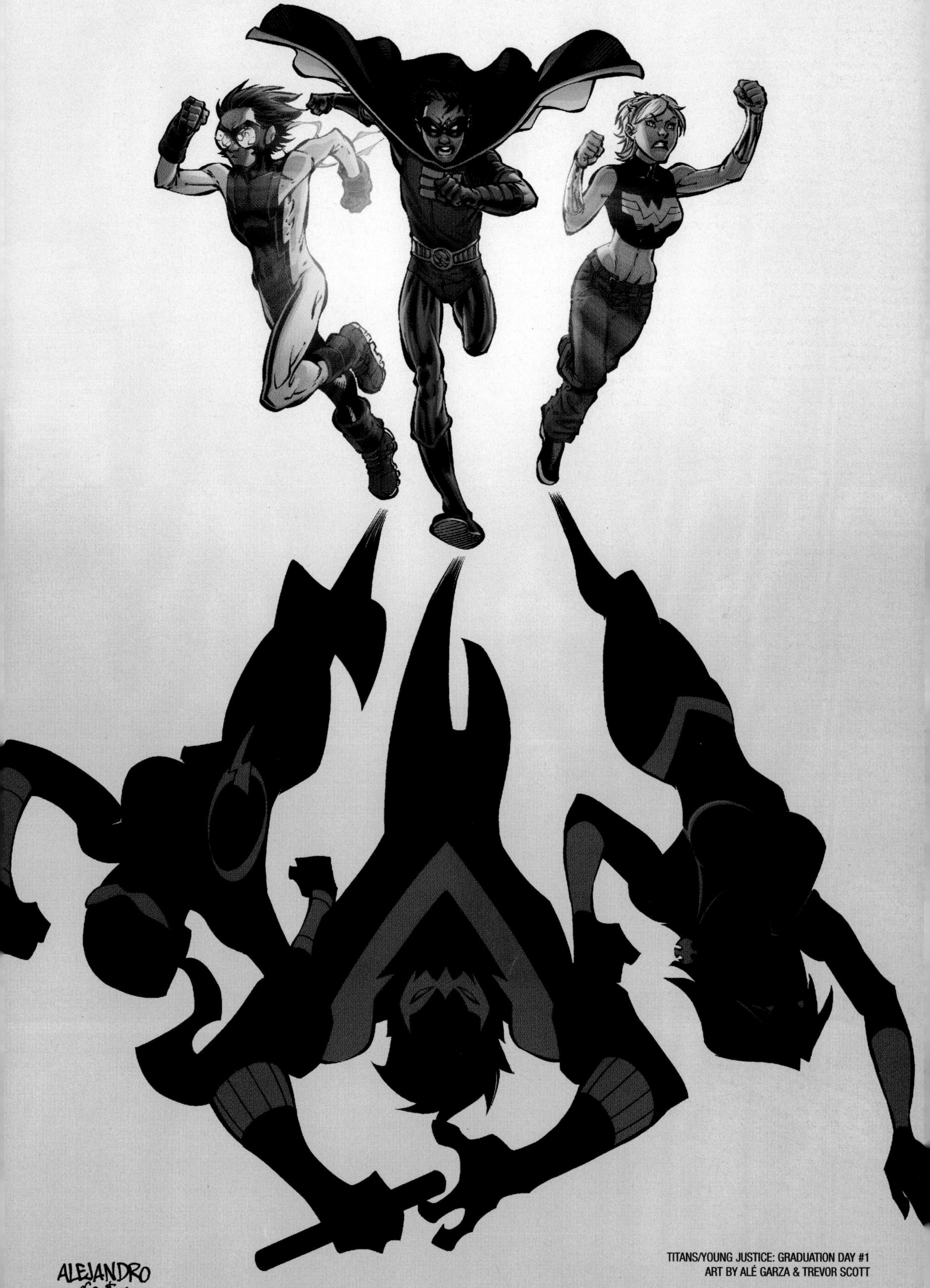
ALEJANDRO

TITANS/YOUNG JUSTICE: GRADUATION DAY #1
ART BY ALÉ GARZA & TREVOR SCOTT

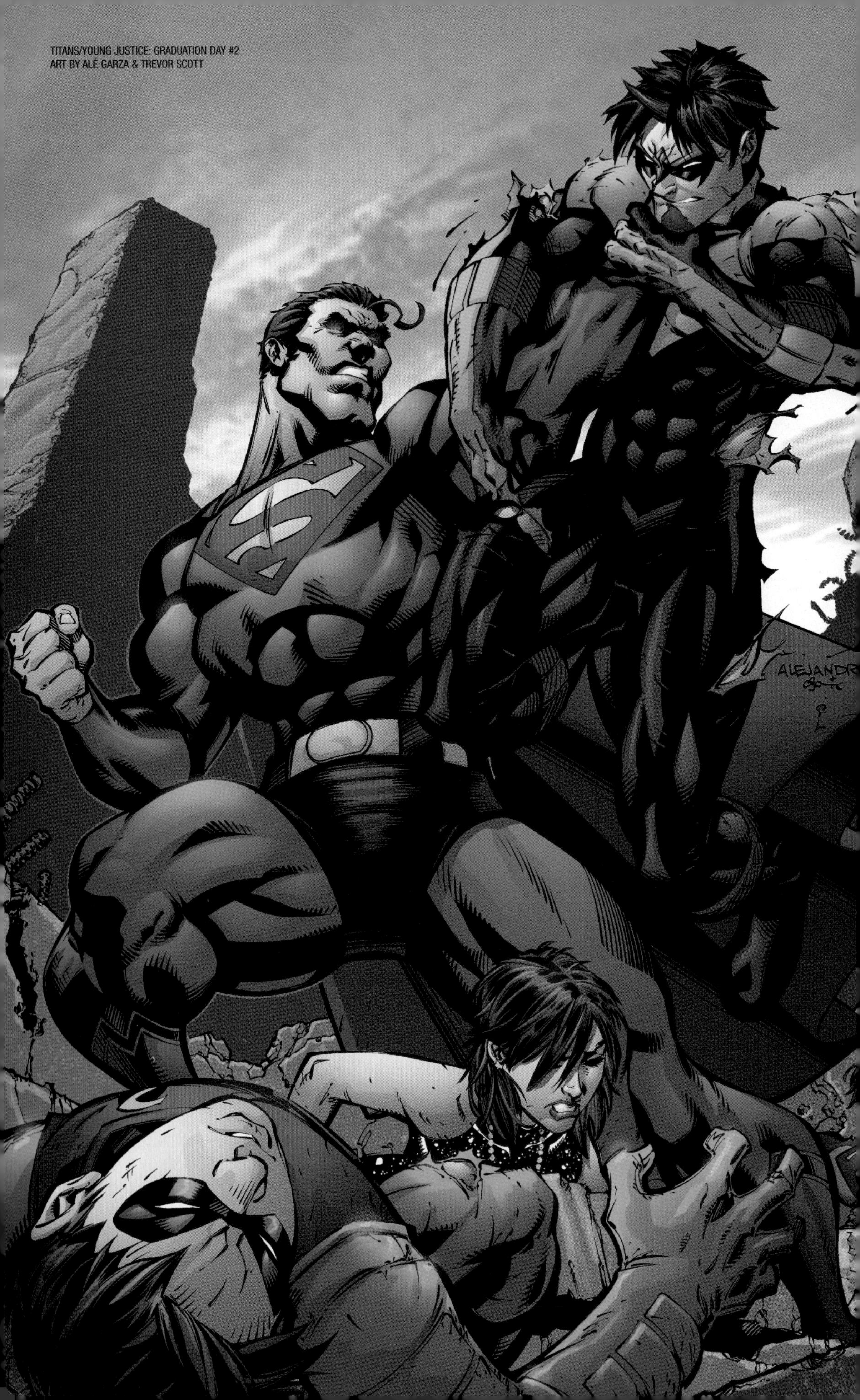

TITANS/YOUNG JUSTICE: GRADUATION DAY #2
ART BY ALÉ GARZA & TREVOR SCOTT

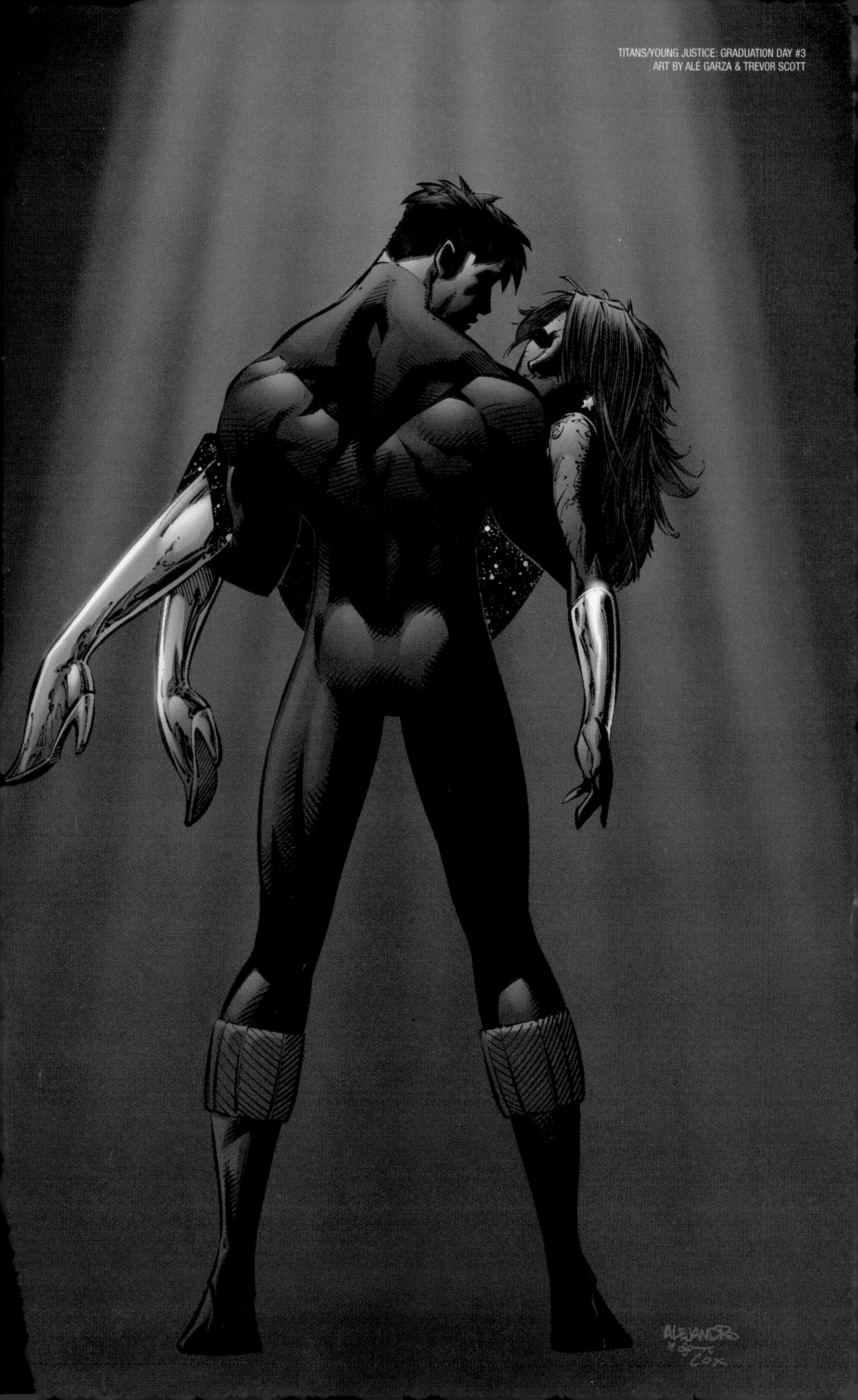
ALEJANDRO
TITANS/YOUNG JUSTICE: GRADUATION DAY #3
ART BY ALÉ GARZA & TREVOR SCOTT

TITANS/YOUNG JUSTICE: GRADUATION DAY COLLECTION
ART BY ALÉ GARZA & RICHARD FRIEND

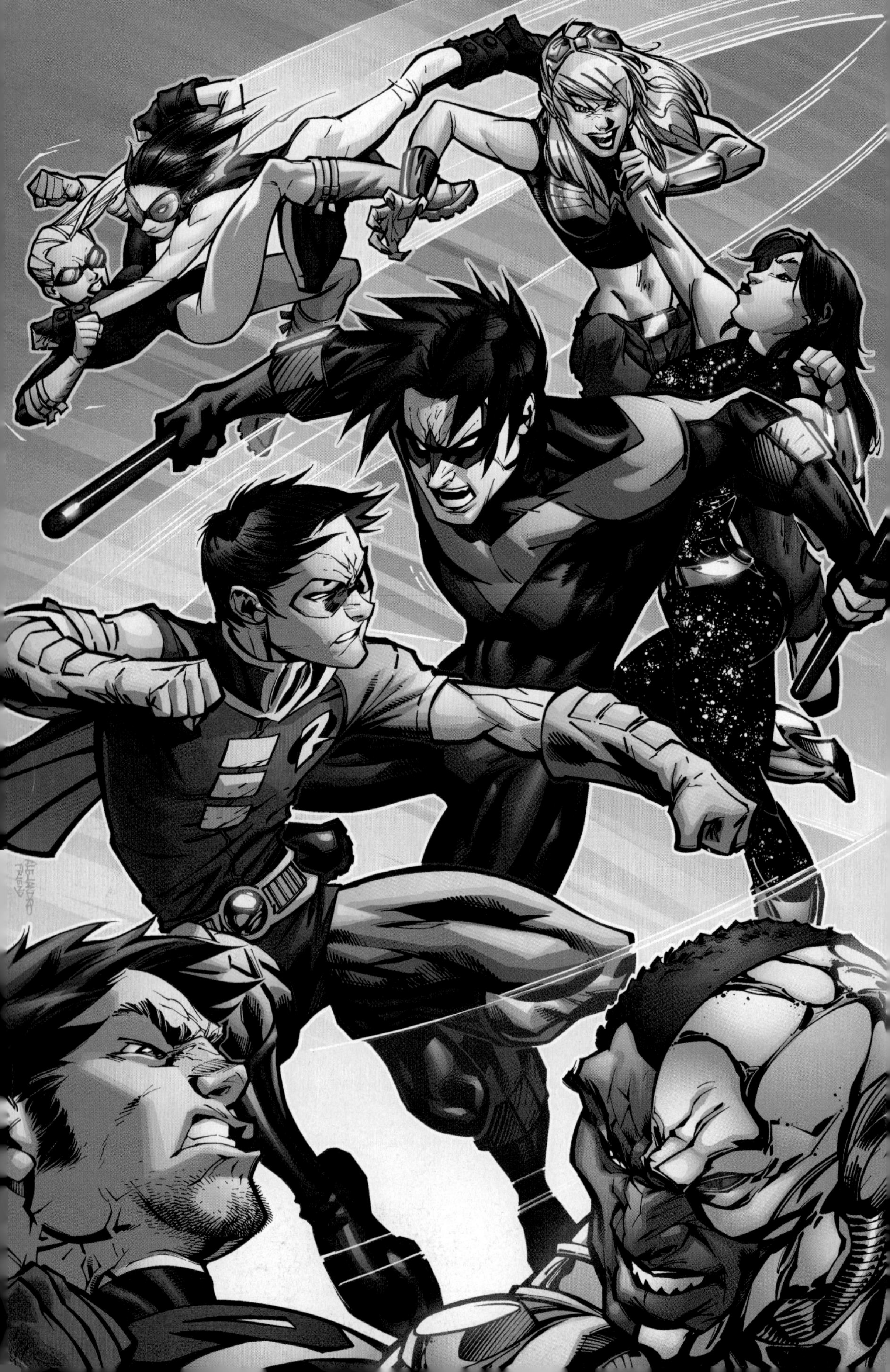

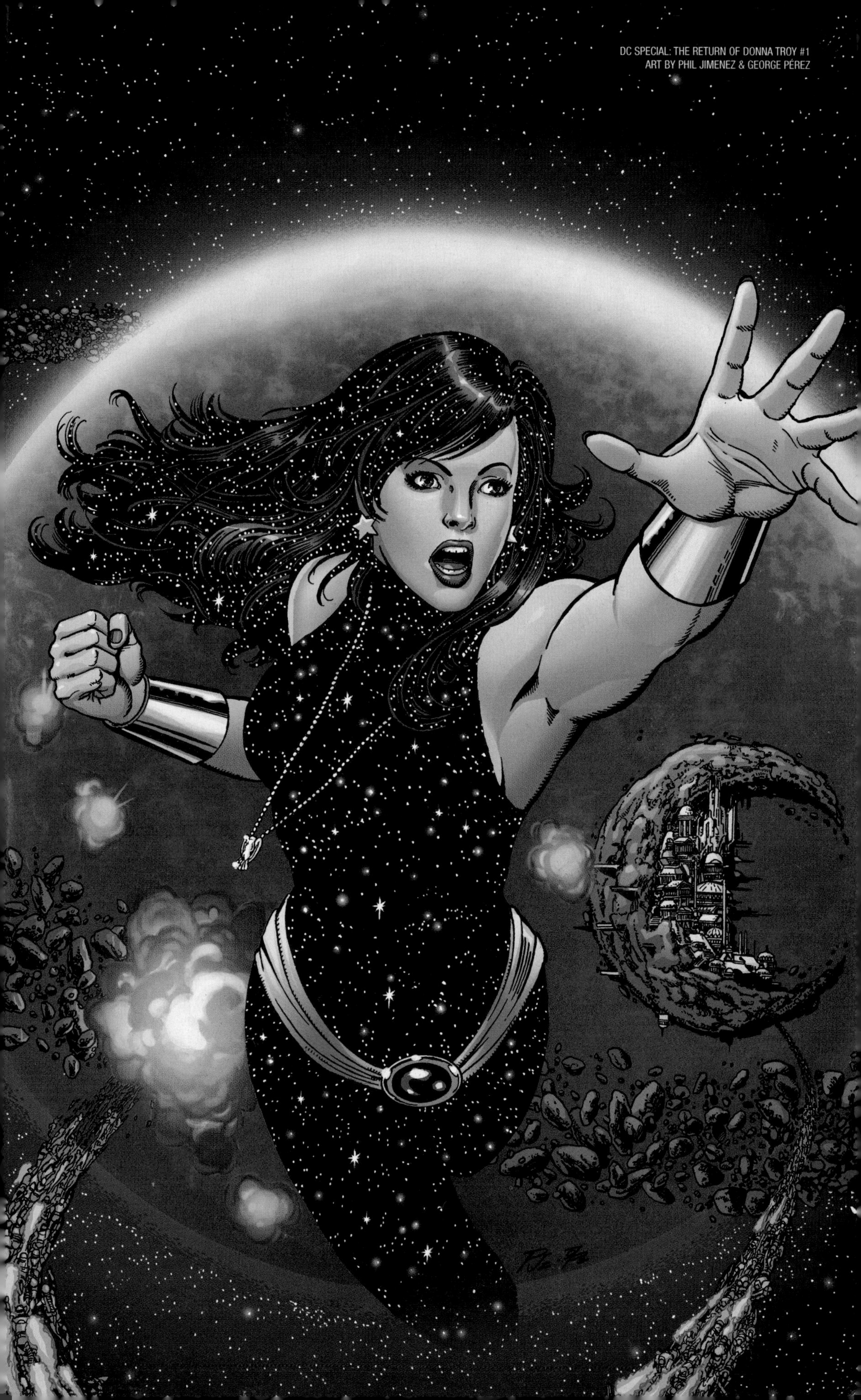

DC SPECIAL: THE RETURN OF DONNA TROY #1
ART BY PHIL JIMENEZ & GEORGE PÉREZ

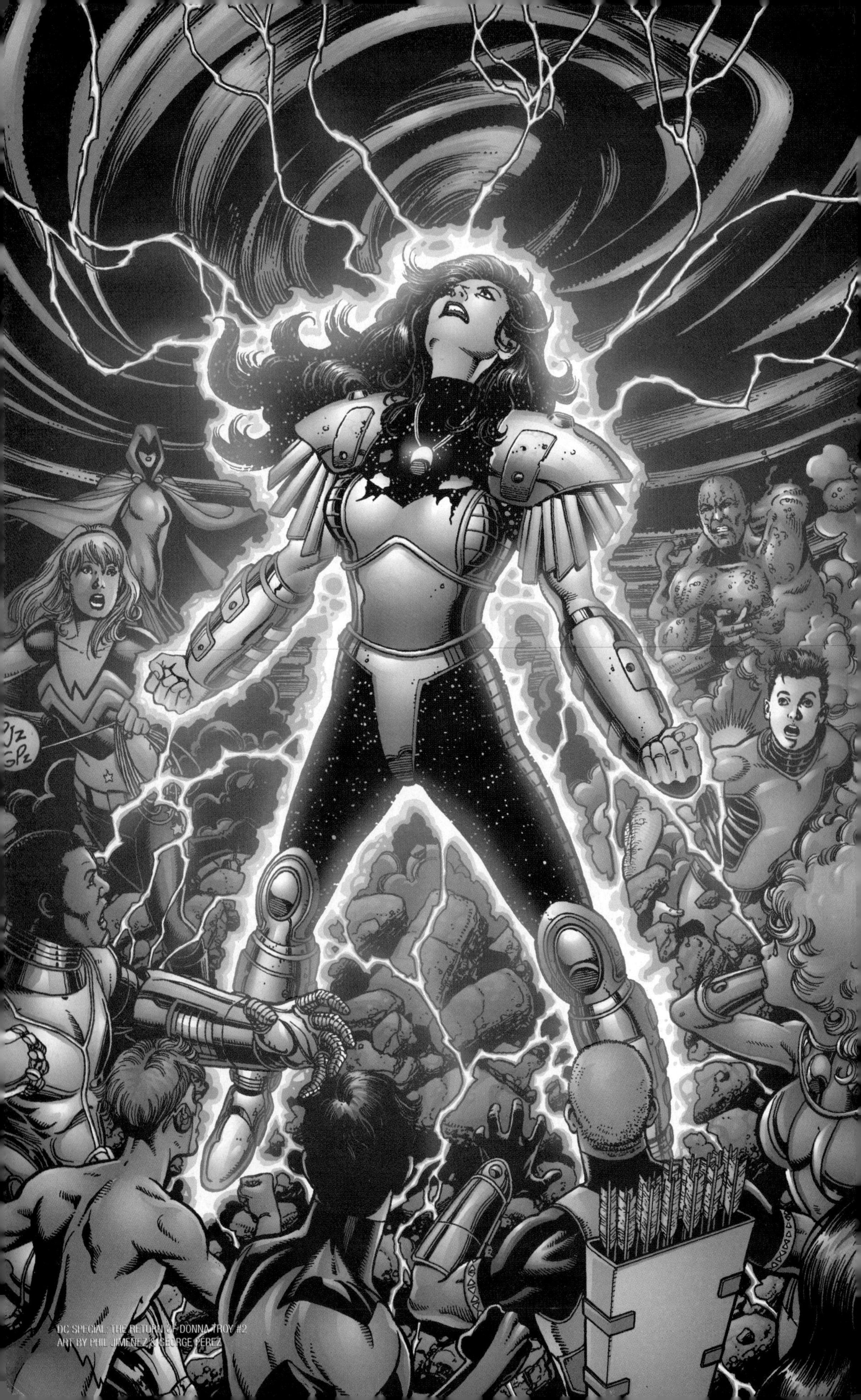

DC SPECIAL: THE RETURN OF DONNA TROY #2
ART BY PHIL JIMENEZ & GEORGE PÉREZ

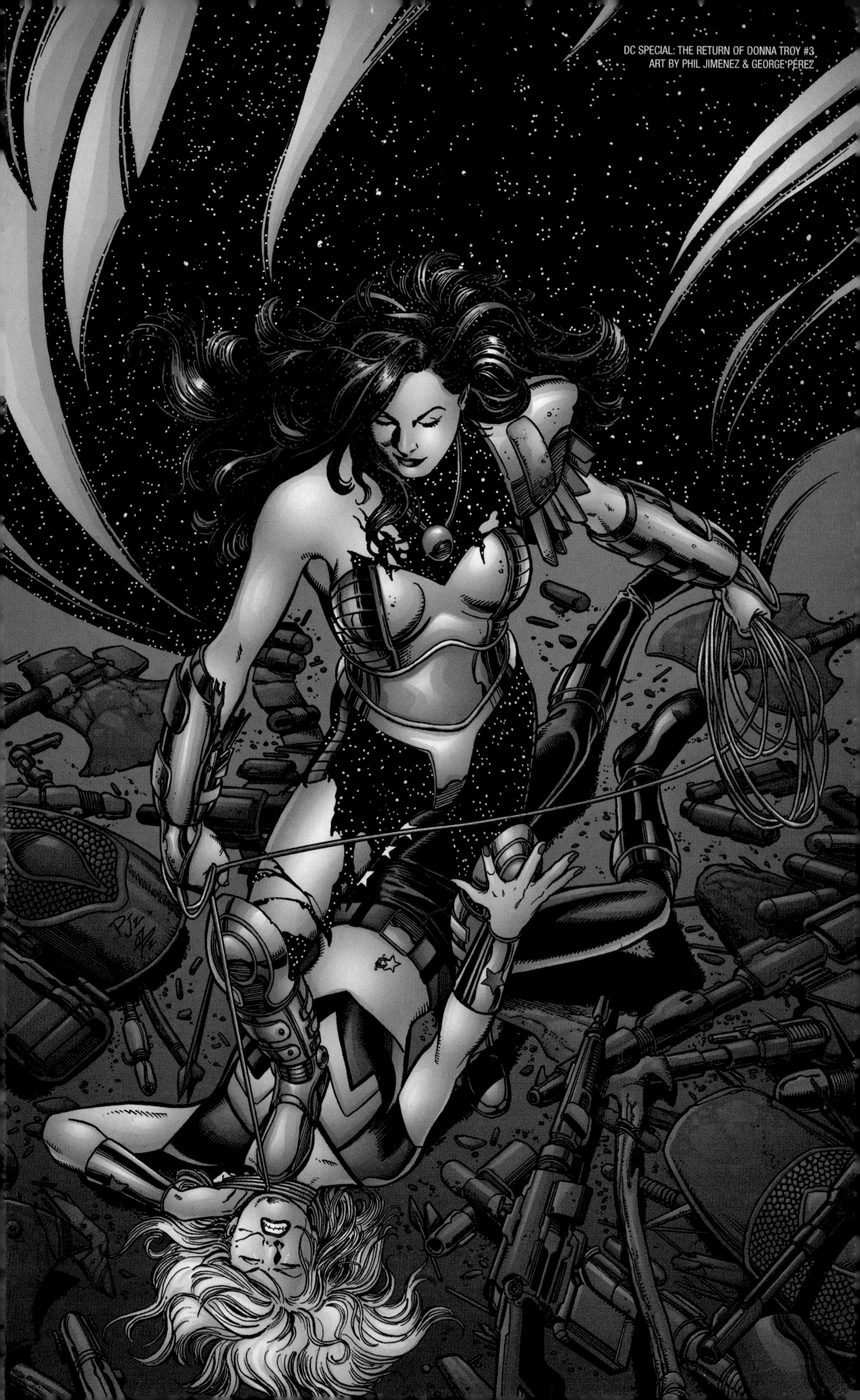

DC SPECIAL: THE RETURN OF DONNA TROY #3
ART BY PHIL JIMENEZ & GEORGE PÉREZ

DC SPECIAL: THE RETURN OF DONNA TROY #4
ART BY PHIL JIMENEZ & GEORGE PÉREZ

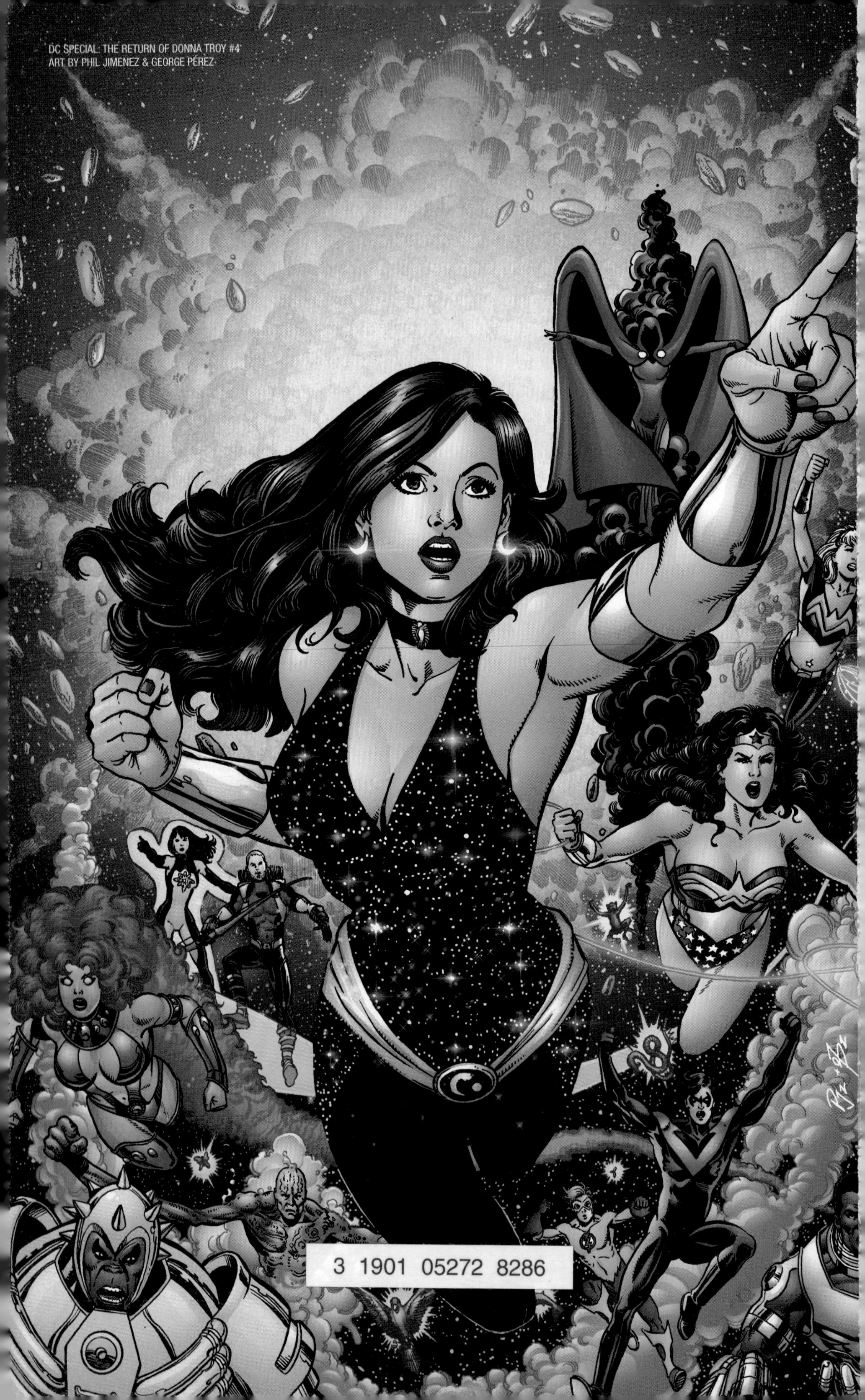